Modern Mummies

Modern Mummies

The Preservation of the Human Body in the Twentieth Century

by
CHRISTINE QUIGLEY

McFarland & Company, Inc., Publishers
Jefferson, North Carolina, and London

The present work is a reprint of the illustrated case bound edition of Modern Mummies: The Preservation of the Human Body in the Twentieth Century, *first published in 1998 by McFarland.*

LIBRARY OF CONGRESS CATALOGUING-IN-PUBLICATION DATA

Quigley, Christine, 1963–
    Modern mummies : the preservation of the human body in the twentieth century / by Christine Quigley.
        p.   cm.
    Includes bibliographical references (p.   ) and index.

    ISBN-13: 978-0-7864-2851-9
    ISBN-10: 0-7864-2851-1
    (softcover : 50# alkaline paper) ∞

    1. Mummies.   2. Embalming.   3. Cryonics.   I. Title.
GN293.Q54   2006
393'.3—dc21   97-43888

Cover photograph ©2006 PhotoSpin

Manufactured in the United States of America

McFarland & Company, Inc., Publishers
  Box 611, Jefferson, North Carolina 28640
    www.mcfarlandpub.com

Acknowledgments

This book would not have been possible without the generous help of the Edward C. Johnson family; Captain Harvey Lee Boswell; Luther Brooks; Lori Lincoln, Georgetown University; Beacham McDougald, McDougald Funeral Home; Brian Price, Taxidermy Unlimited; Paul Sledzik, National Museum of Health and Medicine; and James Taylor, editor of the journal *Shocked and Amazed! On and Off the Midway*.

Thanks to Don McLean Music, BMI, for permission to reprint the lyrics of "The Legend of Andrew McCrew."

Thanks are also due to the following individuals for their invaluable assistance and encouragement: Greg Abbott, Mortuary Management; Michael Ackerman, National Library of Medicine; Caroline Alexander; Edda Ambach, Institut für Medizinisch Physik; Leona Ashe; Robert Ballard, Woods Hole Oceanographic Institute; Mrs. Richard Basgall; William M. Bass, University of Tennessee; Bernie Beichert; Thomas L. Bereuter, University of Vienna; Walter Birkby, University of Arizona; Ian Blair; Stephen Bridge, Alcor Life Extension Foundation; Bob Brier, Long Island University; Gretel Burnett, Mammoth Cave National Park; Lisa Carlson, Funeral and Memorial Societies of America; Tom Christ, Temple University; John Clair, Hydrol Chemical Company; Michael Clem; Eve Cockburn, Paleopathology Association; Joan Carroll Cruz; Fred Dahlinger, Jr., Circus World Museum; Rosalie David, Manchester Museum; Neil Dewhurst; Mike Dodge, Dodge Company; Cynthia M. Dudgeon, Hizone Brands; John J. Dunphy; Dee Durham, Rodrick & Minear Funeral Home; C. W. Eldridge, Tattoo Archive; Jeffrey Ellington; Cherie Emma-Leigh, Commonwealth of Virginia; David A. Evans, the Russell, Kansas, *Daily News*; Chris Fellner, *Freaks!*; Lin Fredericksen, University of Kansas Libraries; Dave Friedman, Calhoun County Fair; David Friscic, National Science Foundation; Stephen J. Frye, Glacier National Park; Josephine Gentile, Jewett Refrigerator Company; Judy Gist, World Apostolate of Fatima; Jan Gregor, Circus of the Scars; John T. Griffith, Jr., Griffith's Taxidermy Studio; Ann T. Harmer, Orange Coast College; Ken Hawkes, University of Tennessee; Tommy G. High, Hatcher & Saddler Funeral Home; John Hochmeister and John Hood, Garden of Eden; Walt Hudson; Bill Huffman, World Fauna Museum; Walter E. Johnson, Tinker's Taxidermy; Wilhelm Kick; Irwin Kirby; Archie Lieberman; John Lovett, University of Oklahoma Library; William Maples, Florida Museum of Natural History; Don Marcks, *The Circus Report*; John Marr, *Murder Can Be Fun*; Pat Mc-Cauley, Barbour County Historical Society; C. Simon L. Ommanney, International Glaciological Society; Susan Paris, Utah State Historical Society; Robert Partridge; Jim Pate, Birmingham, Alabama, Public Library; Harold J. Pavett, Preservation Technology Corporation; Archie Phillips, Taxidermy and Outdoor TV Productions; Rosamond Purcell; Louis Reynaud, Laboratoire de Glaciologie et Géophysique de l'Environnement; Gracey Ra, Summum; Hans Röthlisberger; Barbara Rotundo, Association for Gravestone Studies; Line Schmidt-Madsen, Gyldendal Boghandel; Helen Sclair, Association for Gravestone Studies; Ken Sherman; Duke B. Shumow; the Rev. John Songster, S.J., Georgetown University; Kris Sperry, Office of the Fulton County, Georgia, Medical Examiner; Werner U. Spitz; Dick Stacey, Maplelawn Park Cemetery; James Starrs, George Washington University; John Strausbaugh, New York Press; Debra Stumpf, St. Frances Cabrini Shrine; Ron Temu, Summum; Barkley Thieleman, the *Paducah Sun*; Nick Verrastro, *American Funeral Director*; Louise Tommie, Bessemer Hall of History; Dale Ulmer, University of South Alabama; Ronald Wade, University of Maryland; Kathleen Walczak, National Funeral Directors Association; Max Warren, Warren Monument Company; Jay Wells, Wrangell–St. Elias National Park; James M. Wilson, Georgia Marble Company; Brother Leo Wollenweber, O.F.M. Cap.; Gretchen Worden, Mütter Museum; and the staff of the Italian Embassy.

A special debt of gratitude is owed to my family, friends, and coworkers who indulged my interest without hesitation: James and Sarah Quigley; Donna and Del Gritman; Nicholas and Melissa Heilweil; Cris Hastings; Dorothy Sutton; Jim Miller; Chris Sweeters; Jody Arlington; the owners of Yesterdays Books, Washington, D.C.; and the director and staff of Georgetown University Press.

Table of Contents

Acknowledgments   v

Preface   1

Introduction   3

1. What Has Been, May Be, Can Be, and Will Be Done
   The History, Law, and Science of Modern Mummification   5

2. Lying in State
   Icons, Idols, and Eccentrics   27

3. Occupational Hazards
   Outlaws, Victims, and Local Folks   59

4. Learning About Life and Death
   Teaching Aids, Test Subjects, and Teratology Specimens   103

5. Buying Immortality
   Emulations, Innovations, and Applications   133

6. Accidents of Nature
   Adventurers, Explorers, and a Spelunker   167

7. Acts of Faith
   Servants, Patriarchs, and Believers   195

8. Mummy Miscellany
   Eviction, Collection, and Neglect   217

9. Conclusion   247

Bibliography   253

Index   259

Preface

"Modern mummies" seems to be a contradiction in terms. Mummies are ancient, carried across time by secret preparations, coming at last to rest in a museum showcase alongside other antiquities. As this book will demonstrate, however, not all mummies are old, nor are they all in museums. Modern-day mummies may be found in private collections, where they have come to rest after decades on the carnival circuit. They may be found in the attics and basements of funeral homes, waiting (by now in vain) to be claimed by next of kin. They may be found in the dissecting rooms of medical schools, where they have been chemically fortified to withstand a semester's worth of probing by students. And they may be found under glass in special tombs built in their honor, the most famous of them being Vladimir Ilyich Lenin.

Other modern mummies have been removed from both public and private view. After a long and complicated journey, Eva Perón's well-preserved body was deposited in her family tomb in Argentina. After a legal battle with the U.S. Federal Government, the family of cave explorer Floyd Collins finally succeeded in regaining custody of his body sixty years after his death and having it decently buried. After being discovered in a California funhouse, the mummified body of outlaw Elmer McCurdy was returned to his hometown in Oklahoma for a long overdue funeral and committal service.

Stories like these—of which there are a surprising number—are told in great detail. But *Modern Mummies* is not merely a catalog of preserved people. It is a revealing introduction to the ways in which bodies have been and will be mummified, including reviving ancient Egyptian methods and applying the techniques of contemporary taxidermy. It is an encompassing discussion of how bodies may mummify naturally by freezing, desiccation, or the formation of adipocere. And it stretches the definition of "mummy" to include the male and female cadavers immortalized in infinitesimal detail in cyberspace and the dozens of people now reposing in cryonic suspension.

Within the limited time frame of the twentieth century, *Modern Mummies* is a comprehensive look at the successful prolonged preservation of the human body: accidental and deliberate, scientific and amateurish, traditional and unique. The book is a look behind closed doors, at the techniques and at the individuals to whom they have been applied. Although a complete inventory of bodies mummified in this century would be impossible, the text delves into the stories of many such individuals in as much detail as the author was able to obtain. The case histories are enhanced by information supplied by the custodians of these people whose biographies do not end with death.

1

Introduction

The word "mummy" conjures up the image of an ancient Egyptian pharaoh carefully embalmed and wrapped by his subjects, laid to rest in a pyramid with an impressive array of belongings, and only relatively recently transferred to a less-than-regal glass museum case. The body is dry or "desiccated" and with proper conservation will be preserved indefinitely. Most of the bodies embalmed today are not desiccated, since the natural moisture of the body has been replaced with preservative chemicals that firm the tissues but do not cause them to completely dry out. "The major differences between current funeral practices and those used by the Egyptians are the use of modern chemicals and equipment, and an emphasis on temporary cosmetic restoration rather than preservation of mummies," writes the executive director of Funeral and Memorial Societies of America (Carlson 1987, 37). Mummies can be made today, as this book will show, although this is not the purpose of most embalming. And bodies that have only been restored for temporary viewing may mummify in the grave or crypt due to natural processes that are only enhanced by the embalming chemicals.

Anthropologists are familiar with the preservation of the body by both natural and deliberate means. Some draw the line at referring to bodies preserved naturally as "mummies": "'Mummification' and 'desiccation' are often used interchangeably, but mummification refers to bodies artificially preserved by the deliberate application of the embalming chemicals of ancient Egypt and desiccation results from placing a corpse in a perpetually dry or very cold environment" (Garland and Janaway 1989, 25). Most anthropologists view desiccation as a means of preservation and mummification as the end result. The desiccation may be natural or purposeful and is successful in the areas of the body in which it overcomes the natural tendency of the body to decompose. The final product may be a body that has only partially mummified (perhaps just externally) or a body that has been preserved completely.

Clarence Strub, the author of the well-known embalming textbook *The Principles and Practice of Embalming*, does not dwell on the causes of dehydration or the degree to which a body has dried. He points out that from an embalming standpoint, dehydration and desiccation are interchangeable words (1989, 92). Strub defines mummification as "complete dehydration of the body.... Mummification is a process which reduces the body to a structure light in weight, void of moisture, and not subject to the ravages of decomposition" (1989, 42). For embalmers, the dehydration that leads to mummification is to be guarded against, since it cannot be reversed once it is too far advanced. A body that has mummified cannot be embalmed, but a body that has been embalmed may mummify.

The best approach to the language of preservation may be inclusion. In simple terms, desiccated, mummified, and well-embalmed bodies are those that last. According to the *Oxford English Dictionary*, the word "mummy" has been extended to cover all well-preserved dead bodies. The earliest record of the word being applied to a preserved body dates from 1615. Its first application to a body frozen in ice was in 1727. The word "mummy" is used loosely in this book and includes corpses that have been preserved by injection, immersion, petrification, plastination, refrigeration, cryonic preservation, desiccation, freeze-drying, digitizing, and even the supposed will of God.

The modern mummies described herein have both direct and indirect ties to the ancient Egyptian mummies. Although today's funerary embalmers may distance themselves from the ancient Egyptian methods, which admittedly resulted in a fragile, darkened, withered corpse, an organization called Summum capitalizes on the connection, offering mummification in the style of the ancients and mummiform caskets modeled after the sarcophagi of the pharaohs. (Like the Egyptians, Summum also offers the mummification of pets.) Ancient Egyptian embalming was not promoted but rather replicated at the University of Maryland, where researchers carried out a modern mummification on a cadaver in a successful scientific attempt to reproduce the results of the ancients.

Ancient and modern embalming may be compared in other ways. Modern embalmers offer different levels of service at different prices; so did their ancient counterparts. Both show obvious attempts to perfect their art and to learn by their mistakes. Their subjects, too, have something in common. Like the ancient Egyptian mummies who sometimes became separated from their identities when tombs were plundered, modern mummies—particularly those that toured in the carnival circuit—have been inexactly identified and much of their biographies lost to history. Finally, we can compare motivations, which are sometimes similar. Modern mummies in the form of the cryonically preserved are the remains of those who hope,

like the ancient Egyptians, to one day reinhabit their bodies, which is the reason for their careful preparation.

Modern mummies also differ from the bodies of the ancient mummified Egyptians in many respects. The ancient Egyptian embalmers did not have access to refrigeration or the chemicals, plastics, and polymers used today to preserve the body. They were not compelled to display the mummy, often a driving force in modern mummification when bodies are to lie in state or be placed on display in a museum or mausoleum. The ancient Egyptians worked hard to keep the features of the deceased recognizable, whereas some forms of modern preservation, such as anatomical embalming, do not necessitate preserving the likeness of the individual, and the forms of natural preservation offer no guarantee.

Robert Wilkins (1990, 140) quotes a 1975 embalming textbook: "It is our purpose to serve the living…not to create museum specimens for the amazement of those who may populate the earth many centuries in the future." Although this may be true at the local funeral home, it is not true in the larger sense. The mummies created over the last hundred years may be around for another hundred. The body of Eva Perón will remain presentable even though she is locked in her Argentine tomb; the body of Vladimir Lenin will remain intact whether or not he remains on display in Moscow; and the body of little Rosalia Lombardo will survive as an example of Dr. Alfredo Salafia's work for future generations of tourists to the Capuchin monastery in Sicily. Carnival mummies will continue to change hands as long as they do not disintegrate, anatomical cadavers will remain on the dissection table as long as they are necessary, and cryonics clients will be kept in cold storage as long as funds and liquid nitrogen remain plentiful. Mummies, by definition, are here to stay.

1. What Has Been, May Be, Can Be, and Will Be Done

The History, Law, and Science of Modern Mummification

Mummification has come of age. With the development of superior mortuary chemicals and embalming techniques and the understanding of natural processes, the body may now be preserved in a remarkable variety of ways. The body may be injected with or immersed in preservative chemicals. It may be rid of moisture naturally or artificially by evaporation or sublimation. And it may be frozen or refrigerated. Despite the input of the sciences, funeral embalming, anatomical embalming, and even experimental embalming remain arts requiring more than just manual dexterity. Twentieth-century embalmers have guarded their professional secrets just as their counterparts did millennia ago. Although it will take a few thousand years to determine whether today's mummies will hold up as well as those of ancient Egypt, the twentieth century can lay claim to the successful preservation of bodies such as those of Lenin and Eva Perón that may well rival that of Ramses II.

Anthropologists group mummification into three types. Natural mummification may be caused by a number of natural processes acting alone or in combination. These may include heat or cold or the naturally occurring chemical components of the soil in which the body is buried. Intentional natural

mummification occurs when these natural processes are enhanced or exploited purposefully, for example when a cemetery is located in an area having favorable natural conditions for the preservation of organic materials (Vreeland and Cockburn 1980, 154–57). Artificial mummification is purposeful preservation by other than natural means, although it is usually most successful in climates that favor natural preservation. Artificial mummification includes embalming by arterial injection, immersion in preservative fluids, and many other varieties of intentional preservation.

Traditional embalming is the fixation of the tissues by chemical means. The action of changing the proteins of the tissues is compared to the change in consistency when a raw egg is fried (Mayer 1996, 113). Embalming commonly includes arterial injection and cavity treatment, and may involve evisceration. The body of Lenin was eviscerated before being embalmed by arterial injection and other means kept secret by the Russians, who have now begun to offer their services to the public. The body of China's Mao Tse-tung was also injected with preservative fluid in a method patterned on that used by the Russians. In Italy, Dr. Alfredo Salafia used a fluid that he developed on the unclaimed dead and demonstrated on his own father to embalm a premier, a cardinal, a senator, and a count. In the United States, attempts by embalmers to develop their own fluids resulted in a number of mummified bodies with an equal number of posthumous histories.

The first commercial embalming fluids were arsenic solutions (Strub 1989, 38–39). Bodies embalmed with arsenic were relatively supple, making dressing and positioning of the body easy. Arsenic-based fluid easily penetrated all of the body tissues, even without the drainage of the blood (Johnson et al. in Mayer 1996, 455). Arsenic figures in only a few of the stories in this book, most notably that of outlaw Elmer McCurdy, but its preservative properties are still occasionally seen in the bodies of those whose deaths were caused by ingesting it (Strub 1989, 473–74). Arsenic and other deadly chemicals were superseded by formaldehyde, the hardening action of which was discovered in 1893. At the turn of the twentieth century, formalin (formaldehyde solution) became available at a reasonable price, thus providing the opportunity to eliminate arsenic and other poisons from embalming fluid formulas (Johnson et al. in Mayer 1996, 455). Continued attempts at improving embalming chemicals led to extensive research by the Hizone Company, the Champion Company, and others. By 1996, three embalming fluid companies had announced formulas that replaced formaldehyde (Johnson et al. in Mayer 1996, 457).

In addition to improvement of the chemical formulas, the equipment used to embalm the body became more sophisticated, more automated, and more powerful in the twentieth century. A battery-powered pump for injecting embalming chemicals was debuted in 1914 but was not widely adopted. By the mid–1930s, however, electric-powered injection machines were available and in use. And later in the decade, machines—some with pressure gauges—were available from three different companies. In 1939 the Porti Boy was introduced by the Turner Company and became the most popular of all the injection machines. By the 1960s extreme high-pressure injection machines were on the market (Johnson et al. in Mayer 1996, 455–56).

Other methods of preservation require little in the way of equipment. The body may be easily kept intact by immersing it in a liquid preservative such as alcohol or brine (Johnson et al. in Mayer 1996, 422). The embalming of Joseph Stalin was described by his daughter as "pickling" (Richardson 1994, 255). The tannic acid in tea has a preservative effect, and alcohol has well-known preservative effects and antibacterial activity. In certain instances water alone may result in preserved tissue by the transformation of the body fats to soap (see the discussion of formation of adipocere below). The more traditional formalin solutions are used to soak the bodies of anatomical cadavers, if they are not injected arterially, and to preserve teratology and other specimens. The body may also be preserved, at least in part, by coating it with bitumen, balsam, or another resinous substance. The contemporary organization Summum, which offers mummification to its clients, uses both methods, first bathing the body in a number of chemicals and then painting it with wine, oils, and a coat of polyurethane. Chemicals with the power to preserve the body do not necessarily have to be in liquid form and they do not always have to be introduced into the body. Artificial means of preservation include placing the body on a bed of sawdust mixed with a preservative powder such as zinc sulfate (Johnson et al. in Mayer 1996, 422). Complete desiccation may be achieved by placing the body in contact with lime, charcoal, clay, or other absorbent materials. Alternatively, the body may be wrapped in materials such as cloth, cotton fiber, leaves, and grass that will absorb the body fluids. In the case of Carl Stevens, whose death went unreported for more than seven years, the daily changing of his clothes and bed linens assisted in the drying and ultimately the mummification of the body.

Bodies may be preserved by drying in

air, in the sun, or by exposure to heat. This may and does occur naturally in arid regions, but it can also be done on purpose. The application of simple heat, for instance drying the body in an oven, is an effective means of artificial preservation. Smoking the body will result in its preservation. Alternatively, the body may be skinned, the skin tanned, and the defleshed bones (or other packing material) returned to the skin to fill it out. The methods the Jívaro Indians used to shrink heads—boiling, the removal of the bones, and the application of hot rocks and sand—would be tedious to perform on the entire human body but may have been the method of preservation in the case of two mummies still in existence. The soft tissues of the body may be replaced with plastic materials, clay for instance, with or without fire desiccation or smoke curing. The infamous Edward Gein soaked the heads of the women he exhumed in brine, removed the face and scalp, and then stuffed the resulting "mask" with paper or sawdust to facilitate drying.

Cold is another means by which the body may be preserved artificially or naturally. The body may be stored by refrigeration indoors, or it may freeze accidentally outdoors. Many explorers and adventurers have been victims of weather in arctic and antarctic regions or at high altitudes. Depending on the interval between death and the recovery of the body (if it is recovered at all), frozen corpses are subject to a variety of influences. They may simply remain frozen, they may thaw and refreeze, they may form adipocere (discussed below), or they may dehydrate by the process of sublimation—in other words, freeze-dry. Artificial freeze-drying in a machine, a practice that has been put to use in the preservation of animals, has been planned by one taxidermist and carried out by another as an appropriate and very promising method of preserving the human body. Another method already practiced and having a number of proponents—cryonics—is to keep the body in a perpetual frozen state through the use of liquid nitrogen.

An area that is largely unexplored by those who intentionally mummify bodies is the preservative effect of certain plants. Aromatic spices have antibacterial activity that could lead to tissue preservation. Garlic also has an antibiotic component and the mint plant has antibacterial properties. "Natural plant products with antibacterial action are found in honey, cinnamon, vanilla, anise, black pepper, hops, and red pepper. Foods with antibacterial action include mushroom (*Agaricus bisporus*), cycad (nuts), Laburnum senecia, Crotoleria, Heliotropium, sassafras, and sesame seed. These plant products contain compounds that inhibit bacterial growth, especially when combined under heat with amino acid and simple carbohydrates, as would be present in mummified human remains" (Micozzi and Sledzik 1992, 762). If the body is intentionally or accidentally placed in contact with these materials, or they are used to fill the body cavities, preservation may be achieved.

Preservation may also occur due to exposure to mineral salts, which have a desiccatory effect on soft tissue. Most bacteria cannot exist in a salty environment, so burial in the salt layers found in some arid regions restrains the growth of corruption-causing microorganisms and thus favors the protection of dead bodies (Wang 1996, 61). The preservation of the bodies exhumed from the cemetery in Guanajuato, Mexico, is attributed to the properties of the soil. The bodies removed from the volcanic soil of Naples are also said to be mummified. A naturally occurring salt was used in its solid state by the ancient Egyptians to mummify their dead, a process replicated by Bob Brier and Ronn Wade in the twentieth century.

In many cases mummification is either deliberate or accidental. In some, on the other hand, preservation may be due to embalming, natural causes, or a combination of both. The bodies of people both religious and secular have been disinterred and found to be incorrupt, a condition deemed miraculous. Although this may be true, it may also be true that the treatment of the body at the time of death (often poorly documented) and the conditions of the burial contributed at least in part to the preservation. Even when conditions are right for desiccation or when an experienced embalmer is at work, preservation may fail. There are numerous variables in the recipes for mummification.

WHAT MAY BE DONE

Modern Preservation and the Law

There are many laws governing the licensing of funeral directors and embalmers in the United States, many regulations dictating which chemicals may or may not be used in the embalming process, and numerous ordinances stating the ways in which the body may be transported, but the disposition of the body after it has been lawfully embalmed is generally left up to the poorly defined "standards of common decency" in each community. Lisa Carlson, executive director of Funeral and Memorial Societies of America, speaks of the dearth of legislation in a letter to the author (10 February 1997): "Most state laws are simply mute on this topic....Even though there are often laws requiring that a burial transit and disposition permit be filed within a certain time period, there is rarely a system of checks and balances to see that it is done. That would allow someone to hold a body indefinitely in some states, I suppose. The Yuppies in Utah who are into mummification and the cryonics folks are about the only examples I can think of who take advantage of the silence of such laws."

The Summum organization based in Salt Lake City, which offers contemporary mummification to its clients, positions its services carefully between traditional funeralization and ultimate disposition in a mausoleum. Cryonics organizations are in fact very aware of the laws that govern their unique preservation method and take care to stay within them, at the same time protecting their own interests. When a 1980 opinion of the California state attorney general stated that cry-

onics organizations were not acceptable donees under Section 7153 of the California Health and Safety Code (which gives individuals and designated relatives the right to donate human remains under the Uniform Anatomical Gift Act), cryonics groups—most of them initially based in California—turned to Section 7100, which provides that oral or written instruction related to the interment of one's human remains must be carried out, even though this statute enumerates only disposition of the body or cremated remains by inurnment, entombment, burial in a cemetery, or burial at sea.

In his *Cryonic Suspension Legal Forms Manual*, attorney James L. Bianchi (1986) concludes that the best written directive is a legally executed will that contains the sentence, "I direct interment by cryonic suspension of my human remains," although a holographic (or handwritten) will using these words may also suffice. In the same manual Bianchi points out that cryonic preservation may be designated by the next of kin in the absence of written or oral instructions left by the deceased, but he warns his colleagues to "take care that the person making the arrangements is the person having priority over other relatives and is not opposed by a majority of relatives bearing the same degree of relation to the deceased." A relative with the statutory authority to control the disposition of the remains may direct an alternative method to cryonic preservation but is obliged to do so at his or her own expense, Bianchi points out. Furthermore, to protect his cryonics colleagues against civil liability for the mutilation of human remains, Bianchi instructs that changing the mode of suspension (for instance from full-body to neuro-preservation) must have consent of the relative controlling disposition.

The terms of cryonic suspension are specified in another legally executed document. In a Declaration of Trust, the deceased (or the person in charge of the remains) finances the continued maintenance of the body and may place limits on the power of the cryonics organization to release information about its client and his or her suspension. The cryonics organization is charged with keeping records of the cause of death, medical history, and procedures used for cryonic treatment of the remains, in addition to periodically reviewing the continued maintenance of the remains by the cryonics facility. Determination of when an attempted revival should be made is the responsibility of the cryonics organization. If the revival attempt fails, the organization will determine whether to resuspend the remains, engage alternate services for maintaining them, or direct a traditional form of interment. If the revival is successful, the revived suspension client becomes the beneficiary of the trust.

Because the chances of revival look slim to the public and because large sums of money are involved, Bianchi urges cryonics organizations and those contracting with them to be wary of actions that may result in negative publicity. He suggests that the written directive by the deceased contain a preference for a means of traditional interment, should it be necessary due to physical or financial reasons such as contagious disease, mutilation by autopsy or embalming, direction of a court, lack of a cryonics organization or facility, acts of God, failure of the trust, or exhaustion of funds. In his manual (1986), Bianchi also advises cryonics organizations to protect themselves by being cautious: "It is advisable to back away from situations where the condition of human remains are unsuitable for any form of cryonic treatment, such as remains that sustained burn damage. Otherwise, it will create a public impression that you are less concerned about revival and research than you are about receiving funds from a trust. Such public opinion will seriously affect legislation in the field of cryonic preservation" (11-5). The most important document required by cryonics organizations in California—aside from the Declaration of Trust—is a Disposition Permit issued by the Department of Health Services, although Alcor Life Extension Foundation employee Michael Perry notes in *Cryonics* (November

1992) that neuro-preservations are treated as "tissue samples."

Although cryonics organizations may not be able to take full advantage of the Uniform Anatomical Gift Act, it is the means by which many bodies that are preserved for a prolonged period are donated and received. The Uniform Anatomical Gift Act allows any individual of sound mind over eighteen years of age to make a gift (to take effect upon death) of all of his or her body to a hospital, surgeon, or physician for education, research, advancement of science, therapy, or transplantation; to an accredited medical school, dental school, college, or university for education, research, advancement of science, or therapy; to a bank or storage facility for education, research, advancement of science, therapy, or transplantation; or to any specified individual for therapy or transplantation needed by him or her.

An anatomical gift may be made by will (but is not subject to probate) or by a witnessed document and may be revoked by a signed document, an oral statement, or the destruction of any existing document of gift. If an individual has not declared his or her wishes to the contrary, the body or parts of it may be donated by the spouse, adult children, parents, adult siblings, guardian, or other person authorized in that order of priority to dispose of the body. To avoid a conflict of interest, the doctor who certifies the death of a donor or who accepts an anatomical gift in the absence of a specified donee should not participate in its use. The recipient of a full-body donation may authorize the embalming and use of the body in funeral services and will usually allow the next of kin to have a say in the final disposition of the remains after the stated purposes have been achieved (Iserson 1994, 617–18).

All deaths, regardless of the disposition or donation of the body, require certification and the filing of the death certificate with the proper authorities. Death certificates vary from state to state, but most follow the general format outlined by the United States Standard Certificate of Death (DeSpelder

1983, 280). Although the author does not advocate circumventing social mores to retain control of a corpse, few rules would have to be broken to do so. When embalming is not desired, some states allow persons to care for their own dead and to sign the death certificate as the "funeral director," indicating their relationship to the deceased (Carlson 1987). The body may then be transported by the family in a suitable vehicle—even across state lines—if a transportation permit is obtained from the Health Department, although embalming or the use of dry ice may be required, depending on the weather and the distance (Morgan 1984, 53). These rules allow families to participate in the direct disposition or cremation of relatives and rarely result in their retention of the body.

If professional embalming is desired, or if the body is to be transported by common carrier, the family seeks the services of a funeral director, who is both more familiar with the law and subject to much more stringent regulations. Some states require embalming if the body is to be transported interstate or by common carrier. All states honor the properly acquired permits of other states when a body is to be moved from one state to another, and in many states funeral directors are allowed to serve as deputy registrars outside normal business hours (Carlson 1987, 56–57). Some states require embalming in the event of death by contagious disease, and others require embalming if burial or cremation will not take place within a certain time frame. In a few states, embalming is never required (Gilligan and Stueve 1995).

Earlier in the century, embalmers received their credentials by attending a brief seminar conducted by representatives of fluid manufacturers, who often required purchase of their product in exchange for a diploma (Strub 1989, 38–39). In 1927 national accreditation of mortuary schools was introduced by the Conference of Funeral Service Examining Boards, a national association of state licensing boards (Johnson et al. in Mayer 1996, 453). Today, most states require that funeral directors be certified by state licensing, and all states except Colorado require that funeral directors and embalmers be licensed. Basic educational requirements for receiving embalmer and funeral director licenses vary from state to state but generally include a high school diploma, training at a mortuary college or in a mortuary science program of up to four years of college, and at least one year of apprenticeship. Most licensing requires passing state and/or national board examinations.

The greatest changes in embalming procedures began in the 1980s. The Federal Trade Commission (FTC) adopted rules concerning the necessity for embalming and the need to secure consent. The Occupational Safety and Health Administration adopted rules relating to embalming procedures, protection of funeral home personnel, and public health and hygienic measures. And the Environmental Protection Agency issued rules concerning the use and control of formaldehyde and other chemicals (Johnson et al. in Mayer 1996, 456). Under the FTC's Funeral Rule, funeral directors are not prohibited from explaining that embalming provides a temporary preservation to the body, but they are prohibited from making any claims that embalming (or any other goods or services) will preserve the body for a long or indefinite period of time (Gilligan and Stueve 1995, 106).

Ernest Morgan, an advocate of "simple burial" by the family, makes the following accusation: "Laws governing the care and disposition of human bodies are meant to protect public health and safety, but sometimes their purpose is to promote the interests of the funeral industry. For example, some states have a law that only a licensed funeral director or 'direct disposer' may transport a dead body. Several require embalming under certain circumstances, such as length of time between death and burial and availability of refrigeration" (Morgan 1984, 43). In *Mortuary Law* (1995) Gilligan and Stueve explain that the funeral profession is principally regulated by the states through the enactment of laws by the state legislature. Most states have boards of funeral directors and embalmers that oversee the licensing statutes, investigate and inspect funeral homes, and conduct enforcement actions against those in the profession not in compliance with the laws.

Once a law is enacted, its scope and applicability are interpreted in the state and local court. When a particular issue is resolved by a court, the principle established will control future decisions by that and lower courts. Courts of equity have the authority to settle controversies concerning dead bodies. Many aspects of funeral law that have been established are impacted by common law, a great body of unwritten principles and judicial decisions passed down over hundreds of years and having roots in English and early colonial law (Gilligan and Stueve 1995).

U.S. law now generally holds that the right to dispose of a body rests with the surviving spouse, adult children, parents, siblings, more distant kin, executor or administrator of the estate, or the owner of the house or master of the vessel in which the death occurs, with the exact order of priority governed by state law. The next of kin have a general property right of holding and protecting the body until processed for disposition, selecting the place and manner of disposition (based on the wishes of the deceased, if known), and carrying out the burial or other last rites. These rites also include the responsibility to pay for the funeral expenses. They also have the right to the undisturbed repose of the remains after disposition (Iserson 1994, 557).

Although many states do not legislate the disposition of the body once it is released to the next of kin, failure to hand the body over to the family—even if funeral costs have not been paid—may leave a funeral director liable, although he or she is granted immunity from lawsuits by relatives desiring a different disposition than the one set forth in legal arrangements made by the deceased with the funeral home (Gilligan and Stueve

1995, 20). According to the Department of Health Professions of the Commonwealth of Virginia, human remains are the legal property of the next of kin. Provided they are transported with decency and respect, there are no laws governing what is done with them when they reach their destination. Subject to certain county restrictions, they may be buried in the family's yard or they may presumably be kept in the house or displayed in a glass casket.

Corpses are unique entities under the law. They are not property in the commercial sense, but their legal custodians are provided with a bundle of rights with regard to them (Gilligan and Stueve 1995, 6). Legally, the right of custody is a limited right given for a specific purpose and is subject to revocation if not utilized for the proper purpose. The holding of the body prior to disposition is usually several days, but a longer period may be justified by circumstances (Gilligan and Stueve 1995, 9). There are two scenarios in which the rights of next of kin are superseded by the state or by other relatives. Bodies may not be disinterred without proper authority, regardless of purpose or motive, and to do so against the will of other relatives requires that the custodian of the body persuade a court of equity that the disinterment is required by justice (Gilligan and Stueve 1995, 49). The laws governing legal autopsy take precedence over body donation and may be required by the coroner or medical examiner. Hospital autopsy, however, is at the discretion of the next of kin (De-Spelder 1983, 284), unless it has been provided for in the will of the deceased. If an autopsy is required by law, the relatives may request that it be conducted in a manner that limits the deterioration of the remains. In some states an autopsy may even be prevented by executing a Certificate of Religious Belief indicating that autopsy or any procedure that would allow the body's deterioration or the retention of any body tissues violates religious belief, a tactic often used by those planning for cryonic suspension.

Although regulations are more likely to

be enforced against institutions, violations have been cited against individuals but almost always have resulted in misdemeanors or dropped charges. Ordinances against the display of human remains have resulted in confiscation. Bodies found in the possession of serial murderers are of course recovered and their killers prosecuted for more than "failure to report a death." But in many instances, the law does not come into play. The preservation and display of famous political figures have been sanctioned by the state, as were most of the vagaries of Eva Perón's embalmed body. Many carnival mummies and mortuary relics predate state requirements to certify death or dispose of the dead. Others had their bodies displayed, but only within the confines of a cemetery mausoleum. And still others legally donated their remains for long-term use.

The law may be manipulated to effect the permanent preservation and private display of a body in one's custody, but the point is moot in many of the cases discussed in this book. Whether due to public pressure, difficulty of maintenance or storage, or merely convenience and opportunity, many of the bodies that led an unusual posthumous existence have undergone traditional burials— fitting in some cases and somewhat ironic in others. These burials, as will be shown, may perpetuate the preservation of the bodies but out of the sight—if not out of the minds— of those who cared for them or cared about them with full knowledge of the law or regardless of any legal consequences.

WHAT CAN BE DONE

The Science of Modern Preservation

What can be done and what the Federal Trade Commission allows funeral directors to claim can be done are widely divergent. In 1984 the FTC enacted the Funeral Industry Practices Trade Regulation Rule, commonly known as the Funeral Rule. The rule prohibits funeral directors from represent-

ing to consumers that the goods or services they provide will delay natural decomposition of human remains for a long or indefinite period. Funeral directors are restricted from characterizing embalming as anything other than a temporary preservative treatment. The reality, before and after the legislation, has been that embalming may preserve the body for extended periods. Proficiency and intent may result in a body that circumvents the natural decay processes. Even when a body is not embalmed with the purpose of prolonged preservation, the chemicals alter the natural course of decomposition and cause the body to remain intact far longer than what would be considered "temporary."

Embalming for long-term preservation may involve sacrificing the "presentability" of the body that short-term preservation is known for. Robert Yount, mortician and embalming instructor at the San Francisco School of Mortuary Science, explains: "I can embalm someone now to last for years and years and years....By adjusting the strength of the chemicals I can preserve human tissue very easily, but to preserve tissue so it looks natural, so that it has pliability, that 'lifelike' look, that's another story altogether" (Palmer 1993, 158). There have been many attempts, some of them successful, to achieve the best of both worlds. The embalming textbook *The Principles and Practice of Embalming* (Strub 1989) contains a photograph of a body embalmed with Bisga embalming fluid in approximately 1902. The photograph—which shows a man fully clothed, holding a newspaper, and seated with legs crossed—was taken three months after death and embalming.

Over the years mortuary chemical companies have developed wide ranges of embalming fluids to meet a variety of short- and longer-term needs. These needs include preparing bodies that have already begun to desiccate and bodies that require prolonged preservation. The Hydrol Chemical Company carries a line of injection, arterial, cavity, and specialty fluids that includes Hydrolan, a lanolin moisture conditioner to add to arterial fluid. The promotional literature states, "Hydrolan is especially effective in emaciated cases, aged, and dry bodies. It will be effective on cases where the body is to hold for a long time and all cases embalmed in hot, dry weather." The company also offers Hydrolite, a high index and high firming arterial fluid that is promoted as the strongest fluid on the market today. Used full-strength, it sets the body quickly. The catalog states, "Hydrolite's great strength makes this an ideal fluid for dropsical cases, for bodies which are to be shipped long distances and for bodies which are to be retained in receiving vaults for long periods."

Mike Dodge of the Dodge Company, a manufacturer of embalming chemicals and products, writes, "There are no special embalming fluids produced for the specific purpose of long-term preservation. However, long-term preservation can easily be achieved by using modern embalming chemicals full-strength. For the preservative chemicals to be used full-strength, proper additives must be used, but they are readily available" (letter to the author, 13 August 1996). It is left to the discretion of the embalmer whether to merely restore the body for temporary presentation or to attempt a more permanent result while guarding against the side-effects of the potent preservatives.

Embalming fluids have become complex chemical formulas. Most include the following in varying degrees: preservatives (formaldehydes, phenols, alcohols), which render the tissues unsuitable for bacterial growth; germicides (phenols and ammonium compounds), which kill or inactivate microorganisms; modifying agents (humectants, buffers, water conditioners, and inorganic salts), which control the action of the main preservative agents; anticoagulants (citrates, phosphates, and borates), which reduce the viscosity of the blood; surfactants (wetting agents, surface tension reducers, penetrating agents, and emulsifying agents), which promote diffusion and saturation of preservatives; dyes, which impart a permanent

color to the tissues; deodorants, which displace or convert the unpleasant odor of the embalming chemicals; and vehicles, which serve as solvents and stabilizers for the various ingredients of the fluid (Mayer 1996, 111–12).

Modern embalming seeks to counteract the natural drying of the body due to the surface evaporation that occurs before, during, and after treatment. In addition, significant moisture may have been lost during life due to a number of conditions: slow hemorrhage, febrile diseases, kidney diseases, diabetes, some cancers and localized neoplasms, some first-degree burns, tuberculosis, drug therapy, and chemotherapy (Mayer 1996, 371). Tissue moisture will continue to evaporate through the skin and membranes until the moisture content of the tissues is no greater than that of the surrounding air. More movement of the air will cause greater evaporation, and air that is dry will be more receptive to the moisture (Strub 1989, 92–93).

Although the drying of the body tissues is favorable to natural preservation, it poses a number of problems in artificial preservation: "Regardless of the antemortem or postmortem conditions that have brought about the condition of dehydration, there is only one positive benefit to the embalmer. Dehydrated bodies tend to decompose more slowly, as water is necessary for decomposition. Likewise, in embalming, the reaction of the preservative with the proteins leads to the drying and firming of tissues. Extreme dehydration is called *desiccation*. Desiccation is a form of preservation; however, desiccated bodies are not viewable" (Mayer 1996, 371–72). Loss of moisture causes the skin to shrink and lose its resiliency. The eyelids, lips, and tip of the nose become shriveled and wrinkled. The tips of the fingers turn a yellow-brown, and the skin becomes parchment-like. Desiccation of the exposed mucous membranes occurs even more rapidly than dehydration of the skin itself. The mucous membranes of the eyes and mouth begin to darken. The lips will appear black and wrinkled, and the lips may have drawn back to expose the teeth. Areas of the face such as the forehead and cheekbones take on a yellow to brown discoloration. Discoloration of the skin may range from yellow to brown and finally to black. The skin may appear "suntanned," and small scaly pieces may tend to flake off. The tissues will be tight and hard to the touch (Mayer 1996, 93–95, 371–72).

To prevent excessive moisture evaporation, the lining of the lips, nostrils, and eyelids—and the skin itself—may be coated with a liberal film of massage cream (Strub 1989, 354). If the vulnerable areas are not protected, the embalmer may not be able to counteract the effects. When thin areas such as the ears, nose, and eyelids become desiccated, arterial or hypodermic injection cannot correct the condition (Mayer 1996, 372). Once the dehydrated tissues have discolored, they cannot be bleached. The skin may be moisturized by injections and creams, but the discoloration will have to be hidden by opaque cosmetics (Mayer 1996, 95).

Dehydration may occur as a direct result of the embalming process itself, which is why humectants and other additives are included in the fluid. Chemical dehydration may occur with the injection of an excessively strong arterial solution; direct contact of a concentrated fluid with the membrane of the eyelids, mouth, or nostrils; or the regurgitation of cavity fluid up through the respiratory tract or cervical vessels. Drainage dehydration may occur as the result of rapid injection and continuous drainage (Strub 1989, 291). Whether natural or due to some

The head and shoulders of a fourteen-year-old female embalmed in the 1880s by Dr. Thomas Holmes, the "father of modern embalming," to whom all contemporary embalmers owe a debt of gratitude. Photo courtesy of the National Museum of Health and Medicine, Armed Forces Institute of Pathology. (Accession number 558844.)

other cause, dehydration may hinder the embalming process. The blood becomes more viscous and is therefore increasingly difficult to drain. Moisture from the blood and lymphatic fluids is drawn into the surrounding cells; the postmortem edema that results may pose problems in the distribution of the preservative fluid (Mayer 1996, 95).

Once a body is buried, its preservation is influenced by a number of factors that are quite independent of how well the body was embalmed. Preservation favors bodies that are not emaciated, that do not have wounds, and that are not septic. The cause of death, the state of the body at death, and the time interval between death and burial are also factors (Garland and Janaway 1989, 16, 18). Preservation may also have much to do with the specific chemicals used to embalm. Tissues embalmed with alum may subsequently be preserved through a process of mummification after burial (Micozzi and Sledzik 1992, 762). Bodies placed in a mausoleum crypt will also mummify, rapidly and completely, a condition encouraged as an inoffensive alternative to decomposition and gas formation. The constant stream of clean, fresh air—or in some instances, a chemically dehydrated air—removes the moisture from the body, which tends to desiccate (Strub 1989, 99).

Much depends on whether the body is in contact with the earth or the air, although embalming instructor Clarence Strub (1989, 477–78) has high expectations in both cases: "Embalming, if done as the public has every right to expect it to be done, should insure preservation for months—with very little additional treatment for years and years of contact with the atmosphere and for generations or even centuries after burial." Burial limits the access of carrion insects and may preserve soft tissue for years. Burial in well-drained soil may lead to desiccation, but the casket and the burial garments may dominate or negate the effects of the soil (Garland and Janaway 1989, 16, 18). The casket itself may enhance preservation microscopically. The rusting of a cast-iron coffin may create a hermetic seal and introduce iron oxides that may prevent bacterial decomposition, resulting in remarkable soft-tissue preservation. Lead-lined coffins may produce lead oxides that could have bactericidal effects and allow preservation, especially in the presence of embalming fluids (Micozzi and Sledzik 1992, 762).

The closed environment of a well-sealed casket also has the potential to destroy the careful work of the embalmer. Moisture will tend to evaporate from the body, condense on the casket lid, and drip back down. To prevent this cycle of events, embalming powder, which is both germicidal and fungicidal, should be placed in the casket. A tablespoon is recommended for shipping in hot, damp weather, a quarter pound when the body is to be held in a receiving vault, and a pound when the body is to be buried. If embalming powder is unavailable, paradichlorobenzene (moth crystals), which is fungicidal, may serve as a substitute. In addition to these chemicals, which will arrest mold and mildew, a desic-cating agent may be used. A gallon of anhydrous calcium chloride placed in a wide mouth glass or ceramic jar in the casket and opened just before burial will absorb moisture that would otherwise damage the corpse. If a drying agent is used, the face and hands of the deceased should be protected by applying a thick coating of carbolated vaseline (Strub 1989, 478–79).

"The extent of the preservation has little to do with the expense of the treatment and burial: Sealed containers protecting the body from the environment, be they a sealed steel casket costing thousands of dollars or a cheap container made of plastic or Styrofoam, will result in an amazing degree of preservation, even over long periods of time. I've seen a well-embalmed body—an autopsied body, which makes embalming very difficult—last inside a sealed casket within a burial vault for twenty-seven years, looking as if death had taken place only a day or so before, with perfectly natural features and only small areas of skin slipping from the hands and feet" (Maples 1994, 47). Embalming does not affect the sequence of events in the decomposition process, but it does retard the rate and alter the areas of the body that are affected. Cemetery remains may exhibit mold, especially on the face and hands. Head and facial hair may adhere to the skin and the face may bear the impressions of the fabric from the upholstery of the casket. In time, shrinkage will cause the skin to crack and often to peel, resulting in an "old paint" appearance. The upper body may be better preserved than the appendages, reflecting the dispersal of the embalming chemicals (Berryman et al. 1997, 166–67). The dense tissues of the buttocks and legs are more prone to decomposition than other areas of the body where the embalming fluid has more easily penetrated.

The success of the embalmer's art is revealed upon exhumation. The author of a well-known embalming textbook asks, "We wonder how many funeral directors have had an opportunity to examine a body after a few months' burial in a completely closed casket and/or vault. When adequately protected against moisture condensation, fungus growth, and other forms of post burial disintegration, the body, even when casually embalmed, is usually in excellent condition" (Strub 1989, 478). The same author offers suggestions for the preparation of a subject removed from a receiving vault, mausoleum crypt, or grave. The body should be removed from the casket for a few hours to dispel the chemical fumes, the vaseline coating should be removed from the skin with a soft clean cloth and the use of the warm air from a hair dryer if necessary, the lips should be waxed and other sunken areas restored with tissue filler, cosmetics should be applied, and the subject should be returned to the casket (Strub 1989, 479). If the embalming and the subsequent restoration are both successful, the body may be suitable for viewing by family members despite the time elapsed since death.

"Embalming is a process designed to retard tissue decomposition for a reasonable period of time. Under favorable conditions it is possible to keep a body intact for many years—or even centuries" (Strub 1989, 51). The truth of this statement is borne out in many of the stories discussed in this book. In many cases, the embalming has been an integral component in the preservation, which would not have occurred otherwise. In some cases the body has been preserved through a combination of artificial and natural circumstances. And in other cases the body is kept intact by a natural process of desiccation, with embalming only incidental to the end result.

WHAT WILL BE DONE

Natural Preservation

The preservation of a body exposed to the elements or disposed of directly in the ground depends on a number of factors. Pressure on the body will tend to retard decomposition, so a body that is clothed or buried will not decay as rapidly as one that is neither. A well-known theorem puts this in perspective. According to Casper's Law, the same grade of decomposition will be found in a body buried in earth for eight weeks, a body floating in water for two weeks, and a body exposed to open air for one week (Strub 1989, 96). "Deep burials of approximately four feet or greater, by maintenance of cool temperatures and inhibition of depredation, provide an extremely reduced rate of decomposition. A corpse buried at such depths will remain virtually intact, with minimal tissue loss for a period of at least one year" (Rodriguez 1997, 459).

Like bodies that have been buried, bodies that are tightly wrapped in plastic or finely woven synthetic fabric may be remarkably preserved. In one case, the body of a homicide victim was wrapped in several layers of carpet and plastic sheeting and hidden in a concrete rental garage. Three years later, the body was discovered and examined by the authorities. They found only moderate skin shrinkage and discoloration and good preservation of the internal organs. Forensic anthropologists theorize that initially, bacteria acting to degrade the tissues multiply rapidly. After their by-products, such as ammonia and alcohol, increase and the pH within the closed system changes, the bacterial action is suppressed. Oxygen depletion by aerobic bacteria may also help to retard decomposition (Rodriguez 1997, 463–64).

Bodies may be preserved for longer periods by a range of possible natural agencies or processes. The body may be deposited in a perpetually dry, frozen, or anaerobic tomb environment. The body may be subject to hot (coastal) or cold (highland) temperatures throughout much of the year. The soil or substance with which the body is in direct contact may be highly saline, alkaline, or absorbent (Vreeland. and Cockburn 1980, 155–57). "A buried corpse may last nearly forever in icy ground. Peat and moisture may also retard decay. In dry sand bodies will mummify to durable parchment. In mineral-rich earth they may be impregnated with salts and metals" (Maples 1994, 36). Although these environmental conditions may be purposely exploited to achieve preservation, mummies can and do occur without intent.

The successful transformation of a dead body to a mummy requires that its components reach a state in which they are thermodynamically stable or kinetically inert. In addition, the products of the process have to be unattractive to scavengers and microorganisms. The three fundamental preservation types in which these properties have been observed are mummification by desiccation, transformation to adipocere, and tanning in the acidic bog environment (Bereuter et al, 1996, 265). Freezing preserves the body, but only while it remains frozen.

Desiccation

Desiccation, or the drying of soft tissues, can occur naturally under the right conditions, resulting in mummification. The moisture escapes from the body through the skin and surface membranes, especially those of the mouth and nose (Strub 1989, 47). The weight of the body will be reduced by 70 to 77 percent. The completely dehydrated body of a 150-pound person will yield a mummy weighing approximately 45 pounds, much of which is contributed by the skeleton (Strub 1989, 289). It is more common for the skeleton to survive minus the flesh. "Most human tissue is preserved postmortem as bone. However, natural and artificial processes of desiccation may lead to mummification with partial or total preservation of soft tissue. Immediate postmortem change is essentially a competition between decay and desiccation, and external factors such as temperature and humidity largely determine the outcome of this contest" (Micozzi and Sledzik 1992, 759).

Between its natural state and complete mummification, the human body may exist in any of a variety of degrees of desiccation (Strub 1989, 289). A body in the early stages

of dehydration will have sunken eyes, sunken temporal areas, and shallow cheeks (Strub 1989, 293). Desiccation begins in areas that contain little fluid, such as the scalp, eyelids, nostrils, fingers, toes, and scrotum. The exposed portions of the body such as the face desiccate more quickly than clothed or covered areas. The tissue becomes shrunken, and the skin loses its elasticity, causing it to wrinkle, contract, and sometimes split: "Tightened mummified skin displays a brownish discoloration and a parchment-like appearance, which preserves facial contour and dries and discolors bent knees. Similar drying may be observed in fingers and toes exposed to hot, dry air. Mummified fingers and toes are shriveled with wrinkled, firm, brown skin. The process begins at the fingertips which become spindly. The nail beds shrink and give the erroneous impression that the nails have grown after death. Drying of certain parts of the body may cause shrinkage of the skin to the extent of causing large splits that resemble actual injury. The splits are common in the groin, neck, and armpits" (Perper 1993, 35). Internal organs are usually the last tissues to desiccate, provided they do not decay in the meantime. As the body surface hardens and mummifies, internal dehydration slows, insect activity may continue, and odor may be pronounced. Underlying parts of the body may mold or skeletonize while the upper surface mummifies. Incompletely mummified internal tissues will be dark and viscous (Galloway 1997, 144). A completely mummified body will be dry, brown, hard, and light in weight.

Desiccation occurs when atmospheric conditions are consistently dry and the temperature is above or below that favorable for bacterial growth. Temperature and humidity are the key factors in the desiccation of the body. The ideal conditions for mummification are high environmental temperature, low humidity, and adequate ventilation. Complete mummification of the body is very uncommon in hot, humid conditions, although isolated areas of the body, particularly areas of skin, may mummify (Sledzik in press).

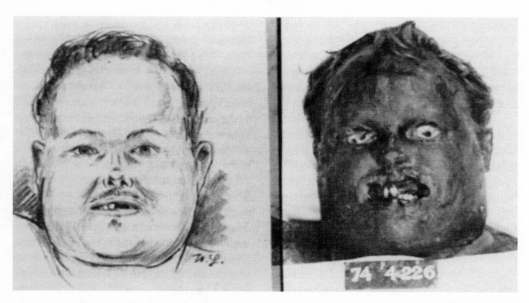

The extremely mummified body of a thirty-four-year-old Caucasian male (right) identified through an artist's sketch published in a major Detroit morning paper (left). Reprinted by permission from *Spitz & Fisher's Medicolegal Investigation of Death (3rd edition),* edited by Werner U. Spitz, Fig. III-6 (Springfield, Ill.: Charles C. Thomas, 1993).

Mummification is relatively rare in the United States because of the high humidity in most sections of the country (Strub 1989, 99). In the desert Southwest, however, burial in warm, dry sand permits the rapid evaporation of body fluids, completely arresting the dissolution of the internal organs, where the process of corruption usually begins (Cruz 1977, 31).

Hot, dry climatological conditions are the most favorable for desiccation. Rapid drying of soft tissues prevents putrefaction by enteric micro-organisms, soil bacteria, and other decay organisms. In "Postmortem Changes in Soft Tissues" (158) Michael A. Clark et al. include a photograph of a thirty-year-old woman found on the roof of a building during a long summer drought. During the three to four weeks since her death, she had totally mummified, with loss of hair, nails, and internal organs. Geographic areas with a preservative climate include the coastal zones of Chile and Peru, the southwestern U.S., and the desert areas of Australia and North Africa (Micozzi and Sledzik 1992, 760). Provided the proper conditions

are met, a body will desiccate entirely. If only part of a body is exposed to the proper environmental conditions, only that portion will mummify. Postmortem disturbance may result in incomplete desiccation (Sledzik and Micozzi 1997).

Desiccation does not always take place outdoors. Air-conditioned and heated dwellings sometimes provide favorable conditions for mummification, especially if insects have no access to the body. When the bodies of reclusive or elderly people are recovered after their unattended deaths, they are sometimes leatherlike, with dried organs and hair still present (telephone conversation with Tom Christ, 14 June 1996). In a case in Canada reported by H. E. Emson in 1991, a body was found in a dry, heated apartment eight to ten days after death. The skin was mummified, but the internal organs had decomposed before mummification was completed (Sledzik and Micozzi 1997). In April 1993, the corpse of a forty-one-year-old man was found lying in an apartment three and a half years after his death from causes unknown. The body had desiccated, but not before some damage by putrefaction and maggots. The better-preserved body of a man was also found in April 1993 lying in an apartment four years after his death from unknown causes. In this case, beginning putrefaction had been arrested by successful desiccation (Bereuter et al. 1996, 269).

The speed with which a body desiccates varies with the weather. "The rate of mummification and its extent depend on the humidity of the air and the intensity of the environmental heat, and its full development in temperate areas generally requires at least three months of postmortem interval" (Perper 1993, 38). In arid regions partial mummification with leathery change of skin may occur in four days (Perper 1993, 35), with complete mummification in as little as two weeks. Because arid conditions reduce insect activity, decomposition in such environments slows and the opportunity for mummification increases (Sledzik and Micozzi 1997). The rate of mummification also depends on whether the body is sheltered. According to a study by Galloway et al. (1989), desiccation in the open air took from two to eighteen months, an average of two to five months. Mummification in a closed structure took between eleven days and four months, an average of one to four months. "As a rule of thumb, one can state that the faster the process of desiccation is, the better the degree of macroscopic preservation will be" (Bereuter et al. 1996, 268).

Once mummification has fully developed, the body remains preserved as a shell indefinitely (Perper 1993, 38) and is resistant to further decomposition. This permanent preservation is possible because the water necessary for bacterial growth has been eliminated. If the mummy is not protected against the elements, it will eventually crumble to dust; if protected adequately, it will be preserved for years or even centuries (Strub 1989, 98–99). If the body remains exposed, the mummified material will be lost, leaving desiccated material and exposed skeletal elements. It is subject to damage by beetles and their larvae that perforate the

mummified skin and desiccated tissue. The desiccated material is most commonly retained at the points of muscle and ligament attachment, such as along the spine and at the articular ends of the long bones. The body is also subject to damage and disarticulation by wild and domestic carnivores (Galloway et al. 1989, 611–12).

The preservation of the soft tissues of a body is often an aid in its identification. A mummified face may allow reconstruction through an artist's sketch or Identi-Kit methods. Mummified fingers can be fingerprinted after being soaked in warm water and injected subcutaneously with water or glycerol to raise the ridges and remove wrinkles. Samples of mummified tissue may be removed for toxicological, serological, and DNA testing. Desiccated tissues may be rehydrated by immersing in Ruffer's solution, fixed in absolute alcohol, embedded in paraffin, and then sectioned and stained according to standard techniques (Fierro 1993, 79, 87, 103).

Cooling and Freezing

A corpse that has remained cold since death may be even easier to identify, if necessary. A body exposed to low temperatures of 32° to 50° Fahrenheit (0° to 10° Celsius) will decompose very slowly, and a body exposed to temperatures consistently less than 32° F (0° C) will not putrefy at all (Strub 1989, 96). A body left exposed during the winter months in temperate areas can maintain a "fresh" appearance for long periods. Cool temperatures slow the decomposition processes and allow time for the body to dehydrate. Insect activity is also decreased.

At temperatures of more than 60° F (15° C), decomposition due to bacterial action is rapid and desiccation must therefore be rapid, and nearly complete in order to allow even limited preservation of soft tissue. But when temperatures are between 41° and 59° F (5° and 15° C), the degree of desiccation required for preservation is reduced, and at temperatures of less than 41° F (5° C), the degree of desiccation required is minimal. "Below 32° F (0° C), no desiccation is required (given sustained temperatures) since freezing is the most effective preservative technique. Prior freezing also retards bacterial growth after thawing at ambient temperature" (Micozzi 1997, 172).

Cold and moist conditions will retard both decomposition and dehydration; cold and dry conditions will cause slow decomposition and rapid dehydration (Strub 1989, 173). Thus in arctic and antarctic regions or at dry, high altitudes, bodies are subject to sublimation or freeze-drying. Bodies of arctic natives, however, are rarely preserved in this way. "The frozen ground makes winter burials impossible; the bodies of those who die are put out for disposal by animals. The permafrost layer is only a few centimeters below the surface, discouraging deep burials even in summer. Cycles of freezing and thawing tend to bring summer burials to the surface, exposing remains to the ravages of climate and animals" (Zimmerman 1996, 90). A process similar to sublimation commonly occurs when bodies buried directly in the ground during the winter months are recovered in the late spring or summer. "The cold temperatures greatly retard or practically halt the decompositional process. As environmental temperatures slowly warm in the spring, the body begins to desiccate similar to the effect of freeze-drying, thus producing mummification of the corpse" (Rodriguez 1997, 460).

Continuous and discontinuous permafrost zones cover 25 percent of the earth's surface, and seasonally frozen ground covers 50 percent (Micozzi 1997, 175). Freezing is an exceptional means of preservation of soft tissues, but the bodies recovered from such conditions often undergo deterioration when removed from the conditions that caused their preservation. As they thaw, bodies that have been frozen are subject to decomposition from the outside in, with decay due predominantly to invasion by external soil organisms. The mechanical disruption of the tissues caused by thawing also weakens the skin, connective tissue, and joints, thus facilitating aerobic decay and skeletal disarticulation, and making internal organs more susceptible to invasion by foreign organisms and insects (Micozzi 1997, 177). In addition, those handling frozen bodies should take special precautions to avoid the remote possibility of contamination by infectious diseases such as smallpox, which may have been preserved with the body.

Preservation in Water

Robert Ballard of the Woods Hole Oceanographic Institute notes that the effect of the underwater environment on human remains depends on a number of factors: whether the water is fresh or salt, the depth of the water (which determines light, pressure, and temperature), exposure to predation, and the presence or absence of free oxygen. A body would have the best chance of being preserved in anaerobic waters where it would be less likely to be defleshed by predators (letter to the author, 20 November 1996). Decomposition will be slower in water than in the air and slowest in water that is cold, unpolluted, running, or salty (Strub 1989, 97). In "Forensic Taphonomy in Marine Contexts" (Haglund and Sorg 1997), Marcella H. Sorg lists the independent variables that decelerate postmortem skeletonization, decomposition, and disarticulation in marine environments: colder water and air temperature; a thick covering on the body; a softer, muddier seafloor substrate; and more mineral solubility and saturation.

Mummification does not occur in water, but the exposed areas of a body drifting in shallow water may be mummified (Spitz 1993, 513). Other areas of a floating or submerged body may form adipocere (discussed below). Just such a case was discovered in a mountain lake in Innsbruck, Austria, in September 1989. An automobile was found submerged in the Achensee 50 meters below the water surface. Inside the vehicle were the skeleton of a man and the torso of a thirty-year-old woman. The bodies had been submerged for fifty years in water that had averaged 39° F (4° C). The preservation of the woman's soft tissues was attributed to her higher fat content (Bereuter et al. 1996, 268).

Bodies that were deliberately disposed of in the water have also been found, and their preservation aids in identifying and consigning them to the sea a second time. A body was found on October 25, 1969, among the mangroves on the western shore of Biscayne Bay in Florida. The forearms and mandible were missing and the skull and upper arms had been defleshed, but adipocere was prominent, and all the internal tissues and neck viscera were well-preserved. Inside the skull, the brain was found to have mummified and shrunken to the size of an orange. The preservation allowed the medical examiner to determine the cause of death (bronchopneumonia) and the fact that the body had been embalmed. A search of sea burial records revealed that the body was that of an eighty-five-year-old man who had been buried at sea nearly a year to the day earlier. After the wooden casket had disintegrated, the body had been transported some three miles to the Bay by tidal currents and then drifted another few miles inland. The body was returned to the funeral home for repeat disposal (London et al. 1997, 618). In March 1993, human remains were found in 700 to 800 feet of water 80 miles south of Block Island, east of Long Island, New York. Although little soft tissue was present, the skin of the torso had been preserved in excellent condition and indicated that the individual had undergone major surgery (from which he had most likely died), been subjected to a medical autopsy, and subsequently been embalmed and buried at sea. The investigation was concluded without identifying the man, since it was deemed unnecessary and possibly traumatic to his family (London et al. 1997, 616–17).

Tanning

Special circumstances advantageous to the preservation of the body are found in peat bogs. The humic acid decalcifies bone and tans the skin. Even the fingernails, toenails, and hair will survive in good condition, although the nails may become separated from the body. The antibiotic properties of sphagnan, an organic component of sphagnum moss, are held to be more important in the preservation of bog bodies than tannin or the wet anaerobic acid conditions (Brothwell 1996, 161). Sphagnan aids preservation by reacting with the digestive enzymes secreted by putrefactive bacteria and immobilizing them on the surface of the peat (Daniels 1996, 173). The temperature of the bog at the time of burial is an important factor in the prevention of decomposition and the activity of the intestinal flora (Micozzi and Sledzik 1992, 760). To prevent rapid decomposition, the weather must be 39° F (4° C) or below. Different types of bogs yield different results. The best preservation occurs in the acidity of raised bogs. In fens, containing lime, and transitional types of bogs, the body is often skeletonized but may form adipocere (Fischer 1980, 177).

A similar means of tanning the skin and soft tissues may occur when a body has been placed in contact with plant materials such as tree bark, pine needles, or decomposing leaves. "Naturally occurring tannins leach out from the plant material under moist conditions, and in sufficient concentrations, tan and preserve the body tissues. Leaching of preservative compounds from leather goods in close contact with the body after death, such as tight boots or a leather jacket, may produce preservation of the tissues" (Rodriguez 1997, 463).

The Formation of Adipocere

One of the ways a body may be naturally preserved in more or less its outward shape, if not appearance, is by the formation of adipocere. "Some of the bodies thus transformed are said to retain the lines of the face, the features and expression, and the hair, but for the most part they are hideous objects" (Cruz 1977, 32). Adipocere is a waxy or greasy decomposition product resulting from chemical changes in soft tissues under conditions of high humidity and high environmental temperature. Adipocere formation usually requires a warm, damp, anaerobic environment but has been observed in buried bodies, dry environments, and cool water submersions (Mellen, Lowry, and Micozzi 1993, 91). It has also been found in corpses released by glaciers and in bodies preserved in bogs.

Sometimes called "grave wax," adipocere occurs in bodies that have been buried or immersed for long periods in moisture, such as a bog or pond, a cave, or a damp grave. Bodies buried deeply or in wet soil or clay typically exhibit advanced adipocere formation (Rodriguez 1997, 460). Traditionally, it was thought that adipocere could only form in a damp environment, but there is ample evidence that it may form in bodies interred in dry vaults, "water-tight" lead-sealed coffins, relatively dry inhumation graves, and other unusual burial places such as caves and beneath floorboards. In these cases, the water required has been derived from the body's own tissue (Garland and Janaway 1989, 23). As water is extracted from the body tissues, the viscera shrink, and the dermal tissues desiccate.

For a long time adipocere formation was thought to be the result of the body turning literally to soap, and that is approximately what happens. Chemically, adipocere consists of fatty acids formed by the hydrolysis and hydrogenation of body fats after death, a process attributed to bacterial action but still not fully understood. Bacterial enzymes from intestinal and environmental sources convert unsaturated liquid fats (oleic acid) to saturated solid fats (hydroxystearic acid and oxostearic acid). The chemical process is called saponification, and the resulting substance is not properly termed adipocere until it remains firm and consistent at room temperature. It is most likely to involve the subcutaneous tissues of the face, extremities, buttocks, and female breasts and may cause the body to appear larger than it did in life. It does not affect bone, affects organs at different rates, and throws off any toxicology studies. Once formed, adipocere is stable for extended periods. The conversion of fat to fatty acids causes the pH to drop, inhibiting bacterial growth. Adipocere is therefore highly resistant to and generally free from putrefactive organisms, so the soft tissues of the body may be preserved for years.

Adipocere is described as having a strong odor, like that of ammonia or rotting cheese, but is much less offensive after it has dried (Mellen, Lowry, and Micozzi 1993, 92). Adipocere "imparts a grayish-white color and soft, greasy, clay-like, plastic consistency to the soft tissues of the body" (Perper 1993, 38). Strub (1989, 99) describes adipocere as either pure white or pale yellow. Both color and consistency may vary. Relatively recent adipocere is white, yellow, or reddish-brown; older adipocere is white or gray. It may be soft and greasy or dry and brittle (Garland and Janaway 1989, 23), depending on whether it is fresh or aged. When first removed from the aquatic environment, adipocere will be doughy. Older adipocere that has been allowed to dry will crumble and split apart. In "Chemical and Ultrastructural Aspects of Decomposition" (Haglund and Sorg 1997, 102–3), H. Gill-King gives a scientific explanation for the different consistencies of adipocere: During its formation, fatty acid chains utilize sodium from the interstitial fluid, forming "sapo durus" or hard soap. As the cell membranes fail, the adipocere takes on potassium, forming "sapo domesticus" or soft soap. The hard soap is crumbly, and the soft soap is paste-like. If the water or soil surrounding the body has a high mineral content, both sodium and potassium may be displaced, producing hardening, an even more brittle consistency.

The visible results of saponification are highly variable. "Depending on conditions, the skin of an adipocered body can become as hard and leathery as bacon rind or an old boot, and eventually the remains take on many of the properties of a mummy" (Ubelaker and Scammell 1992, 150–51). Adipocere formation is not common, and when

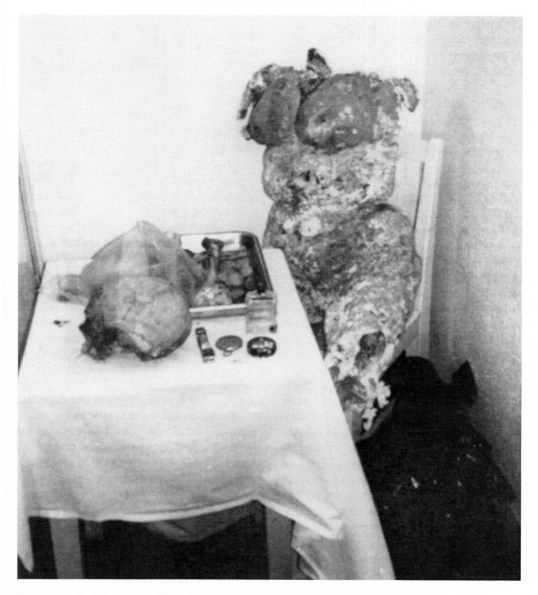

The torso of a thirty-year-old woman converted to adipocere during fifty years underwater in an Austrian mountain lake. Reprinted by permission of James Bereuter from *Human Mummies*, edited by K. Spindler et al. (New York: Springer-Verlag, 1996).

it does occur, it is rarely complete. It is usually more evident in the bodies of babies, women, and obese persons. The bodies of infants are more likely than those of adults to completely saponify. A newborn infant, for instance, was preserved in a near-perfect state of adipocere after eighteen years of burial in a polystyrene coffin containing water

(Spitz 1993, 513). But as with most forms of natural preservation, formation of adipocere depends on many factors, not all of them easily measurable or detectable. Development of adipocere may be accelerated in tissue covered with clothing. "In addition, pre-inhumation conditions of warm weather, fog, or haze may contribute to the process" (Micozzi and Sledzik 1992, 760). Bodies may also react differently under virtually identical circumstances. T. D. Stewart (1979, 73) examined the remains of American soldiers killed in the Korean War. Many of the bodies of the deeply buried soldiers had been converted in different degrees to adipocere, but others found in close association were completely skeletonized.

Although the formation of adipocere does typically take some time, it has been shown to reach completion in as little as three weeks. "Most often it takes at least three months and is usually not observed before six months" (Perper 1993, 35). A study by the National Museum of Health and Medicine (Mellen, Lowry, and Micozzi 1993, 92) determined that the formation of adipocere in human tissue took approximately two months in warm water submersions of 60° to 70° F (15° to 21° C) and approximately one year in cold water at 40° F (4° C). Presence of adipocere suggests that a minimum length of time has passed since death but may not always be useful in determining the postmortem interval.

In an effort to determine how long it takes for adipocere to form in the human body and what conditions are conducive to its formation, Tyler G. O'Brien conducted a study at the University of Tennessee's Anthropological Research Facility. Previous researchers had analyzed the chemical constituents and microscopic properties of adipocere and had even re-created it in the laboratory in nonhuman subjects, but this would be the first study to use human cadavers to simulate underwater decomposition. O'Brien immersed three human cadavers into excavated holes in the earth for three months or until adipocere formed. He recorded gross morphological changes of the tissues and the ambient and water temperatures to determine the relationship between the transformation of the cadavers and fluctuations in climatological and meteorological conditions that included rain and snow. Liquid and tissue samples were extracted and analyzed for fatty acid and microbial composition.

The subjects of the study were acquired from the State Medical Examiner's Office in Nashville. They had either donated their bodies to the University of Tennessee Department of Anthropology or had not been claimed. The cadavers had been stored in a morgue cooler for a period of about three months. The first body was that of a 5' 10" adult white male weighing 188 pounds. He had died after a twenty-foot fall and had not been autopsied. Mold and mildew was present around the neck and the extensive open trauma to the head and the body had multiple bruises. The second body was that of a 5' 8" adult white male weighing 173 pounds. He had died from a self-inflicted gunshot wound to the head and had open trauma on the left lateral and posterior cranial region. The body had not been autopsied and was partially bloated. The third body was a 5' 9" adult African-American male weighing 220 pounds. There was no trauma to the body, and the cause or manner of death was not indicated. No autopsy had been performed.

The site for the study was a level portion of ground near a water source in a partially wooded area. Three holes two or more feet apart were excavated using a backhoe. Hole 1 measured 7' 10" long, 4' 4" wide, and 3' deep. Because large rocks prevented digging any deeper, planks and concrete blocks were used to make a vertical wall around the hole, giving it a depth of 4' 6". The hole was lined with a doubled sheet of 3 mil polyethylene clear plastic. Hole 2 measured 8' 6" long, 4' wide, and 3' 6" deep. Again because of rock, planks and concrete blocks were used to make a vertical wall, giving the hole a depth of 4' 4". The second hole was also lined with plastic. Hole 3 measured 9' long, 3' wide at the bottom, 5' wide at ground level, and 4' deep. The soil, which is primarily clay, was found to hold water, so no plastic was used to provide a control for the study.

On October 20, 1993, the unclothed bodies were placed in a supine position on specially built support trays. The trays measured approximately 6' × 3' and were constructed of wire fencing nailed to an untreated pine frame with four cross-beams. The holes were filled with water using a garden hose. The cadavers were observed and photographed, climatic conditions were documented, and water temperature was measured. The trays were lowered into the holes using lengths of rope that had been attached to each corner to facilitate access for observation. The body in hole 1 sank within thirty minutes. The body in hole 2 remained floating with exposure of the anterior thighs, upper arms, abdomen, thorax, neck, and head from approximately the ear forward. The body in hole 3 remained floating with exposure of the face, shoulders, upper arms and thighs, and part of the abdomen.

Observations were made three times a week. The decay rate was noted, the drop in water level measured, temperature of the air and water recorded, and the upper half of each body was exposed and photographed. There were no changes during the first week, but all of the holes had accumulated dropped foliage. During the second week, the flesh of the body in hole 1 had softened and begun to decay. The body in hole 2 had also begun to putrefy, becoming swollen and discolored. The skin on the palms and soles had become wrinkled and started to peel and there was evidence of insect activity in the nose and mouth. The body in hole 3 had become covered with a thin layer of sediment and was also discolored.

In the third week, the body in hole 1 was still submerged and continuing to decay. The discoloration of the body in hole 2 had intensified, and it, too, continued to putrefy. In hole 3 puddles of thin, oily film covered the water, which had become thicker. Along the exposed contours of the body was a whitish, milky, oily film. In the fourth week, the body in hole 1 was still submerged beneath a film of leaves that coated the surface of the water. The body in hole 2 had patchy, moldy clusters of brown fungal growth, insect activity around the genital region, and beetles crawling over the exposed torso. The body in hole 3 remained floating and had marked tissue decay. The water had become almost completely opaque, and a thick, viscous film had formed on the surface.

In the fifth week, the body in hole 1 was still submerged, but a thin layer of green alga growth had formed on the surface of the water. In hole 2 the skin below the surface of the water began to slough off in large segments and the skin at the water level became wrinkled and thickened and turned a pale yellow color. The tissue above the water level became "crusty and hardened or mummified" (O'Brien 1994, 39), and the skin became darker red and brown. Maggots infested the upper neck and face. The body in hole 3 was extremely bloated and floated high in the water. Liquid samples were extracted from the cadavers for analysis. In the sixth week, there was little change in hole 1. In hole 2, the exposed regions of the body had become lighter in color and the fungal growth had paled. The tissue just above and below the water level became wrinkled, yellowish-white, and had a "goose-pimply" texture (cutis anserina) on the surface. The oral cavity was still heavily infested with maggots. The body in hole 3 had lightened in color with a small area of cutis anserina near the right elbow.

In the seventh week, the body in hole 1 was green and slimy with algae, and the tissue was soft and soggy. Hole 2 was drying, and the lateral portions of the body had yellowed. The chest and lower abdomen had dried and had pockets of brown and orange mold and mildew. The maggots seemed to be migrating away from the body. There was no change in hole 3. In the eighth week, the water in hole 1 was opaque and the body was unchanged. The swelling of the body in hole 2 had deflated, and the exposed tissue was mummifying. The extremities became lightly colored with hues of yellow and whitish-gray, and the tissue of the abdomen, waist, and shoulders appeared warped and crumpled at the water level. Maggots were still present beneath the water in the oral cavity. The body in hole 3 continued to mummify without remarkable desiccation. It was discolored and patchy with hues of light brown.

In the ninth week, the body in hole 1 remained submerged and unchanged. The bodies in holes 2 and 3 remained floating and had no remarkable changes. Liquid samples were extracted from each body. In the tenth week, a bright orange moldy growth appeared on the chest cavity of the body in hole 2. The body in hole 3 remained floating and deflated. In the eleventh week, the body in hole 2 had lowered slightly in the water and the orange mold-mildew spread to the shoulders and thighs. In the twelfth week, the body in hole 1 remained submerged. The body in hole 2 continued to exhibit cutis anserina at the water level and "remained covered with the orange mold-mildew growth and patched in brown, decomposed, mummified flesh encrusting the area on the top of the cadaver" (O'Brien 1994, 42). Hole 3 had areas of cutis anserina on the arms and upper thighs. Liquid samples were taken from each cadaver.

In the final stages of observation, the submerged body in hole 1 was soggy and covered in algal matter. It had not performed as expected. The bodies in holes 2 and 3 were encased in a yellowish-white caseous material characteristic of adipociferous bodies found in natural aquatic contexts. Thus, two of the three cadavers had presumably formed adipocere during the three months of observation ending on January 22, 1994. O'Brien notes that the body in hole 2 showed the first signs of adipocere formation in the sixth week, when cutis anserina was observed speckling the body in the areas above and below the water level. After this texture emerged, the tissues became denser, the skin rippled, and the color paled to a dull yellow and white. The tissues above the water-level zone (the three or four inches above and below the surface of the water) were mummifying and had hardened and dried. The tissues below the water-level zone were sloughing and macerating. To a lesser degree, the progression of the body in hole 3 followed that of the body in hole 2. O'Brien concludes that temperature is the primary factor in adipocere development and that bacterial evolution within the body is the secondary factor. The study reveals that adipocere formation is most likely to occur in weather and water temperatures ranging from 70° to 113° F (21° to 45° C), the optimum growth temperature for *Clostridium perfringens (welchii)*, the primary bacteria responsible for adipocere formation. Despite the limited sample size, the study confirmed that complete immersion in an aquatic environment is not necessary for adipocere to form.

O'Brien notes that in a textbook example of a drowning, the body sinks within a few moments and remains submerged until gas formation causes it to rise to the surface. Internal decay and predatory action continue, and the epidermis is breached by the hatching of insect larvae. The gases escape and the body submerges for a second time, during which O'Brien believes adipocere formation is at peak progression. The body may subsequently be snagged and remain underwater or become free floating. In either instance, the body will continue to decompose. The bacteria will destroy the cells, which will cause the chemical reaction that forms adipocere. The adipocere will accumulate over time to become an encasing tomb for the bacteria and will reach completion when all the bacteria are dead or there is no more soft tissue to hydrolyze (O'Brien 1994, 58).

Tyler O'Brien's research will be a useful guide to forensic anthropologists investigating the deaths of those whose bodies are recovered from aquatic environments in similar climates. He admits that the conditions were not ideal for his study and that there is more to be learned about adipocere formation. He suggests future studies involving flowing, chlorinated, and salt water; differences in temperature and humidity; differences in age and gender; and the effects of blunt trauma and loss of blood. O'Brien plans to continue his studies of adipocere development to achieve a better means of estimating time since death through the conversion of the body's fats. He will continue to analyze and observe the cadavers in the study, but expects them to remain consistent and stable.

2. Lying in State

Icons, Idols, and Eccentrics

For most people, lying in state means a few days of posthumous repose to allow one's friends, acquaintances, and admirers a chance to pay their respects. For a select few, lying in state is perpetual or comes to an end years or decades after it began. None of the most famous of these preserved people asked for their fate, and many explicitly voiced their objections prior to their deaths. Ho Chi Minh asked his fellow countrymen to avoid the time and expense of a large funeral. Mao Tse-tung had chosen a gravesite with his wife and signed a pledge to be cremated. Vladimir Lenin wrote that doting on the physical remains of great revolutionaries instead of their ideas was vulgar. His wife agreed and begged the authorities to bury him. But when the body can be made to serve a higher purpose, such as symbolizing a country's ideology, it is put to use despite the wishes of its former occupant or his or her next of kin.

Embalming offers a seductive, though mechanical, means of achieving immortality. "Let him be with us always," the public said of Lenin. When the Soviet scientists were able to make this sentiment a reality, other countries—China and Vietnam in particular—followed the example. The decision, often made by committee, has also been made by individuals. "It will remain forever beautiful," the embalmer promised Juan Perón about the body of his wife. Eva Perón's successful preservation precluded total bereavement, allowing her survivors to retain her physical remains instead of just her memory. Unlike Lenin, who has publicly reposed in his mausoleum for more than seventy years, Evita spent most of the twenty-four years after her death on the move or in hiding. Like him, Evita remained in such good condition that her body was thought to be a wax replica.

Other less-prominent individuals are subject to less scrutiny. They are infused with less political importance. And they are, of course, less well known. Samuel Dinsmoor sought a public audience, promising to smile at anyone who paid a dollar to gain admittance into his Midwest mausoleum. Leslie Hansell, on the other hand, just wanted her body to bask in the sun rather than being consigned to the cold ground. Evita's body was finally entombed, and Lenin's body remains—at the time of this writing—on display at the Kremlin. Lenin receives 3 million visitors a year, and his Kansas counterpart has his share of ten thousand. But more important than the number of tourists he draws is the fact that Dinsmoor's decision to have his body embalmed was his own.

ICONS

The embalmers of heads of state face steep challenges. The consequences of failure are dire, yet their success is jeopardized by delay and indecision. First, they may be

The body of Vladimir Lenin lying in his mausoleum in Moscow. Photo courtesy of Reuters/ Corbis-Bettmann.

charged with preparing the body for temporary viewing. Then they may be called upon to restore the body during an unexpectedly prolonged lying in state. At an even later date, they may be required to preserve the body in a lifelike state for an undetermined amount of time. The teams of embalmers, sometimes succeeding each other, may be forced to proceed by trial and error, but any and all errors must be rectified. Their process may evolve, but their subject's external appearance must not change. The result of the embalmer's work will be symbolic of the nation but will in a lesser sense symbolize the state of the art of preservation.

Vladimir Lenin

Russian revolutionary Vladimir Ilyich Lenin died, reportedly of a stroke but possibly of poisoning, on January 21, 1924, at his country estate in Gorki. His body lay upstairs in his sickroom on a sheet-draped table surrounded by flowers and fir branches. A Central Committee plenum began making arrangements for the lying-in-state and funeral, and the Central Executive Committee formed a commission to organize the burial. All regional and republican party commit-

tees were notified of Lenin's death by Communist leader Joseph Stalin.

On January 22 the Central Committee and members of the party and government went to Gorki to pay their respects. Lenin's friends and colleagues formed an honor guard that stood by the body as hundreds of peasants, who had heard the news by word of mouth, came to pay their respects. That same day, V. D. Bonch-Bruevich was given the task of supervising the construction of a suitable tomb. Because it had to be completed in three days, work began immediately and went on around the clock, but shifts were limited to two hours due to the cold.

Lenin's body was autopsied by a large team of physicians led by Dr. A. I. Abrikosov. During the autopsy that lasted four hours and forty minutes, Lenin's internal organs and brain were removed. (The autopsy report was published in detail three days later.) Abrikosov then carried out a normal embalming with the aim of preserving the body for six to seven days. Lenin's hair was darkened a bit to counteract the effects of an extremely short haircut his wife had given him before his death.

On the morning of January 23 another delegation of mourners arrived from Moscow.

A large crowd had gathered outside the villa. Lenin's body was placed in a casket lined with red velvet, his head resting on a red pillow. The casket was carried downstairs and covered with a glass lid. Six men then carried it on their shoulders for four miles through snow-covered woods from the country estate to the Gerasimovka railroad station. Lenin's widow and his sisters Anna and Maria Ilinichna walked alongside the casket until it was carried aboard the train. The train, draped in red and black mourning, pulled out of the station that had filled with mourners.

When the train arrived in Moscow, another large crowd had gathered at the station. The casket, covered with a red cloth and laden with flowers, was carried on the shoulders of eight men—one of them Joseph Stalin—over the nearly five miles from the Paveletsky railroad station south of the city to the House of Trade Unions, north of Red Square. The route was lined with troops and mourners and the procession included wreath-bearers, a marching band, Lenin's family members, honor guards, party members, many delegations, and a military escort.

A funeral march was played as the casket was carried into the Hall of Columns. Lenin's body was placed on a raised platform draped in red and surrounded by potted palms and lilies. Banners covered his body so that only his head, resting on a snow-white pillow, was visible. "Those who saw him say that the face was yellow-white like wax, without the slightest wrinkle. The eyes were closed, but there was a suggestion of someone merely resting, still possessed of an astonishing vitality" (Payne 1964, 614). An honor guard formed around the body and was replaced every ten minutes. For the first few hours, only family, friends, and privileged people were allowed inside the Trade Union House without a permit.

At seven o'clock on the evening of the 23rd, the doors to the Trade Union House were opened to the public. The body remained on view continuously for four days, although authorities had intended to close the gates each night. Lenin's wife Krupskaya kept watch by the body. Hundreds of thousands of people (probably more than half a million) lined up for hours in temperatures of 20 degrees below zero to get a brief look as they passed by the bier. "It seems to me that the Russian people has a far greater special mystical curiosity than other people, some kind of pull to look upon a corpse, a deceased person, especially if the deceased was above the common rank. In the pilgrimage to Lenin's casket there was this curiosity, but undoubtedly there was another impulse as well: to testify before the deceased to one's respect, love or gratitude toward him," wrote Nikolai Valentinov (Tumarkin 1983, 141).

Mourners, some of whom passed by the body more than once, were allowed inside at the rate of three per minute. So many people wanted to serve on the honor guard that its size was increased to twenty-four, and it was changed every five minutes. Mourners remained quiet and expressionless long after they passed by the bier. Most of them had never seen Lenin in person before his death. Hundreds of mourners fainted and were carried away on stretchers. The burial originally announced for four o'clock on January 25 had to be postponed as mourners continued to come from all over the country.

On January 24 the Politburo discussed ways of preserving Lenin for a period of forty days. Lenin's widow, sisters, and brother Dmitry Ilich would not agree to even a temporary preservation of the body. Two men were named to persuade them or, if that failed, to get them to agree to discuss the question in another month. Stalin, on the orders of the Politburo, gave instructions on the same day that the casket containing Lenin's corpse be kept in a vault formed in the Kremlin wall on Red Square and made accessible to visitors (Volkogonov 1994, 437–38). Stalin predicted, "In a short time you will see a pilgrimage by representatives of millions of toilers to the grave of Comrade Lenin" (Volkogonov 1994, 438).

Dr. Abrikosov had been placed in charge of the body. Although he feared the autopsy he had performed might have hindered the possibility of successful preservation, he hoped Lenin's body would remain unchanged for three or four years by keeping the temperature of the crypt at zero, keeping the humidity very low, and keeping the casket completely airtight. Feliks Dzerzhinski, founder of the Cheka (predecessor of the KGB), suggested preserving Lenin's body indefinitely and the Politburo fastened on the idea ("Lenin's Face-Saver," 31). Other sources state that Stalin was the first to suggest the permanent preservation of Lenin's body.

On January 25 the Moscow daily *Rabochaia Moskva* published three letters urging that the body be preserved. One of them read, "Under no circumstances can we give to the earth such a great and intensely beloved leader as Ilich. We suggest his remains be embalmed and left under glass for hundreds of years....Let him be with us always" (Tumarkin 1983, 173). The sentiments echoed those expressed in a meeting Stalin held several months before Lenin's death in which he stated, "Certain comrades believe that contemporary science offers the possibility, by means of embalming, to preserve the body of the deceased for a long time, in any case for a long enough time to permit our consciousness to get used to the idea that Lenin is no longer among us" (Tumarkin 1983, 174). At the same meeting Leon Trotsky and Lev Kamenev both spoke out vehemently against mummification of the remains as an affront to Lenin's memory.

On January 26 the Second All-Union Congress of Soviets met to pay official homage with speeches and eulogies by Krupskaya, Stalin, and several others. Resolutions were taken at this Second Congress and at the almost constant sessions of the Politburo, Central Control Commission, and Funeral Commission to rename Petrograd as Leningrad, to declare the anniversary of Lenin's death a day of national mourning, to erect statues of Lenin in all of the chief cities

of the Soviet Union, to commission his biography, and to compile and publish all of his words and writings. This same day, Commissar of Health N. A. Semashko issued his opinion that Lenin's body should be preserved only until a crematorium could be built and should then be cremated as an example to others. At about this time, however, it was decided that Lenin's body should be preserved indefinitely. "Certainly the overwhelming popular response to Lenin's lying-in-state must have played a significant role in prompting the decision to preserve and display Lenin's corpse" (Tumarkin 1983, 179). Another factor may have been the discovery of the tomb of Tutankhamen in Egypt fifteen months earlier. The foundation for Lenin's tomb had been laid the previous day and the crypt fitted onto it that morning.

On the evening of the 26th, the gates of the House of Trade Unions were closed. During the night, Lenin's body was placed in a red-draped casket. The next morning, January 27 the casket was carried out on the shoulders of eight men, again one of them Stalin, and transferred to the shoulders of eight more men who carried it to Red Square. It remained there while bands played funeral marches and tributes were offered by lower officials, workers, and foreign Communists. Just before four, the banners were removed from the casket. At four o'clock that afternoon, everything in Russia that could make a noise was sounded for three minutes, during which time the men carried the casket down into the wooden vault that had been completed earlier in the day. The crowd did not begin to disperse until the following morning.

Like others, Lenin's widow Krupskaya was very much opposed to Lenin's mummification, which she probably did not learn about until January 29: "...she was an old-style Bolshevik who abhorred personal glorification, as he had, and must have been horrified at seeing the revolutionary regime imitating ancient Russian church practices" (Fischer 1964, 674). In a small paragraph published in *Pravda* on January 30, she wrote, "Great is my prayer to you: do not allow your grief for Ilyich to assume the form of external reverence for his person..." (Payne 1964, 619). Her pleas were ignored, even though they mirrored those of Lenin himself. In *The State and Revolution*, he had written of great revolutionaries: "After their deaths attempts are made to convert them into harmless icons, as it were to canonize them, and surround their *names* with a certain halo for the consolation of the oppressed classes with the object of duping them, while at the same time emasculating and blunting the *real essence* of their revolutionary teachings, reducing them to vulgarity" (Payne 1964, 625). Krupskaya silently protested the mummification by refusing to visit the mausoleum and never mentioning Lenin's preserved body in her writings on him.

Despite the objections, the Politburo set out after the funeral to find ways to preserve Lenin's body indefinitely and debated the technical aspects of the problem. Leonid Krasin was put in charge of the preservation of the body and the construction of the mausoleum in which to house it. A wooden hut was soon built over the temporary vault and for the next several months only security police and the doctors who were embalming the body were allowed to enter. On February 3 the Funeral Commission announced that measures had been taken to protect the crypt from fire and water seepage and that an electric heater had been installed to maintain a constant temperature of zero. On February 4 Krasin supervised the installation of a refrigeration system to circulate cold air into the sarcophagus that had been constructed. The refrigeration unit was built in duplicate in case of mechanical breakdown. The sarcophagus, which had been designed by architect K. S. Melnikov, used glass that had once been the front window of a restaurant.

The preservation methods employed to this point had failed in their objective. The Funeral Commission reported in February 1924 that time had done its work and the skin of the corpse had become discolored, a sign that mold had set in (Tumarkin 1983, 183).

The skin was drying out and the ears were deteriorating. Lenin's face was "waxen gray, wrinkled, horribly shrunken. Beeswax and mortician's fluid had worked a change in him. Yet there was no doubt that this was his mortal body. The viscera had been removed, and the brain was in the keeping of the Soviet Brain Institute...but no one doubted that this face, so wrinkled and waxen, and so worked upon by the doctors, was his authentic face. In the first hours of death he looked strangely calm. Now he looked angry and sullen, tormented by guilt" (Payne 1964, 622).

Professor Vladimir Vorobyov of Kharkov University in the Ukraine read about the problem in the newspapers. He suggested to the authorities that they apply the methods used at anatomical museums to preserve human organs. Vorobyov was summoned to Moscow by Dzerzhinski and allowed to examine the body closely. He agreed to carry out the preservation if he could choose his assistants. Vorobyov formed a team of four assistants: Commissar Semashko, Professor V. N. Rozanov, Professor Veisbrod, and Professor Boris Ilich Zbarsky. They soon came to the conclusion that immediate steps had to be taken. On March 5 and 12 the Funeral Commission charged the scientists with a tall order: to preserve Lenin's body in a state in which it could be viewed and with an external appearance that would preserve the physical features in the way that he looked in the first days after his death. The scientists pointed out that the presence of oxygen would change (and in fact had changed) the color of the skin, that the only way to prevent the skin from drying out would be to immerse the body in liquid, and that contemporary science had not provided a means for solving the problem at hand (Tumarkin 1983, 184).

In early March 1924, construction of a temporary wooden mausoleum that would allow the viewing public access was begun and continued through April. On the 25th of that month, the Funeral Commission announced its intention to preserve the body intact: "At the present time, responding to the desires of the wide masses of the U.S.S.R. and other nations to see the physical features of the deceased leader, the Commission of the Funeral of V. I. Ulianov (Lenin) has decided to take measures, available in current science, to preserve the body for as long a time as possible" (Tumarkin 1983, 185). Once made public, the decision was irreversible and success imperative. The Funeral Commission was renamed the Commission for the Immortalization of the Memory of V. I. Ulianov (Lenin) three days later.

On March 26 Vladimir Vorobyov, who was a professor of anatomy at the Kharkov Medical Institute, headed the work to restore and re-embalm the body. He was closely assisted by another member of the team, Boris Zbarsky, a biochemist. Their efforts were under the general supervision of Leonid Krasin and their fellow members of the medical committee. The two men worked around the clock, resting in turns. Before applying a chemical to Lenin's body, they tested it on cadavers provided by morgues and pathology institutes. It has been hinted that the process they employed replaced the body liquids with a chemical that served as both a disinfectant and an antidehydrant. The result of their tests was said to be a solution consisting of glycerin and potassium acetate. Other accounts list ingredients including formalin, glycerin, alcohol, calcium, ethanol, and some 50 other unnamed additives. A chemist in Philadelphia attributed the preservation to a formaldehyde that produced a chemical reaction to form synthetic resin. Lenin's face was injected with a mixture of vaseline and paraffin that had the consistency of human fat tissue. The skin of the face was then smoothed and sewn. Marks and mold on the skin were eliminated. According to one account (Bortoli 1975), the scientists installed a small electric pump inside the corpse to maintain a constant degree of humidity in the tissues. The mausoleum was heavily guarded as the members of the team did their work. In mid–June, the Immortal-

ization Commission announced that the re-embalming had nearly reached its goal by imparting a uniform appearance to the skin with regard to normal color and consistency, introducing a chemical to hinder autolysis, and replacing the liquid in the tissues with one that would not evaporate (Tumarkin 1983, 186–87).

According to the author Nina Tumarkin (1983, 187), sharing the initial decomposition of Lenin's body with the public shows that the Funeral Commission was not trying to pass off the preservation of the corpse as miraculous. On the contrary, they were celebrating the expertise of Soviet science in restoring it. Two groups of visitors were allowed to see the body before the mausoleum was officially reopened. Delegates of the Thirteenth Party Congress viewed the remains on May 23 and delegates of the Fifth Congress of the Comintern were allowed to file past on June 19, 1924.

The task of re-embalming the body was completed at the end of July. From the 22nd to the 26th of the month, a team of experts inspected the body and reviewed the written records of the scientists. They concluded that the work was scientifically sound and that the body should remain viewable behind glass as long as humidity and temperature were kept at an appropriate level. The entire Immortalization Commission made a detailed inspection of the body on July 26 and held a meeting at the Kremlin later that day announcing the success. The team of experts gave their report, stating that the body would remain unchanged but would require constant attention. The Immortalization Commission resolved that Professors Vorobyov and Zbarsky should attend to the observation and care of the body under their general supervision (Tumarkin 1983, 188).

On August 1, 1924, at six P.M., the mausoleum officially opened to the public after a solemn ceremony. The mausoleum was surrounded by a paved courtyard enclosed with a railing inside which flowers and bushes had been planted. The vault had been enlarged, painted, and carpeted. Guards holding fixed bayonets were posted in the courtyard, at the entrance, and inside. Regulations had been published that visitors were required to arrive in groups according to districts and that all belongings (briefcases, pocketbooks, umbrellas, canes, etc.) had to be checked with the guards. Visitors descended a stairway carpeted in red. A corridor led to the chamber containing Lenin's body, which visitors viewed from a railed gallery along the sides. The casket lay in a red-lined sarcophagus topped with glass. Lenin lay in the casket with his hands crossed above his waist wearing a khaki tunic. The lower part of the body was covered with black and purple satin.

Foreign newsmen were allowed to see the body on August 3, 1924. Walter Duranty reported, "The body is in a perfect state of preservation....Although the medical experts who embalmed the body say that neither wax nor any coloring material was used, the face appears normal in every way, there being no indication of pigmentation of the flesh, emaciation of the body or shrinkage of features" (Tumarkin 1983, 195). Zbarsky told the media that the entire cost of embalming the body had been $7,500 and that the results were expected to last at least three or four decades. If the temperature were kept constant, he explained, "Lenin's body should last forever" (Tumarkin 1983, 196). Lenin's corpse was viewed by his brother on August 24 and said to look no different than when he died.

In April 1926, entries in a competition for the design of a permanent mausoleum were due. Design requirements included a central hall for the body, underground space for the technical apparatus, a chamber to house Lenin's books and manuscripts, a waiting room for up to two hundred people, a podium, and architectural harmony with the Kremlin wall and Red Square (Tumarkin 1983, 202). In the end, all 117 entries were rejected, and it was decided to rebuild the existing wooden mausoleum in stone.

When Nikolai Valentinov visited the mausoleum for the first time in 1927 or 1928,

he was disgusted by the "small lacquered doll with yellow whiskers" that bore no resemblance to the Lenin he had known (Tumarkin 1983, 205). At about the same time, Soviet authorities contacted Dr. Pedro Ara, who had embalmed Eva Perón, and Ara's mentor Dr. Hochstetter of Vienna about the possible restoration of the still deteriorating body of Lenin. "Both seemed to feel that the suggested method, additional injections of alcohol followed by glycerin, would not be effective and declined the offer" (Johnson and Johnson/Part 1 1986, 24).

In July 1929 construction on the new mausoleum began and was finished in sixteen months. The mausoleum was constructed of red-black Ukrainian granite, Karelian porphyry, and labradorite in Red Square with some 30 steps leading down to Lenin's body. At this time, the body vanished from sight for several months but returned with a look of youthfulness: "Not only had the last remaining wrinkles been smoothed away, but the flesh looked firmer and was more vividly colored. The fine-drawn ascetic features, with the high cheekbones, the domed forehead, and the thin beard, suggested an early icon. Gone was the rough-hewn Mongoloid face which habitually wore an expression of determination; the new image was gentle and remote, almost abstract" (Payne 1964, 623). The left hand that had been clenched was now resting on his breast with well-shaped, rosy pink, tapering fingers. The new mausoleum containing the freshly restored body officially opened on November 10, 1924. Lenin now lay beneath a hermetically sealed glass sarcophagus lit from above with the rest of the chamber darkened. In interviews Boris Zbarsky boasted of having produced the effect of a man who is not dead but sleeping.

Publicly, it was rumored that Boris Zbarsky had in fact abandoned the embalming effort, cremated the body, and replaced it with a wax effigy. To dispel the rumors, an official investigation was opened and a German doctor was invited to participate and issue a report. He observed what he called frostbite on the skin, he felt the cheeks, and he lifted one of Lenin's arms. His opinion was that Lenin had been wonderfully preserved. Thus vindicated, the scientists offered to reveal the secret embalming formula in three or four years once they were sure of its effectiveness, but despite reported offers of more than $1 million they never did.

In the 1930s members of the foreign press stated their opinion that the pale mummy was a wax figure, prompting the Kremlin to invite a number of non–Russians, including author Louis Fischer, to the tomb. When they descended into the shrine, Boris Zbarsky alluded to the secret process by which the mummification was achieved and estimated that the body could last a century. "Then he opened the hermetically sealed glass case containing the relic, tweaked Lenin's nose and turned his head to the right and left. It was not wax. It was Lenin. The iconoclast is now a modern Russian icon, and millions queue and gaze in wonder at the miracle of his preservation in the flesh" (Fischer 1964, 675). Many were still not convinced: "The body has, from the first, been the subject of stories and rumors, many of which claim that the figure in the mausoleum is made of wax. There is no way of knowing for certain whether or not the displayed remains of Lenin are indeed his embalmed body. As a rule, the Soviet system's supporters claim they are, and its detractors say the relic is a waxen doll—testimony to the political symbolism with which it is invested" (Tumarkin 1983, 197).

In 1934 Boris Zbarsky (d. 1954) handed down his tasks and techniques to his son Ilya Zbarsky. The responsibility was daunting: "If we made the slightest mistake in manipulating the body, we knew the fate that awaited us....We were sure to pay for it with our lives," the younger Zbarsky recalled ("Lenin's Face-Saver," 31–32). Stalin was given regular reports on the condition of the mummy, which Zbarsky and later his son were responsible to the security services for maintaining in viewable condition. The embalming staff watched carefully for any de-

terioration of the mummy's skin, including peeling, deformations, or darkening. "During the Stalinist days...even the smallest flaw on Lenin's body could earn one a trip to Siberia or worse. Every blemish and bacteria growth that might appear brought terror to the hearts of the embalmers, who would frantically scrub the imperfection off of Communism's central deity" (Tanner 1994, 34).

In 1935 Professor Vorobyov received the Order of Lenin for his part in the development of the embalming process. The younger Zbarsky took over the head of the embalming team when Vladimir Vorobyov died during surgery in October 1937. In 1939 a mausoleum laboratory was opened, and the team was provided with new machines and reagents, most of them from Germany. In 1940 it was reported to the Politburo that an inspection had revealed deviations on the face, a parting of the autopsy incision on the head, and a darkening on the nose (Volkogonov 1994, 445).

Lenin's body remained on display until July 1941, when it was evacuated under the care of Ilya Zbarsky to Tyumen in the Ural Mountains of Western Siberia to prevent its capture by the Germans. The body was transported during the four-day journey on a special train in a casket equipped with shock absorbers to protect it from the slightest movement. The casket was watched over during the entire journey and was accompanied by four scientists, the commander of the mausoleum, and approximately 40 Kremlin guards. For four years the body was maintained and monitored on the first floor of a specially prepared laboratory that had once housed a technical secondary school. Despite the precautions, the body had deteriorated during the journey: the eyes had half-opened and wrinkles had appeared under the arms. Restoration was successful and, according to Zbarsky, the body was in better condition than before its transfer. The scientists made great improvements to the elasticity of the skin and the mobility of the limbs ("Lenin's Face-Saver," 32). Lenin's body was returned to Moscow in 1945 and placed in a new sarcophagus. A new light filter inside the sarcophagus gave the skin a rose-tinted hue, whereas the previously stark lighting had highlighted blemishes.

In 1945 Zbarsky revealed about the re-embalming "that when we completed the job, we did not have complete confidence in it" (Tumarkin 1983, 205). In the 1950s the embalming technique used in the 1920s was perfected: the key to the body's preservation (a state secret until the early 1990s) was a compound consisting mostly of glycerol and potassium acetate, which replaced all the water in Lenin's tissues. The compound has two special qualities: bacteria does not grow in it, and it does not absorb water or evaporate if conditions of 60.8° F (16° C) and 70 percent humidity are maintained (Schemann 1992). Because the arteries had been cut during his autopsy, the compound could not be effectively injected as is done in traditional embalming, so the body was bathed in the solution.

In 1952 Ilya Zbarsky was relieved of his post when his father was arrested. Care of the mummy was taken over by Sergei S. Debov as a sideline to his work as a molecular biologist. Attempts were made several times to convince the authorities and the public of the absurdity of the mausoleum. The glass of the sarcophagus was broken by a visitor in 1959 and again in 1969. (The transparent sarcophagus is now bulletproof.) Concealed explosives were carried in by visitors with deadly results: in 1963 a bomb killed the man who carried it, and in 1973 another bomb killed its courier, a man named Savrasov, and wounded many visitors.

By the early 1970s the laboratory at the mausoleum employed 27 scientists and 33 technicians. "Gradually an entire mechanism was put in place to manage Lenin's embalmed body, which had become vitally necessary not so much for its propaganda value, as for its effect on the psychology of the masses" (Volkogonov 1994, 445). An improved sarcophagus was installed in the

1970s, and the mausoleum continued to be frequently refurbished at a cost of hundreds of millions of rubles over the years. The death chamber is outfitted with color monitors and multiple sensors that constantly report temperature—kept at the suggested 60.8° F (16° C)—and humidity.

The mausoleum's other chambers include a showcase of the weapons and explosives taken from visitors by guards, a lounge for the 10 specialists under the supervision of Dr. Debov, and two identical laboratories with operating tables—one for Stalin (installed in the mausoleum from 1953 to 1961) and one for Lenin. Lenin's body is conveyed on a hospital stretcher to the second lab every Monday and Friday for an examination. Embalming fluid is painted on his hands and head. According to Debov, the body is saturated once a week with a bactericidal solution that does not absorb liquid from the air at the maintained temperature and humidity.

Every 18 months the mummy is undressed and thoroughly examined by a team of five men (an anatomist and his assistant, a biochemist and his assistant, and the commander of the mausoleum). "Women are barred from taking part in the embalming because the authorities consider it improper for them to view the Soviet demi-god naked" ("Lenin's Face-Saver," 31). The catafalque on which the body lies is moved into a sterilized room. The walls are wiped down with antiseptic and alcohol. The laces that tie Lenin's jacket and trousers at the back are untied. The arms, which must be articulated to get them out of the sleeves, are said to retain their suppleness. The special watertight suit that is worn under the uniform is removed and the body is immersed for a month in a glass bath of glycerin and potassium acetate so that it will remain 70 percent liquid.

After the bath the excess liquids are allowed to drip off for a few hours. Any discoloration is wiped away with hydrogen peroxide. When the body is dry, the watertight suit is replaced and preservative solution poured inside the suit. The uniform, which is changed periodically, is replaced on the body. "If a pathologist looked at samples of skin from Lenin and a fresh corpse under a microscope...he could not tell which is which, it's so well preserved. If the conditions in the mausoleum could be maintained, he could be preserved forever," Debov says (Schemann 1992). The body shows gradual changes, but the scientists continue to strive against time.

Care of Lenin's body is now maintained by Boris Khomatov. Custodianship of the mummy is overseen by officials at the Scientific Research Institute for Biological Structures in Moscow (also called the Research Center of Biostructures). Once every four or five years, the body is thoroughly inspected by a commission of senior scientists, who check the body with devices designed to spot changes in the size or color of the skin and take small samples of the skin for testing. There are said to be several signs of progressing decay: fungus has started to grow along the neck and behind the head, the skin around the ears is turning blue, and dark spots are now visible on the pads of the fingers ("Lenin's Face-Saver," 32). Continued preservation would require expensive reagents imported from abroad, which are no longer available to the embalmers for financial reasons. "Nothing lasts forever," says Zbarsky ("Lenin's Face-Saver," 32).

To this day, however, the debate about the authenticity of the body continues. Funeral director and embalming historian Gail Johnson points out that the exact method of preservation has always been a state secret, and Johnson does not discount the long-held belief that the body is made of wax. In response to the suggestion that the exposure of only the head and hands indicates that the body has not been preserved in its entirety, Ilya Zbarsky calls such rumors "quite unfounded" ("Lenin's Face-Saver," 32). "There have been a lot of articles in the press saying that a hand was cut off or that just the head and the hands remain....They ab-

solutely do not correspond to the truth; the body is whole and is preserved to this day," says Zbarsky (Tanner 1994, 34). John Chew, former director of the Institute for Funeral Service Education at Boca Raton's Lynn University, believes the effigy was created using Lenin's skeletal remains. Chew wonders whether the chemicals necessary to preserve the corpse would have been available in 1924. London embalmer Desmond Henley, O.B.E., is skeptical that the Russians had sufficient knowledge of the art and science of embalming, particularly of a body that had been autopsied.

If the body has been preserved, John Chew suggests that the Russians allow an international group of experts access to it to answer questions about whether they really developed a viable method of preservation and whether they are using pumps to exclude oxygen and keep the body hermetically sealed (Cronin 1994, 20). Henley points out that maintenance of the body by periodically soaking it in embalming fluid would have a desiccating effect and render it unviewable. Richard Todd, a member of a British delegation allowed to visit the Lenin Mausoleum privately in 1959, states that although the faces of Lenin and Stalin (who lay by his side at that time) looked waxen, "they were quite heavily stubbled with bristle that must have grown after death. I know nothing of embalming," Todd writes, "but feel sure that no wax model could have hundreds of tiny bristles inserted into it" ("Lenin's Embalming," 24). Others disagree, pointing out that it is common for professional embalmers to replace the hair of the head and face.

After the breakup of the Soviet Union, there was much discussion about whether the display of Lenin's preserved body should continue. The mausoleum had become a place for both Communists and the simply curious (Volkogonov 1994, 441), drawing as many as 3 million visitors a year. "It is likely that people were—and still are—drawn to the Lenin Mausoleum not for spiritual reasons but out of a combined sense of political duty and fascination, or even morbid curiosity" (Tumarkin 1983, 197). Lenin's widow had begged the Communist leadership to bury him rather than enshrining him. Krupskaya had visited the mausoleum less than once a year to spare herself the emotional upset it caused. On her last visit to the tomb in 1938, she had muttered, "He's just the same, but look how I've aged..." (Volkogonov 1994, 441). Krupskaya lamented before her death in February 1939 that her husband's body had become an icon, regretted that people line up for three hours to get a peek at him, and noted that the body vibrates when tanks roll across Red Square.

The Russian government under Boris Yeltsin has tried to bury Lenin twice, once after the August 1991 coup and a second time after the October 1993 destruction of the Soviet-era parliament, but Yeltsin hesitated and the opportunity was lost. "Since the December 1993 elections...Yeltsin has been unwilling to spend the political capital it would take to bury Lenin in his likely final resting spot, next to his mother's grave in St. Petersburg. And in recent months, few have clamored for the burial" (Tanner 1994, 34). Meanwhile, the guard at the mausoleum changes every hour as it has since the tomb was built.

Many, including Moscow Mayor Yury Luzhkov, who ordered the closing of the Lenin Museum, think that Lenin should be buried alongside his mother and sister in Volkovo Cemetery in St. Petersburg. Mayor of St. Petersburg Anatoly Sobchak was willing, but officials of the Russian Orthodox Church objected to the burial of a life-long atheist on sanctified ground. Sobchak feels that Lenin's corpse is viewed out of curiosity, that his mortal remains have become nothing more than a wax or marble statue. He maintains that Lenin deserves burial, rather than being subject to what Sobchak refers to as "continued execution," and that by burying Lenin everyone will be purified. On the other hand, Lenin's niece Olga Ulyanova thinks the body should be preserved (Sternthal 1989). "There's a tendency to destroy everything. I would be sad if this

was destroyed," agrees Debov (Schemann 1992). Ilya Zbarsky, on the other hand, says, "I put a lot of energy and time into this in my life...but as a citizen, I say it's time to bury him" (Tanner 1994, 34).

Joseph Stalin

Just before he died on March 5, 1953, Joseph Stalin cursed the people in the room with a final menacing gesture, lifting his left hand as if he were pointing to something above. His face was said to be angry and full of fear. After his death, his body was autopsied. A witness to the autopsy was one of his guards, a man called Krustalyov. When they opened the head, one of the medics said, "This is obviously a very fine brain, quite out of the ordinary" (Richardson 1994, 253). This made such an impression on Krustalyov that he afterwards collapsed completely, drank heavily, and was fired. Stalin's death was announced on the morning of March 6, 1953. His body had been secretly transferred from Kuntsevo to Moscow during the night.

On the afternoon of March 6, Stalin's body was put on display at the House of the Trade Unions in the Hall of Columns. A giant portrait was hung above the door and graced with evergreen boughs. Stalin lay in state amid a mountain of flowers on a raised bier that, in the Russian tradition, remained uncovered. "He was dressed in his military uniform. The old face was peaceful but still imperious. Beneath the thick brown skin, the cheekbones were still prominent; the outstretched hands still seemed ready to clutch and seize" (Bortoli 1975, 160).

The Hall of Columns was opened to the public. There was a tremendous outpouring of feeling from the people as he lay in state. "His death...inspired...a strange sense of surprise that a leader who had so long been thought of as remote and godlike could do anything as ordinary and human as to die" (de Jonge 1986, 482). The reaction of the Russian people to the death of their leader was filmed by Sergei Gerasimov, but the film that he claimed was "not the official version" was banned because it showed the grieving public. "The later official story was that nobody cried," he said (Richardson 1994, 253–54). The press of the crowd, which the military could not control, continued for three days during which many people suffocated or were trampled to death. After waiting 12 or 14 hours, mourners were borne along by the tide: "There was just enough time to etch in one's memory the coffin covered with red silk emerging from the flowers and palms, and the rigid, uniformed shape, its legendary face so close for the first time, humanized by death" (Bortoli 1975, 167).

A funeral commission of seven people chaired by Nikita Khrushchev was hurriedly making arrangements. On March 7 a decree was issued that Stalin's body be placed in the mausoleum in which Vladimir Lenin reposed. The decree also ordered the construction of a pantheon (that has never been built) to which the sarcophagi of Lenin, Stalin, and all the other heroes memorialized at the Kremlin wall would be moved. Some protested the decision to entomb Stalin in Lenin's mausoleum, but the crowds at his viewing continued. The honor guard around Stalin's corpse was constantly being changed. When the doors were closed on March 8, a line of people still waiting to pay their respects stretched six or seven miles. They remained in place.

The following morning, March 9, mourners carried wreaths and bouquets toward Red Square, and the Kremlin bells tolled. (After the funeral, there were so many wreaths in Red Square that they could not all be placed on the mausoleum.) Six black horses pulled a gun carriage bearing the red-draped casket with Stalin's visored cap on top. His decorations were carried by marshals and generals. Stalin's heirs and family followed, then the heads of governments, ministers, ambassadors. The cortege halted and the glass-topped casket was placed on a catafalque. Eulogies that sounded like political speeches were made by Malenkov, Beria, and Molotov. Afterward, Stalin's

"comrades-in-arms" lifted the casket onto their shoulders with the help of soldiers and carried it into the crypt where Lenin already rested. Stalin's name was already engraved beside Lenin's on the outer wall. Cannons roared, the flag was hoisted to full-staff, and the regiments prepared for a final parade. Newsreels of the funeral filmed by Soviet cameramen remain consigned to the film archives, unavailable for foreign or domestic viewing.

Professor Zbarsky, who had once been arrested by Stalin, began the process of preparing the body for extended display, a job that took several months. Stalin's body was embalmed, possibly by immersion: "They mummified him in a pickle solution for display and deification," says his daughter Svetlana (Richardson 1994, 255). The mausoleum that now contained Lenin and Stalin was reopened to the public in November 1953. "Soviet citizens would then see the two glass coffins standing side by side in the cold, reddish-yellow light of the crypt. Lenin austere in his short jacket, Stalin more massive and flamboyant with his huge epaulettes. His eyes were shut and his hands extended. He looked barely asleep, and there was a touch of imperious irony in the heavy aquiline profile" (Bortoli 1975, 171).

People filed past the preserved body of Stalin for years until January 1962, when the mausoleum was closed and a seven-foot fence erected. The mummified body was removed from the mausoleum as ordered by the Twenty-Second Congress and buried in the Kremlin wall, where it probably remains in fairly good condition. Sergei Debov, who had taken over the care of the bodies of Lenin and Stalin in 1952, remembers, "It was at night....A commission came, bringing a common coffin. We took the body out of the sarcophagus and put it into the coffin, some soldiers hammered it shut and took it into the grave out back. That's all there was to it" (Schemann 1992). Stalin was entombed with much less fanfare than he was funeralized with almost nine years before. At least one

The body of Mao Tse-tung lying in state in the Great Hall of the People in Beijing two days after his death. Photo courtesy of UPI/Corbis-Bettmann.

family member was grateful that Stalin did not share Lenin's posthumous fate permanently. "Thank God...they gave my father a proper burial in the end," said Svetlana (Richardson 1994, 255).

Mao Tse-tung

Chinese Communist leader Mao Tse-tung (or Zedong) died on September 9, 1976, of Parkinson's disease, advanced arteriosclerosis, and old age (he was 83). Wang Dongxing, the chief of bodyguards, announced to Mao's personal physicians, including author Li Zhusui, that the Politburo had decided that the body would have to be preserved for two weeks and that steps to prevent the body from deteriorating should be taken immediately. Li Zhusui, deputy chairman of the preservation committee that was formed, consulted with the minister of public health, Liu Xiangping, and together they sought the help of people at the Academy of Medical Sciences. A meeting took place between Li Zhusui, Liu Xiangping, Yang Chun (party secretary at the Academy), Huang Shuze (a doctor and vice-minister of public health), and two experts in the preservation of human bodies: Zhang Bingchang (research associate in the department of

anatomy) and Xu Jing (assistant research in the department of histology).

The specialists agreed that Mao's body could easily be preserved for two weeks by injecting two liters of formaldehyde into a leg artery. After they returned to Building 202 of Zhongnan-hai to start their work, they were told by Wang Dongxing that the Politburo had now decided that the chairman's body should be permanently preserved. Li Zhisui protested, as he writes later: "'But it's impossible....It just can't be done....Even iron and steel corrode, to say nothing of the human body. How can it not deteriorate?' I was remembering my trip to Moscow with Mao in 1957 and our visit to the remains of Lenin and Stalin. The bodies had seemed shrunken and dry, and I had been told that Lenin's nose and ears had rotted away and been replaced by wax and that Stalin's mustache had fallen off. Soviet embalming techniques were far more advanced than China's. I could not imagine how we could preserve Mao's body" (Li 1994, 18). Wang assured him that the central authority would provide anything they needed in the way of personnel, facilities, and equipment.

Marshal Ye Jianying, a founder of the People's Liberation Army and a member of the Politburo, discussed the preservation with Li Zhisui and suggested he consult with instructors at the Institute of Arts and Crafts about making a wax dummy of Mao in case it was later needed as a substitute for the body. Mao's widow Jian Qing learned of Li Zhisui's skepticism about being able to preserve the body and withdrew herself from the funeral and embalming arrangements. "If Mao's body could not be preserved, she could claim not to have been involved and could turn against those who were" (Li 1994, 630).

Mao's body was moved to a more spacious room, and the temperature of the entire building was lowered to 50° F (10° C), since the rooms did not have individual thermostats. Zhang Bingchang and Xu Jing injected the formaldehyde. They were told about the decision to permanently preserve the body and Xu Jing went to the library at the Academy to research possible methods. She came back and reported a procedure she learned of in a Western journal that would preserve the body for a "relatively long time." The procedure called for twelve to sixteen liters of formaldehyde to be injected within four to eight hours of death. The amount depended on the size of the person, but, "when the tips of the fingers and toes are filled with liquid, enough has been injected" (Li 1994, 19).

They decided to try the procedure, and two men joined the team: Chen (an intern with the department of anatomy at the Academy) helped administer the formaldehyde, and Ma (from the department of pathology of the Beijing Hospital) lent his expertise in the restoration of the dead. By ten o'clock the following morning, twenty-two liters of solution had been injected, six more than the formula called for in hopes that this would provide an additional guarantee of preservation. "The results were shocking. Mao's face was bloated, as round as a ball, and his neck was now the width of his head. His skin was shiny, and the formaldehyde oozed from his pores like perspiration. His ears were swollen, too, sticking out from his head at right angles. The corpse was grotesque" (Li

1994, 20). They decided to concentrate on his face, since his body would be covered by clothing, and began massaging the face with a towel and cotton balls to try to force the liquid down into the body. When Chen pressed a little too hard, a piece of skin on Mao's right cheek broke off, but vaseline and flesh-colored makeup made the damage invisible.

By three o'clock in the afternoon, Mao's face looked normal and his ears no longer stuck out. The neck remained swollen, and when they tried to put his suit on, his chest was so swollen the jacket would not button. "They cut a slit in the underside of the jacket and trousers to accommodate Mao's new bulk" (Li 1994, 20). While the body was being dressed, Xu Shiyou, commander of the Guangzhou Military Region, arrived to pay his respects. He bowed three times, asked some questions, and circled Mao's remains twice, asking, "Why are there bluish bruises on his body?" He bowed three more times, saluted the chairman, and left. When Xu Shiyou raised his question again later, the bruises were explained as "death patches" that appear about four hours after death. In Mao's case they were said to have been caused by three large air bubbles in the left lung and pneumonia in both lungs. After Xu Shiyou's visit Ma touched up the makeup on Mao's face and the embalming team draped the body with the Communist party flag.

Sixteen hours after it had occurred, the death of Mao Tse-tung was announced to the public by the Central Committee of the Chinese Communist party. "No particulars were given. Nothing was said of cremation, burial, or Leninization, the preservation of his body for future generations" (Shearer 1976, 8). At midnight the morning of September 10, the embalmers placed the body—draped with the Chinese flag—in a crystal vacuum-sealed casket. Several members of the Politburo had their pictures taken facing the casket. The casket was then loaded into the back of an ambulance, and Li Zhisui accompanied it through Beijing to the Great Hall of the People.

Mao lay in state for one week at the Great Hall of the People, where 300,000 (according to another estimate 750,000) people filed past the catafalque to pay their respects. A huge portrait of Mao hung in the middle of the crepe-draped hall. A banner read, "Carry on the cause left by Chairman Mao and carry on the cause of proletarian revolution through to the end." At the end of the week of mourning (September 11 through 17) that had been proclaimed, a funeral rally was held at the Square of the Gate of Heavenly Peace. A million people—none of them foreign diplomats—attended the rally on September 18, during which all work stopped and all sirens were sounded for a three-minute period at three o'clock. At the end of the rally, the crowd made three solemn bows toward the giant portrait of Mao atop the gate and dispersed.

In the meantime, Li Zhisui had begun to organize a special team for the permanent preservation of the body. He recruited more than 20 leading specialists in anatomy, pathology, and organic chemistry from medical schools around the country. They investigated historical Chinese methods of preservation but concluded that the ancient techniques would be of no use in this situation. They thought of sending a research team to Russia to find out how Lenin's body had been preserved, but China's relations with the Soviet Union had deteriorated, and this was impossible. They sent two investigators to Hanoi to find out how Ho Chi Minh had been preserved, but no one in Vietnam was willing to explain the process, and they were unable to view the body.

According to researcher I. W. Blair, the Vietnamese did provide assistance to the Chinese in preparing Mao's body, but because they did not want to reveal their dependence on the Soviet Union for the continued maintenance of the body of Ho Chi Minh, they dispatched an ordinary embalmer to China. Blair writes, "The body was duly embalmed and the result seemed highly satisfactory with the restoration of a lifelike and dignified appearance. After a few weeks

had passed, it was noticed that the great statesman was changing color. Slowly his skin began to wrinkle. Shriveling and extreme discoloration followed. The body was removed from public display" (Blair 1994).

The two members of the special team who had been sent to visit Madame Tussaud's Wax Museum concluded that the waxen figure of Mao made by the Institute of Arts and Crafts was far superior to the English wax replicas. After reading scientific journals, the team decided on a plan. Work began after the official period of mourning had ended and was done in the utmost secrecy. Sometime after midnight on September 17, Mao's body was taken in a minibus from the Great Hall of the People in Beijing to Maojiawan and through the guarded entrance to the "May 19" underground complex. They arrived ten to fifteen minutes later at the fully equipped hospital just beneath the 305 Hospital that Li Zhisui directed. The body was placed in one of the clinic's operating rooms. The brain was left intact, but the viscera (heart, lungs, stomach, kidneys, intestines, liver, pancreas, bladder, gallbladder, and spleen) were removed and preserved in formaldehyde. The visceral cavity was filled with formaldehyde-saturated cotton. A tube was inserted into the neck to allow them to replenish the formaldehyde at periodic intervals. The crystal casket was filled with helium. Several days later, the wax figure arrived and was placed in another locked room. Li Zhisui inspected Mao's body once a week for a full year.

In 1977 the Chi-nien t'ang (Memorial Hall) in Tiananmen Square was completed to house Mao's body. The construction of the 112-foot-high building is said to have involved the labor of more than 700,000 people. Xu Jing was put in charge of both the remains and the mausoleum. On September 17, the embalmed body, the wax replica, and the jars containing Mao's vital organs were transferred to the huge vault beneath the public hall. The casket was installed on the floor of an elevator that raises it to and lowers it from the viewing area. The day after

Mao's body was installed in the mausoleum, and a little more than a year after his death, a memorial service was held at Tiananmen Square. At three o'clock that afternoon the whistles of every factory and train sounded for three minutes, followed by three minutes of silence. Today, those paying homage walk up a set of stairs and into an anteroom in which a ten-foot statue of Mao, supposedly inspired by the Lincoln Memorial, is installed. In an inner room, the body lies on a black granite catafalque beneath a trapezoidal crystal. The body appears sallow and the face wrinkled (Iserson 1994, 510).

Several years before his death, Mao had selected a grave site in Papaoshan Cemetery for himself and his wife Jiang Qing. The two of them had visited the spot on more than one occasion. After his death, many people believed that cremating Mao and scattering his ashes over the rivers and mountains of China would be more fitting than burial or enshrinement, and in 1956 he had been the first person to sign the pledge to be cremated (Li 1994, 17–18). In his biography, Ross Terrill remarks, "…mummification in a mausoleum seems to be the last thing he would have wished" (1980, 422). Mao's successor, Deng Xiaoping, tried to distance himself from Mao's legacy. "Mao was mothballed: his mummified corpse remained on periodic display in a crystal sarcophagus in his mausoleum in Tiananmen Square, while his political legacy drifted into a decade-long state of suspended animation" (Schell 1992, 32). Even so, Mao's thought still resides at the center of Party ideology and the Memorial Hall containing Mao Tse-tung's mummified body attracts tens of thousands of Chinese and foreign tourists each day.

Ho Chi Minh

Ho Chi Minh, Vietnamese Communist leader, died on the morning of September 3, 1969, aged 79. His death was not announced publicly until September 5, 1969. "It took them [his associates] two days to mourn his death and to prepare an announcement to the people among whom, they knew, Ho's passing would cause a serious commotion" (Huyen 1971, 314). In his will, Ho requested, "When I am gone, grand funerals should be avoided in order not to waste the people's time and money" (Huyen 1971, 316). He had specified that his body be cremated and his ashes buried on three unmarked hilltops around the country. Despite his wishes, a service took place on September 9 at the Ba Dinh Square in Hanoi, which was crowded with more than 100,000 people. The ceremony included the playing of the national anthem, the stopping of traffic, a eulogy, the reading of Ho's will, a twenty-one gun salute, and a fly-over by a squadron of jets, all accompanied by mass sobbing and crying. After the service, the crowd proceeded past the clear-glass casket containing the body. He was dressed in his familiar khaki suit, lying on a red velvet bed, with his head on a white pillow.

Information about the preservation of Ho Chi Minh's body is difficult to come by. The Vietnamese apparently obtained their knowledge from the Russians, either directly or indirectly. According to one account (Soloviov 1996, 15), the embalming was in fact carried out by Moscow's Scientific Research Institute for Biological Structures. At the time of Mao Tse-tung's death in 1976, members of his embalming team were told confidentially by the Vietnamese that Ho Chi Minh's nose had rotted away and his beard had fallen off (Li 1994, 23). Today he continues to lie in state in a refrigerated tomb in Hanoi that was built to resemble that of Lenin's. The tomb is visited daily by masses of people, many of whom weep when they gaze upon the corpse.

Kim Il Sung

Kim Il Sung died on July 8, 1994, at age 82 after ruling North Korea for forty-six years. His funeral procession was led through the streets of Pyongyang. After the funeral, the location of the corpse was kept a state secret. For months it was rumored

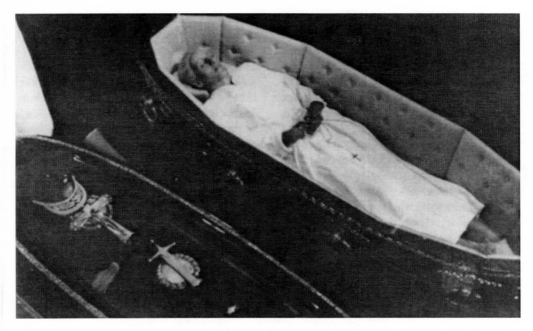

The body of Eva Perón on public view in 1974, nineteen years after death. Her open casket lies next to the closed casket of her husband Juan Perón, who had died less than six months earlier, in the crypt of the Presidential Residence in Olivos, Argentina. Photo courtesy of UPI/Corbis-Bettmann.

that Russian specialists had been brought in to embalm the body. *Mortuary Management* reported in November 1994 that the corpse was supposedly being prepared by Moscow's Scientific Research Institute for Biological Structures in an embalming process that was expected to take from eight to twelve months and cost $300,000 to $500,000.

South Korea's news agency reported that both Russian and Chinese embalmers had been working on the body. North Korean authorities then revealed that Kim's preserved corpse would be displayed in a glass tomb in Pyongyang's parliament building. The body was expected to draw millions, according to the October 1995 issue of *Mortuary Management*.

IDOLS

The bodies of the beloved are sometimes saved from decay. Tenor Enrico Caruso lay in state in a crystal casket for years due to the influence of his friends. Eva Perón, champion of the Argentine masses, was expertly embalmed as desired by her husband. Two-year-old Rosalia Lombardo was remarkably preserved, presumably at the request of her family. The bodies were lovingly cared for, which in the case of Caruso required careful manipulation to regularly change his clothes. Both he and Rosalia were displayed under glass to the public in a dignified and serene setting. But whereas Caruso may have had a saintly voice in life, Evita and Rosalia were saintly after death. The face of the woman did not change during the transition from life to death and for decades afterward. The face of the child seems to be imbued with life to this day except for her lack of breath. Both may be considered their respective embalmers' tours de force.

Eva Perón

As his wife lay dying Argentine leader Juan Perón inquired about enshrining her remains like those of Vladimir Lenin. Eva Perón's attending physician, Dr. Ricardo Finochietto, recommended Dr. Pedro Ara, a Spanish pathologist, professor of anatomy, and cultural attaché at the Spanish embassy in Buenos Aires. Perón summoned Dr. Ara, who was present when "Evita" died on July 26, 1952, aged 33 and weighing only about sixty-five pounds. Dr. Finochietto closed her eyes and placed her face in repose. Juan Perón gave Dr. Ara the keys to the room, telling him that no one would be allowed to enter while he worked. Dr. Ara, who died in 1973, recalled, "Her face…had a tranquil, beautiful look, liberated at last from her cruel suffering" (Barnes 1978, 161).

Dr. Ara had acquired his embalming skills by preparing hundreds of anatomical cadavers. In addition, he had embalmed several bodies for funeral purposes in which he adjusted the features to the standards of modern restoration, techniques not necessary in cadaver preparation. One body was that of the twelve-year-old daughter of one of his Córdoba Medical College colleagues, who was said to have dressed the child and sat her at the dinner table every night (Ortiz 1996, 279). Another was that of an elderly beggar and was later prepared for display as a bust by separating the head and neck from the torso by dissection (Johnson and Johnson/Part One 1986, 24). In his novel *Santa Evita* (1996, 21), Tomás Eloy Martínez puts words in the mouth of Dr. Ara: "I am not a taxidermist. I am a preserver of bodies. All the arts aspire to eternity, but mine is the only one that turns eternity into something visible."

Dr. Ara was first charged with preserving the lifelike appearance of Eva Perón's body for a sustained viewing by the public. She was immediately embalmed with what some accounts claim was a mixture of alcohol and glycerin. The brain and internal organs were not removed. British embalmer Desmond Henley, O.B.E., who corresponded with Dr. Ara, believes that he carried out a "normal arterial injection" and Dr. Ara himself said only that he had used "preservative chemicals" (Johnson and Johnson/Part One 1986, 60). Dr. Ara was accused by an American publication of being present at Eva Perón's deathbed for the express purpose of insuring that her doctors gave her no drugs that would counteract the embalming chemicals (Johnson and Johnson 1987, 18). Another source states that when Dr. Ara heard that Perón wanted him to embalm the body of his wife when she died, he went to Moscow to learn the technique used on Lenin's body (Sava 1976, 175).

Dr. Ara had explained to Perón that the success or failure of the embalming process depended critically on those first few hours. Gabriel García Márquez later wrote in a Buenos Aires newspaper, "He had to proceed with the mummification beginning the instant she died, to render the conservation more convincing and more durable" (Ortiz 1996, 280). After the embalming, Perón viewed the body and was completely satisfied. When he asked how long the body would remain free of decay, he was told by Dr. Ara, "When I have finished with the body it will never decompose. It will remain forever beautiful and graceful as she is now" (Sava 1976, 178). One of Evita's maids arrived to remove the red polish on the nails and replace it with clear polish, as Evita had requested. Evita's dressmaker dressed the body in a flowing white tunic, and her hairdresser Pedro Alcaraz dyed and styled her hair, commenting, "She looks as though she is sleeping" (Barnes 1978, 161). At this time Evita's brother, Juan Duarte, came in and cut off a long lock of her hair to take to their mother. After these preparations, Evita's body was lifted into a silver-trimmed, mahogany casket upholstered in white satin with a full-length glass top. The rosary that had been presented to her by the pope was placed between her crossed hands, a jeweled brooch containing the insignia of the Peronista Party was pinned on her breast, and her body was draped with the blue and white flag of Argentina. Before the casket lid was locked, Dr. Ara sprinkled some detoxicant tablets inside to protect against microbes and insects.

The body was transported in a black van to the Ministry of Labor, where Evita lay in state in a gold-domed room atop a bier of lavender and white orchids. The public converged while a private mass was conducted inside. When the crowds finally broke through the police lines, they were admitted. As the public filed past her casket, some just touched the casket lightly, others kissed the glass, others crossed themselves, and many broke down uncontrollably. No count was made of how many people came to see her, but the estimate was between two and three million. Mourners stood in several lines four to six abreast outside the building, and the lines stretched as many as thirty blocks in different directions. Some waited in line for as long as sixteen hours to pay their respects. In all, there were some twenty deaths in the crush, and thousands of people were injured.

The lying-in-state, planned to last three days, was extended indefinitely and lasted thirteen days. Hundreds of thousands of Argentinean workers appealed to Pope Pius XII to canonize their beloved Evita, but the Vatican politely refused, pointing out that even beatification cannot be conferred until fifty years after death (Sava 1976, 180). During the viewing a mist from the normal evaporation of moisture from the body developed inside the glass plate and had to be cleaned off several times. Workers supposedly then allowed for air to circulate through the casket, which greatly displeased Dr. Ara and was against his strict orders not to expose the remains to air (Ortiz 1996, 280). The casket was sealed on August 9 and taken in procession on an ancient gun carriage to the National Congress Building fourteen blocks away, where it was opened again for one day, and crowds were briefly allowed to file past. At the conclusion the nation's top political leaders said some final flowery words. The casket was again carried out into the street, mounted on a gun carriage, and drawn by fifty workers through two miles of the main streets of Buenos Aires to the headquarters of the National Confederation of Labor

(CGT). At the entrance, a twenty-one-gun salute sounded and bombers and jets streaked overhead. There Juan Perón handed over the body to CGT Secretary-General José Espejo, who promised, "Upon receiving the remains of Eva Perón, I swear to be their custodian today, tomorrow and forever" (Barnes 1978, 166).

In a guarded laboratory on the second floor, Dr. Ara examined his work and "noted a number of problems, including condensation within the glass-covered casket, purge [that indicates there had been no cavity treatment], and some desiccation, although no mold ever was observed" (Johnson and Johnson/Part Two 1986, 22). The body was removed from the casket and placed on a portable table. Dr. Ara carried out a second arterial injection of formalin, glycerin, thymol (an antiseptic and disinfectant), and pure alcohol. In addition, he made several hypodermic injections of the solution. The body was then submerged in a bath containing 150 liters of the same chemicals, but believed by Henley to contain paraffin kept liquid by the application of heat: "...the paraffin within the body and on its surface penetrated all the tissues. When cooled and hardened the paraffin filled out the tissues and prevented dehydration and mold formation" (Johnson and Johnson/Part One 1986, 60). The technique was said to have been developed in Argentina after the turn of the century (Cockburn and Cockburn 1980, 8). The body was then immersed in a solution of acetate and nitro-cellulose dissolved in trichlorethylene. "This solution would leave a thin film of a plastic-like texture on the body surface as it dried, following the removal of the corpse from the solution. It is believed that this final immersion was carried out a number of times in order to build up the thickness of the coating on the body surfaces" (Johnson and Johnson/Part Two 1986, 23). A plastic or rubber cap had probably been used to protect Evita's hair. After the treatment, "...the body began to assume a lifelike appearance with her skin more delicate than in life and her facial expression tranquil and serene, not unlike that of a saint by the old masters of the Renaissance" (Sava 1976, 178). The entire process took a full year and reportedly cost the Argentine government $100,000 plus expenses (chemicals, supplies, laboratory space, and guards).

In Martínez's novel *Santa Evita*, Evita's body is described as giving off a delicate aroma of almonds and lavender and possessing remarkably lifelike qualities: "The transparencies of the body gave off a liquid light, immune to changes of humidity, storms, and the devastations of ice and heat. It was so well preserved that even the tracery of the blood vessels beneath the porcelain skin and an indelible pink tinging the aureole of the nipples were visible" (1996, 17).

Dr. Ara's work was not as well thought of by some. In an attempt to discredit Dr. Ara, various political and medical groups accused him of perpetrating a hoax on the government. Rumors circulated that the body was a mannequin or statue of wax or stone, that it was a composite fashioned out of her head and an artificial (or someone else's) body, or that it was the body of another female of similar physique who had received postmortem reconstructive surgery to simulate her likeness (Gonzalez-Crussi 1993, 24–25). In his novel *Santa Evita* (1996, 44), Martínez makes reference to two copies of Evita's body in Dr. Ara's laboratory, a reclining figure made of wax and vinyl and a seated figure made of fiberglass, and writes that they could be distinguished from the real body by their lighter weight and slightly darker color. Compelled to provide proof of the authentic corpse's identity, Dr. Ara met with a commission of experts who matched the body's fingerprints, teeth, and x-rays of the head and torso with records made of Eva Perón in life. A comparison was also made between photographs taken during life and the x-rays of the skull. The commission reported in 1955 that the corpse they examined was indeed that of Evita.

Evita's body was to lie in state publicly and permanently in a monument 450 feet high to be built according to a design by Ital-

ian sculptor Leone Tommasi. The monument, which was never built, would have required 50,000 tons of white Carrara marble. It was suggested that Dr. Ara embalm four bodies (a descamisado representative of the working class and a member of each of the armed forces) as statuary to carry Evita's preserved body inside the crypt, but Dr. Ara explained that he didn't have adequate time to carry out the preservation of so many bodies. He did, however, continue his work on Evita's remains.

A funerary chapel was set up in Dr. Ara's anteroom, where Evita's family and a few close associates came to view the body and pray. Juan Perón went to see the body only three times. The body, which had been dressed in a sleeveless shift, was attired in a long linen gown and photographed and x-rayed from all angles (Fraser 1980, 163–74). After the Argentine Revolution in 1955, several military men came to see Evita's body in Dr. Ara's laboratory. One of them wrote, "It was the size of a twelve-year-old girl. Its skin was waxlike and artificial, its mouth had been rouged, and when you tapped it, it rang hollow, like a store-window mannequin. The embalmer, Dr. Ara, hovered over it as if it was something he loved" (Fraser 1980, 174–75). Dr. Ara frantically appealed to several embassies to give the body political asylum. The Peronista feminists, whose party had been dissolved, were clamoring for custody of the body so that it could be given a Christian burial, but wherever it was buried was bound to become a shrine, a rallying point for political dissent. "The navy had refused to have her in their cemetery on the island of Martín García, and her family, exiled in Venezuela, ungratefully washed their hands of her" (Main 1980, 282).

The military officers wanted to destroy the myth that was growing around Evita and demonstrate publicly that the body was a fake. It required a second x-ray session and another series of medical examinations, including the excision of a finger from the body, to convince them that the body was authentic. The new junta then met on three-occasions to determine what to do with the corpse. They asked Dr. Ara if it would ever decompose, and he assured them it would not. They asked the Catholic church to make an exception and allow them to cremate the body but their petition was denied. The junta gave up on the idea of destroying the body, but were able to stop construction of the monument and bulldoze what had so far been erected. Other means of disposal were considered, including dropping the body into an active volcano or into the sea, or burying it under the airplane runway on a remote island.

The body was seized again in December 1955 by a small unit of Argentine marines. A welder that had supposedly been hired to seal the casket did not arrive (Ortiz 1996, 283). Two workers lifted the body from its platform and placed it in the casket, which was removed in a truck. If Martínez's fictional account is to be believed, the body spent the next two months in a crate hidden behind the screen of a movie theater and was believed to be a doll by the young daughter of the theater owner: "I couldn't keep my eyes off her. I don't know how many hours went by before I worked up my nerve to touch her. What a surprise I got. She was as soft as could be" (1996, 218). Martínez (1996, 238) then placed it in a military storeroom for three weeks. The head of military intelligence, Colonel Carlos Eugenio de Moori Koenig, was authorized to bury the body in plot number 275, section B, of the Chacarita cemetery. He did not carry out the order, although he later spoke of having buried Evita's body vertically (Ortiz 1996, 284–85). Instead, the colonel delegated the duty of guarding the body to his deputy, who kept the casketed remains in his apartment; frightened of possible reprisals by the Peronistas, the deputy was awakened by movement one night and mistakenly shot and killed his pregnant wife. The body of Eva Perón was reportedly moved to Military Intelligence Headquarters and stored in the attic in a long wooden packing crate labeled "radio equipment." In September 1956 the government filled a number of caskets with ballast and sent them off to Argentine embassies in Italy and Belgium to maintain secrecy, while the real body was sent to the embassy in Bonn, Germany without the ambassador's knowledge. Rumors abounded as to the whereabouts of the body: that it had been spirited off to Rome for burial by twenty-five prominent citizens, each believing the casket they had been given for clandestine burial contained Evita's body. Others believed the corpse had been cremated and the ashes scattered in the sea. When it was suggested that the body had been dropped out of an aircraft into the Rio de la Plata, demands for dredging a large section of the river were made. The more optimistic said that Perón managed to rescue his dead wife's body and that it was now resting in his house in Madrid. In fact, Perón had several times requested custody of Evita's body, and had even asked Generalissimo Francisco Franco to intervene on his behalf, but all requests had been denied.

By this time, Pope Pius XII had reportedly consented to the transfer of Evita's remains to Campagno Jesuit Cemetery near Rome. Instead, the body was transferred in 1957 to the Musocco Cemetery in Milan and buried under the false name of "Maria Maggi de Magistris," a woman said to have died in Argentina five years before being buried in Italy. The plan ("Operation Cadaver") was apparently carried out under the direction of German Colonel Otto Skorzény (d. 1976). In his novel Martínez (1996, 304) describes how Evita's body was prevented from shifting in the casket: "Since the coffin was enormous and she had a tendency to drift about in it, they had immobilized her with bricks: the dust gave a slight red tinge to her hair, her nose, her eyelids." Martínez also writes that copies of Evita's body were buried in several European cities including Rotterdam under different names by people posing as family members of the deceased (1996, 308).

Retired former president Colonel Pedro Eugenio Arambúru—who had authorized the burial of Evita's body—was interrogated in May 1970 by a guerrilla group known as the Montoneros, who were still actively searching for Evita's body. Although Aram-búru revealed the incomplete information that he knew—that the body had been buried in Rome with the help of the Vatican—they shot him the next day for a number of crimes, including "profaning the body of Eva Perón by concealing her location" (Johnson and Johnson/Part Two 1986, 24). According to some sources, Skorzény—prompted by threats of the government to destroy the body or threat of the Montoneros to find and control it for political purposes—arranged to have the body returned to Juan Perón.

In September 1971 Colonel Cabanillas disguised himself and with false papers passed himself off as Carlos Maggi, brother of the deceased, who wanted to transport the body to Spain. The body was exhumed from its grave in plot number 86, section 41 (Ortiz 1996, 299). The outer wooden casing had rotted, but the casket itself (said to be of silver) was in excellent condition, as was the body, whose face could be seen through the glass window in the lid. The man loaded the body into a rented hearse and—without the usual customs formalities—escorted it around the coast of France to Perón's villa in the Puerto de Hierro, 30 km outside Madrid. "All practitioners of funeral service know how much documentary red tape is involved in such a matter, hence it is evident that the Italian government at a very high level must have smoothed the operation" (Johnson and Johnson/Part Two 1986, 24).

Evita's remains arrived safely at Perón's residence with Perón, his second wife, Colonel Cabanillas, the Argentine ambassador, and others including two priests to greet her. "We have no account of its arrival there, but it seems that Isabelita [Juan Perón's third wife], whatever her private feelings may have been, received the body of her predecessor with as much reverence as if it had been a holy relic" (Main 1980, 284). Dr. Ara, who was also living in Madrid, had

been summoned and was present when the casket was opened with a crowbar. Evita's clothing was wet and stained, but Dr. Ara was pleased to find only minor damage to the body after the clothing was cut away. The nose was flattened, the forehead scarred, the ear bent, a fingertip broken off (during the earlier fingerprinting), and there was a crack in the plastic coating across her throat. In his memoirs, Dr. Ara recorded that although slightly wet and dirty, the coiffure given to Evita by her personal hairdresser soon after her death had remained intact. The following day, Dr. Ara made some minor repairs to the body. Isabelita helped Dr. Ara to dry and rearrange the hair and to cleanse the body and dress Evita in a new white gown. Perón was heard repeating, "She is just as beautiful as she ever was" (Sava 1976, 184).

A statement released in 1985 by Blanca and Erminda Duarte, two of Evita's sisters, conflicts with Dr. Ara's account of the damage. They stated that the "gross mistreatment" of their sister's remains included hammer blows to the temple and forehead, a gash on the cheek and another on the arm, a sunken nose and fractured nasal septum, a nearly severed neck, an amputated finger, fractured kneecaps, slashes on her chest, and a layer of tar on the soles of her feet. They also noted that there were three intentional perforations in the casket cover, that the pillow had been ripped apart, that the shroud was stained, that the hair was like "wet wool," and that the body had been covered with quicklime (Ortiz 1996, 300–301).

Evita's body was placed in a new casket that was reportedly kept in the dining room but is also said to have been stored in the attic of the villa (Ortiz 1996, 301). The body remained with the Peróns in Madrid for over a year until Juan Perón returned to power in Argentina in September 1973. He promised to bring Evita's body back to Argentina but never alluded to it again (Ortiz 1996, 302).

When Juan Perón died on July 1, 1974, the Montoneros seized the body of Aram-búru and ransomed it for the return of Evita's remains. Isabelita Perón, who became president, ordered Evita's body to be returned to Argentina. As the chartered aircraft carrying Evita's casket landed in Buenos Aires on November 17, 1974, the guerrillas revealed the whereabouts of Arambúru's corpse. Evita's remains were restored by Dr. Domingo Tellechea, who noted that "her feet were ruined by the vertical position that had to support the body and by the bad treatment" (Ortiz 1996, 303). With the hair restyled and the nails freshly polished, Evita's body (again rumored to be wax) lay in state beside the closed casket of her husband in the Presidential Residence until a pantheon could be built. The government was again overthrown on March 26, 1976, before the pantheon could be constructed, and the new president, General Jorge Rafael Videla, was unwilling to occupy the palace with the bodies there, so Evita's body was at last handed over to her family.

In the early morning of October 22, 1976, Evita's body was loaded aboard an ambulance, which was escorted by two armed trucks under cover of darkness. She was secretly buried in the Arrieta vault (the family of Elisa's husband) in the exclusive Recoleta Cemetery in the most fashionable part of Buenos Aires and in the company of thirteen presidents of Argentina (Sava 1976, 192). The small Gothic tomb stands to the west of the main avenue. An inscription to Major Alfredo J. L. Arrieta and a second plaque to Juan Duarte are accompanied by a long, half-erased list of names that indicates her presence. There is a trapdoor in the marble floor of the tomb leading to a steel-walled compartment of two caskets twenty feet underground, made by a firm that builds bank vaults and outfitted with an alarm system connecting it with Buenos Aires police headquarters. Under that is another trapdoor to a lower compartment in which Evita's casket has been deposited. "There Evita lies, hidden from the eyes of those who believed her to be a saint and might claim her body as a source of miracles. There she lies, out of reach of those who might use her body for political propaganda. There she lies, among the tombs of the oligarchs she hated and who so hated her" (Main 1980, 288).

The installation was paid for by the government, and Evita's sister was given the only key. It is said to be safe from the most ingenious graverobbers and capable of withstanding any bomb attack, including a nuclear one (Fraser 1980, 175–92). Although Evita's remains are seen only by her family and their authenticity is still questioned, the body is probably still intact. Dr. Ara guaranteed that Evita's body "could not be undone by time, ruined by moldy growths, corrupted by bacteria, or any other natural agents. In fact…it would resist immersion in strong acids and would in all likelihood emerge intact from fire" (Gonzalez-Crussi 1993, 25).

If Eva's life and her untimely death were a mystery never to be solved to the complete satisfaction of both her friends and her enemies, her posthumous journey across seven countries and through two continents defies the imagination and borders on the macabre (Sava 1976, 175–76). Of her own desires, it is said, "It is unlikely that Evita expressed a wish to be embalmed or chose her own resting place. Suggestions that she did so merely reflect Perón's response to the many criticisms of what happened to her body after her death. But her desire to die publicly…is beyond doubt. She wanted to thrust the fact of her death, with all its pathos and dramatic circumstances, into the public consciousness, and thus into a niche in history" (Fraser 1980, 160). She has succeeded remarkably, as has Dr. Ara.

Enrico Caruso

After he died on August 2, 1921, of pleurisy and kidney failure, Enrico Caruso was embalmed and laid out between four towering candles in the salon of the Hotel Vesuvio in Naples. Mourners filed past the beloved Italian opera singer for hours, and condolences flooded in. The king of Italy gave orders allowing Caruso's funeral to be held in the Royal Basilica of San Francisco di Paola, the first time it would be opened for a commoner's funeral service. On the day of the funeral, the crystal casket enclosed in wood was transferred from the hotel to a hearse covered with wreaths and drawn by six black horses. All of the shops in Naples were closed. The procession moved along Santa Lucia with a cordon of troops holding back the crowd of 100,000 people who had lined the route and gathered outside the San Carlo Opera House.

After the requiem mass, the glass casket was taken to a temporary chapel in the Cimitero di Santa Maria Del Pianto (St. Mary of Tears) above Naples until a new chapel could be constructed for the Grand Tenor. With Tito Schipa and Caruso's other friends, Antonio Scotti made arrangements to have the embalmed body dressed in new clothes every year. Caruso's widow Dorothy Park Benjamin (d. 1955) had asked to have the casket covered, but the tenor's family had refused: "...it was the Italian custom to display the bodies of their great dead. But visitors from other countries where this custom did not obtain found such a display shocking" (Caruso 1945, 281).

In April 1927 (or as she states in her biography, eight years after Caruso's death), Dorothy appealed directly to the government through Prince Barberini to end the public display of her husband's body and succeeded in having Caruso's sarcophagus closed. "The authorities did not object after a disgraceful episode earlier that year when a party of cameramen, masquerading as tourists, had rampaged for hours round the casket with their paraphernalia" (Jackson 1972, 291). The cemetery confirms that the glass casket was removed seven years after Caruso's death, when his tomb was finally completed. The casket was placed in a white marble sarcophagus in the newly constructed chapel of white granite shaded with cypress trees. Today the sarcophagus—decorated with a bas-relief of two singers, a photograph of Caruso, and a commemorative plaque presented by the U.S. and Canada—is visible inside the locked mausoleum bearing Caruso's name and a depiction of the head of Christ.

Rosalia Lombardo

Rosalia Lombardo is probably the most famous and perhaps the youngest of Dr. Alfredo Salafia's clients. Salafia was trained in chemistry and devised a method of preserving the bodies of animals for permanent display and dissection. He obtained permission to apply his preservative treatment to cadavers in 1892 and spent the next eight years perfecting his formula by trial and error. The formula may have included bichloride of mercury or it may have included arsenic: "...Professor Salafia admits to a sincere admiration of Dr. Tranchina of Naples, who was a forthright advocate of arsenic-content embalming solutions during the early nineteenth century" (Johnson, Johnson, and Williams 1993, 68). Salafia embalmed a number of bodies for funeral purposes, and his method gained popularity because it allowed viewing over an extended period of time. One of these was his father, Filippo Salafia, a military hero. He was soon sought after to embalm important people.

When Italian premier Francesco Crispi died in Naples in August 1901, his body was poorly preserved. The premier's relatives requested that Professor Salafia prepare the body so that it could be viewed prior to being interred in the Pantheon in Palermo in January 1905. Salafia halted the decomposition and restored the appearance to permit public viewing. "It is related that the coffin was opened in May 1910 during the fifty-year celebration of the freedom of Sicily and the remains were found unchanged since their last viewing" (Johnson, Johnson, and Williams 1993, 25).

When Cardinal Michaelangelo Celesia of Palermo died in April 1904, his body was also embalmed by Salafia. The body was viewed by a delegation seven months later. A photograph taken nine months after death shows no physical deterioration. When the body was viewed again in January 1909, witnesses declared that the features, color, and form had been so carefully preserved that the Cardinal looked as if he were asleep. Because of the masterful preservation, the law requiring that ten years elapse between death and burial within a church was waived (Johnson, Johnson, and Williams 1993, 25).

Professor Salafia also embalmed Senator Giacomo Armo, Signora Maria Pareti, Cav. Salvatore Biondo, and the Count of Francavilla. He was assisted by his nephews Dr. Oreste Maggio and Achille Salomone and joined Salomone, who had opened an undertaking establishment in New York, in January 1910. Salafia formed a corporation that would provide embalming services to American funeral directors for $300 per body with a 50 percent discount for stockholders. The Salafia Permanent Method Embalming Company of New York, headquartered at Salomone's

Cardinal Celesia, nine months after being embalmed by Alfredo Salafia. Photo courtesy of the Edward C. Johnson Family Collection.

establishment, offered a $1,000 guarantee of its effectiveness. On April 23, 1910, Professor Salafia embalmed the unclaimed body of John Flinch to demonstrate the efficiency and simplicity of his process. The embalming was carried out at the Eclectic Medical College in New York. Flinch had died some ten days earlier and his body exhibited black and green areas on the face and neck, the trunk, and the extremities. Fifteen gallons of Salafia's embalming fluid were injected distally into the right common carotid artery without draining the blood, treating the cavities, or carrying out secondary injections. The body was stored but not refrigerated.

Six months later in early November, the body of John Flinch was dissected before a group of faculty members, physicians, and funeral directors. The group included an authority on embalming, Professor W. P. Hohenschuh, and New York's most renowned undertakers, Frank E. Campbell and Fred Hulberg, Jr. The discolorations previously noted on the surface had virtually disappeared. "The body was well-preserved, with the skin firm, and moderately hard and dry. All tissue, including fat, was firm and dry. No odor of decomposition, or fecal odor, was present, only the chemical odor of the embalming fluid. Desiccation of the toes was present and in the fingers. No cosmetic effect of the fluid was noted, instead discolored areas seemed to be bleached" (Johnson, Johnson, and Williams 1993, 66–68). The demonstration had been an overwhelming success.

Salafia Method Demonstrated before the New York State Embalmers' Association.

PROF. A. SALAFIA

We, the undersigned, a committee appointed by the New York State Embalmers' Association, this 22d day of September, 1910, for the purpose of witnessing the embalming of the body of David Jenkins at the annual meeting of said Association, do hereby certify that we witnessed said embalming as performed by Prof. Achille Salomone with the Salafia method; that said embalming was done by Prof. Salomone in accordance with his promise and agreement with this Association, by one incision only, viz., the raising of the carotid artery; that said embalming was done by one injection of fluid, the amount injected being six quarts; that said body weighed about 130 pounds and its cavities were in a state of decomposition and the surface of the abdomen was green in color; that in accordance with instructions from said Association, we saw the body, after embalmment, placed in a case, strongly built and with glass sides and top, and saw said case properly closed, secured and sealed with tape and ... and ... that it finally ... and deposited in a safe place, where it is to be kept until the spring meeting of this Association for further demonstration of the results of embalming by the said Salafia process. (Signed) GEO. E. FAIRCHILD, CHARLES C. CARROLL, WILLIAM E. BURNS, WILLIAM A. DRINKWINE, FRANK W. TRAUGOTT, Committee.

We are prepared to do embalming for undertakers anywhere in the United States under a positive guarantee of $1,000 that we will perform all we claim to do. For further particulars address

The Salafia Permanent Method Embalming Co.
338 East 63rd St., New York.

A 1910 advertisement for a seminar on the Salafia Method of embalming. Photo courtesy of the Edward C. Johnson Family Collection.

The Salafia Method was demonstrated a second time that year. On September 22, 1910, a committee appointed by the New York State Embalmers' Association witnessed the embalming of the body of David Jenkins at their annual meeting in Syracuse, New York. The embalming was done by Professor Achille Salomone by his uncle's method. Jenkins' decomposing body weighed approximately 130 pounds, and the surface of the abdomen was green. The carotid artery was raised and six quarts of embalming fluid were injected, a difficult task because of arteriosclerosis. The body was placed without further treatment in a case with glass sides and top. The case was sealed and secured for inspection at the spring meeting of the Association. In April 1911 the body was dissected. "During the second dissection, the basic conclusion reached was that wherever the Salafia fluid penetrated, the tissue was perfectly preserved and where it did not, the tissue decomposed, which is also true today with contemporary fluids and techniques" (Johnson, Johnson, and Williams 1993, 68).

In December 1911 Salafia began selling his embalming fluid to funeral homes for $18 per six gallon case. The fluid had been improved by adding cosmetic dyes and was distributed by American casket companies. By early 1912 the product was no longer advertised and Salafia returned to Palermo. It was there that he embalmed the body of two-year-old Rosalia Lombardo immediately after her death in December 1920. The body was then displayed by special permission (since it had become illegal to bury a body outside a cemetery) at the Capuchin monastery in Palermo. Salafia then died on January 31, 1933, at age 61. "Ironically, he himself died shortly after the embalming [of Rosalia] and took the details of his technique with him to the grave" (Wilkins 1990, 135–36). The only way to deduce the formula Professor Salafia perfected would be a chemical analysis of a tissue sample from the body of Rosalia or one of his other treated cases.

Rosalia remains one of the most recently

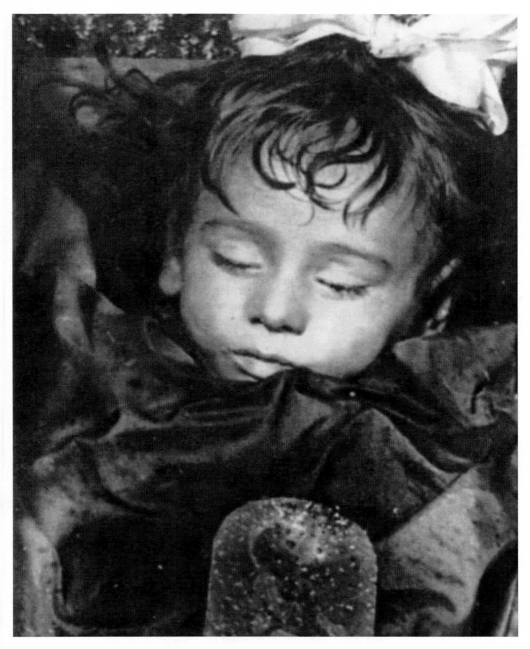

The body of two-year-old Rosalia Lombardo (d. 1920) on view at the Capuchin Monastery in Palermo, Sicily.

deceased persons to be enshrined in the Capuchin monastery. The monks had begun depositing their dead in the monastery in 1599 and had developed a method of drying the bodies, after which they were clothed and placed upright along the walls of the catacomb. The Capuchins later allowed the deposit of the religious of other orders, prominent citizens, and those in government posts. Women, children, and government workers were occasionally placed in caskets in the monastery. Today, the catacomb holds over 8,000 bodies and is divided into sections for monks, priests, professors (doctors, lawyers, and other professionals), adult men, adult women, and children. It was customary for family members to visit and change the clothing of the deceased. Some bodies are arranged horizontally in open wooden boxes, others stand vertically against the white-washed walls and are held in place by ropes around their waists. The monastery is visited by crowds of tourists and by local families visiting their deceased relatives in the catacombs and in the graveyard of the church next door.

Rosalia's body is prominently displayed in a chapel repository for the bodies of children and infants and is perfectly preserved to this day. "I had the impression she was something of a star attraction—there are a few small signs on the walls leading you to her—and that there may be some local-saint sort of tradition attached to her, which would not be surprising, given her remarkable state of preservation," writes John Strausbaugh, editor of *New York Press* (letter to author, February 1996).

Rosalia is displayed at a slight angle in a small casket with a transparent top. She is wearing a light-colored, frilly dress, and her reddish-brown hair is arranged in ringlets. "She's startlingly well preserved—looks asleep rather than dead, the flesh not shrunken or shriveled or dry at all, though it does have a faintly sickly yellowish cast to it," writes Strausbaugh. "She looks like she could be ill, but she doesn't look dead, and she certainly doesn't look like she's been dead for years." Rosalia's body is in sharp contrast to those of the hundreds of other mummies whose skin has darkened and shrunk, whose eyes have sunken, and whose lips have retracted leaving them little more than skeletons. "Appearance and color of the face and head would lead one to believe she had been dead at most a few days. Comparison photographs taken in 1920 and within the past year or two disclose no visible change" (Johnson, Johnson, and Williams 1993, 25). Rosalia's remarkable preservation has ensured a certain immortality for both herself and Dr. Salafia.

ECCENTRICS

Unlike the bodies of idols or icons, preserved out of devotion or admiration, the bodies of eccentrics are embalmed and displayed for reasons as singular as their posthumous settings. A woman in North Carolina wanted to bask in the sun after her lingering death. A man in Kansas became part of his sculptural oddity upon his demise, as he had planned. And the wife of an Argentine doctor was preserved with her husband's experimental fluid, as was her wish. In the North Carolina case, the embalming was successful, but the circumstances cut short the display. In a case in France, a man's plan to have his body embalmed and exhibited was never carried out. In Kansas, Samuel Dinsmoor is still on display in the mausoleum of his own design. The Argentine doctor was unable to find a suitable audience for his deceased wife and her fate is unknown. The moral of the story is that anyone can become a mummy, but planning does not always make it so.

Mrs. Katsusaburo Miyamoto

Dr. Katsusaburo Miyamoto and his wife lived in Rosario, Argentina. When Mrs. Miyamoto died in 1958, her body was preserved by her husband, who was a physician, veterinarian, and botanist. According to Dr. Miyamoto, his wife requested before her death that he use her body to experiment with his preservation system. He used a secret system he had developed himself and referred to as "eonosmia." The technique involved injecting salts and some acids into the body to crystallize the blood and keep the pores open. It began with treatment of the hair, during which time the body was kept wrapped in damp towels. None of the internal organs were removed. Dr. Miyamoto claimed that his technique would keep the remains of his wife in their present lifelike condition forever.

Dr. Miyamoto kept his wife's body in bed with a menagerie of her favorite animals that had been similarly preserved, including lizards, bullfrogs, scorpions, cats, dogs, and a porpoise. In 1960 police discovered the body in Dr. Miyamoto's home, and he was charged with violating municipal regulations regarding the burial of the dead. He was later acquitted by a judge and allowed to retain the body in his home. In 1968 Dr. Miyamoto was on a short lecture tour in Japan. He was forced to remain there due to ill health. He sought authorization to have his wife's body shipped to Japan, but Argentine medical authorities wanted to keep it to research its perfect preservation.

In February 1971 Dr. Miyamoto—then living in Rosario, Argentina—expressed his disappointment that Argentine officials never accepted an offer to display the body of his wife at Expo '70 in Osaka, Japan. He had repeatedly suggested to Argentine government officials that the body

Samuel Dinsmoor standing in front of the mausoleum he built and in which his body and that of his first wife are entombed. Reprinted by permission of the Garden of Eden from *A Pictorial History of the Cabin Home*.

would make an interesting and unusual display at the Argentine pavilion, but his offers were firmly refused. The remains of Mrs. Miyamoto may still present an interesting and certainly unusual display, but nothing is known of her current venue.

Samuel P. Dinsmoor

In 1891 Samuel Dinsmoor—a Civil War veteran, schoolteacher, and farmer—moved onto a quiet residential street in Lucas, Kansas, with his first wife, Frances Barlow Journey. In 1907, at age 64, he began building his eleven-room, two-story "Cabin Home" from limestone shaped into logs; his own "Garden of Eden," a sculpture garden made from 2,273 bags (113 tons) of cement and some wire, limestone, steel, and glass; a forty-foot limestone log mausoleum for himself and his first wife; and several other smaller structures, including an outdoor

Samuel Dinsmoor standing next to the casket he built to house his remains in the mausoleum. Reprinted by permission of the Garden of Eden from *A Pictorial History of the Cabin Home*.

dining hall, a coal house, and a pigeon roost. He opened his home as a tourist attraction the same year and continued his work.

Dinsmoor's first wife died in 1917 and was buried in the mausoleum. None of their five children survive. He married his second wife, Emilie Brozek, in 1924 and they had two children, John and Emily. Dinsmoor's work reached completion in 1929 and includes dozens of unique sculptural creations: a tree of life guarded by an angel; a devil; a soldier shooting at an Indian who is shooting at a dog that is chasing a fox that is chasing a bird that is after a worm that is eating a leaf; a tableau in which a banker, lawyer, preacher, and doctor are crucifying a figure representing labor; a Goddess of Liberty; Adam and Eve; Cain and Abel; children; and an American flag.

Most of the sculptures are perched in cement trees measuring from eight to forty feet high. Of the tree that contains Liberty, Dinsmoor writes, "Say! that tree will be a

beauty. I want to see it in about ten or fifteen years from now. I may be in the Mausoleum. If I am, some dark night I will slip out and take a look at it, or some other people will see it which will be just the same" (*Pictorial History of the Cabin Home*). Dinsmoor is said to have built his garden as a personal statement of his political and religious views (Bergheim 1988, 163), which are characterized as "Free Thought" and "Populism." He explains, "...when I was building this they accused me of being bughouse on religion. I am bughouse good and proper, but not on religion, perpetual motion or any other fool thing that I cannot find out one thing about" (*Pictorial History*).

Dinsmoor decided that his body should be embalmed after death to draw attention to his ideology and hoped that his children would be able to witness the procedure. In exchange for carrying it out, the undertaking establishment would be allowed to place. When Dinsmoor died on July 21, 1932, age

89, the record hot temperatures caused the embalmer to decline the difficult work. Dinsmoor's second wife found someone who agreed to prepare the body if his identity was not revealed, in case the preservation should fail. John Hochmeister, co-owner of the Garden of Eden, explains that Dinsmoor's body was laid out on the kitchen table in the presence of his children, his organs were removed, his body was salted and the body cavity was packed with charcoal, and his face was painted with white lead (telephone conversation with the author, 29 April 1997). The funeral services that followed were handled by the Rodrick & Minear Funeral Home, but Dee Durham says that the funeral home knows nothing about the embalming procedure and that there are no longer any living participants to ask. The funeral record, which is in Durham's grandfather's handwriting, merely states that services were held at 2 p.m. on July 24, 1932, at the Cabin Home on the Garden of Eden grounds (letter to the author, 28 October 1996).

Dinsmoor's body was placed in a glass-topped concrete casket of his own creation. Dinsmoor explains that the casket was made over screen-reinforced no. 6 wire and half-inch iron. The handles have 5-8 iron running full length and are fastened to the casket with wire. The plate glass is fastened to the screen with wire, the entire casket is cemented over with white cement and sand, and the window is covered with a lid decorated with a square, compass, and trowel. After Dinsmoor was laid inside, the large lid was sealed shut with cement. Dinsmoor explains his reasoning: "It seems to me that people buried in iron and wooden boxes will be frying and burning up in the resurrection morn. How will they get out when this world is on fire? Cement will not stand fire, the glass will break. This cement lid will fly open and I will sail out like a locust" (*Pictorial History*).

Dinsmoor's casket was placed above that of his first wife within the pyramidal postrock mausoleum he had erected in a cor-

ner of the garden. According to Dinsmoor's measurements, the mausoleum is erected on a cement foundation six feet deep. It is fourteen feet square at the base, topped by a smaller square of nine feet, and capped by a third square of four feet. At each corner a cement post from eighteen to twenty-one feet long is angled to the top and crowned with a staff bearing a cement American flag. Although the mausoleum was solidly constructed, the body of the man who built it was not as well embalmed. Because the brain had not been treated or removed, a green mold grew on Dinsmoor's forehead within a month of his entombment (telephone conversation with John Hochmeister, 29 April 1997). However, Dinsmoor may be happy to know that his body has not been removed for examination or maintenance since his entombment. His second wife simply had the window in the casket painted over and allowed the tours to continue.

Inside the mausoleum is a room measuring seven by ten feet. A niche two feet above the floor, two and a half feet deep and three feet high, contains Dinsmoor's casket and is fronted with plate glass. The smaller lid was placed on the casket near the foot before the casket was sealed inside the niche. Dinsmoor instructed that a two-gallon cement jug be placed at the foot of the casket and explained, "In the resurrection morn, if I have to go below, I'll grab my jug and fill it with water on the road down. They say they need water down below." Beneath the niche, the body of his first wife reposes in a steel vault cemented in the wall. Dinsmoor's tombstone is to the left and that of his wife is to the right. The guest books that Dinsmoor meticulously kept and had bound are stored above his casket. Dinsmoor explained before he died, "I have a will that none except my widow, my descendants, their husbands and wives, shall go in to see me for less than $1.00. That will pay some one to look after the place, and I promise everyone that comes in to see me (they can look through the plate glass and glass in the lid of my casket and see my face) that if I see them dropping a dollar in the hands of the flunky, and I see the dollar, I will give them a smile" (*Pictorial History*).

The Garden of Eden was a tourist attraction for years before Dinsmoor's second wife sold the property. The mausoleum was locked up and the Cabin Home became an apartment house. In 1967 the Garden of Eden was purchased by an individual who hoped to restore it to Dinsmoor's original intent. He cut the lock to the mausoleum, scraped the paint off the casket window, and discovered that Dinsmoor's body had dried out and was by that time essentially "a skin over a skeleton" (telephone conversation with John Hochmeister, 29 April 1997). The house and grounds were further renovated by investors. Today, the Garden of Eden and Cabin Home is listed in the National Register of Historic Places and is owned and operated by a group formed to preserve it. Dinsmoor's home, creations, and remains (said to be "a bit moldy") may be visited between 10 A.M. and 5 P.M. April through October and between 12 and 4 P.M. on weekends November through March. "Even after fifty years you can look through his glass-sided casket and see the creator of this splendor" (Barth et al. 1986, 194). More than 10,000 visitors take the opportunity annually. In addition, several of Dinsmoor's relatives visit regularly, and the grandchild from his first marriage brings flowers to the tomb each Memorial Day. Despite the draw that the body of the artist may represent, the owners of the Garden of Eden have concentrated on the conservation of the art itself.

"Our concern is the sculpture," says Hochmeister (telephone conversation with the author, 29 April 1997), "Mr. Dinsmoor is on his own."

Maurice D'Urre and Leslie Hansell

Marquis Maurice d'Urre of Aubais died in Paris on May 21, 1927, age 70 and childless. He left his immense fortune to the French government under conditions explicitly set out in his will: "I wish to be seated in an armchair under a glass dome. This dome must be placed facing the sea, in a public place, near a lighthouse and a radio station, and must be perpetually illuminated." His wishes were not carried out, and instead his closed casket was placed in a room in his castle that was turned into a chapel and permanently illuminated. The story was reported in the October 1947 issue of *Paris-Soir* and retold by Philippe Ariès in *The Hour of Our Death* (1981, 386).

Before her death from tuberculosis in 1915, Leslie Hansell requested that she be buried beneath the bright sun. To comply with her last wish, her husband erected an unusual monument in Oakdale Cemetery in Hendersonville, North Carolina. The top of the tomb was constructed of glass, and it was hermetically sealed. Unfortunately, cracks appeared in the tomb walls a few years later. Area residents feared that germs might escape and infect them all, so they hired workmen to reseal the entire tomb with thick tar.

3. Occupational Hazards

Outlaws, Victims, and Local Folks

For decades a sideshow was not complete without a mummy. The bodies were those of outlaws, outcasts, or merely the victims of circumstance. They were seen by hundreds of thousands of patrons and changed hands frequently. The display of carnival mummies fell off sharply with the rise of social conscience referred to as "political correctness." Unlike the bodies of political leaders who lie in state, carnival mummies were exhibited informally and for profit. Their owners did not have consent from them for this display of their bodies and often obtained them through the duping (and sometimes complicity) of those having custody of the remains.

Earlier in this century it was not uncommon for undertakers—now more appropriately called funeral directors—to be asked to hold a body until it could be claimed by family members. The body would necessarily be well embalmed. Often the family members would never appear. Just as often the embalmer would refuse to release the body until he had been paid for his services. The body would remain in the back room until one of three things happened: the undertaker accepted an offer from a showman or collector to purchase the mummy, the undertaker accepted the claim of someone purporting to be a long-lost family member, or the undertaker (or someone of a succeeding generation) decided to give the mummy a "decent burial." During its tenure in the fu-

neral home, the mummy was on exhibit to a more limited audience than it would have had if it were on the road with the carnival. Still, it would inevitably become a popular local attraction.

Today, most carnival and funeral home mummies have been buried or are in hiding. Captain Harvey Lee Boswell is one of the last showmen to exhibit mummies. "As you know," he explains (letter to the author, 17 September 1996), "during the early part of this century all sideshows had a mummy. I exhibited them right up through the 1970s and even into the early 1980s." Dave Friedman adds that when he was growing up, "There were literally dozens of carnival and road show people traveling around with a cadaver. But that was in a different time and a different era. The public has become much more sophisticated now" (Basgall 1989, 195–96). In contrast to their heyday, at which time great lengths were taken to prove their authenticity, the mummies exhibited today are more likely to be fakes or "gaffs," as they are known in the business. Possession of the real thing is usually a well-guarded secret.

OUTLAWS

The bodies of outlaws were particularly prone to being embalmed and put on prolonged exhibit. Not only would they draw a crowd, their families were often reluctant to claim them for burial. Their display was an extension of the common practices of photographing bandits in their caskets and allowing the public to file past the corpses of dead gangsters. When Jesse James was killed in 1882, his mother refused lucrative offers to have her son mummified and taken on tour in Wild West shows. She had his body buried within yards of the family farmhouse to discourage graverobbers. When a body could not be begged, borrowed, or stolen, it could be purchased. Classified advertisements in *Billboard* offered "Mummified Egyptians, Indians, Curiosities" and "Fossilized Outlaw Exhibitions" into the late 1930s. With one notable exception—the body said to be that of John Wilkes Booth—the outlaws circulating in the carnival circuit were of minor status. Their histories were played up and their crimes exaggerated for the paying public.

Elmer McCurdy (a.k.a. Elmer McAudry [Mcuardy, McUardy, McUrday, M'Uardy], Elmer McCready, Frank Amos, Frank [E.] Curtis, Frank Davidson, Frank Davis, Frank Day, Frank Ellis)

There was a price on his head both before and after his death. As a man, Elmer McCurdy was worth $2,000 in reward money. As a mannequin, Elmer was worth $100 a month. In the years between fugitive and funhouse prop, it was somehow forgotten that Elmer was flesh and blood—an oversight excused by the fact that the blood had long ago been replaced by embalming fluid and the flesh covered with several layers of paint.

Elmer's odyssey began in 1911 when he was shot by lawmen in an Oklahoma barn. Elmer had been a soldier (Company E, 13th Infantry), a plumber, a miner, a drinker, a bank robber, and a train robber. Drinking got him arrested at age 25. At age 32 robbery got him killed. Elmer once bragged that he had killed a man in a brawl, but his only arrest was for public intoxication in Iola, Kansas,

in 1905. The events leading up to Elmer's death by justifiable homicide began with his participation in a train robbery in Lenapah, Oklahoma, in March 1911. Although the train was carrying more than $4,000 in silver, most of it was melted by the explosive charge Elmer used to open the safe, and the men only made off with $450. A few days later a heated argument among the five robbers left Elmer with a bad cut across the back of his right wrist.

In September 1911 Elmer followed up his first attempt to crack a safe with the burglary of a bank in Chautauqua, Kansas. The explosive charge was just as excessive, and Elmer and his two accomplices had only enough time to scoop up $150 before making their getaway. Elmer's second and final train robbery was even less successful. He and two other men held up MK&T passenger train No. 29 three miles south of Okesa, Oklahoma, on October 4, 1911. Unfortunately for them, it was not the Katy train due a few hours later that carried a $400,000 payment to the Osage Indians. Their haul was $40, a watch, a coat, an automatic revolver, and several gallons of whiskey.

Elmer was found drowning his sorrows in the barn on the Charley Revard ranch twenty miles northwest of Bartlesville, Oklahoma, three days later. Some believe that Elmer may have been betrayed by one of his accomplices. Others believe that he had not participated in the holdup at all but was passed off as one of the robbers for the reward of $2,000 (even though the reward money was payable only upon arrest and conviction). It is not certain that Elmer was armed, although he was said to have fired first in the hour-long gunfight. It is also uncertain whether the bullet that killed him came from the gun of deputy sheriff Robert Fenton, his brother Stringer Fenton, or posse member Dick Wallace. What is certain is that Elmer McCurdy (alias Frank Amos) was dead. A young man who worked at the ranch entered the barn and confirmed this fact. According to a contemporary newspaper account, he found Elmer sitting in an upright

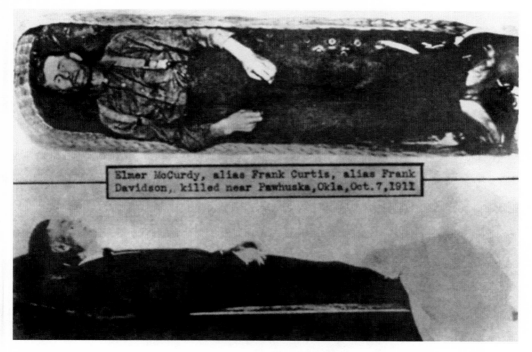

Elmer McCurdy, alias Frank Curtis, alias Frank Davidson, killed near Pawhuska, Okla, Oct. 7, 1911

Elmer McCurdy before and after embalming. Photo courtesy of Western History Collections, University of Oklahoma Libraries.

position with his shotgun in his hands and the two shells he had just placed in the barrels covered with blood.

Elmer's corpse was transported by wagon from the Revard farm to town. Fenton said at the time to a reporter from the *Tulsa Daily World*, "We were over twelve hours in taking the body over the wild and almost impassable roads back to Pawhuska." Once they reached the local funeral home, Elmer was transferred to one of the home's wicker body baskets and carried inside. He was photographed by professional photographer William J. Boag. In the photo Elmer's rumpled hair is graying at the temples with a dark forelock hanging over his forehead. He is wearing black, baggy pants and a long-sleeved, crumpled shirt. His feet are bare and his cupped hands are resting palms-down on his lower abdomen. A dark spot can be seen on the right suspender where the bullet entered.

Because Elmer's identity was in question, prior employer William Root was summoned from Iola, Kansas. Sheriff Harvey Freas asked the funeral director, Joseph L. Johnson (d. 1933), to hold the body until Root arrived. Johnson performed an autopsy to assess the damage caused by the bullet that had entered Elmer's chest. After tying off damaged blood vessels, Johnson embalmed Elmer with an arsenic-based fluid. He closed Elmer's eyes, shaved his face, washed his body, dressed him in a black suit and tie, and combed his hair. The body was covered with a white sheet and stored in the back room until Root arrived on October 12. The body was identified to the satisfaction of the sheriff and photographed a second time, in profile.

Sheriff Freas closed the case but ordered Johnson to hold the body a while longer in case relatives came to claim it. A newspaper article from 1914 reported that Johnson refused to surrender the body or permit it to be buried until he had been paid his fee for its preparation (Basgall 1989, 163). Luckily for the Johnson family, the

Elmer McCurdy three years after his death and embalming. Photo by Richard J. Basgall in *The Career of Elmer J. McCurdy, Deceased* (Dodge City, Kan.: Trail's End, 1989). Reprinted with the permission of Mrs. Richard J. Basgall.

1981, 17) but never accepted any offers to buy it. Charles Custer of Bartlesville, Oklahoma, remembered Elmer propped up in a corner when his family went to the Johnson establishment to make arrangements after his sister's death in 1911. One woman who viewed Elmer, Ethel Louise Boone Thompson, wrote in 1978 that he was wearing an old pair of pants, long underwear, and a pair of suspenders. When she asked the funeral director what he was going to do with the outlaw, Johnson jokingly replied that he was going to place him on top of the new dome at the courthouse as soon as they were finished with it. Another woman, Blanche Lanum, claims that the Johnsons had Elmer rigged on roller skates to come out from the corner when they pushed a button!

A photograph of Elmer, minus gun and shoes, was printed as a picture postcard by the Pawhuska Chamber of Commerce and carried the caption, "The Only 'Dead One' in Pawhuska, Okla." At some point, Elmer may have been taken to downtown Pawhuska, since J. H. Kirshner recalls, as a child seeing him in the front window of a beer and domino parlor called the Smokehouse but the Johnsons deny that the body ever left the funeral home during this period. Ethel Thompson wrote that, in contrast to the rumor that his whiskers continued to grow, Johnson had shaved Elmer because of shrinkage in the face. Despite the careful maintenance, after four years of display Elmer's body had become dry and wrinkled. It had also become coveted.

On October 5, 1916, Johnson received a

corpse held up remarkably well. In the ensuing months after his death, Elmer's tissues had ossified and he was ready for his role as "The Embalmed Bandit" or "The Bandit Who Wouldn't Give Up," "The Mystery Man of Many Aliases" or "The Oklahoma Outlaw." Johnson dressed Elmer in his street clothes, placed a rifle in his hands, and stood him in a corner of the funeral home.

Johnson allowed hundreds of people to view the body and reportedly charged them a nickel apiece for the privilege (Drimmer call from Arkansas City, Kansas. A man named Aver claimed to be Elmer's brother from California and had already spoken to the sheriff and county attorney. He arrived with a man named Wayne two days later and said he was obeying the last wish of his deceased parents to deposit Elmer's body in the family plot in San Francisco. Aver and Wayne inspected and took possession of the body, which they shipped out on the Midland Valley Railway. Elmer's destination was not San Francisco but Arkansas City, where the Great Patterson Carnival Shows were playing. Johnson did not learn that Elmer was being exhibited as "The Outlaw Who Would Never Be Captured Alive" until the carnival had moved on to Texas.

Louis Sonney acquired Elmer's body in 1922 when Elmer's owner, who claimed to have purchased Elmer from an Oklahoma undertaker, defaulted on a $500 loan. "My father put Elmer, the real mummy, in his wax show and said he'd just borrow him for one month and then return him. Well the guy never did come back for him and we owned Elmer for over fifty years," says Dan Sonney (Vraney 1994, 25). The now-mummified Elmer was displayed in a new silk-lined casket and became a part of Sonney's Museum of Crime. Louis Sonney explained to his patrons that rather than be captured alive, the dead outlaw had swallowed poison that had the effect of preserving his flesh. The Museum of Crime traveled to Seattle, Portland, San Francisco, Fresno, and Long Beach. When it wasn't on the road, the crime show was housed in a big building on Main Street in downtown Los Angeles, and extra admission was charged to see Elmer. It was during this time that Elmer's authenticity began to be doubted, probably because most of Sonney's exhibits were wax. In the early 1930s Sonney's son Edward (d. 1968) called in a doctor who made an incision in Elmer's back to settle a $500 bet that the body was a fake (Basgall 1989, 177).

Dorothy Sonney, Louis Sonney's second wife whom he met in 1937, recalls Elmer with fondness: "Poor little old Elmer.

He had shriveled up so much and he was so tiny. He looked like an eight or ten year old child because he had gotten so small. We got very attached to Elmer. He was my buddy. And I wasn't afraid of him at all—being in a casket and everything. When I'd go by, I'd say, 'Hi, ya, Elmer,' and 'How ya doin', Elmer?' Oh, yeah. We took good care of Elmer" (Basgall 1989, 177).

Elmer's next assignment was to pose as a dead dope fiend in the lobbies of theaters showing Dwain Esper's movie *Narcotic*. Esper owned, rented, or borrowed Elmer, depending on whose story you choose to believe. Esper claims he purchased Elmer for $1,000 from a man named Cody, who said he was the coroner of a small Oklahoma town and had been storing Elmer in his barn pending identification. Dave Friedman remembers that Esper leased Elmer from the senior Sonney for $100 per month. Dan Sonney explains, "My dad was pretty good friends with Dwain Esper and loaned Elmer to him for about six months for *Narcotic*. Esper used to tell everyone that he owned Elmer. Even after my dad died and news came out that Elmer had been found, Esper still claimed that he owned it!" (Vraney 1994, 25). Sonney also remembers that Esper didn't think the mummy was real. In any case Elmer was on tour. To promote his film Esper told movie-goers that Elmer was a drug addict who had committed suicide while surrounded by a posse after robbing a drug store. He pointed to the deterioration of Elmer's skin as evidence of his drug abuse. Elmer is remembered by Esper's daughter Millicent, who says he made regular appearances at her Halloween parties.

During his public appearances Elmer had a few notable reunions with old acquaintances. In 1928 Elmer was one of the attractions in a traveling amusement show set up in conjunction with a cross-country footrace called "The Titanic Struggle." Billed as "An Oklahoma Outlaw Who Refused to Surrender," Elmer was not exhibited in Oklahoma. Curious, as were many Pawhuska residents, Bob Fenton traveled to

Tulsa and asked to see the mummy. Seventeen years after they had last met in the Revard barn, Fenton identified the body as the man his posse had brought down. Two years later, Joseph Johnson's youngest son Luke recognized Elmer in a sideshow in Ocean Park, California. Familiar with his father's embalming of the outlaw, Luke countered the carnival talker's claim that Elmer had drunk poison that mummified his body. Luke learned that Elmer had been exhibited in forty states and had been viewed by hundreds of thousands of people for ten cents each.

After Louis Sonney's death in 1949, Elmer went into retirement. He was stored in a warehouse with the other crime museum exhibits until 1964, when Dan Sonney entered into a business agreement with filmmaker Dave Friedman. Elmer came out of retirement in 1966 to be an extra in the film *She Freak*. In the film, which was also distributed as *Alley of Nightmares*, the camera pans across Elmer standing in the corner of a tent. To prepare him for his brief movie appearance, Dan Sonney had to reattach Elmer's arm. According to Friedman, Sonney had severed it to play a practical joke on his secretary and repaired it with wire and electrical tape. Friedman recalls Elmer having a kind of greasy, rubbery feel.

Elmer was warehoused after the filming but surfaced again in 1971. Sonney sold Elmer along with several wax figures to Spoony Singh of the Hollywood Wax Museum for $10,000. Singh made the purchase for two Canadian men who had planned to exhibit Elmer at Mount Rushmore. Sonney said, "...I didn't give a damn where they took him. They could have buried him or they could have sent him up to the moon. He was just another piece of merchandise, like a film can..." (Basgall 1989, 196). Elmer made it to Mount Rushmore, but a windstorm blew the exhibit down, causing the mummy to lose all the fingers on his left hand, the tips of his ears, the big and little toe on his left foot, and one middle toe on his right foot. He was returned to the owner, but Singh didn't think Elmer was as lifelike as

his wax figures and at the same time found him too gruesome for his family-oriented museum.

Singh sold Elmer to E. D. Liersch, who leased space with D. R. Crysdale at the Nu-Pike Amusement Park in Long Beach, California. Elmer's casket had fallen apart, and he now lay in a cardboard box, so Liersch, who later claimed he had no idea the body was real, built a hexagonal casket out of plywood and lined it with red satin. He dressed Elmer in a black suit, laid him out in the new casket, and displayed him on the boardwalk in front of the dark ride he operated. He later topped the casket with glass to prevent his customers from sticking things in the mouth of the mummy he billed "The 1,000 Year Old Man." In 1972 Elmer was confiscated from Liersch and his partner by Long Beach Amusement for nonpayment of rent. He roomed for a while with an electrician nicknamed "Lucky," who stored Elmer in the closet of his apartment. Lucky prepared Elmer for a stint in the refurbished "Laff in the Dark" attraction: he coated the unclothed mummy with red-orange phosphorescent paint and hung it from a noose under a blue light in the funhouse.

The events that unfolded in the funhouse four years later catapulted Elmer McCurdy into the limelight. On December 7, 1976, the amusement park was closed to the public. Universal Television Studios had leased it to film an episode of "The Six Million Dollar Man" in which a secret missile-control room is camouflaged as a carnival attraction. They chose to film in the funhouse and decided to remove Elmer from the set. When Elmer was lifted, his right arm broke off at the elbow and fell to the floor. Deducing that the arm had broken off before and been wired back together, the prop man planned to fix it with electrical tape. He said later that he thought Elmer was just "some crummy dummy" (Basgall 1989, 14). In attempting to repair the damage, he caused another piece of the brittle upper arm to break off, exposing dull, white bone and ending Elmer's posthumous career.

John Purvis, manager of several concessions at Nu-Pike, had believed Elmer to be a wax dummy until he had a close look for himself:

> I wanted to see that bone. And I seen that bone, and I still couldn't believe it. And then I shined it under the arm, and I seen that hair—which that could've been faked. But then I shined it down on his privates. He wasn't in nothin', you know? He had no clothes on. And everything was there—his prick, his balls, everything was there! And I said ... well ... this guy is real!
>
> And then, you know, I got to looking him over, and I shined the light in his mouth. And his mouth, you know, his lips were like this—tight up against his teeth—and you could see where his jaw was tied together. And his teeth was still in there—all of his teeth. I knew then that wasn't no wax dummy 'cause they don't put teeth in a wax dummy's mouth and wire it shut, you know what I mean? (Basgall 1989, 18–19)

Purvis said that Long Beach Amusement, the customers, and even old Lucky the electrician hadn't known Elmer was real. "I guess when you think about it, he wasn't a lousy dummy. He was a damn good one because he fooled everybody," said Purvis (Basgall 1989, 20). It was Purvis who cut the rope so that Elmer could literally be placed in the hands of the authorities. "His days in the sideshows was over," Purvis commented (Basgall 1989, 24).

Sergeant Dan P. Sallmen of the Long Beach Police Department filed report #765-0028 on December 8, 1976, after criminalist E. Williams examined the body at the scene. The report noted that there appeared to be a bone-type structure having bone-like joints beneath the outer covering of the body. The report also noted a small amount of hair on the skull, some pubic hair, and a small trace of hair on the back of the leg. The severed right forearm was delivered to deputy medical examiner Dr. Joseph Choi for examination. In Dr. Choi's opinion, the arm was that of a mummified, aged subject most likely of South American, Indian, or Mexican

extraction. The L.A. County coroner's office sent investigator John Mosbrucker to take possession of the mummy the same day so that its age could be determined.

Mosbrucker took several photographs to document the scene. Elmer had been hanging by his neck from a rope in the ceiling. The hangman's knot pressed against the head, tilting it a little and casting the nearly closed eyes downwards. His nude body had been painted several times with phosphorescent paint, which made him glow in the dark. Streaks of paint had dried on both cheeks under the eye sockets, which Dave Friedman says were empty. The smooth, tightly stretched skin on the high forehead had broken in several places, and the paint had peeled away. Elmer had sutured incisions on his right and left femoral areas and a Y-midline incision in the chest and abdomen. His two big toes were missing, and his feet were skin and bone. Elmer was placed on a stretcher, covered with a white sheet, and wheeled into a van. He became case #76-14812 and was scheduled for autopsy in the morning.

The autopsy was performed by Dr. Choi on December 9. His report describes a gunshot wound through the right chest to the abdomen. The entrance wound on the right anterior chest had been previously sutured. The bullet appeared to penetrate the right sixth rib, right lung, diaphragm, liver, and intestine. According to the trajectory of the bullet, Elmer had been shot while lying down, possibly asleep. The copper jacket—.32 caliber, rusty, and greenish-blue in color—was recovered within the muscle of the left pelvic area.

The body, according to the autopsy report, was completely mummified and weighed approximately fifty pounds. It measured 63 inches in height. There were a few fine short brown hairs on both sides of the head, but the front was bald. Nose and facial features appeared to be Caucasian. Part of the ears, the big toes, and the fingers were missing. The modified Y-shaped incision was noted. The right and left inguinal areas

Death certificate completed the discovery of the mummified body of Elmer McCurdy in after 1976.

showed embalming sutures, each measuring approximately two inches. The right knee and left ankle joints had been separated post-mortem. The back of the body had two holes, which appeared to have been made for a museum stand. A length of the 3/4" rope remained around his neck.

Dr. Choi reopened the original autopsy incision, which had been sutured with black cotton. The abdomen had been filled with a hardening compound. The pericardial sac had been previously opened and the entire heart was in the left chest in a hard, rocklike condition. The aorta showed mild arteriosclerosis. The lungs, trachea, and bronchi were mummified and in their normal positions. They were hard and atrophied. There was some evidence of hemorrhage in the right lung and underneath the right diaphragm. The penetrating wound could not be identified due to mummification, but the right lobe of the liver showed a small indented area appearing to be a gunshot wound. There was no injury in the skull and the dura mater was well preserved. The brain was like a rock, with no evidence of hemorrhage or injury. The closure of the skull's suture lines indicated a man forty or fifty years of age. The external genitalia were mummified and surrounded by a fine pubic hair, which was originally brown before being painted a bright orange-red color.

Sections of the skin, wound, hemorrhagic tissue, various organs, and the perforated rib were preserved for further examination. It was assumed that the bullet had been removed at the time of the original autopsy, but the jacket found was of a type called a "gas check" that was first used in 1905. Lab tests confirmed the presence of arsenic in the tissues, the use of which was prohibited in embalming fluid by the late 1920s. These two findings narrowed down the date of death to between 1905 and 1930. Because his fingers were missing, Elmer could not be fingerprinted. But the contents of his mouth, discovered when the mandible was removed for dental analysis, shed further light on the mystery of the mummy's identity. They included a 1924 penny and ticket stubs from "Louis Sonney's Museum of Crime" and "140 W. Pike, Side Show."

Later on December 9, the *Long Beach Independent* ran a story about the discovery of the mummy. Dan Sonney says that he heard the news on the radio and received a call from police that afternoon. They had traced him after finding the ticket stubs in Elmer's mouth and a tag on the mummy that said "Property of Officer Sonney, the man who captured Roy Gardner." According to

Dave Friedman, he and Sonney read about the discovery of the body in the newspaper and called the *Los Angeles Times* to report its identity. E. D. Liersh read his name in the *Times* and referred the police to Spoony Singh, but Singh was out of town. Through the efforts of Dan Sonney and Dave Friedman, who claims, "I'm the person who made Elmer the most famous mummy since King Tut," Elmer McCurdy's body was reunited with his name.

Also on December 9, Donald Drynan, a spokesman for the L.A. County coroner's office, released a statement. He said that further examination by x-ray, tissue analysis, and dental imprint would be conducted. If the identity of the body could not be established, it would be cremated. "You just can't paint it red and use it for laughs," he said (Basgall 1989, 32). The story of the funhouse mummy made national headlines. Glenn Shirley, the author of more than a dozen books about western outlaws, learned of the discovery and suspected that the body might be that of the relatively obscure outlaw Elmer McCurdy. Then the two photographs taken of Elmer before and after embalming turned up in the Western History Collection at the University of Oklahoma after curator Dr. John Ezell (since retired) was contacted by authorities in California. By December 11, Elmer's story had been pieced together, and what was known of his life, death, and afterlife was made public. Elmer was featured in the *National Enquirer*, the *Star*, and *Variety*. His story was also told by the French, German, and English press. Bud Furillo, a Century City restaurateur and radio talk show host, had 3,000 T-shirts printed up commemorating Elmer and sold them at $4 each.

The L.A. coroner's office was not satisfied. On December 12, they stated that they would hold the body until definitive identification was made and would keep a team of investigators on the case. Two days later they circulated a news release requesting that any of Elmer's relatives step forward to claim the corpse. If it was not claimed within the next few months, they would bury rather than cremate the body. The coroner's office was contacted by several Los Angeles mortuaries who offered to bury the mummy for free, a Western History Museum in Missouri that wanted to add him to their collection, and the Long Beach Amusement Company, who wanted him returned.

It took some work, but Fred Olds, director of the Oklahoma Territorial Museum in Guthrie, Oklahoma, convinced the coroner, Dr. Thomas Noguchi, to return Elmer to the state in which he had lived and died. Olds represented a group called the Indian Territory Posse of Oklahoma Westerners, who had given their unanimous support to bring Elmer back to Guthrie for burial. Olds spoke to chief investigator Bob Dambacher, who was initially skeptical. Dr. Noguchi outlined his conditions for release of the body. He stipulated that the chief medical officer of Oklahoma must agree to accept the body, that the town of Guthrie must promise not to make a Roman holiday out of the funeral, and that Oklahoma must furnish a forensic team to join Noguchi's in making certain that the mummy was McCurdy.

Olds got approval for the plan from Oklahoma governor David Boren. He convinced Oklahoma state medical examiner Jay Chapman to take responsibility for proper burial. He went before the city council for permission to bury Elmer in Summit View Cemetery, which is city property. He had difficulty finding a preacher willing to officiate at the funeral but secured Glenn Jordan, who had been a Methodist lay preacher. Then on April 12, 1977, Fred Olds, Ralph McCalmont, and forensic anthropologist Clyde Snow flew to Los Angeles to assist Dr. Noguchi and his forensic anthropologist Judy Suchey in the positive identification of the body.

Elmer was stored in a room down the hall from Dr. Noguchi's office. He looked like the man in the photographs the Oklahoma team had brought with them, except that his skin had darkened and he had no hair on his head. Picking him up was like lifting

balsa wood, and he was very stiff. His body had been completely sprayed with reddish-orange fluorescent paint, which scrubbed off very quickly. Olds told a friend that the body was like leather and "dark like shoes" (telephone conversation with Max Warren, 14 June 1996). The mummy's age, hair and eye color, and height matched that of Elmer McCurdy. The bunions Elmer was known to have were also said to be present on the mummy (Drimmer 1981, 19). The scar, documented in Elmer's prison record, was noted on the back of his right wrist. The anthropologists conducted a video comparison of Elmer's profile and found the body remarkably similar in bone structure to the photograph.

On April 14, 1977, Dr. Noguchi told a news conference that positive identification of Elmer McCurdy had been made by estimating bone measurements from old photographs of the bandit. At the same news conference, Fred Olds was reported by the *New York Times* (April 15, 1977) as saying, "Elmer will finally be buried at an old territorial cemetery with other robbers and outlaws. He was sidetracked for a long time, but we feel he's part of our history."

More of Elmer's history was learned when six of his tissue samples were analyzed by Dr. Theodore A. Reyman, chief of pathology at Mount Carmel Mercy Hospital in Detroit. Dr. Reyman was startled by what he saw under the microscope. In his report, published as a special supplement by the Paleopathology Association, Dr. Reyman writes, "The preservation of the tissue [by the embalming process] was almost unbelievable. The heart was nearly perfectly preserved.... The coronary arteries were quite normal. Red and white blood cells were easily recognized. The organ appeared normal. Sections from skin, skeletal muscle, and bone were also in an excellent state of preservation." The brain also appeared normal, but Dr. Reyman found abnormality in the lung, which had lost its sponge-like appearance and was heavy and consolidated. This suggested that Elmer had tuberculosis for some time before his death, that he may have had pneumonia when he died, or that he may have aspirated his gastric contents at the time of his death.

Before Elmer was released, the coroner's office took care of a few details. Because it was illegal for anyone to have "owned" Elmer's body, it had to be legally confiscated, a procedure carried out by a lawyer. In addition, Elmer's detached arm was sewn back on. The mummy was wrapped in a black bag and placed on a cart while the paperwork was completed. After a number of confirming phone calls to Oklahoma officials, Dr. Noguchi released the body. He then held a news conference in which he stated: "This case has been of greater interest to the American public than Marilyn Monroe's death or the Manson murder case. People are just fascinated by this Oklahoma outlaw" (Basgall 1989, 237). Elmer spent the night of April 15, 1977, on a loading ramp at Los Angeles International Airport and left L.A. at 8:30 the following morning.

By then nearly 100 years of age, Elmer McCurdy arrived in Oklahoma. He had traveled cargo class and had been shipped C.O.D. for $127. Elmer was delivered to the Smith Funeral Home in Guthrie. Fred Olds and medical examiner Jay Chapman objected to opening the casket before burial, but the body was transferred to a handmade, white pine casket donated by Wes McKenzie, a coffin-maker from Chelsea, Oklahoma.

Two days before the funeral, Fred Olds supervised the machine-digging of the grave, which cost $525. He arranged for a cement truck to be in the cemetery the day of the funeral to show that he had no intentions of allowing the body to be stolen. A horse-drawn, velvet-curtained, glass-sided hearse last used in 1913 was brought from Ponca City, Oklahoma, by the Gill-Lessert Funeral Home. Students in a local history club cleaned and polished the hearse and harness, and rodeo equipment dealer Truman Moody provided two white horses to pull it.

On the morning of the funeral Fred Olds held a news conference, and his wife distributed pamphlets containing a biographical sketch of Elmer. Dr. Snow explained the video process he had used to make the identification. Olds reminded the crowd that the ceremony was to be a real funeral, not a mock one, as though this man had just died. The funeral procession was held shortly after 10 A.M. on April 22, 1977. Elmer's body was transported to Summit View Cemetery, located two miles north of Guthrie. Members of the Indian Territory Posse of Oklahoma Westerners, a state senator, a state representative, the town mayor, and others served as pallbearers and outriders. George Wayman, sheriff of Osage County, where Elmer was shot, rode point, which in the old days meant riding ahead, determining the course, and looking out for hostiles. Olds and Don Odom rode in a Phaeton buggy, followed by another buggy, an antique car, and men on horseback. At the gravesite 500 solemn people had gathered. The pallbearers dismounted and carried the coffin, adorned with a spray of white lilies, to the gravesite, removed their hats, and lined up on both sides of the grave.

Glenn Jordan conducted the service in a little more than a thousand words: "Yet to all of these people, even a Bill Doolin and Elmer McCurdy, we offer understanding and forgiveness. We were not there and we do not know the circumstances and conditions that made our ancestors act as they did. We must be careful to 'judge not lest you be judged.' We simply affirm that all concerned—white and Indian, cattleman and farmer, lawman and outlaw—are a part of Oklahoma's heritage" (Basgall 1989, 251). The coffin was lowered with ropes into the grave, and a member of the history club dropped a single red rose in. Olds placed cardboard over the coffin, and two and a half yards of concrete were poured into the grave. Each of the pallbearers threw in a shovelful of dirt, and the gravediggers filled in the rest. The spray of white lilies was laid near the tombstone. Because rain threatened, everyone left in a hurry.

Gravestone of Elmer McCurdy in Summit View Cemetery, Guthrie, Oklahoma. Photo courtesy of Bill L. Cooper.

Elmer remains buried on Boot Hill next to outlaw Bill Doolin. "It is the place of outcasts—of loners—of men and women who died in poverty and, usually, obscurity, leaving their interment to the goodwill of strangers" (Basgall 1989, 3). Elmer's gray granite tombstone, donated by the Warren Monument Company of Guthrie, reads:

ELMER McCURDY

Shot by Sheriff's Posse
In Osage Hills
On Oct. 7, 1911
Returned to Guthrie, Okla.
From Los Angeles County,
Calif.
For Burial Apr. 22, 1977

Elmer's burial was mentioned that evening on television by Walter Cronkite of CBS. His gravesite is used as the setting for a periodic candlelight memorial service by Becky Luker of Stone Lion Inn and was recently visited by a man from the L.A. County coroner's office. McCurdy's story is still told at the Nu-Pike amusement park where the funhouse has been renamed "The Mummy's Hangout." Elmer McCurdy's working days are finally over.

Hazel Farris ("Hazel the Mummy")

The mummy of Hazel Farris is a small piece of history and has been exhibited as such in the town where she sought refuge from the law. In one morning Hazel shot and killed five men. She later committed suicide, not out of remorse but to avoid capture. Ninety years later she poses no threat to herself or to others.

Hazel Farris lived with her husband near Louisville, Kentucky. They were peaceful for the most part, but neighbors reported

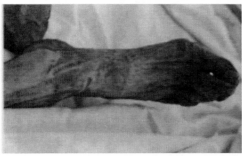

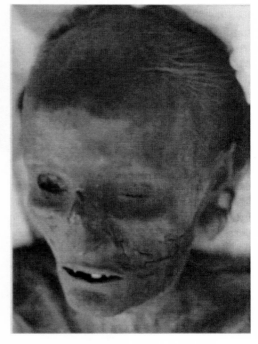

Hazel Farris as she appears today. Note the missing ring finger on her right hand.

that the husband was known to take a drink and that the couple had the occasional fistfight. Such a fight occurred on the morning of August 6, 1905, when Farris declared her intention to buy a new hat. When her husband objected, they came to blows, and Farris shot him twice with a six-shooter. The wounds were mortal, and he died on the living room floor. A modern account of the fatal argument calls Hazel's husband "a victim of his wife's outrage, steel nerve and deadly aim."

Neighbors heard the fighting and the shots and alerted the police. Three officers entered the house and became victims of "the deadly accuracy Hazel was famous for."

A deputy sheriff heard the commotion as he was passing by. He entered the house after being warned by neighbors and tried to overpower Farris, who ran across the room toward him. During their struggle, he stumbled over one of the bodies and his revolver discharged, shooting off the ring finger of

Farris's right hand. Hazel broke free of his grasp and grabbed her pistol. Author Elaine Hobson Miller (1995, 48) writes, "As he stood up, Hazel fired a fifth bullet, and another body was added to the pile." Hazel escaped through the back door of the house. The *Birmingham (Ala.) News* notes, "Hazel's murderous misadventures somehow didn't gain the notoriety of a Bonnie Parker or Lizzie Borden, but the fact that she gunned down her husband, three policemen and a sheriff's deputy in a single day is nothing to be sneezed at."

Hazel fled the state of Kentucky. A $500 reward was offered for her capture, and several hunts for her were launched. In 1906 the twenty-five-year-old Farris turned up in Bessemer, Alabama. She was rumored to support herself through prostitution. She fell in love with a man who soon professed his love for her, despite the fact that she was a fugitive. After Hazel made the mistake of trusting him with her story, the man, whose name is unknown, betrayed her to the local police, probably to collect the reward money. After some heavy drinking, Farris chose to commit suicide by swallowing poison on December 20, 1906.

Farris's body dehydrated in the Bessemer funeral establishment (actually a furniture store) where she was taken after her death. The body became the talk of the town, and "Hazel the Mummy" was viewed in her casket by many of the curious residents, who were charged a dime for the privilege. "No one knows why her body became mummified," declares the *Birmingham News* (March 30, 1974). Some suppose that her body had been embalmed with arsenic, but others believe this was the type of poison she had consumed: "Some local sages figured her preservation was due to a mixture of the whiskey she was so fond of, her passion, and the arsenic they think she used to end her life. Others say it was the repeated injections of embalming fluid" (Miller 1995, 49). Although the current owner claims Hazel had never been embalmed, volunteers at the Bessemer Hall of History are divided:

Catherine Kean has heard stories about Hazel being embalmed over several months with formaldehyde. Louise Tommie, who has spoken to older Bessemer residents and to the daughter of the furniture store owner, says that no one remembers the body being embalmed (Miller 1995, 49).

The author of *Myths, Mysteries and Legends of Alabama* consulted William Counce of the Funeral Service Education Department at Jefferson State Community College. Counce believes that Hazel was embalmed because Alabama had some of the country's earliest legislation requiring embalming and because early fluids were often arsenic-based and very strong: "Arsenic was much more effective than formaldehyde. People embalmed with arsenic tend to dehydrate.... There were recipes floating around where funeral directors could make the fluid themselves. In fact, in 1906, the embalming fluid market probably was not commercially accessible around here like it is today, so it might have been just as easy to make it themselves. That might make it a very astringent arsenic base" (Miller 1995, 49).

Whether or not Hazel's body was embalmed, a question that "remains part of her mystique" according to Louise Tommie and Elaine Hobson Miller, it neither drew any claimants nor deteriorated.

According to the Hall of History, the mummified body was transferred to a furniture store in Tuscaloosa, Alabama, where in May 1907 it was purchased for $25 by carnival showman Orlando C. Brooks. Luther Brooks concurs that his uncle paid a fee of $25 but says that Hazel's body was claimed from the morgue three months after her suicide. In any case, O. C. Brooks stored the body in a garage and set out to Louisville to locate Hazel's relatives. "He did find several people who knew her," relates Luther, "but no one who wanted her body" (Miller 1995, 50). O. C. Brooks had therefore cleared his conscience before making a comfortable living by exhibiting the mummy. The first time the mummy was shown, some 18,000 people

Poster advertising the display of the mummy of Hazel Farris.

saw her for a nickel apiece over a ten-day period in 1911, according to Luther. Records show that during the Depression, the exhibit was bringing in $150 to $200 per week (Miller 1995, 51). Once in show business, Farris was touted as "A Genuine Human Body in De-Hydration" and was toted from venue to venue strapped to the sideboard of a Model T, according to the Hall of History, and later hauled in a 1931 gray Oldsmobile without a backseat, according to Luther. Hazel was said to be "exhibited in the open air so that all may feel and examine the beautiful suit of long, flowing hair." Although she was described as a raven-haired beauty, her hair was and still is red.

O. C. Brooks walked the midway prior to his shows, handing out flyers and urging the carnival patrons not to miss them. Only Farris's face, hands, and feet were exposed to view, but the exhibitor offered $500 cash to anyone willing to examine the body and prove that it was not genuine. The posters boasted that she was insured with Lloyd's of London for $5,000. Farris was "exhibited for the benefit of science—that the world may see what has been accomplished since the art of mummification was lost by the Egyptians centuries ago. Those who have been taught that human flesh must necessarily decay will find that this particular subject is the exception. Persons having no thought save idle curiosity will profit but little by seeing this wonder, which can only be understood and appreciated by the intelligent class." Some female members of this intelligent class accidentally upset Hazel's casket in 1959, dumping the mummy into the sawdust and causing her to lose two gold teeth (Miller 1995, 52).

Among the legends that grew up around the mummy of Hazel Farris was that her hair and nails continued to grow for some thirty-five years after her death. Although the legend is discounted by many, Luther Brooks claims, "My Granny Brooks, who wouldn't tell a lie, said she cut Hazel's hair and fingernails regularly during the five years she was in her west Nashville garage" (Miller 1995,

51). It was in his residence—said to be a corn crib—in Coushatta, Louisiana, that O. C. Brooks's body was found on April 1, 1950. He had apparently died in his sleep, and since he slept atop the pine box that housed Hazel's remains to prevent them from being stolen, that's where his body was found. A then thirteen-year-old Luther Brooks accompanied his father to Louisiana to claim his great-uncle's remains but found that he had already been buried: "People gave us all of my uncle's stuff, including Hazel, so we took her home with us" (Miller 1995, 51).

Luther Brooks was placed in charge of Hazel's mummy and was allowed to keep it in the family garage. "You can imagine how great it was," he told the *National Enquirer* (March 17, 1963). "I was the only kid in school who owned a mummy. It was like being a celebrity." He began showing Hazel at school carnivals and by the time he graduated from high school in 1958, he had organized a small show that included the mummy and some rides, including a ferris wheel. When he was age 18 or 19, Luther inquired about any health permit needed to display the mummy but was told by the medical examiner that no permit was needed. The additional income Brooks brought in exhibiting Hazel at schools, civic clubs, and church carnivals allowed him to get married in 1962 and to house Hazel in a separate location. "It wasn't that my bride was jealous of Hazel or anything like that," he explains, "but people kept walking by our place and pointing" (*National Enquirer*). Luther Brooks sold his show in 1965 but kept the mummy. "Someday, thanks to the people who pay to see her, she'll send my kids through college," he told the *Enquirer*. His two girls helped clean the mummy and occasionally perfumed her and showed her to their friends. Local children liked to comb her hair.

Hazel was examined annually by mortuary science students from Vanderbilt University, who estimated that she had weighed 165 pounds at the time of her death (Miller 1995, 52), although as a mummy she was a mere 33 pounds. The students also took a biopsy from her back or the back of her arm that indicated arsenic in the tissues.

In 1974 the Bessemer Hall of History discovered Hazel (by then retired) and negotiated with Luther to have the body returned to Bessemer as an "educational and scientific exhibit." In its informational material, the museum records that Hazel was willed to Luther Brooks "with the stipulation that she could never be shown commercially, but that she must pay for her crimes forever by benefiting charitable and non-profit organizations," but Luther notes that there was neither a will nor any conditions attached to the mummy. The body was displayed in an otherwise empty downtown building in October of that year and thousands paid fifty cents to see Hazel laid out in a casket and illuminated by an overhead skylight (Miller 1995, 52). Hazel was exhibited by the museum three more times over the next seven years; each exhibit was mounted for about three weeks in the museum, then located in the basement of the city library on Fourth Avenue. In 1981 the fee was raised to $1 for adults and fifty cents for children. After a 10 percent cut to the owner of the mummy, proceeds of several thousand dollars went to the Hall of History (Miller 1995, 53). "Alabama's most celebrated mummy" was also displayed at the Alabama State Fair and, for one week in October 1975, at the University of Alabama's Ferguson Student Center.

Hazel has required little maintenance over the years. Luther Brooks admitted to having accidentally broken her nose as a teenager. And she once fell out of the back of his car when she was being transported but suffered no damage. The finger bones on her right hand are exposed due to the action of rats at some point in the past. She emits a musty odor when confined for too long, a situation that has been remedied at times by adding deodorant to the casket. In preparation for one of Hazel's exhibits at the Bessemer Hall of History, Louise Tommie obtained some cleaning fluid from a local dry cleaner and used it to scrub mold off the mummy, which she laid out on some paper on the floor (Miller 1995, 53). It was also Mrs. Tommie who transported the mummy to and from Luther Brooks's house in her station wagon for her Bessemer visits. That these visits were always scheduled during the Halloween season is chalked up to coincidence. Luther Brooks claims never to have used the mummy to scare anyone, although Mrs. Tommie admits that her children were afraid to ride in the car after Hazel had been in it.

In 1994 the Hall of History borrowed Hazel's mummy from the owner for the first time since 1981. Her most recent exhibit at the museum, now located at the old Bessemer train depot, was held in October 1995. Hazel was shown in a box that was outfitted with an alarm system to warn if it was opened. The public was invited to view her for a modest admission fee: $2 for adults and $1 for children, with special rates for groups of ten or more. Luther Brooks, who now owns an excavating business and raises catfish, has requested that the Hall of History take over as custodian of the remains. "She may have been a bad girl in life, but in death she did a lot of good," he says (Miller 1995, 54). The museum has not yet accepted his offer because they do not want the mummy on permanent display and with renovations pending they do not have a secure place to store her.

James "Slim" Davis ("Gold Tooth Jimmy")

The circumstances of Jimmy Davis' life are obscured, although his death is said to be well documented. His mummy is well known, but usually by his nickname "Gold Tooth Jimmy." Jimmy is reported to have been a bank robber and killer in the 1920s as a member of the Purple Gang. He and fellow gang member Dutch Kapler were ambushed after a high-speed chase and shot on a farm in Canton, Ohio. Jimmy was embalmed by a funeral director who was never paid. The body was sold to a showman and was

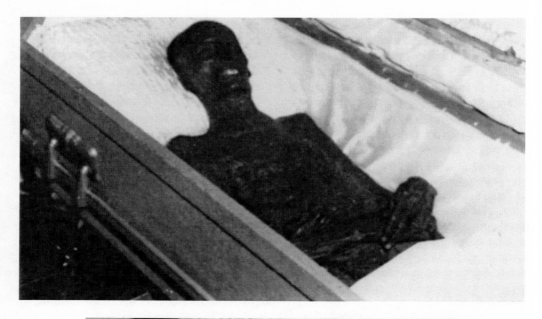

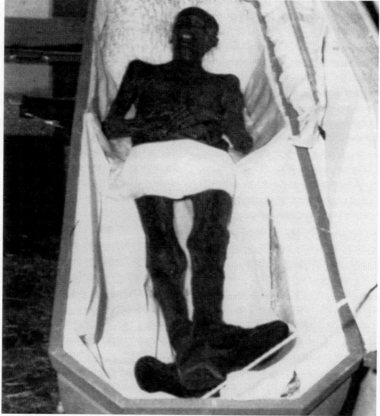

Gold Tooth Jimmy on display in the Palace of Wonders. Photos courtesy of Captain Harvey Lee Boswell.

featured on the two-car railroad show owned by Sam Houston (d. 1957) that played throughout Mexico, the West Coast, and Canada for forty years. (The mummified body of Dutch Kapler was also exhibited.) In the 1960s Jimmy toured shopping centers as a single-o (single exhibit) mobile museum and was the annex attraction in Captain Harvey Lee Boswell's "Palace of Wonders" sideshow. Patrons were charged an admittance fee of fifty cents but paid an additional twenty-five cents to see the mummy. Although the fees were later doubled, so was the attraction: for years Captain Boswell exhibited the mummies of both Gold Tooth Jimmy and Marie O'Day (discussed below) for the same low price. Jimmy's flesh is said to be the consistency of beef jerky. His feet are positioned in a "T" to stand up, but his left arm is said to be nearly detached. Captain Boswell sold Jimmy in the early 1990s, and the mummy is now in a private collection.

John Wilkes Booth (a.k.a. David E. George, John St. Helen, John W. Boyd, J. J. Marr, George D. Ryan, Jesse Smith "The Texas Booth Mummy," "The Bates Mummy")

Questions surround this mummy of many names, or rather photographs of it, since the mummy itself may or may not exist today. There is little doubt that the mummy in most of the photos is the body of a man named David E. George, who killed himself in 1903. Whether David E. George and John St. Helen were one and the same is open to question. The larger question is whether John St. Helen was—as he claimed to be—John Wilkes Booth, assassin of Abraham Lincoln. Despite strong opinions on both sides and the involvement of many who are attempting to remain neutral, the possibility that history may have recorded incorrectly the fate of one of its most infamous villains may never be quelled or confirmed to everyone's satisfaction.

After assassinating President Abraham Lincoln on April 14, 1865 in Washington, D.C., John Wilkes Booth's spur caught in the flag that draped the presidential box in Ford's Theater and caused him to alight in such a way as to break the fibula of his left leg about two inches above the ankle. Booth fled the theater and escaped the city on horseback with the help of his accomplices. On April 20, the War Department offered a reward of $50,000 for his capture and described him as five feet seven or eight inches tall with a slender build, high forehead, black hair, black eyes, and heavy black mustache. On April 24, the fugitives enlisted the help of three Confederate officers. Booth was conducted by one of the officers to the home of the Garretts and introduced to the family as "John W. Boyd," a wounded Confederate soldier. Richard Garrett agreed to let "Boyd" and David Harold, who was posing as his brother, sleep in his barn. At about midnight, the law—in the form of the Sixteenth New York Cavalry—caught up with his unexpected visitors.

The barn was set on fire in an attempt to flush Booth out. Against orders, a shot was fired and Booth fell, fatally wounded in the neck. He was dragged from the barn and died two hours later. Booth's body was compared to photos and checked against the printed description from the reward flyer. "It agreed in every particular," wrote the Reverend Richard B. Garrett in 1907 (quoted by Steven G. Miller in *The Body in the Barn* 1993, 21). Booth had the initials "J.W.B." tattooed on his left hand with India ink, a fact which had limited his choice of aliases. He also had a scar on the back of his neck, from which a large fibroid tumor had been removed. The incision had healed very neatly but had afterwards been broken open, leaving a large and ugly scar. On Booth's person were his diary, compass, knife, pistols, several photographs, a bank receipt made out to "J. Wilkes Booth," and a scarf pin with "Dan Bryant to J. W. Booth" engraved on it.

Booth's body was sewn up in a saddle blanket and examined by many officers and troopers as it was conveyed by wagon to the *John S. Ide*, which was docked at Belle

Plain, Virginia. The steamboat transported the corpse to Washington, where it was transferred to the warship *Montauk*. A limited autopsy consisting of the removal of the three damaged cervical vertebrae was conducted on April 27 by Surgeon General Dr. Joseph K. Barnes. The body was identified by Washington dentist Dr. Merrill, who had filled two of Booth's teeth a few days earlier, and by hotel clerk Charles Dawson, who recognized Booth from his appearance, from the initials tattooed on his hand, from the scar on his neck, and from his clothing. A photograph was said to have been taken at this time, but no copies exist.

The body was also examined by Dr. John Frederick May, who had removed the tumor from Booth's neck. When the tarpaulin covering the body was removed, Dr. May was said to have exclaimed, "There is no resemblance in that corpse to Booth, nor can I believe it to be that of him." But he then described the neck wound exactly before seeing it. After the body was placed at his request in a sitting and standing position, Dr. May was finally able to imperfectly recognize the features of Booth, writing in 1909:

> But never in a human being had a greater change taken place, from the man whom I had seen in the vigor of life and health, than in that of the haggard corpse which was before me, with its yellow and discolored skin, its unkempt and matted hair, and its whole facial expression sunken and sharpened by the exposure and starvation it had undergone ... although the circumstances connected with his capture all tended to corroborate the belief that he had been killed, yet from the body which was produced by the captors nearly every vestige of resemblance of the living man had disappeared. But the mark made by the scalpel during life remained indelible in death, and settled beyond all question at the time, and all cavil in the future, the identity of the man who had assassinated the President. (Wilson 1929, 206-7)

Dr. May noted that the left lower limb was greatly contused and black from fracture of one of the long bones.

The body identified as John Wilkes Booth's was taken by rowboat from the *Mon-* *tauk* to the Old Penitentiary (also called the Old Arsenal) on April 27. It was buried in a locked storage room in the old Capitol Prison in what is now Fort McNair in Washington, D.C. The remains were exhumed in 1867 and reburied in a locked storeroom in Warehouse 1 at the prison. The body was released to the family on February 15, 1869, by President Andrew Johnson and removed to J. H. Weaver's Funeral Parlors in Baltimore. At this time the body was identified by John T. Ford, Harry Ford, Norval E. Foard, Dr. Theodore Micheau, Henry W. Mears, Joseph T. Lowry, Colonel William M. Pegram, members of the Booth family, and many of the hundreds who assembled outside. The body reposed for two days in the back room of the funeral home in a mahogany casket with a hinged lid and a glass plate (Bryan 1940, 310). The remains were buried in the family plot in the Greenmount Cemetery in Baltimore.

Memphis lawyer Finis L. Bates later claimed that the man killed in the barn was a double who had unwittingly stepped in to take Booth's place when sent to return to the Garrett barn for articles left behind. The man's name was said to be "Ruddy" or "Robey," but author Francis Wilson claims that the man of this name, Franklin Robey, proved to be alive many years after his alleged death, and several sworn statements attest that he was still living in 1889. After Booth's body was brought to Washington, the *Constitutional Union* published a statement that Booth had escaped and that the body brought in was not his. Other rumors circulated that Booth was alive and well in Ceylon. The government ignored the rumors. Bates believed that if the government was sure of its identification, the body would have been placed on public exhibition rather than held in secret. Wilson counters that the positive identification of the body precluded the need for public identification, which he contends would have led to a riot.

Finis Bates stated that a man named John St. Helen, of Granbury, Texas, first confessed to him in 1872 (and again later in

1898) that he was John Wilkes Booth. St. Helen showed him the nicked or uneven surface of his shin and explained the details of his escape after the assassination. He also had a penchant for reciting Shakespeare, expert elocution, and an intimate knowledge of the details of theatrical work (Bryan 1940, 335). Bates traced the man to Leadville, Colorado (where he went in 1878), and then to Fresno, California. A man named Mr. L. Treadkell identified a photo of St. Helen as a man called Jesse Smith, whom he had employed as a teamster in early 1867. In Fort Worth, Texas, in 1885, General Albert Pike was said to have recognized a man as John Wilkes Booth. From 1896 to 1899 the man purported to be Booth lived in Oklahoma, calling himself George D. Ryan. Bates relates that while tracing St. Helen, he learned that a man living in Lexington, Kentucky, and calling himself J. J. Marr in 1868 did not deny being John Wilkes Booth when asked, and thereafter the man moved to Texas, where Bates had met St. Helen.

In 1900 Bates submitted a claim for the reward money originally offered for the capture of Lincoln's assassin. He inquired of the secretary of war whether the War Department would be interested in evidence that Booth had survived but was informed that the matter was of no importance to them. He then addressed the matter to the Department of State, who merely acknowledged receipt of his letter with thanks.

On January 13, 1903, in Enid, Oklahoma Territory, a seemingly unrelated event occurred. A man registered at the Grand Avenue Hotel as David E. George committed suicide by ingesting strychnine. Researcher Ken Hawkes, an autopsy assistant in the Department of Pathology at the University of Tennessee, has learned that a week before his suicide, George had gone to the theater where Booth's niece was acting in a play. He slipped a note under her door asking her if she "would like to meet Johnny," but was spurned with the assertion that her uncle was dead. George then left, became morose, and purchased the poison. Hawkes points out

that if George and Booth were not the same man, the visit to the niece was certainly a bold move on George's part.

George's body was taken to the W. B. Penniman funeral establishment, and the death was noted in the local newspapers. According to one account, Jessica Harper of Enid read about the suicide, sent her husband the Reverend E. C. Harper to view the body, and became convinced that the corpse was that of a man who had confessed to her in El Reno in April 1900 that David E. George was not his real name—that he was in fact John Wilkes Booth. After the Reverend Mr. Harper shared his suspicions with Penniman's assistant William H. Ryan, Ryan was quoted as saying, "Of course I took special pains with the body after that. I did the best job of embalming I've ever done. If it was Booth's body, I wanted to preserve it for the Washington officials when they came" (Bryan 1940, 338). Bates saw the newspaper accounts of the suicide and learned of Mrs. Harper's revelations. According to another account, St. Helen had left a note for those who found his body to contact Finis Bates in Memphis.

In any case Bates took the train to Enid, viewed the remains himself on January 24, and announced that David E. George and John St. Helen (whom he had last seen twenty-six years earlier) were the same person, which therefore led to the conclusion that David E. George was John Wilkes Booth. According to Bates, surgeons examined George's body and stated that the man was of the same age Booth would have been at that time and that his leg had been broken in the same place and in the same manner as that of Booth. Bates writes that two government agents compared the body with photographs of Booth and appealed to the Territorial legal authorities to compel the burial of the body, but Bates says that when he was recalled from Memphis to Enid, he "found the body unburied and in a state of perfect preservation, still being held for further identification..." (Bates 1907, 293).

David E. George's body had not been claimed after his death. Author Francis Wilson finds this peculiar, if Bates's suppositions are correct, since Edwin Booth would almost certainly have claimed the body if it were that of his uncle. Contemporary accounts state that it was Bates who had George's unclaimed body embalmed at the Penniman establishment and who urged the funeral director to embalm the body particularly well. "The body was embalmed most thoroughly with a formalin content fluid called Argon—one of the early formaldehyde fluids. The funeral director, W. B. Penniman, and the embalmer, William H. Ryan, upon learning the possible identity of the deceased took great pains to insure complete preservation" (Boffey 1978, 26). According to Ken Hawkes, arsenic was added to the embalming fluid at the time of the initial embalming or some time later and "petrified the body" (letter to the author, 1 June 1996).

About a month after his death, the body of David E. George/John St. Helen was photographed with open eyes, seated in a chair holding a newspaper. The photograph (captioned "Is This J. Wilkes Booth, Assassin of Abraham Lincoln?") appeared in a full-page advertisement that the Durfee Embalming Fluid Company of Grand Rapids, Michigan, ran in the April 1903 issue of a professional journal. The body remained wired to a chair in the window of Penniman's Mortuary for the next two years, awaiting a relative to claim it, in accordance with the waiting period prescribed by Oklahoma law at the time. The body was viewed by many people, including members of the Booth family (Boffey 1978, 26). According to George S. Bryan in *The Great American Myth* (1940, 339–40), the body remained on display to the public but in the rear room of the funeral home. In 1905 Finis Bates went to court and secured custody of the embalmed body as John St. Helen's beneficiary. He had the mummy shipped to midtown Memphis in a wooden box and invited numerous people to view it, but none of the Booth relatives accepted his invitation. Bates supposedly

offered a $1,000 reward to anyone who could prove it was not Booth. He continued to badger the government with reward claims and in 1907 published a book entitled *The Escape and Suicide of John Wilkes Booth*, which sold some 70,000 copies.

As proof of his claim of John Wilkes Booth's survival, Finis Bates circulated a tintype given to him by John St. Helen. He claimed that the photograph had been taken at Glenrose Mills, Texas, in 1877, twelve years after the assassination, and that the subject of the tintype had been identified by many, including Booth's nephew Junius Brutus Booth III, as John Wilkes Booth. Francis Wilson's examination of the photos shows that the tintype of John St. Helen is a fake made up from a later tintype of David E. George. As further evidence that St. Helen and George were not the same man, Wilson points out that their accounts of the escape after the assassination differed, George saying he had been hidden in a trunk and spent ten years in Europe. Other researchers counter Bates's claim that both St. Helen's and George's eyes were black like Booth's by pointing out that William H. Ryan, who assisted in embalming George's body, noted that George's eyes were a cross between blue and gray. Wilson also notes that at George's death no mention of the tattooed initials as made by Bates, the undertaker, or his assistant or any of the eager newspapermen at the time. James O. Hall has compared signatures of David E. George with the handwriting of John Wilkes Booth and finds no comparison. "Pick any name you like and use it. Of course, David E. George could have been David E. George, born at French Camp, Mississippi, on 14 June 1844. We may never know for sure. But John Wilkes Booth he was not," writes Hall (*The Body in the Barn* 1993).

Bates stored the mummy in his garage in Memphis: "And when Bates could, he rented him and leased him and let him out for hire. Small fairs and cheap sideshows proclaimed him—with acknowledgments to Bates. Every now and then Bates tried to sell

The body of David E. George, who claimed to be John Wilkes Booth, embalmed and seated in Penniman's Funeral Home in Enid, Oklahoma, ca. 1903. Reproduced from the collections of the Library of Congress.

him" (Bryan 1940, 340). In 1900 the *Dear-born (Mich.) Independent* offered for $1,000 a mummified body said to be that of John Wilkes Booth. The body was owned by a citizen of Tennessee and the offer included "affidavits and a wealth of circumstantial detail as an accompaniment" (Wilson 1929, 259). In 1920, Henry Ford became interested in the Booth mummy, delegated an employee to investigate its history, and was advised against purchasing it. At one time Bates had hoped to enter into a partnership with G. E. Smith, who had known David George, to exhibit the remains (Bryan 1940, 350).

On January 23, 1923, Finis Bates died. His wife sold the Booth mummy for $1,000 to a traveling carnival that toured the South, the Southwest (Texas and Oklahoma), and parts of the Midwest. The body was transferred from one carnival to another over the years, since each carnival that exhibited the mummy experienced difficulty (one had a fire, another went bankrupt). Wilson writes in 1929, "It [the mummy] has never been buried, and until recently it might have been seen at Memphis, Tennessee, housed in a garage. The writer was lately authoritatively informed that it has been sold to 'parties in the West'" (Wilson 1929, 278–79). By this time John St. Helen, the most famous of the "Booth mummies," was also the most conspicuous of the twenty or so people reputed to be the surviving assassin John Wilkes Booth (Bryan 1940, 332).

In 1931 the Chicago Press Club heard that the Booth mummy was being exhibited locally and commissioned a team of six doctors to examine it. Under the direction of Dr. Orlando Scott, the doctors (Louis K. Eastman, Charles K. Barnes, Bernard Conway, Charles E. M. Fischer, and Edward L. Miloslavich) conducted an external examination of the body, made total body x-rays of it in Dr. Scott's office, and signed a statement detailing their findings. The team found that the mummy had a scarred right eyebrow that arched upwards, a thickening on the knuckle joint of the right thumb, and a piece of skin missing from the back of the

neck (which they learned had been removed to determine the presence of scar tissue). X-rays of the head, hands, and legs showed a thickening of the tissues over the right eyebrow, a thickening in the bones of the right thumb, and a marked thickening of the left fibula at its lower end, indicating an earlier fracture. The doctors stated to the Chicago Press Club that the results were supportive, but could not be considered conclusive, in the identification of the body. Dr. Scott, however, admitted that he believed the body to be Booth's and encouraged exhumation of the body buried in Baltimore.

A photo was taken of Dr. Scott with the mummy at the time of the examination and later published in Curtis D. MacDougall's *Hoaxes* (1940). In the photograph the mummy is shown to have long, slender, straight legs (in contrast to Booth's that were known to be bowlegged). The text describes the mummy as "remarkably embalmed" (MacDougall 1940, 164) and notes that although it bears a resemblance to Booth, impartial authorities have never accepted it as genuine. The mummy was still on display at carnivals in 1940 when the book *Hoaxes* was published. After some correspondence with Dr. Scott, author George Bryan came to the conclusion that the team had looked for no identifying marks other than those mentioned in Finis Bates' book. "No mention is made of height, facial structure, and other standard forms of identification. Those of us who have seen pictures of the mummy would be hard-pressed to identify it as Mr. Booth," he writes (*The Body in the Barn*).

In 1932 the mummy was purchased by Joseph B. Harkin, a tattooed man who joined Jay Gould's show in 1936. Harkin asked twenty-five cents at the gate, and his wife exhibited the mummy along with an x-ray showing a ring with the letter "B" on it in his stomach. Mrs. Harkin maintained the mummy by combing its white hair and by applying vaseline to the dry skin. The mummy was dressed in khaki shorts, and Mrs. Harkin obligingly turned him over so that the customers could look inside through

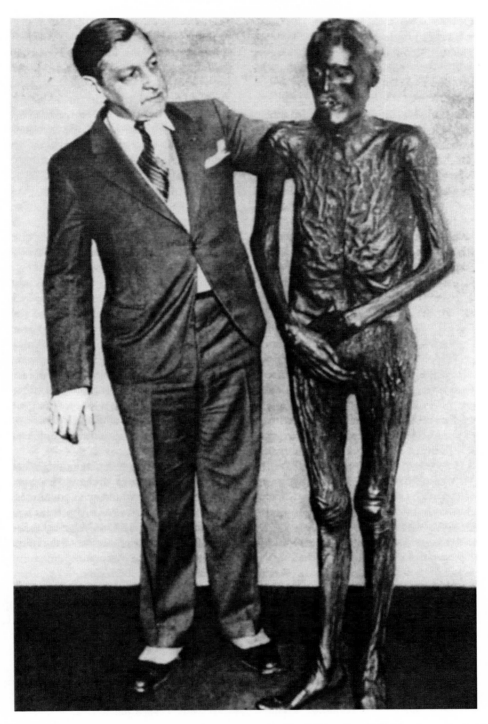

Dr. Orlando Scott with the mummy purported to be John Wilkes Booth during its examination in Chicago in 1931. Reprinted from *Hoaxes*, by Curtis D. MacDougall (N.Y.: Dover, 1958; orig. published by Macmillan, 1940).

a flap in his back. At night the Harkins wrapped the mummy in an Indian blanket and stored it in the truck where they slept.

In the late 1930s the Booth mummy was seen by James D. MacNair when he was a child. He writes: "While attending the annual Nassau County Fair held in Mineola, New York, back in 1937 or 1938 (as best I can remember), I spent 10 cents—which was a princely sum in the depth of the Depression—to visit a sideshow tent which claimed to have on display the mummy of John Wilkes Booth. I managed to prevail on my mother that attending this sideshow was very valuable—we entered the tent, examined the mummy which lay on a special table where the manager carried on a long spiel while turning, rolling over and otherwise allowing one to view the body" (*The Body in the Barn*).

In 1937 the mummy was purchased by Jay Gould's Million Dollar Spectacle for a reported $5,000 and was exhibited at carnivals throughout the country. The last authenticated sighting of the Booth mummy was in the 1940s as part of the Jay Gould show, according to researcher Nathaniel Orlowek. According to John Lattimer, the Booth mummy disappeared from the Chicago area sometime during World War II, apparently stored away due to wartime travel restrictions (*The Body in the Barn*). There have been sporadic unconfirmed sightings in the 1950s in Ohio and Los Angeles.

As the mummy toured with Gould's show, it was kept in the camper of the show's promoters, Mr. and Mrs. John Harkin. When the Harkins left the show, they took the mummy with them. They brought the mummy to Philadelphia in 1963 and kept it in the apartment they found. When they were unable to pay the rent, the landlady accepted the mummy as collateral and kept it in her own apartment. The Harkins moved or were evicted a short time after moving in, and the mummy remained with the landlady. The landlady had a lover who apparently visited on an annual basis. He saw the mummy and offered to buy it but did not have the money

with him. He offered to bring the money the following year, but when he returned the apartment complex had been demolished! (telephone conversation with Ken Hawkes, 1 June 1996).

The mummy was reported to have been viewed in Ohio in 1965, but it is believed that the body of Gold Tooth Jimmy was mistaken for the Booth mummy, which is now rumored to be stored on a farm in Indiana. Kenyon Gordon, a motel clerk in Clarion, Pennsylvania, claims to have paid about fifty cents to see the Booth mummy at a fair in New Hope, Pennsylvania, in 1975 or 1976. He described the mummy as being clad in khaki shorts with skin "like parchment" or "waxy." The mummy had a mustache and hair as white as snow that the promoter would occasionally brush. The body was displayed in a large wooden box with a glass top, and the box was angled upward on a table for easier viewing. Gordon explained that the exhibit included x-ray photos showing a signet ring with the letter "B" in the stomach and that the promoter was offering the mummy for sale at a low price to everyone who entered the tent. In Gordon's opinion the exhibit was undignified and tasteless.

It was in the 1970s that Finis Bates' cause was taken up by Nathaniel Orlowek of Silver Spring, Maryland, who convinced the television show *Unsolved Mysteries* to feature the story in 1991. Orlowek cites the findings of the 1931 examination of the mummy and claims that the physicians' affidavit was verified in 1976 by Dr. Charles K. Barnes, the only living signatory. Orlowek states that the mummy's possession of such identifying marks was further corroborated by Fred F. Bloodgood of Madison, Wisconsin, and Viola Gould of Glencoe, Minnesota, both of whom had seen the mummy many years ago. He is convinced that several generations of historians "have not done their homework."

In May 1995 a petition by researchers and Booth descendants to exhume John Wilkes Booth's remains from the Greenmount Cemetery in Baltimore was heard in

Maryland. Those involved in the petition include the chief medical examiner of Maryland, Douglas Ubelaker of the Smithsonian Institution, and Paul Sledzik of the National Museum of Health and Medicine. Sledzik states that he is neutral about the issue of whether the buried body is that of Booth but wants to be sure any scientific investigation is done accurately. He notes that the museum does have an interest in the case, having performed the initial (partial) autopsy on the body (personal conversation, 7 June 1996). The scientists would like to perform tests on the remains, which Sledzik says were already skeletonized at the time of the reburial in 1869. The tests would include photographic superimposition (which can be done with 99 percent accuracy), x-rays to examine the bones for the injuries Booth is known to have sustained, and comparison of any remaining hair to the color Booth was known to have. The request was denied.

An appeal was heard on May 8, 1996. Each side was allowed to make a twenty-minute oral presentation, after which the judge asked questions. Although he said a decision would be rendered in about two months, the judge turned down the appeal less than a month later on June 4, 1996. The Booth descendants have access to only one more appeal: the Maryland Supreme Court. It is also likely to be turned down unless additional evidence is found, for instance the mummy itself. This case may set a legal precedent, since the right to exhume a body usually resides with the family and not the cemetery. In this case all proven lineal descendants are in favor of Booth's exhumation, but the court has ruled in favor of the cemetery.

Nathaniel Orlowek is in favor of the exhumation and examination of what is purported to be John Wilkes Booth's body from Greenmount Cemetery. If the remains are determined to be Booth's, the question will be settled. If the remains buried in Baltimore are not those of Booth, the mummy (which may or may not be that of the man embalmed in 1903) may be Booth's remains. Orlowek

is one of many searching for the Booth mummy, which may be in the hands of a private collector who is not eager to reveal ownership, and claims to have received some recent leads. He has told journalists that the photographs of the St. George mummy seated holding a newspaper are being compared by forensic photo experts to photos of Booth.

According to James Taylor, editor of *Shocked and Amazed! On and Off the Midway*, no one in the carnival circuit believes that David E. George was really John Wilkes Booth. The mummy was simply exhibited to make a buck and later disappeared. Finding the mummy may answer some questions. Ken Hawkes offers assurance that modern techniques would verify whether any mummy located is in fact that of Booth. Hawkes has been searching for the Booth mummy since September 1990. He understands that there are at least two Booth mummies, since some photos show the left hand crossed over the right and others show the right hand crossed over the left, and suggests that any existing mummies may have been destroyed in the late 1970s when authorities began enforcing laws prohibiting the display of human remains in carnivals. Nevertheless, his opinion is that the St. George mummy is in the home of a collector. He has obtained information, some of it over the Internet, leading him to believe this collector lives on the East Coast. In Hawkes's mind the identities of the mummy and the body buried in Baltimore are secondary. Of primary importance is simply sorting them out. "The rumors are so persistent and the question so equivocal that there is too much evidence to ignore," he explains. "The answer needs to be proven one way or another" (telephone conversation with the author, 1 June 1996).

After the exhumation hearing and a subsequent Baltimore television appearance, Ken Hawkes received telephone calls from two different men claiming to have seen the Booth mummy recently and giving very similar details about its current whereabouts.

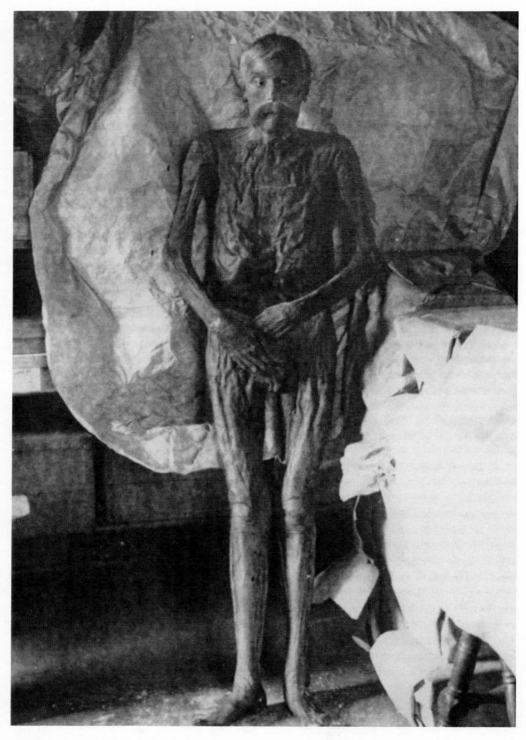

The John Wilkes Booth mummy. Photo courtesy of the E. H. Swain Papers, Special Collections Division, Georgetown University Library, Washington, D.C.

They both maintain that the mummy is in a room of its own in a private home. It is displayed in a glass-like coffin or box. Above the box is a sign indicating that it is the Booth mummy and containing a picture of the six Chicago doctors gathered around it in 1931. The second caller remembered that the walls of the room in which the mummy is kept are white. Both callers had been required not to reveal the location of the mummy as a condition for being allowed to see it.

Ken Hawkes, who is trained in pathology and forensic anthropology, would like to convince the owner of the Booth mummy that he has the credentials to examine it and that he could be trusted to do so. Although he would willingly purchase the mummy, Hawkes would be content to borrow it for a few days for an examination. He would be willing to guarantee the owner complete anonymity and would adhere to any reasonable requests, but would like permission to videotape the mummy and the tests performed on it.

If allowed to examine the Booth mummy, Hawkes would take a total body x-ray with emphasis on the ankle and thumb. From this he could determine if any irregularities were breaks or deformities and whether they occurred during life. He would also conduct an external examination of the hair (for color and texture), the size of the foot (to extrapolate size during life), and height. He would compare the mummy's DNA to a known Booth relative but explains that because all surviving relatives are of patrilineal descent, the results would only be supportive and not conclusive as in the case of matrilineal comparison. He would also do a photographic superimposition by putting an x-ray of the skull on a big screen television and projecting onto it an enlarged photograph of Booth at the same angle. Although photo superimposition is a test of elimination only, all the tests together would be conclusive.

The question of whether John Wilkes Booth lived on for years after assassinating Lincoln will not rest until the scientists have their say based on physical evidence. It is unlikely that the courts will allow them to open Booth's grave in Baltimore, which means that the evidence with the potential to end the controversy will remain underground. Meanwhile, the mummy or mummies billed as Booth remain in hiding. Without either the skeletonized or the mummified remains to examine, speculation will continue that John Wilkes Booth died at his own hand rather than Boston Corbett's and that his show-business career lasted well into the twentieth century, history books to the contrary.

VICTIMS

Although live acts ("No mummies! No Dummies!") were more of a draw, mummies were a mainstay in what were called museum shows or still shows, a mobile version of the dime museums popular in the late 1800s. The museum shows were often truck-mounted, giving their owners the freedom to pull into a town and open the doors separate from any touring carnival. The shows charged an admission fee up front or requested a donation upon exiting. One such show was the Marie O'Day Palace Car. For a small price, the body of a victim of spousal abuse that had supposedly mummified naturally could be visually examined. Those in the medical profession were offered an even closer inspection.

Another victim of violent crime, a mummy known as "Spaghetti," who ironically had been a carnival worker himself, did not have his own palace car but merely a corner in the funeral home that embalmed him. And a third victim, known only by the nickname "Sylvester," carved a well-known niche in the corner of a curiosity shop in Seattle. "Spaghetti," "Sylvester," and Marie have all shared a certain amount of fame but have not shared the same fate. Marie O'Day and "Sylvester" are still above ground. "Spaghetti" has been laid to rest.

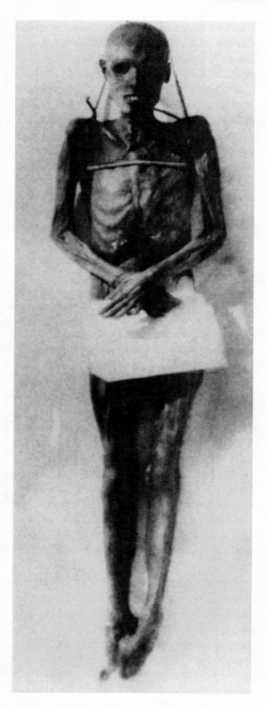

**Cancetto Farmica, also known as "Spaghetti,"
as he appeared at the McDougald Funeral
Home before a case to house his remains was
constructed. Photo courtesy of the Journal**
Shocked and Amazed! On and Off the Midway.

Cancetto Farmica ("Spaghetti")

In 1911 a man variously referred to as
Frinnizzee Concippio (McHargue 1972,
147), Forenzio Concippio (Lewis 1970, 231;
the *Laurinburg Exchange*), Frezzo Con-
sceppo (Associated Press), Formico
Cansetto (the *Washington Post*), or Cancetto
Farmica (letter to the author from Beacham
McDougald, the embalmer's grandson, 3
May 1995) came through the town of Mc-
Coll, South Carolina, with a carnival, as a
musician (possibly a trumpet-player). He
and another performer had an argument—
either over a woman or a letter both were
trying to read—and Farmica ran from the
tent. When Farmica fell down accidentally,
the other carny picked up a tent stake and
struck him on the head. The injured man was
brought to the hospital over the state line in
Laurinburg, North Carolina. He was operated on unsuccessfully and died some ten or
twelve hours later on April 28. The assailant
was acquitted as having acted in self-defense, according to some, or released because it was more economical than conducting a trial, according to the local
newspaper. No state death record is on file
because the death occurred prior to the filing
of death certificates in North Carolina.

Farmica's body was taken to nearby
McDougald Funeral Home in Laurinburg. In
a quote ascribed to the embalmer's son, Hewitt McDougald (d. 1995), by an author who
never interviewed him, Farmica was "a
young fellow 'round twenty-five years old,
dark-complected, black hair and a nice set of
teeth. Built slight, possibly five feet six and
couldn't have weighed more than one hundred thirty-five pounds, if I recall" (Lewis
1970, 230). Although Farmica's date of birth
is not known, the funeral home record notes
Farmica's age as twenty-three. The body of
the young man was laid out on the embalming table and immediately embalmed to
await claim by relatives. The carnival left
town without him.

A couple of weeks later, an old Italian
man arrived with a companion who translated

for him. He believed the dead boy was his son who had run off to join a carnival. When shown the body, he broke down and cried and identified it as that of his son. When John McDougald asked him what he wanted to do, the father said he wanted the boy to be laid out and given a Christian burial. He chose a coffin, made a partial payment of fifteen or twenty dollars, and promised to send the balance with instructions very soon. McDougald embalmed the body by injecting a formaldehyde-based fluid into the carotid arteries, but hesitated to proceed because not only hadn't he been paid in full, he was not certain of the family's religious affiliation.

John McDougald waited several weeks for the father to return or contact him by mail. The funeral home learned the young man's name, but there was no trace of his family. Because the local residents could not pronounce the Italian name, they affectionately dubbed the corpse "Spaghetti." McDougald tied a rope around the body and hung it from the wall of the embalming room, where it gradually dried out. Farmica's embalmed body, covered with a loincloth, was later placed in a plain pine coffin with a glass front and sealed airtight. In 1939, McDougald reportedly declined an offer of $500 from the Italian government to bury the mummified body. Instead, it was moved with the mortuary to new quarters. McDougald stood the coffin up against the back wall of the funeral home's garage, where an overhead bulb provided light for viewing. Visitors were allowed inside upon request. One of these was a young Harvey Boswell, who had hitchhiked to the funeral home and would later exhibit mummies of his own.

While doing research for the book *Carnival* (incidentally maligned by many of those in the carnival business and noted by Beacham McDougald to contain numerous inaccuracies), Arthur H. Lewis decided to investigate Farmica's story, although his investigation apparently fell short of actually visiting the mummy (letter from Beacham McDougald to the author, 18 April 1997). Lewis had heard several rumors about why

Farmica was never buried: that he was half-man, half-ape and to bury him in sacred ground would have been sacrilegious or that he was so large that burial required two plots and the family had only purchased one (Lewis 1970, 226). Instead, he found that the body was not disfigured and had been expertly embalmed:

> Grandpa McDougal's [*sic*] skill had created a figure far more lifelike than any of the statues I'd seen in Madame Tussaud's Wax Museum. The murdered carny was clad only in a loincloth and his olive skin, from head to beautifully manicured hands and feet, had a healthy glow.
> His hair was still jet-black and completely covered his scalp. His cheeks had a pinkish tint and his eyebrows were bushy. Slightly flared nostrils and a flowing mustache made you know he must have been quite a dashing fellow in his day. Except for the protrusion of a set of white, even teeth which spoiled the symmetry of his face, I had the feeling I was viewing a delicate piece of sculpture (Lewis 1970, 231).

The body was short, lean, and muscular, and Beacham McDougald corrects Lewis' description: "His skin was the color of tanned leather, his nose was not flared, there was no hair on his head (it was shaved for surgery), and there was no mustache" (letter to the author, 28 April 1997). In a corner of the coffin was the tent stake he had been killed with.

Ann Groff (stage name "Flame LaMarsh"), a carnival dancer who grew up in Laurinburg, supposedly reminisced to Lewis, "When I was a kid we used to be scared to death of him. It's been quite a while since I been back home and by now they might have given him a Christian burial. I haven't seen him for nearly thirty years, but I've never been able to eat spaghetti without thinking about that poor devil" (Lewis 1970, 226).

The *Laurinburg Exchange* reporter Florence Gilkeson told Lewis about her experience in 1954: "One of the earliest feature articles I ever did was on 'Spaghetti,' and I nearly muffed it…. I maneuvered an assignment to do a piece on the poor old corpse. I took my camera with me, but when I looked at the body, I was almost sick to my stomach, and when I 'shot' the coffin with my flash, all I got was glare" (Lewis 1970, 232). But the newspaper liked and printed her story. According to Gilkeson, Farmica was a legend even back in the 1950s: "People come from all over the country to see him and I'll bet there's not a month passes without a few hundred of the curious traipsing into Mc-Dougal's [*sic*] garage" (Lewis 1970, 232). She claims Spaghetti was stolen for a brief time but was returned to the funeral home without having been removed from his coffin. She denied that the funeral home ever charged an admission fee to Spaghetti's visitors, telling Lewis, "Anybody who wants to can take a look as long as they behave themselves. People from Laurinburg don't bother anymore; they're sort of used to Spaghetti by now. He's just about our city's oldest citizen..." (Lewis 1970, 233).

In mid–September 1972, in response to negative publicity and suggestions by his peers, Hewitt McDougald removed the mummified body from the garage of the funeral home and suspended public viewing. He is quoted in a UPI story (Sept. 3, 1972) as saying, "I have closed him up. He's in the same box he was in. He is laying horizontal." Charles Phillips, executive director of the State Board of Funeral Directors and Embalmers, and Bill Hoke, the board's attorney, investigated the case but declined to file suit against the McDougalds. The board considered them in compliance with the law, despite a rather obscure and untested statute declaring it unprofessional to indecently expose or exhibit a dead human body in the custody or control of an embalmer. The North Carolina association of funeral directors, however, declared that continued exhibit of the mummy would embarrass the embalming profession at both the state and national levels (UPI, Sept. 3, 1972).

Farmica received his long-delayed burial on Saturday, September 30, 1972. Prior to the burial, the casket was opened and the remains viewed by the chief of police and other reliable Laurinburg residents. After this measure to insure against "doubt that the casket did in fact contain the body, that [Hewitt] McDougald had too strong a sentiment for the corpse to bury it" (the *Exchange*, October 2, 1972), the casket was sealed permanently. Farmica was laid to rest in Laurinburg's Hillside Cemetery. The tent stake used to take his life was buried with him. His pallbearers included Beacham McDougald, Sam McInnis, Mac McInnis, and Leon Butler of the McDougald Funeral Home; Harold Odom of the Pate Funeral Home; and Ward Sutton of the McHask Funeral Home (the *Exchange*, October 2, 1972). A casket wreath of red and white flowers was provided by Hewitt McDougald and was supplemented by three additional flower arrangements. A graveside service was conducted over the closed casket at 10 A.M. by the Reverend Frederick Gilbert of the nearby Hamlet Roman Catholic Church, who said mass and sprinkled holy water on the grave. (It was assumed that because he was of Italian parentage, Farmica was raised a Catholic.) The service was attended by an estimated 200 people, most of them dressed in their Sunday best. One of these was S. A. Bridger, who had attended the carnival in McColl as an eleven-year-old child. He had nearly witnessed the killing of Farmica but had been pushed out of the way by adults when the fight between the two carnival employees had begun (the *Exchange*, October 2, 1972).

Farmica's solid bronze casket was lowered into the porcelain vault that had been installed in the grave. At 10:30 cement was poured on top of the vault to prevent any vandalism that could have been provoked by the publicity. "We don't want anyone to dig him up," Hewitt McDougald is quoted as saying (the *Exchange*, September 29, 1972). the *Exchange* (October 2, 1972) reported, "As the wet cement was being smoothed, coins were sprinkled into the grave by a dozen or so onlookers, who remained at the site almost an hour after the service had ended." A flush stone and bronze grave

The stone marking the grave of Cancetto Farmica in Hillside Cemetery in Laurinburg, North Carolina.

marker was provided by Hewitt McDougald and records the dates of Farmica's death and burial in addition to his supposed age.

Some suggest that Farmica's burial was the result of pressure exerted by an Italian congressman. In fact, Representative Mario Biaggi (D-New York) did express outrage that the body of a fellow Italian had remained unburied for years when he learned about "Spaghetti" in mid–1972 (the *Exchange*, October 2, 1972). Biaggi brought his concerns about "ethnic prejudice" to the North Carolina congressional delegation without any action being taken. He then appealed to fellow congressman and funeral director Charles C. Diggs, Jr. (D-Mich.), who brought the issue before the state association, North Carolina Funeral Directors, Inc. Indirectly, Biaggi's actions resulted in the involvement of the state attorney general, Robert Morgan, whose deputy and assistant met with Hewitt McDougald. As a direct incentive, Biaggi mailed a $25 check to the McDougald Funeral Home. Although this approximated the unpaid balance for the services for which Farmica's father contracted more than sixty years earlier, it did

not begin to cover contemporary expenses and would not even have paid for the digging of the grave. The storage fee alone, billed at twenty-five cents a day, amounted to more than $5,000 (the *Exchange*, September 29, 1972). The McDougalds returned the check to Biaggi.

Others insist that pressure to bury the mummy came as a direct result of the publicity generated by *Carnival* author Arthur Lewis. Hewitt McDougald insisted at the time of the burial that it had not resulted from political or other pressures but merely arose out of a local offer to pay the expenses. He stated that he had long ago agreed to inter the body if suitable arrangements were made, but none of the many inquiries he had received had been accompanied by offers of payment. He reminded the media that there was no law compelling him to bury the mummy (the *Exchange*, September 29, 1972). The burial expenses were paid for by residents of Scotland County, North Carolina, who had asked to remain unnamed.

In an interesting postscript to the story, the *Washington Post* reported that a Virginia man named Lawrence K. Mooney, who hoped to open a museum, had been swindled by Freak Enterprises of Wisconsin into paying for the mummy that was by then already in the ground. Mooney made a downpayment of $1,000 on the asking price of $6,500. He filed suit against the mail order firm that had never owned or had custody of Farmica's body. "The whole thing is rather embarrassing," Mooney is quoted as saying. "All I want is my money back…. It was the first and only time I tried to buy a mummy. They just don't come on the market very often. There just aren't that many of them left."

"Sylvester"

One mummy still on display is that of a murder victim discovered in the Arizona desert shortly before the turn of the century. In 1895 two cowboys riding through the Gila Bend Desert discovered an unclothed, half-buried body in the sand. The body was removed to nearby Yuma and spent some time propped up in a secondhand store but was never identified. The man had apparently been killed, at about age 45, by a gunshot wound to the stomach. The drying action of the sand and the effects of great heat and low humidity had reduced his 225-pound body to 137 pounds within what scientists estimate to have been about twenty-four hours of his death. The mummified body retained its hair, mustache, eyelashes, nails, and teeth — everything but its identity.

The mummy was dubbed "Sylvester" and shown at Seattle's Alaska Yukon Exposition in 1909, San Francisco's Panama-Pacific Exposition in 1915, and numerous sideshows across the country. In Texas during the Great Depression, the mummy was sold to a physician from San Jose, California, for $25. The doctor was stopped by police outside Amarillo as he drove Sylvester home but was allowed to proceed when he produced a bill of sale. Once he was home, the man stowed the mummy in a compartment inside his living room sofa and took great pleasure at asking his guests to look under the cushions on which they had been

sitting. After the doctor's death — and presumably traditional interment — Sylvester was back in show business. The doctor's heirs hired him out to carnivals, which billed him in a variety of imaginative ways: as an illegal alien murdered by those who had guided him into the U.S., as an Arizona cowboy who passed out in the sun after some heavy drinking, and as the remains of John Wilkes Booth. Although he is still on display, Sylvester is no longer on the road. The mummy was acquired by Ye Olde Curiosity Shop in Seattle in 1955 and may still be seen under glass at that establishment.

Marie O'Day

Marie O'Day, a nightclub entertainer, was killed by her common-law husband, who stabbed her in the back and cut her throat (for which he was sentenced to ninety-nine years in the Utah State Penitentiary). He threw her in Utah's Great Salt Lake, where her body remained for twelve years. It had washed ashore but remained covered with salt, silt, and sand. When discovered in 1937, her body was said to be "mummified, but not petrified" due to the more than 20 percent salt chemical content present in the water of the lake. A stitched incision in her neck appears to be a stab wound, and the stab wound in her back is also still visible. The mummy was exhibited by Charlie Campbell, Professor L. O. "Hoot" Black, and at least two other showmen. Over the years, O'Day toured thirty-eight states and Canada in the "Marie O'Day Palace Car." In 1955 the chief of police in Springhill, Louisiana, vouched for the authenticity of the mummy in a letter to a fellow officer of the law: "The doctors and nurses here all agreed that the exhibit Marie O'Day was an actual body and was once alive." Admission in the early 1970s was fifty cents. "The remarkable thing is the hair is still growing," claims the advertisement.

O'Day's body was said to be leatherlike: "…you will see that the body is still pliable, you will note the beautiful red hair

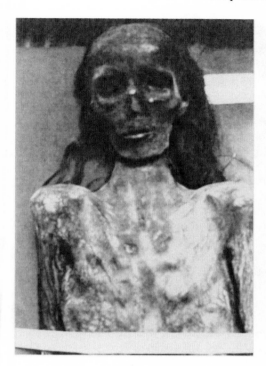

Marie O'Day, above and opposite, as she appears today, in the collection of her custodian, Captain Harvey Lee Boswell. Reprinted with permission of Captain Boswell.

upon her head, which is still growing. The well-preserved teeth, you will see her finger nails, toe nails—even the corn upon her toe." The exhibitors offered an inspection to doctors, nurses, or undertakers who desired to convince themselves of the authenticity of the body. In 1975 Black sold the mummy to Captain Harvey Lee Boswell. Boswell took ownership of O'Day but had to abandon her Palace Car in the adjacent state. He also removed her from the traditional casket in which she had been exhibited, having found that it offended the public, particularly the recently bereaved. O'Day became part of his Palace of Wonders, billed as "The World's Largest and Strangest Tented Museum." She took a celebrated place among the sideshow's shrunken heads, five-legged and two-headed animals, live snakes, and other exotic and domestic wonders. In the late 1980s Captain Boswell was contacted by a vice president of Ripley's Believe It or Not®

The Palace Car in which Marie O'Day was exhibited.

who felt that Marie met their museums' "acquisition criteria" and would greatly enhance their collection. But after more than twenty years with the Palace of Wonders and a veritable lifetime in show business, Marie O'Day—like Captain Boswell himself—is on the verge of retirement.

LOCALS

What do an insurance salesman, a factory worker, a farmhand, a deaf man, and a hobo have in common? They were all mummified. Not because they were murderers or even murder victims, but because their embalmers were trying to do right by them or by the embalming profession. In the cases of the insurance agent, the deaf man, and the hobo, the families could not be located. In the cases of the factory worker and the farmhand, there was no family to locate, so their bodies were used to perfect preservative techniques. In four cases, the mummies were well cared for at the funeral home. They were well dressed and their conditions monitored and maintained. Offers by showmen to buy the mummies were refused, although local residents were given private audience upon request. Each of the four had, and in one case still has, a secure posthumous home. Only the hobo continued his wanderings after death.

Charles Henry Atkins ("Speedy")

"Speedy" Atkins of Paducah, Kentucky, got his nickname by being a fast worker at Dixon Tobacco Factory. He was also said to be a womanizer. He died a pauper on May 30, 1928. Accounts claim that he drowned while fishing in the Ohio River, but Dick Stacey of Paducah's Maplelawn Park Cemetery corrects this error: "Actually, it was the Tennessee. The two rivers join at the foot of our main street to become the Ohio on to the point where it empties into the Mississippi, but he actually slipped off the bank on the Paducah side, before the rivers join" (letter to the author, 13 April 1995). He was in his fifties when he died.

Speedy had no family or close friends except A. Z. Hammock, the funeral home owner. Hammock embalmed Speedy with fluid of a secret recipe, which Hammock took with him to his grave in 1949. According to Speedy's death verification, Hammock had made arrangements for the body to be buried in Oak Grove Cemetery, but this was never done. Hammock sought permission from the local coroner at that time to use Speedy in his embalming experiment. It was typical of funeral homes in the 1920s to keep bodies for several weeks while the often poor families raised money for the funeral, and this is apparently why Hammock wanted to perfect his technique. Hammock was also fascinated by ancient Egyptian mummification. *Mortuary Management* (November 1994) reported that "The mixture turned Atkins' body a rusty color, his yellowed teeth visible through drawn-back lips in his gaunt face."

Speedy became a tourist attraction: "Through the years, visitors to the funeral home gawked at the mummified body, which

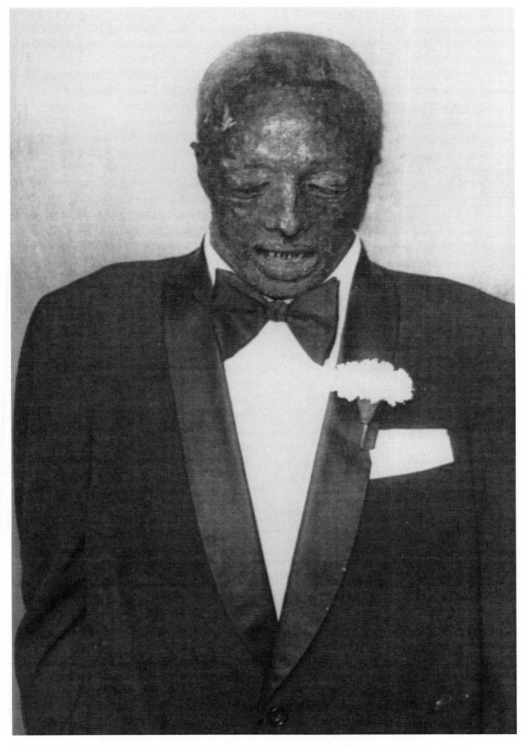

Charles Henry "Speedy" Atkins prior to his burial. Photo courtesy of the *Paducah Sun*.

was stored propped against a closet wall and carefully washed and dressed three times a year to keep mold off" (*Mortuary Management*, November 1994). Hammock's widow, Velma (who spells the family name Hamock), now jointly runs the funeral home that she inherited from her husband. In an interview with *Jet* magazine (August 29, 1994), she said, "It was all an experiment, but it was a success. Speedy's never been duplicated, he's the only one that we know of. He's not stinking, nothing. The amazing thing is he really hasn't lost all of his features. He doesn't look like a corpse laying up in the casket for 66 years. I never saw a dead man bring so much happiness to people." Mrs. Hamock intended to bury Speedy quietly in 1991, but plans never materialized.

"Atkins became the pride of the community around the funeral home. Some of those at his funeral wondered why scientists hadn't expressed more interest in Hammock's embalming technique," writes *Mortuary Management* (November 1994). Velma Hamock and funeral home co-owner Clifton C. Bowles, Jr., felt it was time to bury Speedy and that a proper burial was their responsibility. Velma says, "We didn't want it to change on us. Sixty-six years is a long time to be with somebody. And we just thought it was time to let him be laid to rest" (*Jet*, August 29, 1994).

Speedy's funeral, steel casket, flowers, and burial plot were all donated by local businesses. The funeral at the Washington Street Missionary Baptist Church in Paducah was well attended: "About two hundred people, some of whom posed for pictures beside his open coffin, bade him a rousing farewell with spirituals and sermons" (*Mortuary Management*, November 1994). Speedy was dressed in a black tuxedo and bow tie. A bouquet of red carnations was laid atop the coffin. The eulogy was delivered by the Reverend H. Joseph Franklin of Washington, D.C., who praised Speedy as "a man born with nothing, but who had love, admiration, and respect from people all over the world when he left" (*Jet*, August 29, 1994).

Speedy was interred in Maplelawn Park Cemetery. The church plans to place a historical marker in the town in Speedy's honor.

Anderson McCrew (a.k.a. Andrew McCrew, Sam, "The Amazing Petrified Man")

Anderson McCrew was a one-legged African-American hobo. He hopped a freight train heading north in 1913. As the train passed through Marlin, Texas, McCrew fell out of the boxcar he was riding in. His other leg was severed and he bled to death. The morning after his death, his body was found and taken to a funeral home in Marlin. Knowing that he would never be paid for his services, the funeral director decided to try an experimental embalming fluid on the body of the indigent man. The fluid was successful, but its chemical content was not recorded.

A carnival owner heard about the mummy and purchased it from the funeral home for expenses. Before featuring it as an attraction in his carnival, the showman dressed McCrew in a tuxedo. He was billed as "The Amazing Petrified Man" and was reportedly called by Ripley's Believe It or Not® "The Eighth Wonder of the World." Admission to see the mummy was a dime. When the carnival began losing money and disbanded in the early 1930s, McCrew was sold at a warehouse sale, along with other holdings, to a wealthy man who collected show business paraphernalia. The mummy—with peg leg attached—was wearing a brown tuxedo and was laid out in a pineboard coffin. Fascinated by the mummy's appearance, the collector uncovered what was known about McCrew's life and death.

In 1964 McCrew's body was found in a Houston warehouse. Mrs. Elgie Pace, a relative of both the collector and the rediscoverer, agreed to store the mummy. She wanted to give him a decent Christian burial because, as she said to her sister, "He's a human being. You just can't throw a body in a ditch" (Wallechinsky, Wallace, and

Wallace 1977, 451–52). However, she was unable to afford the cost of burial, so she nicknamed him "Sam" and kept him in a casket in her basement in Dallas for several years.

Mrs. Pace mentioned her predicament to Dallas morticians Frank and Judy Lott. In May 1973 the Lotts buried McCrew at no charge. Because Mr. Lott could not find a period tuxedo, he had dressed McCrew in a plain black suit. Mrs. Pace reported that the service was beautiful and very dignified. Unfortunately, she was dismissed from her position as a vocational nurse for the County Board of Health after her employers and the county health authorities discovered that she had kept the mummy of a black man in her house.

According to another story, the fifty-one-year-old Mrs. Pace had been fired from the Dallas County Mental Evaluation Center in April 1973 for bringing to light the inhumane treatment of patients there. Her dismissal was protested by ten members of the staff who were then also fired. At the height of the scandal, it was learned that Mrs. Pace had the mummy in her basement. Although a friend had suggested that she protect herself against any possible criminal charges by getting rid of the mummy, she reacted with horror and declared that "Sam" was almost a member of the family. The revelation of the storage of the body resulted in police investigation and harassment but also in the burial offer by the Lotts. Mrs. Pace tried to win reinstatement, and her evidence was corroborated by the FBI, but she was unsuccessful.

Folk singer Don McLean read about McCrew in the *New York Times* in May 1974. "I knew there was a song there somewhere, but I wanted to wait until I found just the right approach. I wanted to write it with pathos, humor and morality," he said (Calloway 1974, 18). He had been reading Jack Kerouac's *Final Third* at the time and conceived the idea to do an album called *Homeless Brother* about hobos as metaphors for Americans cast adrift after the Vietnam War.

He wrote a song called "The Legend of Andrew McCrew," changing the mummy's name to make it rhyme. The song was recorded at Regent Sound Studios in New York and was included in McLean's fifth album for United Artists that was released in late 1974:

Introduction:
There was a mummy at the fair
All crumpled in a folding chair
The people passed but didn't care
That the mummy was a man
So tell me if you can,

Chorus:

Who are you, who are you
Where have you been, where are you going to?
Well Andrew McCrew must have lost his way
Cause though he died long ago, he was buried today.

Down on nightmare alley
Where the shady people sway
A hobo came a hikin'
On a salty summer day.
He hopped a freight in Dallas
And he rode it out of sight
But on a turn he slipped
And lost his grip
And he fell into the night.

(Chorus)

Well Andrew had one leg of wood
The other leg was small
But when he fell off of the train that night
He found he had no legs at all
They found him in a thicket
And the undertaker came
And they mummified his body
For a relative to claim.

(Chorus)

Well no one came to claim him
'Til the carnival passed through
The carnies took him to their tent
And they decided what to do.
They dressed him in a worn out tux
And put him on a stand
And millions saw the legend
Called the famous mummy man.

(Chorus)

Well what a way to live a life
And what a way to die
Left to live a living death
With no one left to cry,
A petrified amazement
A wonder beyond worth
A man who found more life in death
Than life gave him at birth.

(Chorus)
But what about the ones who live
And wish that they could go
Whose lives are lost to living
And performing for the show?
Well at least you got the best of life
Until it got the best of you
So from all of us
To what's left of you
Farewell Andrew McCrew.

(Words and music by Don McLean, lyrics reprinted with permission of Don McLean Music, BMI)

McLean later learned that Lee Hayes (now deceased), bass singer for the quartet "The Weavers," had seen McCrew in a tent show as a child in Arkansas in the 1930s. McLean's song was played on the air by Roy Leonard of WGN in Chicago in November 1974. After several listeners called to express their interest in McCrew, Leonard contacted Mrs. Pace and McLean. They were interviewed by Bob Williams of Chicago's Jensen Corporation. Williams then called Leonard with an offer to purchase a headstone for McCrew.

McCrew was reburied in Dallas' prestigious Lincoln Memorial Cemetery on Sunday afternoon, December 8, 1974. A eulogy was offered by the Reverend Harold King, and the choirs of Bishop College and Southern Methodist University participated in the ceremony. The headstone, donated by a Chicago gravestone manufacturer, reads: "Andrew McCrew, 'The Mummified Man,' Born 1867/Died 1913/Buried 1973." The inscription also contains the fourth verse of McLean's song and mentions Elgie Pace, Don McLean, and WGN Chicago. *People* magazine wanted to do a feature about the song and the mummy and asked McLean to pose for a photograph standing over McCrew's open grave, but the story idea was dropped when McLean refused to do so.

George Stein ("The Stone Man")

George Stein was a German immigrant who settled in the Midwest. He worked as a salesman for the Prudential Insurance Company, then in a planing mill, and finally as a porter in a downtown saloon. Stein died at the local hospital on October 25, 1902. He was 65 and had suffered a heart attack twenty-three days earlier. The cause of death on his death certificate reads, "Senility. Immediate cause heart failure and exhaustion."

Stein left instructions that he should not be buried until his relatives in Pennsylvania and Germany sent for his body or came to claim him for burial. To withstand the wait, his body was injected daily for three weeks with an arsenic-based preservative fluid. The funeral home never received communication from the family. The *Chicago Tribune* (November 17, 1975) reports, "By the third week ... Stein's body resembled a life-like piece of sculptured stone." He remained in a satin-lined metal casket in a garret storage room of the funeral home and was at various times and for extended periods (including from 1949 to 1954) exposed to the air.

Stein was never buried because his family never claimed him, and the township trustees did not pay funeral directors to bury the indigent at that time. The funeral home received an offer from a carnival to purchase the mummy for $10,000, but the owner refused to sell. Over the years articles about Stein's mummy have appeared in publications like the *Star* and the *National Enquirer*.

Despite the fact that his presence is not publicized and he has no regular visitation hours, Stein's body has been seen by thousands of visitors from around the world. A funeral home attendant told the *Chicago Tribune*, "People as far as India have made special efforts to view him.... And countless Germans have visited his casket, verifying his claim of aristocratic ancestry, but denying all knowledge of the relatives' whereabouts." In the 1970s two busloads of tourists arrived at the funeral home unannounced from a black church in a nearby state. Rather than turn them away or shuttle them up to the attic to see Mr. Stein a few at a time, the funeral director had the casketed body brought down in the freight elevator for the unscheduled viewing.

George Stein (d. 1902) reposing in his casket in a Midwest funeral home in 1996.

Stein was well known to local residents as the "Stone Man," and rumors about him included the fiction that his hair and fingernails continued to grow. In earlier times a rubber mallet was provided for those interested to tap on the mummified body. The current owner of the funeral home learned from an eighty-year-old man (now deceased) that the chip out of Stein's nose was caused by a friend of the man who had tapped the mummy too forcefully during their visit as children. Stein was especially popular among tavern patrons at closing time and among fraternities and sororities on April Fool's Day. The tavern patrons would make wagers about going to see him; the students would give each other a message to return a call from "Mr. Stein" at the telephone number of the funeral home.

Stein still reposes in the Midwest funeral home where his body was prepared, although he has moved with them to new establishments on two occasions (once in 1929 and again in 1996). Prior to the most recent move, the younger members of the staff urged the director to bury Stein. Although a local cemetery has offered free space, the director decided against burial after many sleepless nights. He plans to continue as Mr. Stein's caretaker.

Stein's skin has darkened over the years and he has shrunk a few inches but is well-preserved. He wears a white shirt, a black suit, and a red tie. He is still contained in the same metal casket, the upper half of which is sealed with a panel of glass through which the body can be viewed. The seam between the glass and the casket is taped to keep out dust and his original death certificate is contained in a frame nearby. An earlier director of the funeral home explained to the *Chicago Tribune* that Stein is an ideal tenant: "In all this time, we've changed his casket lining once, given him three tuxedos, and dusted him off occasionally. Otherwise, he's not much bother." Stein was redressed most recently in 1984. He is not shown to the public except by specific request.

William Lee ("Deaf Bill," "The Alton Mummy")

Bill Lee was a fisherman on the Mississippi River who drank hard during his life and spent time in jail. He lived among the factory workers in a neighborhood of tar-paper shacks near Alton, Illinois, that became known as "Dog Town." Lee had some hearing loss and was known locally as "Deaf Bill." He was occasionally teased but was able to defend himself. John J. Dunphy, a freelance writer who has researched Lee's story, recalls his late great grand-uncle telling him how young "toughs" taunted Lee by whispering abusive and foul language behind his back with the assumption that the mockery would go unnoticed. Lee waited a few moments, then wheeled around and decked one of the boys with a powerful punch, saying, "Bub, there ain't nobody in this world who's that deaf" (the *(Ill.) State Journal Register*, June 23, 1996).

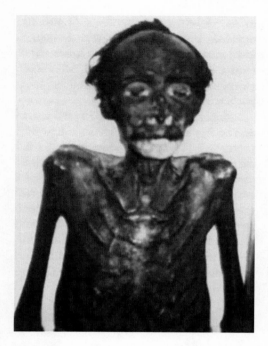

William Lee, also known as "Deaf Bill," prior to his burial in 1996. Photo courtesy of John J. Dunphy.

Legends and anecdotes punctuate memories of Bill Lee. "The story behind the dried-up little gentleman in question comprises one of the most bizarre twists in the history and folklore of southern Illinois," writes Dunphy (*Springhouse Magazine*, October 1986). Lee was known to like preaching fiery sermons, and did so on both the Illinois and Missouri sides of the river, but usually when he was intoxicated and often without invitation. According to Dunphy, he would barge into the meetinghouse of his choice on a Sunday morning, remove the minister from his pulpit, and preach a "guest sermon." Parishioners who objected received a torrent of curses, and those who tried to sneak out were said to have received "multiple bruises and lacerations, courtesy of the Reverend William Lee" (*Springhouse Magazine*, October 1986).

Lee died on November 13, 1915, at age 52 on the Madison County Poor Farm, where he had been taken earlier in the year when his health began to fail. Rather than being interred in the potter's field like most of the other residents of the poor farm, Lee was embalmed by the undertaking establishment of Bauer and Hoehn in the hope that one of the relatives he was rumored to have would claim his body. The preserved corpse was held for six weeks, but no family members claimed him. Just before the body was to be consigned to a pauper's plot, a traveling curiosity show offered the funeral home $2,500 for it. The funeral directors rejected the offer, saying that it would be illegal to sell Lee's body, but wondered why it had been made. "The shrewd entertainers candidly replied that they could make a fortune exhibiting the body, perhaps passing it off as a 'mummy' plundered from a tomb in the Old World," writes Dunphy in the *St. Louis Post-Dispatch* (June 3, 1996). Following this discussion, the funeral directors opted to keep Lee above ground—not as an exhibit with an admission fee but to bring an unusual measure of fame to their establishment.

As a "permanent guest" of the funeral home, Lee became a local attraction over the years and was seen by thousands of visitors. He was clothed with a sheet around his groin. Dunphy writes that Lee was "clad only in a large diaper as a mild concession to propriety and good taste ... although it is difficult to imagine how the sight of a mummy in a closet could be any more startling!" (*Springhouse Magazine*, October 1986). His darkened skin was stretched tightly over his bones. He once stood 5' 9" tall, but his mummified frame measured only 5' 3". Although a wiry 160 pounds during his life, after mummification his weight had dropped to a mere sixty pounds. His scalp was still covered with black hair, and he had a prominent mustache. Township supervisor Donald Huber first saw "Deaf Bill" thirty years ago when Huber was a grade-school student. Lee was also seen by sixty-eight-year-old retired engineer Dick Harris in the late 1930s. In the *State Journal Register* Harris described the visit: "Well, I was a little shocked. I don't know if I'd even ever seen a dead person at that age. It was a pretty courageous thing for a young boy to do, and we talked about it for a long time." Another man caused some minor damage to the mummy as a young boy when he brought several girls to see it. He shoved Lee toward one of them to give her a scare, but rather than catching the body she jumped out of the way. Part of Lee's ear broke off when he fell to the floor. The story has been documented by Dunphy, who writes in a letter to the author (9 April 1997), "How's that for a youthful jest gone awry? Unfortunately, I was unable to learn the fate of that missing piece of ear."

An eccentric during his life, Lee took on several other personae after his death. Dunphy documents the tall tales that circulated over the years but claims that they would have infuriated Lee as taking liberties with his name and reputation (*Springhouse Magazine*, October 1986). Lee's mummified body was said to be the remains of a Wild West gunslinger. Another story maintains that the mummy was the body of an English nobleman who was murdered under mysterious circumstances during a visit to the Midwest. A third version of the mummy's origin places him on Smallpox Island in the Mississippi River, where Confederate prisoners of war, of which he was said to be one, were interned.

The funeral home that had housed Lee's remains for decades was purchased by Thomas "Bud" Burke in 1948. Burke died in 1972, but the establishment was retained by his wife Dallas Burke, the Madison County coroner. Mrs. Burke was too busy to allow curiosity seekers to view Lee's body, which was still housed in a closet on the first floor and tried to donate the mummy to the Alton Museum of History and Art. "Too bad Deaf Bill can't afford a fulltime social secretary to handle his appointments," wrote Dunphy (*Springhouse Magazine*, October 1986), who noted in the same article that Lee probably would have been pleased to remain permanently in the public eye. In August 1996 the Burke Funeral Home merged with the Fine and Quinn Funeral Home, another mortuary a block away owned by Brian Fine.

Lee had been kept in a specially built closet at the funeral home for more than eighty years, "providing perverse amusement to thousands for generations." The Associated Press wire story questions why the spectacle was allowed to continue for so long, but Huber explains, "It's not something that anybody here sees as a social injustice. He just got left there and nobody knew what to do with him." Residents of Alton note that it would have been easy for such a thing to happen to an impoverished man, since there is no law in Illinois requiring funeral directors to bury a body. In fact Dunphy blames Lee's mummification and exhibit on economic discrimination: "Would someone with adequate financial means have been embalmed, then consigned to a closet where he could be gaped at?" he asks (*St. Louis Post-Dispatch*, June 3, 1996).

Huber states that Lee's dignity over the years was maintained and that the atmosphere was not one of a freak show. Nevertheless, after taking over the management of both funeral homes, Fine decided to have Lee interred. "I just felt it was time he was laid to rest," he told the *State Journal Register*. Interviewed by Dunphy for the *St. Louis Post-Dispatch* (June 3, 1996), Fine explains, "He was a human being with a mother and father. I don't feel it is right to keep him standing in the closet." Dunphy agreed and referred to Deaf Bill as a "cultural dinosaur."

On June 24, 1996, Lee was dressed in a donated turn-of-the-century tuxedo and laid in a gold casket for his final viewing at the funeral home. Cosmetics were used to restore Lee's face and hands to a normal flesh tone. Later that day, a graveside service was held at St. Francis Cemetery in Portage Des Sioux, Missouri, a community across the river from Alton where Lee's parents may have lived. Lee was buried in the cemetery that contains the 1884 grave of a four-and-a-half-year-old boy who may have been his brother. His gravestone was donated by Alton Memorial Sales. Dunphy, who first saw Lee when he was fourteen, concludes,

"Our community is acquiring a social conscience. We no longer believe that human beings should be subjected to such exploitation. I think it represents tremendous personal growth for the city of Alton" (the *State Journal Register*).

George Bailey ("Bill")

According to newspaper accounts published at the time of his much-delayed burial, George "Bill" Bailey worked as a farmhand until his death at age 45. He died in 1899 in Waterloo, New York, of apoplexy as stated on his death certificate. With no survivors to claim his body, it was used to teach apprentice morticians the methods of preservation. Charles A. Genung, owner of the local funeral home, developed a method of arterial injection, and Bailey reportedly became one of the first bodies to be embalmed in this way. The successfully preserved body was exhibited in a wooden casket in a shed behind the funeral home, along with a stuffed monkey and an embalmed calf, according to a UPI news report (July 27, 1971). John Genung, the embalmer's grandson, finally decided it was time to lay Bailey to rest. "We now feel George is entitled to a decent funeral," he explained (UPI, July 27, 1971). After a change of clothes, Bailey was buried in the Genung family plot on Friday, July 30, 1971.

4. Learning About Life and Death

Teaching Aids, Test Subjects, and Teratology Specimens

There is a widely scattered group of bodies that have been preserved not because of who they were but because of how they can help the rest of us. There is no vanity in being a cadaver. Identity is often reduced to age and gender. Idolatry of cadavers and specimens is nonexistent. And greed toward them is rare. Part of this group is constantly being renewed, as dissections and experiments are completed and the remains are buried, cremated, or returned to the families. Other members of the group are permanent installations in schools, museums, or laboratories. The common denominator is the use of the donated or unclaimed body for a scientifically valid purpose. Whether this purpose is ongoing or limited to a single anatomy class, the bodies must be properly prepared and maintained. Embalming is often by immersion or with fluids used at a more concentrated strength than used in funerary embalming. Preservation of a single body may involve a combination of methods, including refrigeration. The methods themselves are constantly being improved, sometimes as a result of experiments employing cadavers. And occasionally, the preservation of bodies that end up in museums is the result of unique experimental methods.

When the bodies of infants and adults — preserved by whatever method — are put on public display, conservation takes on a particularly important role. But even more important are the ethical issues surrounding the exhibit of human remains. The families, even when they are aware of the display, are not often a factor. It is the influence of those who find a particular exhibit or display in general objectionable that makes the curator's job more difficult. His or her task is to provide a respectful forum where people can learn something from the remains while at the same time addressing their understandable curiosity. When this task is insurmountable, the bodies usually remain in the collection but are housed in storage areas rather than in the public eye.

TEACHING AIDS

Anatomical cadavers are rarely the objects of public concern. It is understood that doctors and other professionals must dissect the human body as part of their training. Those who donate their bodies for this purpose are considered even more generous than organ donors. Rather than dwell on its fate at the medical school or mortuary science college, the family may consider the donor's body "borrowed" for a time. Dissection is an admittedly grisly task, but it is just as necessary today as it was two hundred years ago. Fortunately, modern embalming techniques make the cadaver less offensive to work with. Plastination, in which the moisture of the body is replaced with a polymer, makes the tissues and organs odor free. Digitization, in which the body is scanned slice by slice into the computer, renders the corpse even further removed, though more visually accessible. But the "visible man" won't usurp the place of the tactile corpse. Most doctors agree that the cadaver on the screen will augment, but won't replace, the cadaver on the table.

Anatomical Cadavers

A corpse makes the transition to cadaver only if certain conditions are met. A person may designate whole-body donation prior to death, or his or her body may be donated by the next of kin. Anatomical cadavers are usually donated to willed body programs carried out under the Uniform Anatomical Gift Act, adopted in all fifty U.S. states since 1964. Bodies may instead be donated to a specific school. Each of the United States—with the exception of Alaska, Montana, and Wyoming—has at least one medical school that accepts donated bodies. If next of kin cannot locate a nearby medical school, there is a National Anatomical Service with headquarters in New York and St. Louis that will make arrangements with a local funeral director to refrigerate the body until transportation to a school can be provided (Carlson 1987, 49). Another source of cadavers is the bodies of the unclaimed dead.

The use of a cadaver is determined by its condition. To be considered for student dissection, a corpse must not be "irregular" in any way. Bodies that are missing limbs or organs, severely burned, decomposed, emaciated, mutilated, diseased, contagious, too young, too old, or have had surgery at or near the time of death may be used instead for research or other purposes. Bodies may be rejected altogether for their size: large bodies may be impossible to store in existing facilities, and obese bodies are difficult to preserve, handle, and dissect. After bodies are accepted, they are usually tested for contagious diseases, particularly when the medical history is unknown. The results of the

tests are recorded, as are the names of the people who have worked with each specimen. In all cases, identification tags of copper, brass, or stainless steel are attached to the ankle and wrist to permit next of kin or other authorized persons to claim or repossess the body at any point in the process of preparation, storage, or dissection.

After the bodies are accepted and tested, the business of preserving them begins. The preparation of cadavers for dissection has varied from school to school and has changed over time. Variables have included the chemicals employed, the amounts of the chemicals injected, and the storage techniques used to minimize dehydration between the preparation and the use of the body. In general, the bodies must be thoroughly embalmed with strong chemicals to effect long-term preservation. The embalming itself may take three days (Carlson 1987, 48).

Today, cadaver preparation is usually done by one-point arterial injection with preservative chemicals. First, the body is washed with antiseptic soap and positioned. The nasal and buccal cavities may be plugged with cotton to avoid leakage during or after embalming. An incision is made to expose the femoral or carotid artery, the artery is raised, and a cannula is inserted and connected to tubing from which the air is removed. The chemicals are injected through the use of a gravity-tank apparatus fixed three to four feet above the body or an embalming pump. Typically, the blood is not drained, and there is no aspiration or injection of the trunk cavities. The body is embalmed over the next eight to twenty-four hours, depending on the ability of the body to accept the fluid.

The skin of the body is observed during the embalming process to assess the effectiveness of the chemicals. Blistering on areas of the body surface indicate that the fluid is being injected at too high a pressure. Small white splotches will appear on the skin in the areas that have been effectively embalmed and will usually disappear within several hours. Regions of the body that do not exhibit such splotching (typically the lower extremities, back, and gluteal area) may be injected directly using a hypodermic needle. The fingers, toes, face, and other areas may also be injected with extra fluid.

The preservative fluid contains a variety of chemicals, including liquified phenol (for primary preservation and the prevention of mold); methyl, ethyl, or isopropyl alcohol (for additional preservation and to promote penetration); and ethylene, methylene, or propylene glycol (to retain flexibility and resist dehydration). Glycols are now used more frequently than glycerin, which causes mold, and formalin (usually 10 percent buffered formalin) or glutaraldehyde is sometimes used as a substitute for or augmentation of phenol. Amphyl, sometimes used to color the blood vessels, also functions as a disinfectant.

After embalming, the body may be stored in liquid or under refrigeration. The cadaver may be totally immersed with other bodies in a tank containing the same preservative chemicals as the injection fluid. In some institutions the bodies are left unwrapped; in others the bodies are coated with petroleum jelly and wrapped in layers of cotton and plastic before being submerged. An upright position may be maintained in the tank by attaching a device resembling a pair of ice tongs into the aural meatus and, in effect, hanging the bodies by their ears from racks that can be operated manually. Although more bodies could be accommodated this way, it was found that vertical storage led to excess fluid in the lower extremities. As an alternative to immersion, bodies may be wrapped and stored on trays or racks in large coolers until needed.

In the preparation of anatomical cadavers, the emphasis is on embalming rather than restoration. The features are not adjusted and the eyes and mouths are not closed, so the results are not recognizable individuals. Care is taken, however, to prevent the bodies from deteriorating over the next few months or the next couple of years. Embalmers at the University of California, Irvine, medical school "put a great deal of effort into improving the quality of the embalming so that specimens can withstand varying degrees of handling, drying, and the extended periods of time the cadavers are exposed during dissection in medical anatomy courses. The cadavers are kept at room temperature for study and dissection for one to five years." A wetting agent consisting of glycol, phenol, and alcohol is applied to the cadavers during their use to keep the tissues soft and flexible (UCI College of Medicine Web page).

At the Georgetown University Medical Center, cadavers are prepared by a licensed funeral director who serves as the embalmer/morgue technician in the Department of Anatomy and Cell Biology. Each of the body donors designated Georgetown University, so any surplus of bodies is not shared among local medical schools. The only condition for acceptance is that the donated bodies be at least eighteen years old. The bodies are processed in a well-lit room. They are positioned on gurneys and—except for their outstretched arms—are covered with heavy canvas sheets. Each of the bodies is given a number, and this number is penned on the skin in several places when the body is received. The body is washed and disinfected. After it has dried, most of the head and body hair is shaved with clippers, and the skin is swabbed with a mold preventative solution. The embalming begins with the arterial injection under pressure of a pre-embalming solution. Then six or seven gallons of Tufts Human Anatomical Solution are injected over the next several hours. The solution is purchased premixed in large barrels and consists of 55.2 percent isopropyl alcohol, 16.3 percent propylene glycol, 14.3 percent phenol, and 4.1 percent formaldehyde by volume.

The blood drains from a vein as the fluid is injected, and the progress of the embalming is measured by consistency and color. As the solution penetrates, the tissues harden and the skin blanches. The suitably embalmed cadaver is rubbery and firm. Success of the embalming depends on the cause of death, the medications the deceased was taking, the size of the body, and many other factors. In more difficult cases, blisters may form under the skin. The blisters, fluid-filled and up to several inches long, are drained. Smaller formalin blisters up to about an inch in diameter may form for several reasons, including injecting under too much pressure. If a body needs additional treatment, a trocar or hypodermic needle is used to inject anatomical solution directly into the tissue, but making additional punctures in the body is avoided if possible. When embalming is complete, the hands, feet, and face of the cadaver are coated with vaseline and wrapped in plastic bags. The entire body is then sealed in a large bag.

The Georgetown cadavers are stored in a large, walk-in cooler until they are needed. The cooler is kept at a temperature of about 50° F (10° C) and holds 120 bodies horizontally on trays. Approximately fifty bodies a year are needed for student dissections. The cooler becomes increasingly stocked as the bodies of donors are prepared and the new school year approaches. The bodies are kept in the cooler for at least four months to "cure" before being used. In August the bodies for use in the anatomy class are requested by the professor, and the required quantity are chosen by the morgue technician. Those that have been insufficiently or less successfully embalmed remain in the cooler, including at least one body that has been passed over several times and dates from 1993.

The covered bodies are placed on gurneys and wheeled two at time up a rough elevator and down several hallways to the dissecting rooms. There they are transferred to the many metal tables. Prior to the dissection, the students are provided with the gender, age, and cause of death of their cadaver. The rooms are crowded with several articulated skeletal models on vertical stands and plenty of bag-lined boxes for the disposal of tissue. Tissue from the dissections is picked up by a mortuary service periodically and incinerated unless the family has requested return of the remains. In these cases a box is placed beneath the cadaver on the gurney and all tissue removed from the body during dissection is retained rather than disposed of in the communal disposal boxes. Organs and tissues are also sometimes retained by professors studying a particular part of the anatomy, such as the eyes or temporal bones. In a recent instance one of the professors was studying bowlegged knees.

Adjacent to the student dissecting rooms is the room in which prosections are done. A prosection is simply a dissection performed by a professional, in this case a university professor. Most prosections are done on bodies unfit for student use. They may have been inadequately embalmed and show signs of decomposition, they may have been autopsied, or they may have a physical deformity. When they are not in use, bodies in the process of being dissected or prosected are covered first with a sheet soaked in anatomical solution, then with plastic, and finally with a heavy canvas sheet to hold the coverings in place. The skin of the bodies is darkened, but they are still flexible and all the nails remain intact. The organs retain a dark red or brownish color.

In November, after the students have finished with the cadavers, they are returned to the morgue. Each of the dissected bodies is separated into smaller components and placed in its own plastic-lined cardboard box measuring about two and a half feet square. The boxes, marked with the numbers given to each cadaver, are picked up by a mortuary service. The remains are cremated and the ashes interred in Georgetown's plot at Mount Olivet Cemetery.

"Aunt Mary"

Unlike the typical cadaver, some bodies have a longer tenure at the school to which they have been donated. The body of an elderly female was embalmed at least

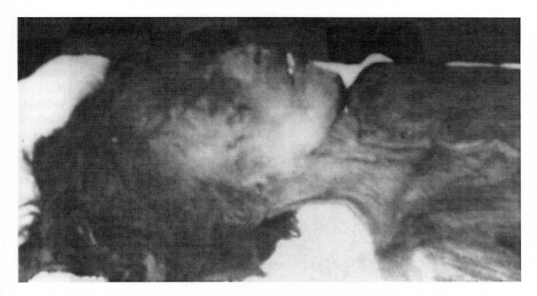

Female cadaver exposed to the air for years after being prepared for use at an American school of mortuary science.

seven days after death at an American college of mortuary science in about 1924. The embalming procedure consisted of injection through a single point at the carotid artery. The blood was not drained and there was no cavity treatment. The body was stored uncovered in the embalming room and intended for dissection but was never used. Students affectionately dubbed the cadaver "Aunt Mary."

The body continued to dry out until it resembled an unwrapped Egyptian mummy in both color and the preservation of the features. The tissues were desiccated and closely resembled wood in texture. No additional treatment was provided over the years. The body was placed in a glass-sided cabinet in 1946. Although specially constructed, the cabinet was not airtight, and the temperature inside it was not controlled. The mortuary college moved in the 1970s, and a local funeral director became the custodian of the body, which was later cremated circa 1974.

Plastination

Plastination is defined by the International Society for Plastination as "the use of polymers to infiltrate and preserve any material for teaching, research or diagnostic purposes." The patented process was developed in East Germany by Gunther von Hagens and has been available in the U.S. since 1981.

Dr. von Hagens, a polymer chemist and pathologist, devised a process whereby biological specimens can be dehydrated and subsequently infused with a polymer, which is then allowed to cure, creating a firm but flexible, dry, nontoxic specimen that is nearly indestructible. "Because of the problems linked to formaldehyde fixed specimens, such as toxicity and suspected carcinogenicity, plastination has proven to be most valuable," vouch R. Fiori and M. Cannas in the *Journal of the International Society for Plastination* (1995, 17).

Plastination is inappropriate for preserving intact adult bodies but is ideal for the preservation of embryos and fetuses. This has been done successfully on individual systems of the body such as musculature, the digestive tract, or the circulatory system preserving the skeleton as an armature, by von Hagens, whose controversial exhibit of "anatomical artwork" has been

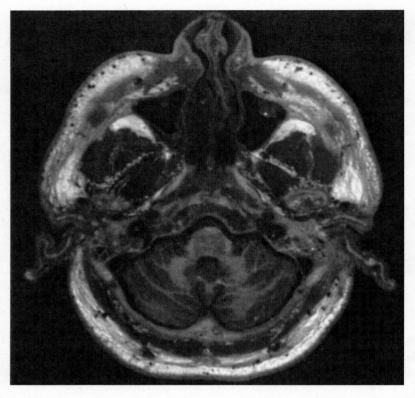

Plastinated cross-section of a human head. Photo courtesy of the National Museum of Health and Medicine, Armed Forces Institute of Pathology.

viewed by more than 200,000 in Mannheim. The specimen may first be fixed by any method, but formalin in concentrations between 5 and 20 percent over one to three days is common. Embalming fluids containing glycerol or other long-chain alcohols must be removed before dehydration (or may be effectively removed during dehydration, if ethanol is used) or they will spoil the final specimens. The specimen is then dehydrated and defatted by either stepwise dehydration in graded ethanol (which may cause considerable shrinkage but will defat the specimen at the same time) or freeze substitution with acetone. If freeze substitution is used, specimens are precooled to 41° F (5° C) and immersed into acetone cooled to -13° F (-25° C). They freeze immediately, so their shape is stabilized. The acetone is changed two to three times during the next three to five weeks until the specimens

have become completely dehydrated. They are then defatted in a bath of acetone or methylene chloride at room temperature (von Hagens, Tiedemann, and Kriz 1987).

The intermediary solvent that has replaced the water and lipids within the specimen is then replaced by curable polymers through forced impregnation. This is done by placing the specimen into the polymer solution, allowing it to stand overnight, and then applying vacuum pressure, causing the solvent to be extracted out of the specimen in the form of gaseous bubbles. The vacuum pressure is monitored and adjusted if necessary. The class of polymer used determines whether the finished specimens will be flexible or firm and opaque or transparent. With silicone rubber, impregnation is done in a deep freezer at -13° F (-25° C). With epoxy and polyester resin, impregnation is carried out at room temperature. After impregnation the specimens are removed from the polymer bath, drained and wiped off, and then cured (or hardened). Gas curing is used for silicone specimens, which are placed in a closed chamber with a stock solution. A gaseous hardener evaporates from the solution, saturates the atmosphere, and may be continuously circulated by means of a small pump. The specimens cure from the outside in. From start to finish, standard silicone plastination takes up to twelve weeks. Specimens impregnated with epoxy resin or polymerizing emulsion may be fully cured at 122° F (50° C). The curing of polyester-copolymers is initiated by UVA-light, followed by heat treatment at 122° F (50° C) (von Hagens, Tiedemann, and Kriz 1987). Once curing is complete, specimens can be stored indefinitely at room temperature.

Plastination of a whole cadaver would require that the skin be pierced numerous times, since skin is not as easy to penetrate as the porous internal organs. In addition, the organs would need individual treatment to remain lifelike. A more effective use of plastination to preserve an entire body is to plastinate horizontal slices and reassemble them. As of 1995 East Coast College had been plastinating for about a year and a half and was in the process of creating an entire cross-sectioned, plastinated cadaver for use in teaching cross-section and gross anatomy (letter from Ann T. Harmer, 5 July 1995).

The University of the Orange Free State in South Africa revised its formula for embalming cadavers in cases where bodies are to be sliced and plastinated. The modified formula of ethanol, formalin, glycerin, water, and phenol is injected into the radial artery under pressure. After five weeks, an injection of 25 percent ammonia solution is immediately followed by a 750 ml injection of latex colored with Rubine Toner. After the latex has congealed, the body is placed in a freezer for approximately three days, with the addition of dry ice over the last twelve hours or so. It is then ready to be prepared (*Journal* 1995, 35–36).

Two plastination techniques are used to prepare body slices. The polymerizing emulsion (PEM) technique results in an opaque and firm—but not unbreakable—specimen and is especially suitable for slices between 15 and 30 mm thick. Forced impregnation of PEM-polymers can be done at room temperature. The finished specimen is transparent to varying degrees. Sheet plastination preserves large (up to 50 × 25 cm) and thin (down to 2 mm) slices of whole bodies. After fixation, dehydration, and forced impregnation with epoxide or polyester resins, the slices are cured between polyester foils, tempered glass plates, or glass plates covered with polyester foils (von Hagens, Tiedemann, and Kriz 1987).

There are two methods of sheet plastination. In the "draining method" the fixed tissue is cut with a rotary meat slicer into 2.5 mm thick slices. The nuclei or connective tissue may be stained. The slices are dehydrated in graded ethanol and transferred to acetone as an intermediary solvent. They are then impregnated with epoxy resin. The impregnated tissue slices are placed between polyester foils, covered with glass plates, and clamped together. Curing is done at room temperature or at 122° F (50° C). A "sandwich" of as many as 40 slices between foil and glass is placed in a slightly oblique position to allow surplus resin to drain off. The entire procedure takes from three to five days (von Hagens, Tiedemann, and Kriz 1987).

The second method of sheet plastination, the "filling method," takes as long as two weeks to prepare a few slices (unless the amount and size of the equipment is increased). Fixed or unfixed specimens are frozen before being prepared. The size of the slices is limited only by the cutting height of the band saw, but the optimum thickness is 2.5 mm. The slices are stacked between plastic nettings and grids and are not allowed to thaw or to dry. They are dehydrated by freeze substitution with acetone, defatted in methylene chloride, and immersed in a reaction mixture before being impregnated under vacuum pressure. Each slice is placed in a flat chamber composed of two glass plates separated by a flexible gasket and held together by clamps. The chamber is filled with resin, air bubbles are removed by vacuum, and the slice is cured by the application of UVA-light and/or heat (von Hagens, Tiedemann, and Kriz 1987).

Plastination results in specimens that are easily handled (they are nontoxic, noninfectious, do not exude fumes or fluids, and do not require the use of gloves), easily stored and transported (they do not require immersion or refrigeration and will not deteriorate), and are very lifelike (they can be made to retain the color, flexibility, porosity, and texture of the natural specimen). Sheet plastination retains the contrast between the loose areolar and adipose tissue, the muscle tissues, the organ tissues, and the blood. The relationships between connective tissue fibers and bony structures are maintained without the bones being decalcified. Filling the blood vessels with a contrasting polymer allows their branching to be followed down to the arteriolar level and allows them to be studied in an uncollapsed state (von Hagens, Tiedemann, and Kriz 1987, 413). Transparent body slices are of clinical relevance in comparing them to MRI and CT-scan images. The fiber patterns of various muscular systems and the textural changes caused by pathological conditions can also be studied in detail. "One of the main advantages of transparent body slices is that the arrangement of all tissue components can be studied in their undisturbed context" (von Hagens, Tiedemann, and Kriz 1987, 415). The use of plastinated specimens will not replace dissection in the gross anatomy laboratory, but the specimens are considered very helpful during dissections.

Plastination offers a welcome alternative to wet specimens and the offer has been taken up by many institutions. The technique is being applied in more than 150 departments of anatomy, pathology, forensic science, and biology throughout the world (von Hagens, Tiedemann, and Kriz 1987, 411). Al-though the technique is patented by Dr. von Hagens and the labs themselves are franchised, producing plastinated specimens for educational purposes is not restricted, as long as they are not sold commercially. Not only does Dr. von Hagens share his technique, he stands by it. He, like a percentage of the people who have seen the models in his exhibit, has made arrangements to be plastinated in slices after death because he finds it the most aesthetic way to remain intact for use in teaching.

The Visible Man and the Visible Woman

Joseph Paul Jernigan, a thirty-nine-year-old high school dropout, was executed by lethal injection and pronounced dead at 12:31 A.M. on August 5, 1993, at the state prison in Huntsville, Texas. The lethal dose of chemicals was administered through an intravenous catheter attached to his left hand. Jernigan was sentenced to die after being convicted of killing Edward Hale, age 75, who had interrupted Jernigan's burglary of his home in Dawson, Texas, in July 1981. Jernigan stabbed Hale several times and shot him three times with a shotgun.

Jernigan donated his body to science without knowing the use to which it would be put and "...now in the virtual world he has been resurrected—with his prior consent—to star in the National Library of Medicine's gruesomely fascinating effort to create a comprehensive digital atlas of the human body" (Waldrop 1995, 1358). Jernigan, a muscular man with a thick neck and a dragon tattoo on his chest, became the Visible Man.

The project, funded by a $1.4 million federal grant, is directed by Michael Ackerman and was inspired in 1987–88 during a series of lectures he gave on the uses of computers in medical education. He formed a plan to digitize "midlife normal" male and female cadavers aged twenty to sixty, of average weight, without surgical scars or

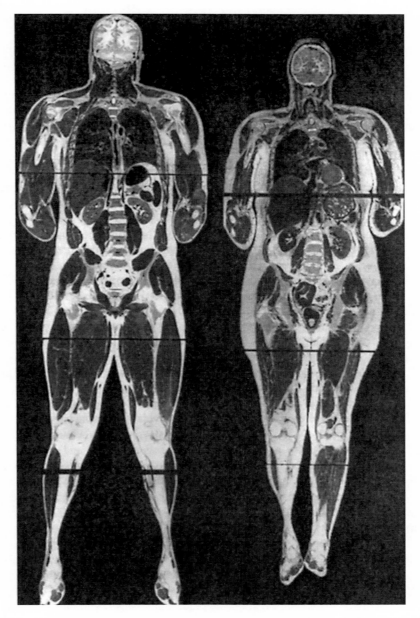

Cross-section of the Visible Man and the Visible Woman, one of the many images available on the Internet. Photo courtesy of the National Library of Medicine.

traumatic injuries. Each would be imaged top to bottom via high-resolution MRI and CT. Then they would be frozen solid in blocks of gel, sliced with high-precision machine tools and photographed with digital cameras. The images would be stored in computers and distributed over the Internet.

The planning stages took several years and involved selecting a contractor for the project. The National Library of Medicine held a national competition and asked finalists to provide cross-sectional pictures of a medium-sized animal. The pictures underwent a peer review by scientists who regularly use medical images. The University of Colorado Health Sciences Center was chosen with Victor Spitzer (head of the Center for Human Simulation) as principal investigator for the project. It then took two and a half years to find satisfactory cadavers. The average age at death of body donors in Colorado is seventy-six and in an older body, the organs and structures have shrunk and are more difficult to see. The availability of younger bodies, in which there is good muscle tone and healthy anatomy, is usually due to accidents that cause damage.

Of the bodies flown to Colorado by several state anatomy boards, three males met the standards of the project. One of these was Jernigan's body, which weighed 199 pounds and measured 5' 11" tall. All three bodies underwent several methods of head-to-toe medical imaging: x-ray, magnetic resonance imaging (MRI), and computerized tomography (CT-scan). The various scans verified that the bodies did not have any internal damage or anomalies. In addition, they would provide images that could be compared with the digitized images of the body. Jernigan's body was chosen by a committee that met in Colorado.

Thirty-three hours after his execution, Jernigan's body was prepared. First, the body was separated horizontally into four sections, each less than twenty inches tall, with a handsaw so that it would fit on the cutting equipment. The sections were placed in aluminum molds that were filled with blue gelatin and frozen to -94° F (-70° C). Starting with the feet, each section was packed around the sides with dry ice and placed beneath three specially designed high-resolution cameras. One millimeter at a time was planed off using a cryomacrotome, the surface was cleaned with compressed air and sprayed with alcohol, and the image was photographed. Each of the 1,871 cross-sections took between six and ten minutes to prepare and photograph. "The rhythm was very important…. We wanted the top to be the same temperature every time we took a picture," said Spitzer (Wheeler 1996). The

work took four months, after which Jernigan's remains were cremated.

The finished product was released in December 1994. Less than a year later, the National Library of Medicine had licensed the data to almost 300 sites in twenty-three countries. As of February 1996, some 400 licenses had been issued. Sample images are available on the Internet, with the complete data available after a license and password have been obtained. The data are also available on tapes for $1,000 to $2,000. "Now the tiniest details of Mr. Jernigan's body are regularly displayed on computer monitors around the world, portrayed in commercial CD-ROMs, and manipulated by artists, medical students, and radiologists" (Wheeler 1996). The Visible Man can be manipulated without the maintenance that a physical body would require: "Unlike a real cadaver, the digital kind can be expanded, shrunk, dissected, and reassembled over and over. Students will even be able to navigate the body's interior as if it were a building. And a digital cadaver will last forever" (Bylinsky 1993, 123).

Several programs have been developed to assist viewers to manipulate the images three-dimensionally and isolate bones, organs, arteries, and muscles. The data are being used by the U.S. Army to simulate damage caused by shrapnel and by engineers to simulate the effects of automobile accidents. The images are also used by oncologists and others searching for noninvasive ways to detect cancer. Future applications include virtual surgery, and future enhancements include animation, "…full-bore, supercomputer-level simulation in which the bones articulate, the muscles contract, the blood flows, and the organs shift" (Waldrop 1995, 1358). Spitzer hopes to one day be able to alter the body's age and size, to show people what will happen to their bodies if they don't take care of them (Wheeler 1996, A14). The most noticeable thing that the Visible Man lacks is labels for the organs, bones, and other structures. "It's difficult to learn any anatomy from him," agrees Spitzer, although it's very useful if you already know anatomy (Wheeler 1996). This shortcoming is being remedied by researchers at several companies and universities.

The computerized images of Jernigan's body are beautiful to some and grotesque to others, but they will not decay. "In its current form—as 15 gigabytes of data—Mr. Jernigan's body may be as close to immortal as one can get" (Wheeler 1996).

This "Adam" was soon joined by an "Eve." A fifty-nine-year-old female muscle-builder who died of a heart attack has become the first Visible Woman. Her body was supplied by Maryland's Anatomy Board, directed by Ronald Wade. She had donated her body to biomedical research, but her identity has been protected. Her body was prepared at the University of Colorado using the same process as the Visible Man, but slicing the body three times thinner. More than 5,000 cross-sections were made over the course of a year.

The Visible Woman's digitized remains were released in late 1995. The Visible Humans have sparked the interest of veterinarians and researchers in creating digital anatomical maps of animals, including a dog, a dolphin, and a mouse. "Mr. Ackerman says the library will concentrate on 'the human animal.' He wants to wait before adding another human cadaver, because he believes researchers are already saturated with data. Eventually, he might like to add a pre-menopausal female" (Wheeler 1996). Others would like to see a range of ages, from embryos to the aged. The next century may see a whole library of Visible Humans.

TEST SUBJECTS

In an age when testing on animals raises eyebrows, scientific testing on human cadavers keeps a low profile. The testing of embalming fluids requires a human subject. The modern replication of ancient Egyptian embalming techniques would not have been definitive without one. In both tests the object was to preserve the body, but one did so with the latest chemicals, the other with the most ancient of salts. Both experiments required cooperation between two organizations, in the first instance two businesses and in the second two schools. Both tests took time, the latter weeks and the former years. And both experiments confirmed the validity of using human remains to prove or improve something.

Embalming Research

Because there are no test animals for the embalming of human remains, bodies embalmed in the course of normal practice are observed, and improvements are reported in various categories, including ease of blood removal, penetration of the fluid, bleaching, even distribution of the dye, and resulting firmness of the tissues. The results are opinions rather than scientific evaluations. Experience is the greatest teacher.

The Dodge Company tests experimental embalming chemicals in their Cambridge, Massachusetts, laboratories. The preliminary work is carried out on different types of meat, depending on the purpose of the chemical being tested. These tests are run until they are completely satisfied that the products do what they are supposed to do chemically (preserve tissue, firm tissue, penetrate quickly). Mike Dodge explains, "Thus, by the time any of our experimental chemicals are tested on human bodies, we are absolutely certain that no harm can come to the body from using these new chemicals" (letter to author, 13 August 1996).

After testing on meat, tests are performed on human bodies to determine skin texture produced, rates of diffusion in different bodies, and (what Mike Dodge considers to be most important) whether the embalmers perceive a new product to be an improvement or not. The bodies for these tests are obtained in several ways, the most common being the use of bodies donated to medical or mortuary schools. (After embalming, Dodge explains, they can be used by medical

The body of a man eight years after being embalmed in 1929 with Hizone fluid at the Palms Memorial in St. Petersburg, Florida. Photo courtesy of the Edward C. Johnson Family Collection.

students in their studies.) The bodies of indigents are also sometimes used. And families will sometimes give permission for this type of embalming. When this is the case, the embalming and any other necessary preparation is done at no charge.

The length of a test may vary from as little as a year for some types of products to as long as seven or eight years if they are having difficulty fine-tuning a product to achieve a particular intended result. Mike Dodge writes, "The shorter periods would be for a product that is intended, for example, to prevent leakage from wounds. In such an instance, it is pretty simple to determine whether the product works better than whatever else might be currently available for the same purpose" (letter to the author, 13 August 1996). After the tests are completed, most donated bodies are cremated. Other bodies are cremated or buried, depending upon instructions given by the individual or by his or her next of kin. Mr. Dodge states that the Dodge Company has used essentially the same testing procedures for at least the past forty years.

Another mortuary chemical company, Hizone Products of Wilmette, Illinois, also has a long history of testing their embalming fluids. Hizone worked with Maynard Duryea of the Palms Memorial Mortuary of St. Petersburg, Florida (now out of business), to develop superior embalming chemicals. An advertising supplement by Hizone dating from approximately 1937 contains "an unretouched photograph of a fine old gentleman who was embalmed September 25, 1929 and still in a state of perfect preservation." The photograph shows a lean, white-haired man reposing on a mattress wearing a suit and tie. His hand and head are visible and show no signs of deterioration. Nine other bodies embalmed from one to nine years earlier were kept in sealer caskets in a vault in the funeral home at the time the supplement was issued. The chemical company claims, "They will keep as long as the caskets last" and notes that copper caskets will last in the ground more than 4,000 years.

The embalming consisted of the use of Selco preinjection fluid, Nasco fluid medium, Sandow cavity fluid, and Paulex powder. The blood was thoroughly removed. "They did not use anhydrous calcium chloride as the drying agent but instead a washed wool sponge about the size of a large grapefruit placed on several layers of brown butcher paper about 20" × 20" in size." The sponge absorbed moisture from the air and acted as a dehumidifier. The supplement mentions that the same technique and fluid combination were used by Mr. Moyer on the body of the Reverend Francisco Olizable, which was shipped and shown all over the United States over one summer. Their advertising copy points out that the advantage of permanent preservation to the mortician is the increased sale of sealer caskets. The advantage to the family is in knowing that the vault protects the casket and the casket protects the body.

Despite years of research and development, no means of mass embalming exists. Bodies are still preserved one by one. In *Embalming: History, Theory, and Practice*, Edward C. Johnson writes: "In the wake of Hiroshima and Nagasaki and other major disasters such as airline crashes, earthquakes, mudslides, and building collapses, a search was instituted for some new means of quickly processing (preserving) huge numbers of dead. Over the years, different means of processing (preserving) the victims of such tragedies were devised, tested, and found unsuitable for a variety of reasons. Experiments were conducted with processes using ultrasound, radiation, atomic bombardment, and ultra-cold. No process tried seemed to be capable of preserving a tremendous number of bodies in a brief period. The search continues!" (Johnson et al. in Mayer 1996, 456). The search for even more effective embalming procedures and chemicals also continues.

Experimental Egyptian Mummification

Ancient Egyptian embalming attempted—often successfully—to preserve the corpse by removing the water from it.

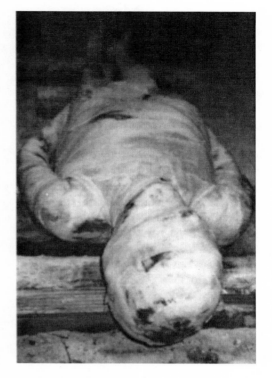

The subject of an experiment by Bob Brier and Ronald Wade to replicate ancient Egyptian embalming techniques on a contemporary cadaver, shown after first wrapping. Photo courtesy of Ronald Wade.

Bob Brier, professor of philosophy at Long Island University, decided to attempt a replication of the ancient method to test the tools that the Egyptians employed, to carry out the procedures that have been described by Herodotus and others, and to assess the properties of the dehydrating agent known to have been used. A "mental mummification," in which the process was simply thought through, presented certain practical problems that an actual mummification would solve.

Brier discussed the idea with Amy Wray, a producer of the television program *National Geographic Explorer*. "It's worth doing because it's history.... Like any historical research, the more we understand the better," Wray was later quoted as saying (Ollove 1994a). Ronald Wade, director of the Anatomical Services Division of the

University of Maryland's School of Medicine, learned of Brier's plan through Wray. Wade realized Brier would have difficulty obtaining a body on which to carry out the experiment. As head of his state's Anatomy Board, Wade was aware that whereas Maryland has a surplus of body donors, New York has a shortage. Brier had not elicited any interest from the medical schools in his area, and if Maryland provided the body, transporting it to a facility other than a medical school would present bureaucratic problems.

After considerable thought about the merits of the experiment, Ronald Wade decided to offer a solution. He proposed to Donald E. Wilson, the dean of the Medical School, that the project be undertaken at the University of Maryland, and he received a positive response. "As a major research institution dedicated to developing new knowledge, we also have a commitment to verifying the old…. This represents a unique opportunity to provide information about an ancient process lost to mankind," said Wilson in a written statement (Ollove 1994b). After several conversations with Brier, it was agreed that the Anatomy Board would provide the donor body and bear the costs of preparation and storage, that Brier would pay for the costs of the materials and tools, and that the mummification would be performed in Wade's laboratory.

Bob Brier traveled to Egypt to collect materials. These included five of the seven sacred oils—lotus, cedar, palm, frankincense, and myrrh—used by the ancient Egyptians (the names of the other two oils have not been successfully translated). The spices were purchased at the Khan al-Khalili spice market in Cairo. The palm wine was obtained from Nigeria. He also procured several hundred pounds of natron, the naturally occurring salt on the banks of the Wadi El-Natroun 100 km west of Cairo. The salt occurs naturally in the soil, goes into solution when the lakes rise, and is deposited on the shore. The natron, made up of sodium chloride, sodium carbonate, and sodium bicarbonate (the chemical composition of baking soda and table salt), was—and would be—used in its solid form to draw the moisture out of the body by osmotic pressure. Modern experiments on the mummifying effects of natron had been carried out on birds and rodents (and on a dog in 1985) but never on a human being.

The tools and equipment needed for the experiment were made to order based on examples that survive from ancient Egypt. Obsidian blades and bronze tools were made, ceramic vessels were crafted, and a wooden embalming table was constructed using the exact measurements (150 × 220 cm) and description of an embalming board excavated by H. E. Winlock from the tomb of Ipy dating to 2000 B.C.

The ideal subject for the mummification would be the body of a young man who had not been damaged by long-term disease, had not died violently, and had not undergone surgery (Ollove 1994a). Ronn Wade briefly considered using the body of John Thanos, a forty-five-year-old murderer who had donated his body to science prior to his execution in May 1994, but Wade realized that would be a public relations disaster. Instead, they chose the body of a seventy-six-year-old white male from the Baltimore area who had died of a heart attack in the spring of 1994. The man, whose identity has not been revealed, had been athletic and trim with no history of disease or surgery. Upon his death the man's body was received into the donor program at his own prior request and without objection from the family. According to the usual policy, the family were not told exactly how the body would be used. They were informed that it would be part of a long-term program, due to which the ashes of the deceased could not be returned. When asked about their possible objections to the experiment, Ronn Wade replied, "My first thought … is that we're treating this man like a king" (Ollove 1994a).

The experimental mummification began on May 21, 1994. The body was weighed at 85 kilograms (188 pounds). After practicing on the heads of cadavers, which were then x-rayed, the team inserted a sharp instrument into the nose of the donor body and used a mallet to penetrate the ethmoid bone. They used a long, curved tool known as a brain macerator and a bladder-like irrigation syringe to liquify the brain tissue, a process that took twenty minutes. The body was then rotated to allow the head to drain. Using the same tools, the cranium was cleaned by swabbing it with strips of linen.

A small incision was made on the left side of the abdomen using an obsidian blade, an implement known by the ancient Egyptians as an "Ethiopian stone." Through this incision, the internal organs were removed: stomach, liver, kidneys, lungs, and intestines. The combined weight of the organs was 14.1 kilograms (31 pounds). The organs were placed in shallow bowls and covered with natron. The heart was left in the body cavity as was done by the ancient Egyptians. The thoracic and abdominal cavities were washed with myrrh and palm wine and filled with twenty-nine linen packets containing natron and myrrh. "The packets had to be small enough to fit through the three-inch abdominal incision but large enough to hold sufficient natron to absorb significant amounts of body fluids" (Brier and Wade 1995, 11). The brain cavity was packed with linen and frankincense.

The prepared body was moved to a sealed room (4 × 2.7 meters) in the University's Gray Laboratory, which had once been Ronn Wade's office. It was arranged on the embalming board on a layer of 95.5 kilograms (211 pounds) of natron. An additional 264 kilograms (583 pounds) of natron were heaped over the body. The height of the feet on the embalming board left them protruding from the natron, so they were encased in surgical foot covers containing the salt. The bowls containing the removed organs were placed at the corners of the embalming board. (In all, 273 kilograms of natron were used.) The temperature was kept at 104° F (40° C), and two dehumidifiers were used to maintain 30 percent relative humidity. The body was left undisturbed for thirty-five days.

On June 25, Bob Brier and Ronn Wade entered the room in which the body had been dehydrating. They realized that they were the first people since the ancient Egyptian embalmers to see the tangible results of natron on the human body, and both found this moment to be a high point in the project. The natron, which had absorbed the fluids of the body, had solidified and turned brown and had to be broken up from around the body and shoveled or brushed away. "As the natron was removed and the hands, feet and head emerged, we were struck by how similar they were to those of an ancient mummy. They were a very dark brown, nearly black. There was no evidence of moisture to the touch and the hands and feet were rigid, fingers and toes incapable of being flexed. The head still retained the hair and, though desiccated and shrunken, all facial features were essentially unchanged" (Brier and Wade 1995, 15–16).

The organs had been completely dehydrated. They were removed from the natron, wrapped in bandages, and inserted into Canopic jars. The natron packets were removed from the body cavity where they had successfully done their work. The natron had dehydrated the flesh in temperatures that would normally have ensured an advanced state of decomposition. The skin of the mummy had the consistency of soft leather. "The skin on the arms and legs of the mummy was still somewhat supple, though leathery, and the limbs could still be flexed. The quadriceps were pliable to the touch, suggesting moisture still remained in these large muscles" (Brier and Wade 1995, 16). Only the underside of the body remained moist, and the natron beneath the lower torso and buttocks was like wet sand. The body emitted an acrid smell, but not one of decay, and no signs of decomposition or putrefaction were found. Its weight had been reduced by half to 35.9 kilograms (79 pounds). Cultures were taken from the cranium and abdominal cavity.

The body was transported by hearse to a laboratory in the basement of the medical school several blocks away. The skin of the mummified body was oiled, and biopsies were taken for further study. The body cavity was packed with spices and wood shavings to keep its shape, and the abdominal incision was covered with a small metal plate. The mummy was then wrapped with an initial layer of muslin bandages that were held in place with dabs of shellac.

To achieve further desiccation, the body was returned to the drying room for three months without natron. Afterward, it had lost another 12.72 kilograms (28 pounds) of fluids and had thus been reduced to 23.18 kilograms (51 pounds), one-third of its initial body weight. It still had a moderately strong odor, but not one of putrefaction. The arms of the mummy had become too inflexible to be crossed in the royal position, so they were arranged at the sides with the hands over the pubis and tied in place. At this time tissue samples were taken from the lungs, liver, spleen, kidneys, stomach, small intestine, colon, and buttock to determine their state of preservation. On November 12, 1994, more wrappings were applied, including a magical wrapping containing hieroglyphs and amulets, a neat wrapping with wider strips of linen, a final wrapping with a wide swath of cloth, and a finish wrapping of eight horizontal and diagonal bands patterned after that of the pharaoh Tuthmose III. In all, the muslin bandages weighed twenty pounds. The wrapped mummy was placed in a Zeigler box (a metal casket), and the transparent lid was screwed on.

The filmed mummification was aired on *National Geographic Explorer* on August 28th, 1994. Although highly satisfied with the experiment itself, Ronn Wade was disappointed with the *National Geographic* segment. He found the title "Mr. Mummy," which he had been led to believe was a working title, rather disrespectful. In addition, the credits did not include thanks to the anonymous body donor without whom the experiment could not have been carried out.

The experiment drew both praise and criticism. "It's a very clever thing to do," commented Rita Freed, curator of the Department of Ancient Egyptian, Nubian and Near Eastern Art at the Boston Museum of Fine Arts. On the other hand, Betsy Bryan, an Egyptologist at Johns Hopkins University, was quoted as saying, "I think it's macabre, and I do think it's tasteless, and I don't think there's a great deal of scientific value." Mark Hanson, a spokesman for the Hastings Center, objected on ethical grounds: "It strikes me as ethically questionable.... A donation to an anatomy service should not be a blank check for any kind of experimentation" (Ollove 1994b). Maryland's health secretary, Nelson J. Sabatini, did not take issue with the experiment but rather with comments Ronn Wade allegedly made to the media (such as referring to the mummy as "E. M. Balm"), which he found "cavalier," "unprofessional," and in "poor taste."

Aside from the controversy, several useful conclusions were drawn from the experiment. The "Ethiopian stone" used by the ancient Egyptians was not merely a ritual element. Obsidian stone proved to be more effective for cutting, since the bronze tools dulled quickly. The four-foot width of the embalming table, at first thought to be excessive, was necessary to accommodate the mounding of the natron over the corpse. Natron was successfully used in solid form rather than in the form of "brine," as has been incorrectly translated from Egyptian texts. And the brain was liquified and poured out rather than being extracted in solid form through the nose. The team hypothesized that the ancient embalmers either positioned the arms of the corpse before the natron was applied or intentionally left some moisture in the body that would later evaporate naturally through the bandages. They showed by example that a single application of natron was sufficient, that the natron did not need to be changed during the drying process. And their results suggested that the seventy-day preparation time written of by Herodotus was the period from death to burial, not merely the time spent in natron.

After the mummification, cultures from the cranium and abdomen tested negative for bacteria (both aerobic and anaerobic), viruses, fungi, and mold. Desiccation had precluded decay. The tissue samples were analyzed and found to be of a state of preservation comparable to the ancient Egyptian mummies, with the exception of the stomach, which was better preserved. Bacterial action had taken place in the colon and intestines. The mummy also underwent a CT-scan. It will be housed at the University of Maryland indefinitely and used for future analysis and study. Ronn Wade points out, "If we wrap this up and one or two years from now there is decay, we will know that we missed something, that there was something else key to the process.... If this doesn't work, we may never know how they really did it" (Ollove 1994a). The mummy makes an ideal control subject in historical comparisons, since the mummification procedure was well documented and the donor's entire medical history is on record. Most recently, the sural nerve in the back of the leg was removed in early 1996 for study and comparison.

Ronn Wade would like to see the mummy stored in a sarcophagus that could be put on public display. At this time it can only be seen by special arrangement or on a fifty-two-minute videocassette titled "Resurrection of an Ancient Art: Mummification," available from Brier-Wood Video. If the storage and study of the body is discontinued, Wade intends to have it buried in the University's gravesite in Sikesville, Maryland. The mummy will have the distinction of being the only donated body to be accorded an intact burial rather than interment of its cremated ashes.

MUSEUM HOLDINGS

Modern mummies acquired by museums are far outnumbered by the mummies of ancient Egyptians and Peruvians in their holdings. Although there are occasional ru-mors of contemporary bodies being passed off as Egyptian mummies in the last century — and it would be difficult to distinguish between a late nineteenth-century and early twentieth-century mummy — most museum mummies are well documented and date far earlier. In one case, however, the bodies of two men were preserved at the turn of the century by means that predate the men and their preparer. The bodies of the so-called "little men," purchased by an American museum, were on display for years until deemed "sensitive materials." In contrast to the little men, who are awaiting burial at the time of this writing, a collection of twentieth-century petrified bodies may still be visited in Milan, and its future does not appear to be in question. Although some may dispute whether either group is (or was) an education exhibit, much can be learned from these mummies, not the least of which is how they were prepared.

Jívaro Mummies

Until the early 1980s the preserved and shrunken bodies of two men were on display in New York's National Museum of the American Indian, which became part of the Smithsonian Institution in 1989. "Though they were the only two shrunken human bodies ever documented, the museum had removed them, in part because they were deemed a little too ghoulish for the taste of an increasingly sensitive public, in part because they represented unorthodox extremes of Jívaro head-shrinking art, and in part because they were growing mold. The bodies, therefore, had been placed in 'deep storage' in the bowels of the building" (Alexander 1994, 100).

The bodies (acquisition numbers 12/6201 and 11/1830) are regarded as "sensitive materials" and are not listed on information cards or available through photographs. Caroline Alexander, who researched the story of the little men, explains that her request to obtain actual photographs from the museum's negatives brought unexpected

The "little men" preserved in the Jívaro style by Gustave Struve. Reprinted from *Indian Notes*, 1926 (Museum of the American Indian, Heye Foundation).

results: "The head of the Smithsonian himself made an unsolicited call to tell me that 'what I was doing was disgusting' and to deliver a little lecture on betraying the 'human dignity of these unfortunate men.' In fact, the Museum's carefully stored negatives have been used to produce the best-selling postcards of the unfortunate men, sold for years in the Museum gift shop" (letter to the author, 3 July 1996).

The photographic negatives reveal one of the men to be well proportioned with Afro-style hair; he was labeled a mulatto and his height was registered as twenty-six inches. He had been obtained in 1922 by the Heye Foundation for $600 from a Polish mining engineer named Juan Krateil, who lived in Lima, Peru, and was president of a petroleum company. Krateil claimed he had obtained the specimen from a Spaniard en route from Callao to Panama. The specimen may be the same one that had been displayed as a shrunken tribal chief in 1898 at an exposition in Guayaquil, Ecuador.

Pictures of the shrunken man were circulated in newspaper articles the following year announcing the establishment of the museum, and he soon became one of the most well-known items in the collection. The museum was soon contacted by the lawyer of a Dr. Gustave Struve of Ecuador, who claimed the shrunken man had been stolen from him in 1920. After inquiries and investigations led nowhere, the museum paid Dr. Struve $500 for the mummy "shunken by the Jívaro Indians of Ecuador." At this time Struve offered the museum a second specimen of a shrunken man measuring 31 inches tall. The second man has white hair on his head and chest and a large mustache, and he was noted to have been a Spanish military officer. He was displayed with the mulatto and more than a dozen shrunken heads. "Postcards of these curiosities became especially popular items in the museum gift shop" (Alexander 1994, 174).

When the men were acquired by the museum, they were said to have died in 1898. Alexander notes that Struve made and sold the mummies in the 1920s: "He had apparently made them specifically for a lucrative sale of this kind. I am a little uneasy with the idea that he held on to them for twenty-odd years before making his move" (letter to the author, 3 July 1996). The memory Struve's son has of "papa making the mummies" would imply that they were prepared just before 1920, but the exact date is still in question and may hinge on when yellow fever raged in Guayaquil, Ecuador, since the bodies may have been victims of this epidemic.

The mummies are said to be hollow, light, and as stiff as leather. The bones had been left in the feet for stability but also appear to have been left in the hands. "They were chilling," said Carmelo Guadagno, who had photographed and handled the mummies. "They look like dolls, but you know they aren't. There is no question that they are human beings" (Alexander 1994, 174). Although their ethnic origin is doubtful, they

may become part of the deaccessioning of human remains provoked by the 1990 Native American Graves Protection and Repatriation Act. Ray Gonyea, head of the museum's repatriation program, says, "We are seeking to do the proper thing, and the appropriate thing in this case would be interment. We are investigating appropriate places for burial" (Alexander 1994, 179).

It would have been difficult to prepare an entire human body in the manner that the Jívaro (properly known as the Shuar) prepared human heads. The body would have to be boned and the skin boiled in water to extract the skin's natural oils, but for not more than half an hour or the hair may fall out. The skin would be air-dried, turned inside out, and scraped of all remaining flesh. It would then be turned right side out and all incisions and orifices, including the mouth, would be sewn shut. The eyelids would have to be sewn shut or large seeds or other objects placed behind them. Stones heated in a fire would have to be applied repeatedly over several days to the inside of the head, body cavity, and extremities. The stones would be followed by repeated applications of hot sand once the skin had shrunk. Flat, hot stones would have to be used to smooth and mold the facial features, the facial hair singed off, and the skin polished and blackened with charcoal. "The entire skeleton would have to be removed, much in the manner in which a fish is filleted. Tireless applications of stone and sand would be required. The whole procedure sounds preposterously complicated..." (Alexander 1994, 175).

Nevertheless, such shrunken bodies were said to have been prepared by remote tribes of the Rio Negro and Orinoco, and the museum's ethnologist Dr. Marshall Saville had reportedly been searching for such a specimen for twenty-five years prior to the museum's acquisition. The heads of the unclaimed dead in Guayaquil and Panama were made by unscrupulous entrepreneurs into shrunken heads or *tsantsas* that were sold to tourists in the early part of the twentieth century. Michael J. Harner (1984, 225) writes, "Sometimes they went so far as to shrink the skins of entire bodies, a practice which, when I described it to Jívaro informants, was greeted with incredulity."

In fact, journalist Caroline Alexander has uncovered evidence in an interview with Struve's still-living son that the mummies were made in the style of Jívaro shrunken heads, but by Struve himself, who had learned the art of head-shrinking from the Indians, whom he had lived with for several years. According to Olaf Holm, director of the archaeological Museo del Banco Central, Struve and fellow medical students in Guayaquil could easily have obtained unclaimed bodies of people who had died in the yellow fever epidemic of the time and experimented on them as a joke. Alexander concludes, "It later occurred to me that, having mastered the complex and painstaking art of shrinking human bodies, Struve might have been loath to neglect the lucrative skill once he left South America. My inquiries about the existence of shrunken figures in Chinese museums, however, have so far come to naught" (Alexander 1994, 179).

The National Museum of Health and Medicine was unsuccessful in an attempt to acquire the two mummies. Plans were underway by the Heye Foundation of the National Museum of the American Indian to have them buried in a Native American cemetery in Seneca, New York. The head of the Committee on Repatriation volunteered Iroquois traditional lands for the burial, but no concrete plans have been made, possibly due to budget constraints. According to a spokesperson at the museum (telephone conversation, 28 March 1997), the burial is being handled by their repatriation office, is being negotiated with various tribes, and will also include interment of other unaffiliated human remains. So the mysterious little men remain unburied.

Petrification

Giuseppe Paravicini, an Italian doctor and psychiatrist, claimed to have developed a secret formula that, if properly injected into a corpse, transformed it into a kind of "everlasting wax statue." The bodies he prepared survive him and bear out his claim. Paravicini began his experiments in Milan in 1901 in an attempt to petrify entire bodies as well as internal organs. He obtained the cadavers and organs from the mortuary of the mental asylum of Mombello, then located on the outskirts of Milan and now called Instituto Hospitalario Provincial Psiquiatrico "Paolo Pini."

In 1906 Paravicini became director of Mombello. In 1914 he petrified a patient who had suffered from senile dementia, Angela Bonnette, who had died on June 3 of that year. In 1917 he embalmed Evelina Gobbo, an epileptic who died of pneumonia on November 16. "Even Cardinal Andrea Ferrari, Archbishop of Milan, who died in 1921, participated in the work of conservation, and today his body is still in perfect condition" (Albert n.d.).

Paravicini's method apparently involved intervention shortly after death to cause the blood to continue to circulate by pressure from a pump. He made an incision in the femoral artery and introduced mummifying liquid that may have been made from balsamic oils and some fixative (according to Antonio Allegranza, retired director of Paolo Pini) or wax and solvents (according to Dr. Carnevali, present curator of the bodies). On his death in 1927, Dr. Paravicini bequeathed the petrified bodies of Bonnette and Gobbo to the Centre, as well as some busts, heads, and numerous brains.

Paravicini carried his secret formula with him to the grave. In reconstructing his history researchers were unable to discover the duration of the experiments, the components of the formula, or the reason for his obsession in keeping all his notes and discoveries so secret. The case of Paravicini's petrification was presented as an authentic medical enigma during the First Congress on the Historic Development of Italian Neurology in 1987 by Professor Antonio Allegranza,

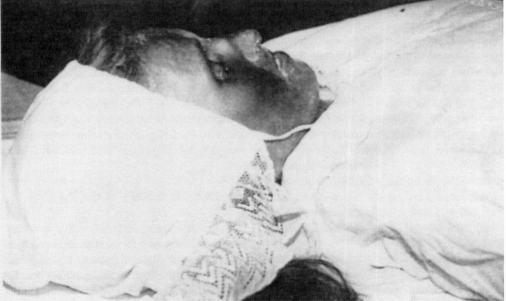

Top: The body of Angela Bonette, petrified by Giuseppe Paravicini in Milan in 1914. *Bottom:* The body of Evelina Gobbo, petrified by Giuseppe Paravicini in Milan in 1918.

who is now retired. Allegranza had collected all the petrified remains that he could and ordered the construction of glass cabinets and wooden support frames to house them in a small (200 square meter) museum above the mortuary in Paolo Pini, which he directed. Only specialists were allowed to view them. The collection was transferred in 1982 to the stores of the Centre for the Study and Investigation of Deviations and Marginalisations, popularly known in Milan as "Brefiotrofio" and later moved to closed rooms of the Faculty of Veterinary Science in Milan.

Researchers visited the Faculty of Veterinary Science and were shown into the gloomy room where the cases and cabinets were stored by Professor Carnevali. It contained the perfectly conserved bodies of Gobbo and Bonnette, which looked like wax statues. "The hands, face and feet had a yellowish colour that contrasted strongly with the white night-clothes that they had on the bodies. Nothing could hide the look of surprise which was obvious on both faces, and which was captured by the cameras" (Albert, 42). From out of boxes Carnevali pulled human heads split down the middle to show the cranial cavities, busts of women which still maintained the color of their hair and the expression on their faces, human brains somewhat reduced in size and grayish in color, and flasks of formalin containing heads and human fetuses. "Since they have been here, nobody has shown any interest in them, perhaps in part because they are such an uncomfortable sight," explains Dr. Carnevali (Albert, 43). Allegranza intended to extract the secret from the human remains but was unable to do so. No analysis has been able to confirm the ingredients of Paravicini's solution, and his work has remained shrouded in mystery.

The intentions of Paravicini—and the source of his experimental material—are not without precedent. Prior to the turn of the century in Philippi, West Virginia, an embalmer named Graham Hamrick (d. 1899) requested permission to try an experimental embalming method that he later patented. The method involves placing the body in an airtight box, draining it through a small incision in the abdomen, injecting it through the same incision with saltpeter dissolved in water, and repeatedly perfusing it with sulfur fumes. The local judge allowed him to try the method on the bodies of two adult women who had died in the state hospital for the insane. Upon examination fifty-five days later, there were no signs of decomposition. The success of his method thus proven, Hamrick attempted to donate the mummies to the Smithsonian Institution, but the offer was declined when he refused to reveal the ingredients of the formula he had used. The mummies reportedly toured Europe with P. T. Barnum before returning to Philippi, where they were exhibited at local fairs and later purchased by Frank "Bigfoot" Byrer (d. 1991). When the area flooded in 1985, the bodies of the two women and a baby that Hamrick had also preserved were taken to the local funeral home for restoration. The mummified baby was not salvageable, but the mummies of the women were cleansed of the "fuzzy gray mold" that covered them. Byrer donated the mummies to the City of Philippi shortly before his death, and they were placed on display at the Barbour County Historical Museum, with proceeds benefiting the local library and a scholarship fund. After another flood struck Philippi in 1997, the mummies were removed to the local funeral home for safekeeping until repairs could be made to the museum that continues to house them.

TERATOLOGY SPECIMENS

Perhaps the embalmed bodies with the most colorful past and most uncertain future are those of deformed fetuses. Publicly accessible teratology collections are few and far between. The specimens at the National Museum of Health and Medicine in Washington, D.C., have been worked into the exhibit on developmental anatomy. At the Mütter

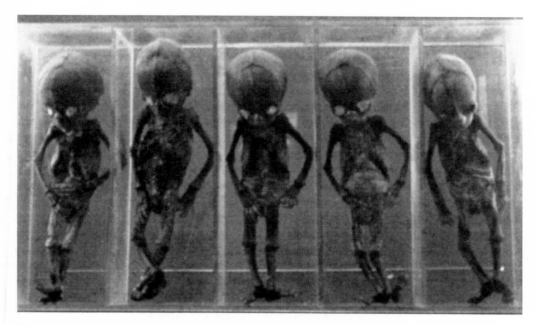

The bodies of quintuplets delivered by Mrs. Oscar D. Lyon of Kevil, Kentucky, on April 29, 1896. Despite the attention the Lyons received after the birth, all five male babies died within fifteen days. Their bodies were embalmed, but Mrs. Lyon was afraid to bury them for fear the grave would be robbed. In November 1915, she wrote to President Woodrow Wilson offering to loan the babies, then "in a mummified condition," to the government for educational purposes. Her letter was answered by the curator of the Army Medical Museum, who offered to purchase them or accept them as a donation. A price of $100 and payment of the shipping charges was agreed upon, Mrs. Lyon was given instructions for wrapping and packaging the bodies, and upon receipt they were placed on display in the museum. Mrs. Lyon was assured that her babies were "perfectly secure from evilly disposed persons," that they were of considerable interest to museum visitors, and that they would be brought to the attention of the president if he should visit. They remain today in the National Museum of Health and Medicine, Armed Forces Institute of Pathology. Photo courtesy of the National Museum of Health and Medicine, Armed Forces Institute of Pathology. Accession number 43411.

Museum in Philadelphia, the teratology specimens may be seen and even photographed, but the photos may not be published. Collections at some other institutions have been shelved entirely or are off limits to the general public. In earlier decades, teratology collections rolled into town with the carnival. Shows advertising the world's strangest babies drew crowds of curious onlookers who could still be appeased if they knew where to look. But it is this unabashed staring at the abnormal, especially in the informal environment of a sideshow, that has drawn the criticism that rains down on all teratology exhibits.

Museum Collections

The term *teratology*, the scientific study of monstrous births, was coined by French naturalist Étienne Geoffroy Saint-Hilaire (d. 1844), although the collection of such specimens predates the word by centuries. In the environment of the modern museum, these specimens are not exhibited as "monsters" but as the unfortunate results of congenital defects and other deformities. Although the teratology exhibit in the typical medical museum is not highlighted, it is carefully maintained and the specimens labeled with explanations meant to be understood by the layperson.

The fetuses in the collection of the National Museum of Health and Medicine (NMHM) were acquired within a thirty-year time frame, approximately 1890 to 1920. All of the specimens at the museum were stillbirths. They were often collected by doctors and donated to the museum. This was prior to today's notion of informed consent, so in some cases the mothers were not aware of the disposition of their stillborn babies. In other cases the specimen was sold to the museum by the mother. The museum has been visited by the mother of a baby born with an ectopic heart; the woman, who was in her nineties, and her family welcomed the opportunity for a brief reunion with the infant and took photographs to mark the occasion.

The specimens at the NMHM are stored in a standard 10 percent formalin solution, which ideally should be changed regularly. A typical bottled specimen will last indefinitely, but the fluid—especially if it is alcohol based—tends to evaporate. A product called "Ruffer's Solution" is used to rehydrate specimens if necessary. The specimens are held in glass or Plexiglas jars. Glass is preferable because the seams in the Plexiglas eventually fail, which happened to one container in late May of 1996.

The teratology collection as a whole was removed from display at the NMHM because the way the specimens were exhibited no longer fit the mission of the museum, not because there was any public reaction, according to curator Paul Sledzik. Some of the specimens were worked into the current display of developmental anatomy. The specimens currently on display include examples of anencephaly (lacking a brain), cyclopia (having one eye), achondroplasia (abnormal bone growth that results in dwarfism), sirenomelia (fusion of the lower limbs), and conjoined twins (one pair joined at the head and the other at the chest). The twins joined at the chest show evidence of having been autopsied, and Sledzik explains that the decision to perform an autopsy depended on the doctor and whether the anomoly was common.

Other museums worldwide are known for their teratology collections. The Mütter Museum at the College of Physicians in Philadelphia keeps approximately half of their teratology collection on display. The specimens are preserved in Shine's Solution, which is said to give better color preservation than formalin, and those that are not in very good condition are not exhibited. Most recently, the museum acquired a thirty-week fetus with acrania in 1991 from an obstetrician working as an attending physician in Trenton. The mother was a seventeen-year-old Guatemalan illegal immigrant and had signed the necessary consent forms. The Museum Vrolik at the Amsterdam Medical Center has one of the world's largest collections of teratology specimens. About forty specimens are said to be on display, including examples of cyclopia, anencephaly, and varieties of conjoined twins. The teratology collection at Tulane Medical School, which also contains specimens of anencephaly and conjoined twins, is housed in a hallway gallery and lined with mirrors so that the backs of the specimens can be visualized.

Such museums are not often crowded, allowing the patron to confront the specimens one on one, as F. Gonzalez-Crussi (1995) describes: "You find yourself in an old-fashioned museum of anatomical and pathological specimens. Most likely, you are alone: establishments such as this are usually dusty and desolate nowadays. You turn a corner and discover, locked in a yellow twilight of decaying liquid fixative, the strangest, most extraordinary beings imaginable. Impossible to look at them without a shudder, but mixed with fear there is curiosity, pity, and astonishment. And you cannot ignore them, either. They seem to grab you by the scruff of the neck and tell you: 'Look at us.' You obey, and your dearest preconceptions crumble. Gender, identity, number, human nature: All these ideas have lost their meaning." Malformed fetuses may disgust but more often provoke wonder and questions of what and why. If the specimens are displayed with respect and the questions are answered truthfully and scientifically, the exhibit has social and scientific legitimacy.

It is both the viewing and the presentation of teratology specimens that are at issue in today's politically correct atmosphere. Although museums are in general unable to discourage those who have come merely to gawk, they can arrange the display and augment it with other materials in such a way that the patron will learn something about human anatomy and fetal development. Paul Sledzik of the National Museum of Health and Medicine explains that in the early twentieth century museums diverged from the "pathological cabinet," which was simply a display of monsters, to use their material for research and educational purposes. He says, "This is the conundrum we face at the NMHM—how to use the unique wet tissue material, which is inherently powerful and visceral (no pun intended), in an educational context" (letter to the author, 21 June 1996). In fact, Sledzik sometimes wishes the teratology exhibits were not on display, since he feels that normal fetal development is more educational.

The now-defunct Weird Museum in Los Angeles was less of a museum and more of a pathological cabinet, offering exhibits to titillate rather than educate the public. The collection, exhibited by Sharon Viedma Aguilar, was housed in a ten-foot by twenty-four-foot space in the rear of a shop called Panpipes that is still located on Cahuenga Boulevard. The collection had reportedly been assembled originally by a carnival performer named Blyth, who had purchased most of the specimens from other collectors and passed ownership on to Aguilar, one of his students, at his death. The exhibits included two desiccated corpses, one said to be the 3,600-year-old body of an ancient Egyptian who had been buried alive, and several deformed fetuses in jars. The L.A. County coroner's office found the Weird Museum's display of human remains objectionable and—acting under provisions of the state Health and Safety Code—confiscated several of the specimens, including a set of conjoined twins. Ironically, a few of the specimens that were seized were destined to remain on display in what some would consider a more appropriate forum. According to Craig Harvey of the L.A. County coroner's office (telephone conversation with the author, 26 September 1996), many of the specimens were destroyed, but some were retained by the coroner's office as "teaching specimens."

Sideshows

The display of teratology specimens in sideshows is much more casual than their display in the museum. The anencephalic infant is the "frog boy," the conjoined twins are the "two-headed baby," and the sirenomelia is a "mermaid." Collectively, fetuses and deformed babies are known by showmen as "pickled punks," a punk being slang for a young thing. Despite their informal jargon and the informality of the presentation, the showmen claimed to be educating the public with their exhibits. Although they were usually congenital, the deformities of the fetuses were said to exemplify the dangerous results of drinking and drug abuse (especially while pregnant), promiscuity, incest, and malnutrition. As James Taylor writes in *Shocked and Amazed! On and Off the Midway* (vol. 3): "The freak baby shows were often pitched as warnings to unwed mothers of the horrors of premarital sex, warnings to expectant parents to stay off drugs, warnings to everyone of the dangers of incest, anything to make the shows palatable to the stiff-necked or squeamish members of the community." The display of embryos and fetuses that weren't deformed illustrated normal fetal development.

Sideshow banners proclaiming "Born Alive" or "Born to Live" often gave the misleading impression that the exhibits inside the tent were alive. Of course, they were in jars just like the specimens in museums. Shows without live acts were in fact called "museum shows." Until the early twentieth century, teratology specimens could be found among the objects and live acts in the dime museums that operated out of buildings or store fronts. When a show specializing in teratology went on the road, it became known as a life show, a baby show, an unborn show, a bottle show, or simply a freak baby show. At a carnival, the baby show operated as a "grind show" or walk-through exhibit.

A teratology specimen (a two-headed baby) was first exhibited at a carnival attraction by Walter K. Sibly at Coney Island in 1893, but Lou Dufour (d. 1977) was the first to put together and exhibit a baby show in 1927. Dufour had seen a medical exhibit depicting the development of the human fetus and borrowed the idea for his own shows. Soon he had twenty or thirty lucrative exhibits touring the United States and Canada, including shows at Niagara Falls and at the New York World's Fair in 1939–40. The attractions at first catered only to adults and were billed as "The Scroll of Life" and "Nature's Mistakes." According to an anonymous carnival authority quoted in the *Lake County (Ill.) Suburban Tribune* (August 5, 1977), the fetuses were easy to come by: "At the time these flourished, you could readily obtain fetuses from hospitals. They threw them out. Or you could order them. You could assemble a complete set of fetuses showing their development."

Because of the inception, growth, and popularity of his baby shows, Dufour became known as the "King of the Unborn." He prided himself on operating his life museum in Niagara Falls behind a cleanly presented theater marquee. His show took an academic approach that he said appeals to all age groups. "Man is fearfully and wonderfully made," Dufour wrote in a treatise. His show presented the story of life from its first visible form. Diagrams and other visual aids filled out the story and female lecturers explained the entire process of fertilization, development of the embryo, growth of the fetus, and birth of the baby. Although the auxiliary materials rounded out the show, the patrons' eyes were surely fastened on the babies in the jars arranged sequentially by size.

Other showmen later followed in Dufour's footsteps. In 1970 Ward Hall convinced the owner of Gooding's Million Dollar Midway to let him exhibit a baby show on their secondary route. Although the show included a two-headed baby made of wax, Hall also displayed a real double-bodied baby that he had purchased in 1969 from a woman in Indianapolis, whose father had exhibited the specimen during the Depression. After Hall convinced Gooding's to let him exhibit the baby show on the main unit, he purchased some fetuses from the Museum Supply Company in South Carolina to bring the total in the show to twelve or fourteen. Patrons were lured into the show with the following "grind," as recounted in issue no. 3 of the fanzine *Freaks!* "Children of forgotten fathers … *they* did not ask to be born!…. Is the *pill* right? Is *abortion* the answer? *You* be the judge! But first, come in and see the World's Strangest Babies!" In 1976 Hall booked his baby show into the Ohio State Fair. "…I have photographs showing people lined up two abreast clear across the midway waiting to get in that thing," he boasts (*Freaks!* no. 3). According to *Shocked and Amazed! On and Off the Midway* (vol. 3), the popularity of freak baby exhibits allowed showmen to double their incomes.

Ward Hall and his partner Chris Christ charged seventy-five cents for admission into the "World's Strangest Babies" show. A few of the babies were normal, but most were grossly deformed and were labeled according to their physical appearance: "Frog Boy" (a baby described as having a flat skull and bulging eyes whose mother was said to have been afflicted with venereal disease), "Fish Boy," "Elephant Nose Baby," and "Cyclops." To lend some dubious credibility, a sign in the exhibit read, "All babies and fetus specimens in this display preserved in formaldehyde and on loan to Wondercade, a nonprofit corporation, through the courtesy of the U.S. Bureau of Educational Exhibitions."

When the baby show played the five-day Lake County Fair in Grayslake, Illinois, in 1977, it was seen by a young girl who mentioned the exhibit to her mother. The shocked mother went to see the show, and afterward alerted county coroner Robert Babcox. "At first I thought these would be plastic models.... I didn't believe down deep these could be human remains," Babcox told the *Lake County Suburban Tribune* (August 5, 1977). He sent two men to check the show and when they visually verified that the remains were human, Babcox obtained a warrant from circuit court Judge Thomas Doran for the arrest of Christ, owner and operator of the show. Christ was arrested on July 29 for unauthorized transportation and display of human remains. He was released on $2,000 bond pending a circuit court appearance.

Twenty jars were confiscated from the show three days after the fair had begun. The jars were removed to the basement of the morgue in Waukegan, and their contents were x-rayed by a pathologist who determined that they were actual human remains. The formaldehyde had turned the skin of the fetuses gray. Babcox assured the public that the remains would not be returned to Christ and would be properly disposed of. He commented to the *Tribune*, "Yes, as far as I know, he was doing a brisk business.... It's the most hideous thing. The thought behind these tragic births and the thought that they are displayed for profit. The whole concept is overwhelming." County officials tried unsuccessfully to contact the "Bureau of Educational Exhibitions" mentioned in the show and were unable to uncover the source of supply for the exhibit. Christ told the officials that he had purchased the specimens from another carnival that had gone out of business three years earlier. Authorities suggested that the remains had been obtained from hospitals years ago, when the disposition in such a manner was not illegal.

News of the raided show hit the wire services with photos of the coroner standing next to the jars and later burying a dozen or more carnival babies in tiny coffins. Reporters claimed to have found a similar exhibit titled "Nature's Mistakes" at the Knox County Fair, but the bodies had been replaced with rubber replicas and animal fetuses before the authorities could be summoned to the scene. After he learned that Christ was in partnership with Ward Hall, Babcox contacted the police in Hall's home state of Florida. The Tampa sheriff's office, armed with a search warrant, entered Hall's home and removed the bodies of fourteen fetuses or infants wrapped in newspaper and preserved in formaldehyde. The remains were turned over to the Hillsborough County medical examiner and the *Tampa Tribune*'s headline declared Hall "The Ghoul of Gibsonton."

Ward Hall claims that the arrest and confiscation were a publicity stunt by the coroner, who was to be replaced by a medical examiner and was therefore going to run for sheriff. Hall fought the charges against Christ and the case went to trial. The judge ruled that the fetuses were not "corpses." Since they had been issued neither birth certificates nor death certificates, it was legal to own, transport, and display them. Christ was acquitted. Hall and Christ had made rubber molds of the babies, so with these substitutions the show was out of business for only a week, although the negative publicity caused several of the fairs to cancel the show during the rest of the season. The authentic teratology specimens were never returned (*Shocked and Amazed! On and Off the Midway* vol. 1, 12–13). "But, we did not ask for the babies back," Hall explains. We didn't need them. We had the rubber ones. They were easier to handle; you didn't have to have formaldehyde, and so on" (*Freaks!* No. 3).

Fake babies—"bouncers," as they are known in the business—were not new to Ward Hall. Back in 1950, when he was nineteen, he crafted his own conjoined twin to use as a "blow-off" attraction (one for which customers were charged an additional admission fee) in a sideshow with the Stevens Brothers Circus. He glued an extra head on a rubber doll, painted it brown, and put it in a large jar filled with water that he clouded with ink. When a customer exposed the fake baby, he had a better replica made of wax by the B. W. Christopher Waxworks in St. Louis. He showed the wax baby with the Wallace & Clark Circus for donations, which he culled from the crowd by explaining that it had been born to a woman in India with twenty-one other children whom the money would help support (*Freaks!* no. 2).

As the "World's Strangest Babies" show began its 1978 season, the events that unfolded revealed the downside to displaying bouncers. The first spot of the season was in Ohio, the explicit laws of which state that one cannot exhibit a faked freak. Before the show opened, its manager Henry Valentine, mindful of what had happened the year before, demonstrated to the inspector that the specimens were made of rubber. Because they were not real, the inspector would not issue a license for the show! Although he set up an indoor show with Christ on the Seaside Heights, New Jersey, boardwalk in 1979, it was shortly thereafter that Hall decided to get out of the baby-show business.

Several years later Ward Hall changed his mind and built another baby-show, less elaborate than the first. Ward Hall is one of only a handful of showmen, including Bobby Reynolds and the owners of the Harmur Sideshows, still exhibiting deformed fetuses. In 1987 his museum show "World of Wonders" began touring the major fairs in the Northeast every summer. After seeing the show at the York Fair in Pennsylvania in 1992, James Taylor published a description in *Shocked and Amazed! On and Off the Midway* (vol. 1, 21): "On the platform were the World of Wonders bouncers, each floating in its couple gallons of clear fluid. The tape on the boom box, Ward's voice announcing that he was doctor somebody or other, ground out a lecture about 'these replica freak babies,' the word 'replica' spoken so softly you could hardly hear it spoken, the lecture going on to tell of the horrors of drug abuse." The babies in the baby show were no longer authentic but still had a following and therefore still turned a profit.

Ward Hall's "World's Strangest Babies" show had been seen years earlier by a teenage Walt Hudson, who later became a showman in his own right: "The first grind show we stopped at was a show housed in a 20' × 20' tent. It had four large banners—two on either side of a single ticket box.... Each banner pictured a small freak baby: the frog baby, the lobster baby, a two-headed baby and a cyclops baby. 'They didn't ask to be born!' 'Children of forgotten fathers!' 'Drug abuse baby!' These slogans, and others, helped to sensationalize the attraction. Everything was done to lead the public into thinking they were going to see live babies. They were not live—nor were they real" (*Shocked and Amazed! On and Off the Midway*, vol. 2). Hudson believed that the babies were made of wax and rubber. Colored liquid obscured them in the jar and articles and photographs culled from medical journals were displayed to lend credibility. Hudson realized that a baby show, with little overhead and no salaries to pay, was a lucrative operation. He acquired a rubber two-headed baby in anticipation of owning his own exhibit. "I planned then and there that I would acquire at least one curio a year for my collection. Maybe some day I'd frame my own show. I was really feeling good! After all, how many sixteen-year-old kids own a two-headed baby?" (*Shocked and Amazed! On and Off the Midway*, vol. 2).

Unlike the first bouncer that Ward Hall fashioned out of a doll, many replicas or "gaffs" are quite sophisticated and made from molds of authentic teratology specimens. Once in circulation in the sideshow, they passed from hand to hand and show to show. Showman Tim Cridland explains in *Freaks!* no. 4, "As sideshow owners retired or moved on, collections were sold and exhibit origins became obscured; even the operators couldn't tell the bouncers from the punks." Whether they are real or believed by the viewer to be real, "monster babies" are part of a long history of exhibition. According to Jack Hunter in *Inside Teradome* (1995, 15), the recognition, treatment, and display of human anomalies as special beings is an institution that dates back in one form or another to the beginnings of recorded history, in every civilization across the world. Whereas the medical museum is generally thought to be a more appropriate forum for the display of teratology specimens, the carnival baby shows have become scarce not just because of pressure from the public or a more savvy audience, but because rides with their repeat business are more lucrative than a sideshow attraction. Touring all the medical museums and visiting each of the sideshows will give you a representative look at teratology specimens, but even if you have seen one, you haven't—and never will have—seen them all.

5. Buying Immortality

Emulations, Innovations, and Applications

What sets apart the mummies in this section is that most of them have engineered—or at least financed—their own fate. They have taken advantage of modern technology to effect their own physical immortality. To make this goal a reality, they have had to plan in advance—and indeed many are still in the planning stages. The means of preservation is a matter of personal choice and the choices are growing along with their respective clienteles. Thus, this is a group of mummies and mummies-to-be and methods that are proven in some cases and merely promised in others.

Most of the preservation techniques offered for sale require expertise and many require upkeep. For these reasons, to underwrite continued research and development, and to pay for sarcophagi and other accoutrements, they are expensive. But the clients need more than a bank account, they must have the desire—ranging from the spiritual to the egotistical—to be mummified. Many of Summum's clients are health-conscious during their lives and believe that preserving their bodies will allow their souls a smoother transition into death. Most cryonics clients believe that deep-freezing their bodies will facilitate their reanimation at a future date, although frozen embryos (microscopic mummies?) may have a better chance of being revived.

Some of the methods of purchased preservation are concerned with the more immediate future: keeping the body presentable until a funeral can be held or a mausoleum can be built. In other methods, including Summum's mummification, a patented method of sealing the body in glass, and the application of taxidermy to the human body, the mummy *is* the monument and is meant to remain on display. The result is a work of art, illustrating the fact that embalming, despite a wealth of technology and technical know-how, remains an art rather than a science.

EMULATIONS

Whether or not you choose to live like a king, you may now die like one. You don't have to be a Russian revolutionary to be embalmed as carefully as Vladimir Lenin. You don't have to be an Egyptian pharaoh to be painstakingly prepared and wrapped. The Scientific Research Institute for Biological Structures and the Summum organization, respectively, are willing to treat your dead body like royalty ... for a fee. For an additional premium you may buy periodic maintenance or personalize your mummiform sarcophagus. The purchase of such products and services may call into question the clients' vanity. The secrecy surrounding the formulas and techniques, maintained to keep them commodities, raises doubts about their validity.

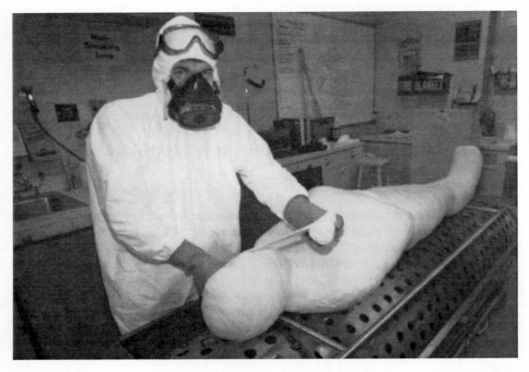

John Chew at Lynn University in Boca Raton, Florida, demonstrating the wrapping that will be performed on Summum's human mummification clients. Photo courtesy of Andrew Itkoff.

Mummification by Summum

A nonprofit organization named Summum (Latin for "sum total") claims to have revived the ancient Egyptian art of mummification. The company was begun by aerobics instructor and wine maker Summum Bonum Amen ("Corky") Ra, age 52 [in 1997], formerly known as Claude Nowell and now a licensed funeral director in the state of California. Ra teamed up with Salt Lake City, Utah, mortician Ron Temu (formerly known as Ron Zefferer), age 49 [in 1997], to develop a mummification process that they feel is far superior to that of the ancient Egyptians. They tested it on chicken eggs, rats, birds, cats, and dogs, sometimes shaving the bodies to approximate human skin and usually using animals that had been killed accidentally on the road. They also mummified Ra's dog and cat (which had died of old age and feline leukemia, respectively) before going public in 1987 as "thanatogeneticists."

Summum now has a home page on the World Wide Web and headquarters in a three-story pyramid in downtown Salt Lake City. Ra and Temu patented their formula, trademarked the company's name, and registered the words "mummification," "permanent body preservation," and "eternal memorialization" as their service marks in all fifty U.S. states. Summum currently provides the only commercial mummification service in the world. "The idea at first seems out of place in today's society. However, people may come to find that it fulfills a certain need and Summum feels that the time is fitting for the revival of this particular brand of corporeal conservation," reads the information on their "Modern Mummification" Web page.

At a funeral industry convention in Las Vegas in the late 1970s, Ra and Temu had been introduced to John A. Chew, age 64 [in 1997], then a mortuary sciences professor at Lynn University in Boca Raton. Chew was put in charge of Summum's human mummification division, now based in Florida. At the time of this writing, however, all of Summum's human clients are alive. "We're ready to go," says Chew. "All we're waiting for now is for someone to die" (Bowen-Jones 1993, 48). In a 1990 interview, Chew admitted that Summum advertised its services for free in some California papers and had made contacts with medical examiners and anatomical boards to obtain a body. By 1993 Chew and his students had experimented on cadavers. According to the *San Jose Mercury News* (June 17, 1996), Summum's embalmers had practiced on thirty cadavers purchased from a medical school and claim, "There has been no breakdown of tissue at all" (Rivenburg 1993). Summum insists that their unique solution "stops biological deterioration dead—but beautifully—in its tracks."

Corky Ra is assisted by his second wife, Gracey Ra, 52 [in 1997], a body-builder who hikes, bikes, swims, skis, teaches aerobics, and has also signed up to be mummified. Of the 139 people enrolled in Summum's mummification program, 38 [as of April 1995] plan to become mummies themselves and the rest plan to have their pets preserved. Summum's human clients range in age from their late twenties to their mid-fifties and include a celebrity musician whose identity has not been revealed. All of their clients are physically fit and none are handicapped, but Gracey Ra notes, "We accept clients in any condition." Chew, who plans to be mummified by Summum, comments, "It's not for everybody. Not everyone wants to be memorialized. But some people do. And some people ought to be. Regular embalming goes just so far, but the body eventually turns to dust. Our process will make the body last forever" (Klinger 1991, 12). The Summum brochure reads, "Mummification is thorough and detailed, but well worth the effort, for the results represent the ultimate personal transformation.... Mummification does not represent a break with tradition: *it can only enhance it.*"

When a client dies, the body may be embalmed and a traditional funeral held. The corpse will then be flown to what Summum's brochure calls "a designated sanctuary" at Lynn University and washed with a sacramental wine made at Summum headquarters. The internal organs will be removed through a ten-inch incision beneath the ribcage and cleaned. The brain will be left in place and a chemical preservative will be injected into the cranial vault to harden the organ. The body and the internal organs will be soaked for as little as a week or as long as a month (usually 7 to 12 days) in a stainless steel vat filled with a fragrant solution of salts (to remove moisture), oils (to replace it), and chemicals (to improve the absorption of the oils). The solution includes phenol (a preservative acid) and dimethyl sulfoxide or DMSO (a solvent and penetrating agent). Chew explains that they have applied modern technology to the mummification process. According to Summum, today's modern chemistry allows them to preserve the genetic message in each cell to a very high degree and for an indefinite amount of time—what they call a "sumsoshoeugenic state" that will keep one looking "healthy and robust for millenia."

The bath in which the body and organs will soak includes the same chemical genetic engineers use to preserve tissues, according to Ra. The secret formula is said to contain—in addition to the above-mentioned phenol and DMSO—a small amount of formaldehyde, fluoride, alcohol, and various salts. Other sources include carbonated water, borax, and other chemicals in the mix. The liquid preparation is followed by a final preparation using two types of natron and taking 7 to 14 days, depending on the weight of the body. After the mummification, the body will supposedly remain soft and supple—just as the person was during life—indefinitely. Chew explains, "The body breaks down through two processes—its own chemistry, powered by oxygen, and bacteria. By saturating and inactivating every cell, driving out the oxygen and replacing it with our formula, we've eliminated both processes" (Stone 1990, 10).

When the body is removed from the bath, it will have a rubbery consistency but will get firmer as it dries. The organs will be coated with polyurethane, wrapped in linen, and replaced in the body cavity that has also been polyurethaned. The body will then be painted repeatedly with a mixture of glycerin, wines, and oils, followed by several coats of polyurethane. It will then be wrapped with 200 feet of linen gauze that has been seasoned with herbs and spices, coated with polyurethane or latex rubber, and covered with a layer of cast fiberglass. It may be covered with a veneer of gold leaf, placed in a standard casket, or sealed inside the sarcophagus previously chosen along with any items the client has designated. The sarcophagus will be welded shut and purged with argon, an inert gas that replaces the oxygen, after which the purging holes will be sealed. The entire process will take a minimum of thirty days.

The sarcophagi or "mummiforms" (a word also trademarked by Summum) are made by local artists and are available in a choice of styles: Egyptian, Art Deco, Renaissance, or custom-made (which may cost $500,000 or more). They are first modeled in clay from which molds are made. From the molds, they can be cast in bronze, stainless steel, gold, or a metal of the client's choice and inlaid with gems or enameling. The face of the mummiform can also be personalized by casting the client's face or by modeling the mask after a photograph of the client, for instance at an earlier age. The designs on order for customized mummiforms include an Oscar statue, a three-piece business suit, various military uniforms, a graduation cap and gown, and a wedding dress. Temu's mummiform will be custom-made: "It's going to be very plain, very smooth, very modern looking; almost a capsule, but with a slightly defined body and my face..." (Stone 1990, 9).

The mummiforms may be displayed alone or with others in a walk-in mausoleum available from the Georgia Marble Company: "These buildings may be utilized for mummiform caskets by modifying the design and not including any interior applications," explains cemetery products manager James M. Wilson (letter to the author, 11 May 1995). The mausoleum may also house the prized possessions of the clients, although most admit that they are not sure whether they will be able to use them in the afterlife. Legally, the mummified bodies are considered the property of next-of-kin, and there must be a final disposition in a cemetery. Eventually, Ra plans to build a mausoleum in Utah's Manti-Lasalle Mountains to house the mummies he has created in their own vaults. Clients will be able to purchase a private granite sepulchre (3' × 10' starting at $10,000) or a family room (10' square starting at $25,000), each equipped with a six-inch-thick glass viewing window. Summum is convinced that the services they offer (and those they plan to offer) represent a heightening of our cultural standards. "Mummification is such a profound and exact science, its re-emergence may very well change the course of humankind" ("Mummification: A Philosophical Examination," Summum Web site).

The cost of becoming a "museum-quality corpse" (Rivenburg 1993) is at least $33,000: $7,700 to $10,000 for the services and $26,000 or more for the sarcophagus. The cost may be covered by buying a universal life insurance policy. The method is said to be scientifically sound. After reviewing it, pathologist Michael Zimmerman of Philadelphia's Hahnemann University declared that a corpse preserved by Summum "should last indefinitely" (Rivenburg 1993). Unlike freeze-drying or taxidermy, in which the moisture in the body is removed, Summum preserves the membranes and cells in the body by saturating them with chemicals. The mummified body will not decay, but the question of whether it will last forever is not important to Ra. He points out that at some time in the future the sun will "go nova" and the planet will be destroyed.

Summum's page on the Web claims that statements in the Holy Bible about the preparation of Jesus Christ's body with spices and linen proves that he was mummified, although embalming historian Edward C. Johnson disputes this and notes that spices were used to mask the odor of decomposition. "It [mummification] was practiced by people who at the time appeared to be at a height in their personal development," says Summum. They liken mummification to a caterpillar wrapping itself in a cocoon: "We can do the same as a caterpillar, except on a grander scale.... A chrysalis of time—your time—for all time." They use the example of out-of-body experiences to suggest that the body remains aware and capable of feelings after death but is disoriented: "Your sense of time and space has changed.... You have mental abilities but are unclear how to deal with the current conditions. You look for anything familiar that will help reduce your fears and the body you just left is the most familiar thing to you."

Ra's beliefs are a mix of ancient Egyptian philosophy, New Age thought, and extraterrestrial influence he says he has received through visions. In his view the mummified body can serve as a familiar reference point for the disembodied spirit after death, as it was for the ancient Egyptians, making it more comfortable and therefore enhancing the odds of an auspicious reincarnation (Weiss 1992, 30). He believes that even after death, an ethereal bond exists between the body and the soul and that mummification can effect a directed change and prevent "postmortem panic." Ron Temu agrees: "I'd like to keep my body intact for as long as possible.... It might help me if I have a few more days to hang out after I die rather than being stuffed into the ground or into a fire. It's like hedging your bets" (Bowen-Jones 1993, 48). Ra, who plans to be mummified by his own technique, suggests that, unlike the ancient Egyptians, today's mummies seem to be motivated by vanity: "When you're buried in a cemetery, you're covered with dirt and forgotten. With mummification, you're remembered" (Rivenburg 1993). His wife says in an interview in *Hardtimes*, "Actually, for those who have the consciousness to take their bodies to the ultimate, it is only fitting that they preserve them permanently for time and all eternity. After all, the Egyptians may have been right. You can take it with you." Mummification, she concludes, offers eternal memorialization.

Client Kay Henry, age 48 [in 1997], a former radio talk-show host living in Salt Lake City, says of her mummification, "I figure it's going to cost me $50,000, but it's worth it. It's going to be fabulous" (Klinger 1991, 12–13). Client Lydia Campuzano of Santa Ana, California, age 35 [in 1997], a neonatal nurse, has already had her parrot mummified and at age 29 had a life mask made for her mummiform. She says, "Future generations can go in and visit you and see what you were like.... It's the burial of kings" (Rivenburg 1993). She hopes that many people will visit her body in the sepulchre. Campuzano decided as a child that "it would be too traumatic to see my body being buried and dirt being thrown on top of me, or to watch my body go up in flames. I'd like to see something more beautiful, like being soaked in nice wines and chemicals, and being wrapped with tender loving care" (Bowen-Jones 1993, 48).

Client Julie Garvin of Stanton, California, notes that important world leaders such as the Dalai Lamas have had themselves mummified. She says, "If it's true as some Christians say that on Judgment Day Christ will call us up from the grave, then I want to be in the best shape I can" (Johnson 1988). Client Janet Greco, 44 [in 1997], a nurse from Kearns, Utah, concurs: "I work out and eat right and take care of myself, and to just discard the body seems silly" (Weiss 1992, 30). She is also convinced that the soul remains with the body for a time after death: "I believe that when someone is dead their spirit is aware of what's going on. I'm always very careful about what I say and do around my patients when they've just died" (Bowen-Jones 1993, 50). Greco would like to have her mummiform installed in Ra's proposed mausoleum. Client Sue Parsons, age 46 [in 1997], a music teacher at the University of Utah, also intends her mummiform to be placed in a mausoleum. "I don't think my sons would like to have me in the living-room," she says.

Client Bernie Beichert, age 39 [in 1997], explains, "I don't like the thought of me rotting away in the grave" (Johnson 1988). Journalist Rick Weiss (1992, 30) counters, "...in this recycling-conscious age, many may bristle at the idea of hanging around in the environment indefinitely like some glorified lump of Styrofoam." But Bei-chert was no more attracted to incineration than he was to burial: "...I never liked the idea about being buried in the ground. I also did not like the idea of being cremated. The idea of mummification appeals to me." Bei-chert goes on to say that he, too, believes that the spirit remains in the vicinity of the body after death and that how the body is handled after death has an impact on the spirit. He clarifies, "I have chosen mummification not so much for the preser-vation of the body, but for the effect pre-serving the body has on the spirit of the de-ceased. I see death as a transition in my existence, and my being mummified will en-able that transition to be more of a directed, guided change—and in the end, I will arrive at a destination that will be more instru-mental to my continued growth and evolu-tion, which otherwise would not be possi-ble" (letter to the author, 5 July 1995).

Beichert plans to have his custom mum-miform placed temporarily in a cemetery mausoleum until Summum's mausoleum is completed. "I have no objection to allowing access to my mummiform by all visitors," he writes, "however, I do plan on making arrangements that at some time after my death (this could be a few years or many years), my mummiform will be off limits al-together." In the event that his corpse is dis-membered or not wholly recoverable, Bei-chert will be cremated and the proceeds of the life insurance policy he has taken out to fund his mummification will be donated to Summum (letter to the author, 5 July 1995).

Advocates of mummification find it more practical, dependable, and cost-effec-tive than cryonic preservation. "The only way to stick around even half as long [as mummification] is to get frozen.... Of course, the problem with cryopreservation is you have to worry about thawing out," says Ron Temu (Weiss 1992, 31). On the other hand, those who are mummified have no chance of future revival, as Temu makes clear: "We can preserve the body's genetic message so people may someday have them-selves cloned, but we have to make it clear that this isn't like cryonics; people aren't going to be reanimated. This is simply an option for people who don't want to allow their bodies to fall into corruption after death" (Stone 1990, 10). Beichert views cry-onic preservation as an attempt to cheat death that is driven by a fear of death. "I do not hope to reanimate my body," he says. "When I am done with this one, it is on to a better one" (letter to the author, 5 July 1995).

But after years of Hollywood films fea-turing mummies as monsters, traditionalists are skeptical that Summum's services will catch on. Gregory Jewell of Service Corpo-ration International, America's largest owner of funeral homes, told the *Wall Street Jour-nal* (Johnson 1988), "I think most practical people would find mummification repul-sive.... I hope no member of my family would consider it." Howard Raether, former executive director of the National Funeral Directors Association, agrees: "To be diplo-matic, I'd have to say this is not an especially popular option.... What I've seen so far is that it is on the extreme end as far as osten-tatiousness and cost are concerned" (Weiss 1992, 30).

Ra is not deterred by criticism. Nor is he concerned about future archaeologists ex-cavating the mummies he has created. He says in *Cremation Chronicles* (1991, vol. 1, no. 1: 15), "That's a matter for the people who live a thousand years from now to work out. I do think mummification would be fan-tastic for genealogists because they could see *exactly* what your great-great-great-grandfather actually looked like." If the mummiforms are dismantled, the wrappings painstakingly removed, and the remains found intact, the mummies will evidence what great shape their bodies were in: "I'm not excited about the idea of decomposing," says Ra. "I spend a lot of time keeping my body in great shape. I do aerobics, lift weights and I'm proud of it…. Grace is five-foot-four and 134 pounds with just 6 percent body fat…. She wants that body to stay" (Klinger 1991, 14). Beichert explains that he is not bothered (and is in fact fascinated) by the idea of future scientists examining or even cloning his body and that such possibilities have no bearing on his decision to be mummified (letter to the author, 5 July 1995).

Ra points out the misconception that people who are embalmed by traditional methods are permanently preserved: "…that isn't true. You spend lots of money for a casket, and then you decompose" (Stone 1990, 8). Beichert explains, "I do know enough about modern embalming techniques to consider them just a method to slow down deterioration in order to allow for viewing and funeral services which [are] intended more for the living rather than the dead" (letter to the author, 5 July 1995). Humor columnist Dave Barry (1988) writes, "Mr. Ra expects the concept to really take off as the public becomes more aware of the benefits that a deceased consumer can derive from being a mummy, as opposed to a regular civilian corpse. One benefit, of course, is appearance…. The idea is that with conventional embalming methods, even a really youthful-looking corpse, even the Joan Collins of conventionally embalmed corpses, is going to look pretty unattractive after just a short time in the coffin environment."

If mummification does become popular, Summum will consider developing a special training program and offering franchises to funeral homes, though they concede that the services they offer may not easily grab a foothold in the funeral industry. Ra

hopes that mummification will capture a portion of the market like cremation did twenty years ago. He explains in *Cremation Chronicles* (1991, vol. 1, no. 1: 15): "Mummification may not have the same call as cremation—it's not as economical. But the wonderful thing about mummification is the pre-need involvement. The design of your mummiform tells your personal story." Beichert's father at first objected to his plans to become a mummy, and most of his family and friends see it as a bit unusual, but they have accepted it as his decision if not their own: "None of my friends or family have decided on mummification, but I would say there is a possibility that could change" (letter to the author, 5 July 1995). If, on the other hand, Summum goes out of business, the wishes of its clients must, under current U.S. law, be carried out by another company (Bowen-Jones 1993, 48).

Russian-Style Embalming

With the possibly imminent burial of Vladimir Lenin, his embalming team may soon be out of work: "…in the wake of the disintegration of the Soviet Union, and word that Lenin has been condemned to mortal earth burial (next to his mother), the embalmers have lost their only customers and are looking for new ones" (Cronin 1994). The embalming specialists at the Scientific Research Institute for Biological Structures (also called the Research Center of Biostructures) number a reported 150, earn about $30 per month, and were forbidden to talk about their work until a few years ago. The team has embalmed many foreign Communist leaders, including Klement Gottwald (d. 1953) of Czechoslovakia, Georgi Dimitrov (d. 1949) of Bulgaria, Agostinho Neto (d. 1979) of Angola, and (for a price of $1,000,000) North Korea's Kim Il Sung. They now hope to sell their services to wealthy foreigners, since the institute is no longer subsidized by the Russian government. "We're not dealing with every request," explains Yuri Romakov, deputy head of the institute, "We only do embalmings that require high qualifications" (*Washington Post*, November 28, 1993).

The Scientific Research Institute is well equipped, with embalming and research facilities, rooms to simulate any climatic conditions, and a museum containing approximately 100 anonymous embalmed bodies stored as control specimens. The first of the control corpses was embalmed in the 1940s by the same method used on the body of Vladimir Lenin, and they serve as experimental subjects in the search for new methods and solutions. According to Romakov, the scientists plan to offer their exclusive service in the United States for $250,000 to $350,000 and up to $1,000,000 depending on the level of continued maintenance (*Mortuary Management*, Oct. 1995). The *Washington Post* (November 28, 1993) reports that the institute has entered into an agreement with a Western-style funeral home called Ritual Services, headed by Alexander Kruglyak, to provide preparation of the corpse including its specialty: long-term embalming. The same article quotes Romakov as saying, "We provide a full guarantee of the quality of our work. Our experience of embalming, especially for long periods, is unique."

Provided the chemicals meet U.S. health and sanitary laws, the process would take six months and the body would be maintained with visits from institute specialists every couple of years. According to Romakov, "There is no one as qualified or as experienced as this institute. It has unique personnel trained for seventy years of Soviet power and has accumulated the world's leading experience in this field" (Cronin 1994). Without details of the secret process, Gail Johnson, embalming historian, is not convinced of its validity. Jacquelyn Taylor, president of the San Francisco College of Mortuary Science, remains unconvinced that the idea will appeal to Americans. "...I've gotten questions about mummification, but I think it's more a matter of curiosity," she says. "And I'm not sure they could promote it successfully. The general public doesn't even know what embalming is anyway, and I just don't think there are that many people that rich and vain" (Cronin 1994).

In Russia, however, one doesn't need to be rich to afford services by the Center, and there is plenty of vanity among the friends and relatives of the thousands of gang members who are killed each year. Whereas the families often spend $5,000 on malachite gravestones with lifesize full-length etched portraits, up to $20,000 on customized caskets, and hundreds of thousands on the funeral itself, embalming by the institute runs them a comparatively minimal $1,500, provided it does not take more than a day (The *New York Times Magazine*, April 13, 1997). The price goes up when the lethal gunshot has caused damage to the face, which may take up to a week to restore, but the institute prides itself on its reputation for the restoration of severely damaged bodies.

INNOVATIONS

Modern mummies may be encased in glass blocks or metal capsules. The former method may be patented, but the latter is actually practiced. With the help of liquid nitrogen, bodies are preserved indefinitely in large canisters known as dewars. Rather than being monuments to memory, the frozen corpses embody the hope that thawed, repaired, and revived, they will live again. For this reason, those in cryonic suspension are akin to the mummies of Egypt, who hoped to reinhabit their bodies. But many scientists believe they are as deluded as their ancient counterparts. The cryobiologists put their hopes not in the revival of the human body, but the *potential* human body—not the corpse, but the embryo.

Cryonic Preservation

The idea of freezing the human body in the hope that death and the condition that caused it may be reversible at some future time is attributed to Robert Ettinger, age 78

The wrapped body of an Alcor client being hoisted in preparation for lowering into a dewar for cryonic suspension in liquid nitrogen. Photo courtesy of the Alcor Life Extension Foundation.

[in 1997], although the term "cryonics" was coined by Karl Werner. Ettinger read about French experiments to preserve frog sperm in 1947 and conceived the idea of applying such concepts to the human body. He thought others would come up with the same idea, but by 1960 no one had. After a few unsuccessful attempts to generate interest, Ettinger wrote up his proposal and had it privately printed. Doubleday published a revised edition entitled *The Prospect of Immortality* in 1964. In arenas where the book was not completely ignored, it was considered controversial (Harrington 1969, 218–21). Within the cryonics movement, which it spawned, it is considered a classic.

Robert Ettinger founded the Cryonics Institute and the Michigan Cryonics Society and made plans for his own suspension. The First Annual Cryonics Conference, which addressed the potential difficulty of quickly initiating cryonic procedures after death, was held in New York in March 1968. Ettinger thought cryonics would catch on in the 1960s but now believes that the idea was too revolutionary at the time. Alan Harrington (1969, 217) writes: "To arrest our impending decay in frozen capsules and hold mortal humanity in a suspended state, actually planning for bodily resurrection, can hardly avoid being a revolutionary concept. Yet it sometimes appears to be a limited sort of revolution." Despite a slow start, cryonics has grown, although it cannot be considered popular. Today, there are five cryonics organizations in the U.S. One of the largest, the Alcor Life Extension Foundation, has 360 members, 30 of whom were in suspension as of October 1996. In all, less than 100 cryonic suspensions have been performed, and some 600 people worldwide have made arrangements to be cryonically preserved.

Dr. James H. Bedford has the distinction of being the first human in the world to be put under cryonic suspension of his own free will under controlled conditions. Dr. Bedford, a retired psychology professor at Glendale City College, became interested in cryonics, donated $200,000 to establish the first cryonics laboratory in Los Angeles, and volunteered to be the first to undergo cryonic suspension. He was aware that the chances of his reanimation were not good, despite estimates that his body could be preserved for several hundred million years, and wanted his suspension to be conducted with privacy and dignity.

To carry out Dr. Bedford's wishes, members of the Los Angeles Cryonics Society (LACS) were on hand when he died in a small convalescent home in Glendale, California, on January 12, 1967. His death at age 73 was due to lung cancer. Bedford was pronounced dead shortly after 6:30 P.M. by his personal physician Dr. B. Renault Able, who was also interested in the possibility of cryonics. Dr. Able connected Bedford's body to a heart-lung machine and flooded it with nutrients and oxygen to keep the brain from degenerating. He injected Bedford's body with heparin to prevent the blood from clotting. With LACS member Dr. Dante Brunol, Able intravenously injected dimethyl sulfoxide (DMSO) to prevent ice crystals from forming in the body tissues. The men packed Bedford's body in dry ice and turned off the heart-lung machine when the body temperature had reached near freezing.

By 2 A.M., the temperature of Bedford's body had been lowered to -100° F (-73° C), equal to that of dry ice. A horizontal cryogenic storage capsule manufactured by Cryocare Equipment Corporation was brought into the room. The stainless steel cylinder was seven feet long and had been constructed with double walls to insulate the body. Bedford's frozen body was wrapped in aluminum foil, enclosed in a sleeping bag, and placed inside the capsule. The inner container was welded shut. "The chamber was filled with liquid nitrogen, a liquified gas with a temperature of about 320 degrees below zero, and within seconds Bedford's tissues had become as brittle as glass" (Kurtzman and Gordon 1976, 109). The space between the inner and outer container was evacuated.

Robert Ettinger learned of Bedford's suspension, flew to Los Angeles, and held a press conference to announce that a person had been cryonically suspended. As soon as reporters discovered Bedford's identity, they besieged his family, physician, and those who had participated in or observed the suspension. The Bedford family began litigation to withdraw the funds Bedford had earmarked for cryobiological research.

Bedford's body was stored at the Cryonics Society of California (CSC). The vacuum between the inner and outer containers was maintained over the years with a pump. The liquid nitrogen, which would have boiled off completely in seven months, was refilled at intervals of three months. In 1971 Bedford's body was transferred to a new horizontal capsule manufactured by Galiso of Fullerton, California. When the facilities of the CSC were investigated in 1980, it was found that the nitrogen in the capsule had been depleted. The body was successfully transferred to the Alcor Life Extension Foundation then based in Riverside, California.

By 1991 Bedford's capsule was found to take up too much floor space, and the vacuum insulation was difficult to maintain. The capsule was retired after a record twenty-one years, and Bedford's body was transferred to a new dewar on May 25. The old capsule was cut open at one end. Bedford's body was cut loose from the stretcher on which he lay, lifted out in its wrappings, and placed in a large, open foam box filled with liquid nitrogen. The body was wrapped in an additional sleeping bag and strapped inside an aluminum pod that had been assembled around the nitrogen bath. The pod was riveted shut and hoisted by overhead crane into a nine-foot upright, cylindrical dewar (called a "Bigfoot") designed to hold four bodies.

The dewar containing Bedford's body was moved with the rest of Alcor's twenty-seven clients when the facility relocated to Phoenix, Arizona. The dewar was lifted from the top using chains and loaded by forklift onto a trailer with three others (with the neuropatient vaults and the forklift itself on a second trailer). Everything was strapped down, chained in place, and covered with tarpaulins. The dewars were hauled the 350 miles to Phoenix and put into place in the new facility with the forklift.

Like James Bedford, many cryonics adherents are well educated. A disproportionate number of cryonics clients have math, physics, or computer backgrounds. Most of them are atheists or agnostics, but a few are religious. The majority of them are male. But the expense of cryonic preservation may be prohibitive to those who do subscribe to its concepts. The Cryonics Institute preserves only whole bodies at a cost of $28,000. Other organizations charge upwards of $100,000. This fee is reduced by half if only the head is preserved. "Neuropreservation" requires the assumption that future scientists will not only be able to re-

vive and repair the body but will have the technology to grow new ones for those that need them. Nearly two thirds of Alcor's clients opt for neuropreservation. Most clients fund the procedure they have chosen by taking out a life insurance policy that benefits the cryonics firm. Once the financial arrangements are made, the way is paved for another modern mummy.

James Bedford was the first of the several dozen bodies (or heads) to be frozen over the next thirty years. Some of the cases are discussed in the cryonics literature, often using pseudonyms. In September 1968 the body of a twenty-four-year-old student who died of complications following surgery was preserved by the Cryonics Society of New York. In January 1969 the body of Ann Deblasio was also put in suspension by the Cryonics Society of New York. In February 1985 the head of a woman from Madison, Wisconsin, who died of lymphoma was preserved by Alcor. In June 1987 Alcor preserved the head of a twenty-nine-year-old rock musician who had died of AIDS. In December 1988 the body of Richard "Dick" Clair was suspended by Alcor. In June 1990 Alcor suspended the body of Arlene Chamberlain of Sonoma, California, who died of cancer at age 68. In August 1992 Jim Glennie of Fort Collins, Colorado, who had died of a brain tumor, was suspended by Alcor. In April 1993 the head of a man who died of AIDS and lymphoma was also preserved by Alcor. In February 1994 the body of Jerome "Jerry" B. White, who had died at age 55, was suspended by Biopreservation for the American Cryonics Society, of which he was a founding member. In April/May 1994 a ninety-one-year-old woman from New York was preserved by Alcor. In January 1995 the head of Paul Genteman, age 47, a computer programmer and former director of Alcor who died after surgery for Crohn's disease, was preserved by Alcor. And in June 1995 the body of Anatol Epstein, age 66, a history professor from New York, was placed in suspension by Alcor.

In November 1995 the cryonic suspension of the body of Stanislas Penska was performed by the Alcor Life Extension Foundation and featured on the television program "Immortality on Ice," which aired on the Discovery Channel in October of the following year. Penska died on November 26 in upstate New York. He was ninety-nine. Penska had arranged for full-body preservation and purchased a large freezer, which he stocked with bags of ice to facilitate the immediate cooling of his body after death. Within eleven hours of his death, the ice was used to pack around his corpse in a casket and his body was transferred to a local mortuary. There his blood was drained and his circulatory system was flushed with an organ preservation liquid made by Dupont. Twenty hours after his death, Penska was flown to Phoenix for perfusion. An Alcor ambulance transported him to the cryonics facility.

Thirty-two hours after death, Penska was prepped for surgery. His chest was opened and he was attached to a heart-lung bypass machine. Cryoprotectants were perfused throughout his circulatory system until the level of glycerol reached 5 percent. Several holes were drilled in his head for the insertion of temperature probes to measure the cooling of the brain. The holes were left open for five days. During the perfusion, a blockage occurred in an artery, but the pressure was lowered and the problem resolved itself. After 32 quarts of cryoprotectant were pumped in, Penska's chest was closed. Stan was wrapped in plastic bags with wires connected to his brain. He was placed in a vat of liquid silicone with bottles filled with sand as ballast. With the addition of dry ice, the temperature of the silicone was gradually lowered from -17° F (-27° C) to -108° F (-78° C) over three days. He was then wrapped in a sleeping bag hosed with liquid nitrogen and marked with his number "A1478." The bag was used to prevent his body from chipping and protect it from temperature variation within the tank. He was sealed in a metal body pod and placed in a holding tank for five days. The temperature of the liquid nitrogen is -320° F (-196° C) and will preserve the body for centuries. Two weeks after

death Penska's frozen body was finally placed in a permanent dewar that already held five heads and three bodies.

Not all cryonic suspensions go according to plan or as smoothly as Stanislas Penska's did. In September 1967 Marie Phelps Sweet (Mrs. Russ LeCroix Van Norden), age 74, was stored in a mortuary at 30° F (-1° C) for two to three days after her unexpected and unattended death in a Santa Monica Hotel until she could be frozen by the Cryonics Society of California (Harrington 1969, 222–23). Of the eleven whole-body suspensions and nineteen neuropreservations that have been performed by the Alcor Life Extension Foundation, seven of the clients died without warning. Ideally, preservation requires immediate postmortem intervention. When an elderly German woman made arrangements with the Cryonics Institute to be preserved, the institute made advance plans with London funeral director F. A. Albin to have the body transported on ice in a specially designed stainless steel chamber.

But even when technical difficulties are foreseen and prevented, the families of the clients may object to their disposition. Alan Harrington (1969, 225–26) puts their point of view into words: "Without faith, the arrangement seems cold and unsatisfying. To the families left behind, the suspended bodies of their parents may be likely to represent a dead selfishness entombed in an endless future. Families who feel this way will not want to share the faith, or keep it, and the tendency among many will be to obstruct frozen interment." Some relatives have done just that. A woman identified as "Sylvia Graham" arranged with Alcor for full-body suspension, but the paperwork was completed by Mrs. Graham's husband after she became too ill. When Mrs. Graham died in 1990, her sister brought suit to have a Christian burial arranged and the case went to trial. The court found that Mrs. Graham could not have given informed consent for the procedure and revoked her husband's right to donate her body to Alcor for suspension. A court order was issued, and the body was transferred to California for burial.

Cryonics clients face other legal difficulties. Although they are classified as cadavers and placed in suspension through the Uniform Anatomical Gift Act, they are subject to mandatory embalming and/or autopsy. Autopsy damage was one of the reasons that Althea (Mrs. Larry) Flynt was not placed in suspension after her death, despite her full-body contract with Alcor. A crisis of greater magnitude (and a lot of negative publicity) was generated when the fateful decision was made to allow eighty-three-year-old neuropreservation client Dora Kent to "deanimate" (die) at the Alcor facility in Riverside, California, in December 1987. Shortly thereafter, Kent's chest was opened, her body perfused, and her head surgically removed. The unusual circumstances of the death, in the absence of a physician, drew the attention of the county coroner, who launched an investigation. After conducting an autopsy on Kent's headless body, the coroner ruled the death a homicide. He demanded the frozen head for autopsy, and his deputies detained several Alcor employees during their search for it. The employees had removed the dewar containing the head from the premises before it could be confiscated and later succeeded in having a temporary restraining order and a preliminary injunction issued against the destruction or damage of the frozen remains maintained by Alcor. The case, which went all the way to the California Supreme Court, was settled out of court in favor of the Alcor employees.

Despite the inherent physical and legal difficulties, the clientele of cryonics organizations continues to grow. The majority of cryonics clients are still alive and include James Baglivo, age 25 [in 1997], of Hammonton, New Jersey, who was gravely injured, but not completely disabled, in a car accident in 1991 and plans to be preserved by Alcor; Alcor founders Fred R. Chamberlain III (whose father was Alcor's first client in 1976) and Linda Chamberlain (whose mother was suspended by Alcor in June 1990); New Yorker Tom Hazard, who has signed up for suspension with Alcor; Californian Alan Lovejoy, who has chosen Alcor; Paul Segall, a Berkeley physiologist, age 54 [in 1997], who has signed up with Trans Time; Joe Tennant of California, who has made arrangements with Alcor; H. Jackson Zinn, president of the American Cryonics Society, who has arranged for preservation with Trans Time; Brent Schieding of Connecticut, age 20 [in 1997], and Blaine Mulestein, age 14 [in 1997], whose mother works for Alcor, two of Alcor's youngest clients; and Paul Michaels, owner of a Bedfordshire, England, vitamin company, who— along with his wife and son—has arranged for cryonic preservation with the Cryonics Institute.

At the Alcor Life Extension Foundation, the staff leaps into action when a client is known to be near death. A transport team is dispatched, and a transport kit (containing a customized shipping container and a supply of Viaspan, a blood replacement solution used in stabilizing transplant organs) is air-shipped to the client's location. Arrangements are made with a local funeral director for the use of facilities and services. Immediately after death, the body is packed in ice, transport medications are administered, and cardiopulmonary resuscitation without ventilations is performed until the body can be removed to the mortuary. At the mortuary CPR is taken over by a mechanical device, an IV catheter is installed (if it has not been already), and medications are given unless the blood has clotted. While awaiting air transport, a cutdown to the carotid and femoral arteries is performed. The blood is flushed out of the body, and about ten liters of Viaspan (preferably cooled beforehand) is introduced. The patient is packed in the transport container surrounded by ice and insulating material.

The body is flown to Phoenix via commercial airlines or an air ambulance and transported to Alcor's facility in an emergency vehicle. The body is placed on an operating table atop several cooling blankets. The chest and head are shaved. One or more small burr holes in the skull (later sealed with bone wax) are made with a power drill to observe the brain surface for signs of edema and to measure its temperature. The chest is opened with an electrocautery, the exposed ribs are sawn apart, and the pericardium is opened to give access to the heart. A bypass circuit is attached to the aorta and a blood sample taken. The circuit is opened and the blood is pumped out of the body over the next ten minutes, if it has not already been drained. A cryoprotectant glycerol solution is then pumped in over the next three or four hours in gradually increasing concentration.

The perfusion replaces 60 percent or more of the body's water with glycerol and leaves the chest, eyes, cheeks, and nose noticeably bloated. It gives the skin a lurid orange glow. Long wires are connected to internal temperature probes in the skull, throat, and rectum. Two clear plastic bags are unrolled over the body and vacuum sealed. The package is lowered into a whirlpool tub filled with silicone oil cooled by dry ice. A computer-controlled regulator will gradually chill the silicone oil to -110° F (-79° C) over the next day and a half. The body is wrapped in a sleeping bag. The body is then submerged, head down, in a stainless steel tank filled with liquid nitrogen at a temperature of -320° F (-196° C). If neurosuspension is chosen, cephalic isolation (the separation of the head from the body) is performed with a sterilized panel saw at the base of the neck between the sixth and seventh vertebrae. The head is wrapped in a pillowcase and synthetic wool. Each full-body dewar holds four patients, and neuro units can hold ten heads.

The bodies in suspension await a future age and a future knowledge. Their greatest hope is the development of nanotechnology, the theoretical use of molecular surgical tools to repair the damage to the cells. Whereas skeptics ridicule the idea of reversing the pervasive damage caused by freezing, and point out that science has not yet been able to freeze and thaw individual human organs, advocates of cryonics argue that the suspended bodies can wait *indefinitely* for scientific technology to advance. Steve Bridge, the president of the Alcor Life Extension Foundation, points out that his institution is under an obligation to at least try to bring the patients back to life when that becomes a possibility.

Although the objective of cryonic preservation may never be reached, cryonics organizations have developed an extraordinary method of preserving the corpse in its entirety. One thing is certain: successful cryonic preservation ensures that the deceased will never decay as long as the liquid nitrogen is replenished: "Already, numerous bodies have been prepared in this way and stored in lockers at low temperatures. This technique may or may not work, but it will surely supply excellent specimens for research by paleopathologists in the future!" (Cockburn and Cockburn 1980, 8). At its temperature of 320° F below zero (-196° C), molecular motion is extremely slow, and decay is essentially nonexistent. According to an article about cryonics in the *Saturday Evening Post* (Ben-Abraham 1989, 60), degeneration that would take one second at normal temperature would take 30 trillion years.

Cryopreservation of Human Embryos

Although a collection of a few cells may not constitute a "body" in the same sense as the other mummies in this book, the cryogenic preservation of the human embryo bears mentioning in these pages. Thousands of embryos that have been fertilized in vitro or flushed from the womb are being frozen each year for later thawing and implantation. They join the tens of thousands of embryos currently in frozen storage. The first birth resulting from the implantation of a frozen embryo occurred in Australia in 1984. By 1990 the more than 3,000 frozen embryo transfers that had taken place in the U.S. had resulted in more than 300 births (Kimbrell

1993, 89). The success of the technology has led to a number of ethical questions about the future of cryobiologically preserved embryos that, unlike those about the revival of cryonically preserved adults, are not merely theoretical. The questions concern whether the frozen embryos have intrinsic worth as living entities, whether they should be viewed as property, and what should be done with them in the case of death or divorce (Kimbrell 1993, 90). Unlike adults who purchase their own mummification, these potential people are not masters of their own destiny. They have been preserved not after death but before life.

Sealing the Body in Glass

Joseph Karwowski, a Russian laborer residing on 233 Perry Street in Herkimer, New York, applied for a patent for his method of preserving the dead on October 13, 1903. His application included three diagrams but no actual model or specimen. On December 29, his invention was registered by the United States Patent Office as Patent #748,284, a method of preserving a dead body in a sealed transparent block of glass.

Karwowski's intent was to provide a full, clear, and exact description of his technique to allow others to perform it. His invention was a means by which a corpse could be hermetically encased within a block of transparent glass. By excluding the body from the air, it would be maintained for an indefinite period free from decay and in a perfect and lifelike condition. Karwowski describes his method as follows: "In carrying out my process I first surround the corpse with a thick layer of sodium silicate or water-glass. After the corpse has been thus inclosed within the layer of water-glass it is allowed to remain for a short time within a compartment or chamber having a dry heated temperature, which will serve to evaporate the water from this incasing layer, after which molten glass is applied to the desired thickness. This outer layer of glass may be molded into a rectangular form ... or, if preferred,

cylindrical or other forms may be substituted for the rectangular block which I have illustrated." Karwowski also points out that the head alone may be preserved in a transparent block if preferred. The use of glass to enclose the body (or head) allows it to remain entirely visible. In the diagrams illustrating his method, Karwowski shows a deceased man modestly dressed in a suit and tie.

APPLICATIONS

Certain methods of preservation are desired when survivors do not want to relinquish the body of a loved one. Families inquire about taxidermy when they want to keep the body around the house rather than in a mausoleum. To mount the body by conventional means would require applying the preserved skin over a form or mannequin. The tattooed torsos of human beings have in fact been preserved in this way but are in some cases deteriorating. A newer and easier method is to freeze-dry the corpse, an idea being considered in Colorado by one taxidermist and marketed in Arizona by another. Occurring naturally under the right circumstances, freezing and sublimation may be coerced with the right equipment. Less elaborate equipment—simple freezers and refrigerators—may be used instead if the intent is prolonged rather than permanent preservation. And the most simple of tools, fire, may also be used to keep the corpse in the community of the living.

Smoking the Body

In Papua, New Guinea, the natives in remote areas still practice the custom of smoking the bodies of the dead, despite an attempt by missionaries to abolish the practice in the 1960s. The Kukukuku people of the village of Aseki cover the corpses with red ochre to keep away evil spirits. They then put them in bamboo cages atop a fire built in a specially made hut. After one week in the smokehouse, the bodies are pierced to let the fluids

No. 748,284.   Patented December 29, 1903.

UNITED STATES PATENT OFFICE.

JOSEPH KARWOWSKI, OF HERKIMER, NEW YORK.

METHOD OF PRESERVING THE DEAD.

SPECIFICATION forming part of Letters Patent No. 748,284, dated December 29, 1903.

Application filed October 13, 1903. Serial No. 176,922. (No specimens.)

To all whom it may concern:

Be it known that I, JOSEPH KARWOWSKI, a subject of the Czar of Russia, residing at Herkimer, in the county of Herkimer and State of New York, have invented certain new and useful Improvements in Methods of Preserving the Dead; and I do declare the following to be a full, clear, and exact description of the invention, such as will enable others skilled in the art to which it appertains to make and use the same, reference being had to the accompanying drawings, and to the figures of reference marked thereon, which form a part of this specification.

This invention relates to certain new and useful improvements in methods of preserving the dead; and it has for its object the provision of a means whereby a corpse may be hermetically incased within a block of transparent glass, whereby being effectually excluded from the air the corpse will be maintained for an indefinite period in a perfect and life-like condition, so that it will be prevented from decay and will at all times present a life-like appearance.

To this end and to such others as the invention may pertain the same consists in the steps of the process whereby this result is attained, all as more fully hereinafter described, shown in the accompanying drawings, and then specifically defined in the appended claims.

The invention is clearly illustrated in the accompanying drawings, which, with the figures of reference marked thereon, form a part of this specification, and in which—

Figure 1 is a front elevation of the corpse as it appears after the first step has been taken in carrying out my process. Fig. 2 is a perspective view of the completed glass block, showing the corpse incased therein; and Fig. 3 is a like view of the transparent block of glass, the same being shown as incasing a human head.

In carrying out my process I first surround the corpse 1 with a thick layer 2 of sodium silicate or water-glass. After the corpse has been thus inclosed within the layer of water-glass it is allowed to remain for a short time within a compartment or chamber having a dry heated temperature, which will serve to evaporate the water from this incasing layer, after which molten glass is applied to the desired thickness. This outer layer of glass may be molded into a rectangular form 3, as shown in Fig. 2 of the drawings, or, if preferred, cylindrical or other forms may be substituted for the rectangular block which I have illustrated. In Fig. 3 I have shown the head only of the corpse as incased within the transparent block of glass, it being at once evident that the head alone may be preserved in this manner, if preferred.

It will be at once noted that a body preserved in this way may be kept indefinitely, as the body being hermetically inclosed within the outer glass covering it will be impossible for air to reach it, and hence it will be effectually preserved from decay. The glass surrounding the corpse being transparent, the body will be at all times visible.

Having thus described my invention, what I claim as new, and desire to secure by Letters Patent, is—

1. The process of preserving the dead, which consists in first surrounding the corpse with a coating of sodium silicate or water-glass, and then surrounding the same with an outer coating of molten glass, substantially as shown and described.

2. The process of preserving the dead, which consists in first providing a corpse with a surrounding coating of sodium silicate, evaporating the water from the coating so applied, and afterward incasing the same in molten glass, substantially as described and for the purpose specified.

In testimony whereof I hereunto affix my signature in presence of two witnesses.

JOSEPH KARWOWSKI.

Witnesses:
ALEXANDER JAWOVOSKI,
TOZED TOWOVOWSKI.

Above and opposite: **United States Patent for a Method of Preserving the Dead issued to Joseph Karwowski in 1903.**

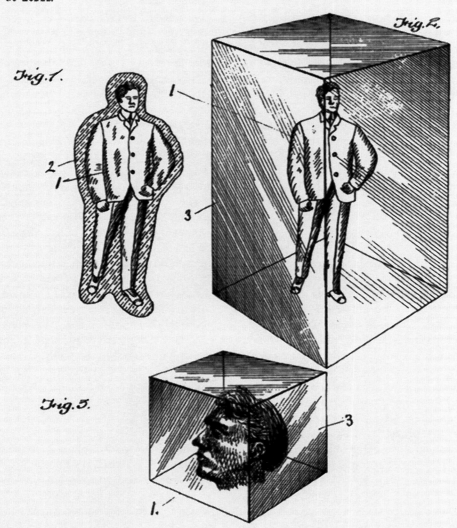

escape. After two weeks, the process is complete. According to the account in *Fortean Times* (no. 94, Jan. 1997) most of the bodies have been preserved in the same poses in which they died. The bodies are placed in a seated position on a trellis that rests on a ledge 3,280 feet up a cliff towering 11,500 feet high. Newer additions join mummies more than 100 years old. Some of the mummies have been washed away by rain and landslides, but those that remain include warriors holding their spears and a woman cradling her baby in her arms. At their post high above the village, these mummified elders are believed to protect the living from evil spirits. The Buang tribes of the north coast of Australia are also said to smoke-dry the bodies of the dead (Cockburn and Cockburn 1980, 195).

Tanning the Skin

Whether as infamous as the stories that surfaced after the Holocaust or as obscure as the occasional news report, instances of the human skin being preserved often cause a sensation. The outer aspect of the body may not constitute the body itself, but human leather in bits and pieces may suggest a semblance of the whole that would be possible through taxidermy. In taxidermy the skin is removed, tanned, and replaced on a mannequin. In the stories below only the first two steps are practiced. Instead of clothing a mannequin, the tanned skin is displayed by the men who harvested it—displayed on themselves.

On July 6, 1995, Associated Press carried the story of a twenty-one-year-old Ukrainian man accused of murder. The newsworthy aspect of the crime was the fact that he crafted a brassiere and shorts out of her skin. According to the news report, he told a court that he did it to calm his nerves. Another man attempted to allay his grief by tanning his wife's skin. Andan Kazir of Dhaka, Bangladesh, was so distraught when his wife died that he had her skinned so that he could wear her pelt as a coat. The news

story, which originally appeared in the *Sunday Express* (March 19, 1995), commented that since the woman weighed 27 stone, there was plenty of skin for the tailor to work with. What the infamous Ed Gein lacked in a single subject, he made up for in volume.

Edward Theodore ("Eddie") Gein lived alone on a small Plainfield, Wisconsin, farm after the deaths of his father (1940), older brother Henry (1944), and mother (1945). Gein read books about the Nazi atrocities of Ilse Koch, cannibalism and head-shrinking in the South Seas, and the bodysnatchers of nineteenth-century England. He was fascinated by a story in the newspapers of a man who had undergone a sex-change operation. And he read and clipped the local obituaries. In 1947 Gein began to satisfy his anatomical curiosity by exhuming and examining or dissecting the corpses of recently deceased women, middle-aged or older, whose deaths he had read about in the paper. After digging he worked the caskets open with a crowbar. In some cases, he took the bodies home. In others he removed the parts he wanted (usually the head and sometimes the vagina) and returned the mutilated body to the grave.

On November 16, 1957, he committed the crime that led to the public exposure of his hobby. Gein shot Bernice Worden, the owner of the Plainfield hardware store, in the head with a .22 rifle and took her body home. He had cut off her head and dressed her body out like a deer by the time Sheriff Arthur Schley and Captain Schoephoerster followed the trail to Gein's farmhouse. Parts of Worden's body were almost destined to join the gruesome handcrafted articles for which Gein became known. He had attached the ends of a wire into each of her ears with a nail in preparation for hanging her head on the wall.

When police searched Gein's house, they found several body parts used for decorations (skulls in whole or part and lips) and others collected in boxes (vulvas, some of which had been sprinkled with salt, and noses), so many that they were unsure of the number of victims. Gein had also made several household items and ornaments (chair seats, a drum, and a knife sheath) from human skin. And he had crafted items to be worn, including several pairs of leggings made from human legs and a vest complete with breasts made from the upper torso of a middle-aged woman. Displayed on the wall or stored in plastic or paper bags—and at times worn—were masks made by peeling the skin of the face and scalp from the heads of nine women. The masks had holes where the eyes had been and the hair was still attached. They had been stuffed with paper or sawdust to facilitate drying. Gein later explained that he had cured the heads that were found in brine. "A few of the masks looked dried out, almost mummified. Others seemed more carefully preserved, as though they had been treated with oil to keep the skin smooth. Some of them still had lipstick on their mouths and looked quite lifelike. For those who knew their faces, it would not have been hard to tell the identities of the victims" (Schechter 1989, 89–90).

Gein's collection was packed in cardboard boxes, transferred to the State Crime Laboratory's Mobile Field Unit, and unloaded at the University of Wisconsin in Madison. The heads and skulls were compared to the dental records of a missing woman, but there was no match. Based on the number of face masks and the "extra noses" found in the house, police estimated that the relics were the remains of fifteen women. Some of the body parts smelled of formaldehyde, which led to speculations that they had either been disinterred from the cemetery or that Gein was an amateur taxidermist. The death mask of one victim, a woman named Mary Hogan who had never been buried, smelled unmistakably of embalming fluid.

Gein's farm and the town of Plainfield were besieged by reporters eager for news about "the mad butcher of Plainfield." Gein was arrested and thirty hours later (during a total of nine hours of interrogation) acknowledged killing Worden but said he had done so in a daze. He also admitted, in the face of overwhelming evidence, that he had killed Mary Hogan, carved up her body in the summer kitchen, and cremated the parts he didn't want to keep in his potbellied stove. He insisted that he hadn't looted a grave since 1954 and had never practiced cannibalism or had sexual intercourse with any of the bodies. During questioning Gein revealed that he wore the skinned faces as masks, securing them to his head with a cord. He donned the mammary vest, wrapped his legs in the crudely stitched skin stockings, and covered his penis with a preserved vulva. "Then, decked out from top to bottom in his corpse costume—a crossdresser who derived his pleasure not from donning women's clothes but from wearing their skin and hair—he would parade about the cobwebbed rooms of his house or, on warmer nights, strut about in the moonlight" (Schechter 1989, 140). He said the ritual gave him great satisfaction.

Gein was charged with murder and armed robbery and sent to the Central State Hospital for the Criminally Insane at Waupun (now the Dodge Correctional Institute) for a thirty-day examination period. He underwent a series of physical and psychological tests and was also given a polygraph test at the State Crime Laboratory. Among other things Gein frequently complained of smelling "bad odors" that he described as "like flesh" (Schechter 1989, 209). He was diagnosed as a schizophrenic personality of the chronic undifferentiated type with several neurotic manifestations. "He admitted to feelings of excitement during the grave robberies and describes periods when he felt he should return the bodies. There were also feelings that the bodies should be preserved and that he should care for them," reads a report on Gein's social history by hospital social worker Kenneth Colwell (Schechter 1989, 212). After examining Gein, the hospital's chief of medical services, Dr. R. Warmington wrote "The motivation is elusive and uncertain but several factors come to mind—hostility, sex, and a desire for a substitute for his mother in the form of a replica or body that could be kept indefinitely. He has spoken of the bodies as being like dolls and a certain comfort was received from their presence, although ambivalent feelings in this regard probably occurred" (Schechter 1989, 217).

Residents of Plainfield refused to believe that Gein had assembled his collection from the town's graveyard, "that the faces, vaginas, and other parts found in the squalor of his farmhouse were the relics of their own closest relations, the mummified scraps of their departed sisters, wives, and mothers" (Schechter 1989, 168). But Gein had admitted to making some forty visits over the years to Plainfield Cemetery, Spiritland Cemetery in nearby Almond, and Hancock Cemetery. Only nine of the visits resulted in disinterments and he returned the bodies in a few instances. To confirm parts of his story, police decided to exhume the remains of Eleanor Adams, who had been buried on August 26, 1951, and Mabel Everson, who had died on April 15, 1951. Both caskets were empty.

At a sanity hearing in early 1958, Gein was found insane and committed indefinitely to the Central State Hospital. His farmhouse was burned to the ground on March 20 of that year, and his farm and personal property were auctioned off ten days later. The contents of Gein's "collection," augmented by another pile of human bones found by workmen on the property in May 1960, were buried in 1962 in a cemetery plot purchased by the state of Wisconsin. Bishop William O'Connor of the Madison Archdiocese had objected to their proposed cremation.

In 1968 it was decided that Gein was competent to stand trial. The case was reopened, but Gein was found not guilty by reason of insanity and recommitted to the Central State Hospital. In 1974 Gein's petition to be released from the facility, claiming that he had fully recovered his mental health, was denied. In 1978 Gein was moved with nine other patients to the Mendota Mental Health Institute in Madison. A year later former patient of the Central State Hos-

pital Pervis Smith bludgeoned eighty-six-year-old Helen Lows to death in Milwaukee, gouged her eyes out, and attempted to peel the skin from her skull. Smith told police he had learned many interesting things about murder, mutilation, and the manufacture of human face masks from his best friend at the hospital, Eddie Gein. In 1984, at age 87, America's most notorious amateur taxidermist died of respiratory failure. He was buried the following night in an unmarked plot in Plainfield Cemetery reported to be next to that of his mother.

Because they are in the unfortunate company of Eddie Gein and Ilse Koch, collectors of human skin keep a low profile. However, not all skins are obtained by murdering their occupants. A little-known museum at Tokyo University, the Medical Pathology Museum, contains human skins collected since 1926 by Dr. Masaichi Fukushi, a doctor of medicine specializing in pathology. Dr. Fukushi had previously worked at a hospital in downtown Tokyo, where many of the patients were tattooed in the old Japanese tradition. In addition to his medical interests, Dr. Fukushi had become intensely interested in the highly developed art form of the Japanese tattoo. He cataloged more than 2,000 designs and collected 3,000 photos. As many of the tattooed people died of illness or old age, Dr. Fukushi performed their autopsies and preserved the tattooed skins as specimens. He devised a method of special treatment to preserve only the dermal layer containing the tattoo, stretched under glass in a frame. He had the full cooperation of the tattooed people, who shared his regret that such painstakingly acquired works of art would otherwise be lost. He even extended financial assistance to those who could not afford to have their extensive tattoo work completed.

Dr. Fukushi's photographs and documentation housed in the university medical buildings were destroyed during air raids in 1945, but the tattoo specimens themselves were stored elsewhere and survived intact. His son Katsunari also became a pathologist (specializing in cancer) and continued Dr. Fukushi's tattoo research. Dr. Katsunari Fukushi has collected twenty specimens, which brings the total in the collection to 105. "People who have willed their tattooed skins to him do so as a donation for the purpose of medical study, much as more familiar donors of eyes, heart, and so forth" (Hardy 1988, 77). The tattooed skins have not been actively collected for some fifty years, and most of them were acquired in the 1920s, 1930s, or early 1940s. Dr. Katsunari Fukushi aims for quality rather than quantity: "Numbers are not important; I have limited this collection only to tattoo masterpieces which cover the entire body, to hand them down to posterity.... I would like to devote myself to finishing the fine specimens of tattooed skin I have preserved and to the medical study of them. I feel this would be an appropriate memorial to all those souls who volunteered their skins to me and a duty on my part for their bereaved families and all who are concerned with the subject of tattoos" (Hardy 1988, 77–78).

The museum is not open to the general public, but the collection may be viewed by special advance appointment and letter of introduction. An example of the art of Japanese tattooing, mounted on a dummy torso, could be seen until recently at the National Museum of Health and Medicine in Washington, D.C., but was removed from display and replaced with a photograph because it is in bad repair. Dr. Katsunari Fukushi is aware of the sensational aspects of the Tokyo collection. When articles about his father's work appeared in *Life* and various men's magazines in the 1940s and 1950s, the photographs were treated with a "freak show" bias and accompanied by copy largely invented by overimaginative writers (Hardy 1988, 77). The collection and the field of study established by the Fukushis are unique, and there is apparently no one to continue their work.

Taxidermy

The word "taxidermy" is from Greek, meaning to order, arrange, or prepare the skin. The specimen to be mounted (a word preferred to "stuffed") is skinned, the hide is cured, a mannequin is prepared, the skin is fitted over the mannequin, and the finishing touches are applied. With some slight modifications, the techniques used to preserve animals could be used to preserve the human body. Although few taxidermists would be willing to ply their trade on their fellow humans even if it were legal, the occasional news report indicates that one or two have already tried and succeeded. Most recently in late 1996, the wife and two children of German taxidermist Erhard Vonner were found perfectly preserved in the basement of his house in Bonn. Although human skin—particularly when it is tattooed—has been tanned for legitimate as well as illegitimate purposes as discussed above, there have apparently been no sanctioned finished mounts of humans in this century. There has, however, been the odd request.

In 1985 English taxidermist Neil Dewhurst of Bridgnorth, Shropshire, received a telephone call from a woman who asked if he undertook human beings. "The enquiry was unbelievable ... but I'm sure the woman meant it. I had to refuse, though, because I thought it might be illegal," said Dewhurst (De'ath 1993, 158–59). The woman explained that her grandfather had passed away and the family had decided to have him "stuffed," standing at attention in the hallway. He had been from a military family and, rather than bury him, they wished to have him preserved in his uniform complete with medals. "At that time ... I thought it was quite macabre," writes Dewhurst, "so I suggested she approach an embalmer, which she thought was a good idea and rang off after thanking me. We did not hear from her again" (letter to the author, 12 February 1996).

In 1992 Dewhurst received a second inquiry. A man called asking the preservation costs of a large ape. Dewhurst needed to know what kind of ape in order to provide an accurate estimate. "However, he was reluctant to actually tell me the species but insisted it was the size of a human, so I thought he was possibly meaning a gorilla. After more discussion on the subject he did finally admit that the query did refer to a human being!" writes Dewhurst (letter to the author, 12 February 1996). After asking more questions, Dewhurst learned that the entire family had agreed to the proposed preservation if it were financially possible and that they had made legal inquiries and been granted permission to have the work carried out in one of two English establishments. The body was that of a man in his late thirties who had been killed in a car accident. "What this documentation consisted of and from where I did not ask but he certainly seemed to have gone into it with great scrutiny," writes Dewhurst. "I am not easily shocked but I could not understand how a family could possibly want to do this." Hoping to discourage them, Dewhurst quoted what he thought was a high price of £5,000–6,000 but was told that this was less than the family had expected to pay! The man promised to call him back but never did, so Dewhurst was spared having to decline the job.

Theoretically, a human body could be mounted using the same principles for mounting large game animals, except that a mannequin—available commercially for most animal specimens—would have to be made by hand. "The actual practice would be very similar to the mounting of various apes throughout the museums of the world," writes Walter E. Johnson of Tinker's Taxidermy in Poolesville, Maryland. Johnson also makes the point that the term "taxidermy" has come to include replicas of specimens using many different media and states that one could even consider wax figures a form of taxidermy (letter to the author, 6 May 1995). Taxidermist John T. Griffith, Jr., of Waldorf, Maryland, contends that human skin is too thin to arrange by conventional methods of taxidermy. He also points out that it would be against the law without a mortician's license (letter to the author, 30 April 1995).

Neil Dewhurst believes it would be possible to preserve the human body by means of taxidermy and that the procedure would resemble that of the domestic pig, which has a transparent skin once removed and dry. "One would have to perfect a flesh coloured form or artificial body on which to fit the preserved skin. Once the skin dried it would be possible to see any deformities underneath," he writes. He suggests the use of a finely modeled wax figure. "However, it certainly would not be a job I would care to undertake," he states (letter to the author, 12 February 1996). Brian Price of Taxidermy Unlimited in Vienna, Virginia, would not welcome such a task either but believes it would be similar to the preparation of a primate.

If a human body were to be prepared by an amateur or professional taxidermist, the skin would first have to be removed from the body. The incisions in the skin would be made where they would be least likely to be seen. If the finished mount were to be displayed seated or standing, the body would be skinned as it lay on its stomach. A vertical incision would be made from the middle of the back of the head all the way down the back. The skin would be peeled away from the body on the neck, shoulders, all the way around the torso if possible, and the buttocks. The skin of the arms and legs should pull off like gloves, although incisions would have to be made at the wrists and ankles to remove the bones, since the hands and feet would not invert.

The head would be skinned out by pulling the skin from the previously made incision over the skull, cutting it away as needed and taking care not to tear it. The flesh of the lips and nostrils would be cut close to the skull and trimmed afterward. The ears would be separated from the skull with a knife and left attached to the skin. Once the skin was completely freed from the body, any excess flesh would be trimmed away from the inside. The lips would be split and opened up, to be folded back into place later. Unlike the ears of large mammals like deer, human ears are too detailed to turn inside out and remove the cartilage. The skin would be spread out with the flesh side up, on a slanted surface in a cool, shady place. A heavy layer of noniodized salt would be applied to draw out the moisture, which should not be allowed to pool on the skin. Any additional fleshing would be carried out after the skin had been salted for at least twelve hours and resalted if necessary. When the skin had finished draining but was not completely dry, it would be rolled up until it was ready to be tanned.

Tanning is a tedious and painstaking process carried out most efficiently by a commercial tannery. To prepare for tanning by hand, the skin would be unrolled, soaked in water, and drained to remove the salt. Soaking would be kept to a minimum; borax and soap would be added to the water to speed up softening, if needed. The skin would be laid over a shaving board or smooth beam, and any hard or thick spots would be shaved off the flesh side using a currier's knife or large butcher knife to bring the skin to a uniform thickness.

The tanning or "pickling" solution would be purchased or mixed by dissolving two pounds of salt and one pound of alum in four gallons of water. The skin would be placed in the solution at room temperature and stirred several times a day. It would be tested when the skin had turned white by cutting a tiny piece from the thickest edge. When the skin had become white all the way through, it would be removed from the solution and rinsed in a mix of one ounce of borax to each gallon of water, followed by a rinse with plain water. Without wringing, the skin would be squeezed out and hung to drain until it is only damp. It would then be laid out on a smooth surface flesh side up and painted with a thin coat of nondetergent laundry soap. After the soap had soaked overnight, a thin coat of warm neat's-foot or tanning oil would be applied to the flesh side by hand or with a cloth or sponge. Afterward, the skin would be rolled up flesh side in and left overnight or until the skin had

shrunk and begun to darken but had not completely dried.

To finish the skin, if prepared by hand, it would need to be stretched in order to soften it. To do so, it would be pulled back and forth over the shaving board, over the top of an upright post, or through a metal ring suspended from the ceiling or wall. This would be carried on steadily and vigorously in all directions in a shoeshine motion, with more oil being applied with a sponge during periodic breaks. Finishing, which could take many hours, would be complete when the skin had become completely dry and soft. If the skin were too oily, it would be given a mild detergent bath and dried by working in sawdust or cornmeal and then shaking it out. If a commercial tannery were used, the tanned skin would be rehydrated, drained, and "sweated" (left in a sealed bag) to soften it.

The mannequin on which the skin would be mounted could be made by making a mold in which the mannequin or form would be cast or by building up a form out of other materials. In both cases measurements from the skinned body would be taken and sketches of it would be made before it is dismantled or discarded. A mold could be prepared most easily in one of two ways:

(1) The skeleton could be used to create an armature on which the form would first be modeled in clay and then molded in fiberglass. The flesh would be cut off the bones and the skeleton would be roughly cleaned, soaking or boiling if necessary but not long enough to make the joints come apart. Using strong wire or iron rods tied to the bones, the skeleton would be posed in the desired position. The torso and legs would be partially filled in with wire netting and covered with strips of burlap dipped in fiberglass. Then, according to the previously made measurements and sketches, the body would be modeled with clay by building up the bulk of the form and then adding detail. When the right proportions had been reached, the surface would be smoothed with a paintbrush dipped in water.

The model would then be partitioned into four or more sections by forming walls between each section with inch-wide strips of metal or clay pressed into the clay model.

Fiber glass would be applied to each section in turn. When one section had hardened, the partition between it and the next would be removed, notches cut in it so it could be properly lined up later, a coat of shellac and then a coat of stearin applied to the edge so the wet fiberglass in the adjacent section would not stick to it. The mold would be left on the model for several hours, and then the sections would be carefully pried apart and removed. The film of clay inside would be washed off and any air bubbles filled in. The mold would be assembled, tied together, and allowed to dry completely. After several days the inside surface of the mold would be given one or more coats of shellac.

(2) A mold could be made directly from the carcass of the specimen if it had been carefully skinned. The viscera would be removed through an incision in the trunk wall and any blood or fluids wiped from the body cavity, which would then be filled with excelsior and sewn closed. The body would be posed using wires run up through the flesh where possible and wooden supports where necessary. All fleshy areas could be injected with a formaldehyde solution to harden them, or sunken areas could be injected with water and the entire carcass frozen. The eyeballs would be removed and the eyesockets filled with clay but left in a concave shape. The lips and nostrils would be arranged with clay as desired. The walls to partition the mold into sections would be made by attaching strips of corrugated cardboard to the body with wire and coating the cardboard with shellac. The walls of each section and the carcass itself would be painted with stearin before applying fiberglass as described above.

To prepare the mold for use, a release coat of stearin would be applied to the inside surface. The mannequin or form could then be cast most easily by mixing urethane foam, pouring it inside, and allowing it to harden. The form would then be roughed up for better adhesion of the skin, and detail, especially in the hands and face, would be cut in. To make an excelsior form—which would not require making a mold—the skull and the bones of the legs and arms would be first be cleaned and treated with borax. They would then be assembled with wire and rods and attached with staples or U-bolts to a center board made from wood cut to the appropri-

ate size and shape. When the framework had been set up in the desired position, the bulk of the body would be built up with wire netting and covered with a layer of fiberglass and burlap. The body would then be modeled by winding excelsior and string around it. A final thin coat of papier-mâché would be added if additional detail were desired.

After the mannikin was prepared, glass eyes would have to be obtained from a prosthetic supplier or custom-made by a taxidermy supply house and would be positioned with clay. The skin would be soaked in warm borax water until it was relaxed. It would be squeezed out, drained, and trimmed around the eyes, nose, and lips if necessary. The skin would be slipped over the mannikin and arranged loosely in place. A commercially available adhesive would be applied to the torso of the model, and, without stretching the skin too much, it would be pulled into the proper position on the body of the mannikin. The ears would be anchored to the head of the mannikin with clay. Adhesive would be applied to each leg, the skin pulled into place, and any incisions sewn closed with small stitches. Adhesive would also be applied to each arm, the skin pulled into place, and incisions sewn closed. The finger and toe hollows in the skin could be filled out as needed with clay before the incisions were sewn. More adhesive would be applied before the skin was brought up around the neck, the face, and over the head.

The main incision would be pulled together and sewn beginning at the head. Pliers could be used if the skin did not come together easily and any excess skin at the union of the legs and body could be stuffed into a slot cut into the form for this purpose. A slot would also be cut in which to tuck the skin of the mouth when the lips are turned back inside. The body would be inspected for any air bubbles, which would be pierced with an awl or hypodermic needle and the air forced out. Excess skin could be formed into a series of small wrinkles rather than one large fold. Pins could be used to keep any hollow spots in place until the adhesive set up. Any adhesive would be washed off the skin and out of the hair before it dries.

The mount would then be clothed if desired. The hair would be combed, and the mouth and eyes would be modeled with a blunt instrument to make them look natural. Straight pins could be used temporarily to hold the shape of the mouth and eyes. The mount would be allowed to dry completely, and any pins would be removed. Creases around the eyes would be filled in with epoxy, and any excess clay on the skin or around the eyes would be scraped away. Live models and photographs of the deceased would be important for reference. The natural color of the face, and particularly the lips, would be restored with water-based or lacquer paints. The specimen would then be ready for display.

Freeze-Drying

A less labor-intensive method of preserving the human body would be freeze-drying, or lyophilization, that would convert all liquid to gas and remove it by vacuum. Freeze-drying was first used to preserve diseased human organs for pathologists and is now used by taxidermists, particularly when the animal to be preserved is small, highly detailed, or difficult to mount by traditional methods. Freeze-drying would not require skinning the corpse, although the entrails could be removed and the body cavity packed. The skeleton would be left in place for support and it would not be necessary to remove the brain.

The body would be posed and wired into position if necessary. A filler would be injected to restore muscle that has dried and shrunk. The prepared figure would be placed in a commercially manufactured freeze-drying chamber. It would be removed from the chamber periodically and weighed. When the weight had stabilized, which in the case of a human body may take many months, the process would be complete. Taxidermist Archie Phillips of Fairfield, Alabama, estimates that, depending on the size of the freeze-drying machine, a human body could be prepared in approximately six months (Phillips 1981). According to Brian Price of Taxidermy Unlimited, a freeze-drying equipment salesman he spoke to at a trade show claimed to have received an inquiry from serial killer Jeffrey Dahmer. "If he got hold of one, he'd probably still be in business," says Price (telephone conversation with author, 1 May 1995).

In fact, there is a man who would like to extend his business to the legitimate preservation of the body by means of freeze-drying. Bill Huffman of World Fauna Museum, a wholesale taxidermy establishment in Aguilar, Colorado, would like to practice his craft on humans, but has almost given up on the idea because of the lack of a body on which to work. He states that the technology exists and says that his firm would gladly crate the body and transport it to his laboratory to be prepared. The story became a sensation after he was interviewed by a Detroit, Michigan, paper. When asked if he would be willing to preserve a human body, he admitted that he had "considered the idea strongly" (telephone conversation with the author, 15 October 1996).

After it had been embalmed by a licensed funeral director, the body would be freeze-dried in its entirety, as is done with primates and other animals. The body would first be frozen to a temperature between 0° and -10° F (-18° to -23° C) in his twenty-five-cubic-foot freezer. It would then be placed in a freeze-dry chamber that would remove approximately 90 percent of the body's frozen moisture, including that in the bones, by means of vacuum pumps. The moisture would be pulled into another chamber maintained at -65° F (-54° C) and defrosted every couple of days. The freeze-dry process would take a year or more. There is one complication. Because Huffman's largest freeze-dry machine is only five feet six inches long, the body of a six-foot individual would have to be bisected at the knees. The legs would be reattached after freeze-drying was complete. Huffman said he does not consider this desecration but merely what needs to be done to reach the objective. Any evidence of the amputation would be covered by clothing or by the lower half of the casket. After freeze-drying was accomplished, the body would be placed in a cradle-type tank and submerged in a chemical bath for about six months. The bath would have two purposes. First, it would chemically remove the oil that remains in the body with a solvent, since fat tissues cannot be freeze-dried. Huffman explains that even a ⅛" layer of fat would leach out through the skin and ruin the specimen within months by making it look "like it has had oil poured over it" (telephone conversation with author, 15 October 1996). Second, the bath would include a pesticide preparation (the exact makeup of which needs enhancement according to Huffman) that would permeate the body to prevent insect damage. Huffman assures that the bath would not introduce any moisture back into the body.

After the bath the body would be dressed and released to next of kin. Huffman claims that the freeze-drying would cause little or no shrinkage. The skin may lose some color, but cosmetics could be used just as they are in traditional funeralization. Huffman points out that at the funeral home silicone is injected into the cheeks and other areas to fill them out and that regularly embalmed bodies are prone to shrivel when dry.

Huffman believes that the whole idea, if it catches on, would be a money-maker. Setup costs for the procedure would run $100,000 to $200,000, including special tanks for the chemical bath, but he already owns four freeze-dry machines worth $28,000 apiece. Another expense is electricity, which currently runs Huffman $500 per month. His charge to clients would be a minimum of $10,000 and possibly as much as $40,000 to $50,000.

Huffman also notes that such treatment is legal in many states but assumes that he would receive regular visits by the health inspector. In Colorado, there are no legal restrictions once the body is embalmed. In California, on the other hand, his proposed procedure would be illegal. Even where legal, it could be dangerous, as reported in *Mortuary Management* (March 1996). Huffman admits, "There is the possibility of the ongoing presence of microorganisms.... When the organs are removed, one would have to follow the same precautions as a pathologist would follow. There is a danger of HIV, hepatitis B or tuberculosis. Those organisms could survive the death of the body." The body itself would survive indefinitely. Huffman says, "Properly cared for— by which I mean you don't leave it out in the rain or allow the dog to chew on it, it should last for years" (*Mortuary Management*).

Huffman says that because we are used to seeing the dead in caskets, he would likely present the bodies lying down but would consider positioning them seated or in a favorite pose. He feels that to put the body in a rocking chair, for instance, would not be proper. In his opinion allowing the body to repose in a glass-topped casket inside a crypt would be more respectable. By freeze-drying the deceased, the family would be able to have Grandpa around for generations. "A lot of people will find the idea disturbing," admits Huffman, who has been considering it for several years. "I believe a number of people would like the opportunity to devote a room upstairs to the remains of someone they cared about, perhaps a young child who died, where they could visit it occasionally."

As far as Huffman is aware, no one has preserved an entire adult body by his intended method. He has, however, had to retain a patent attorney to counter claims of infringement by professors at Michigan State University who freeze-dry individual organs. Other than the legal obstacles, there still remains the problem of a body on which to practice his craft. Huffman would have to obtain either the body of a volunteer or a cadaver from a medical school and admits that it would bother him to prepare the body of a child or a person he knew. Huffman has been asked by a magazine published in Paris to write an article about his proposed method

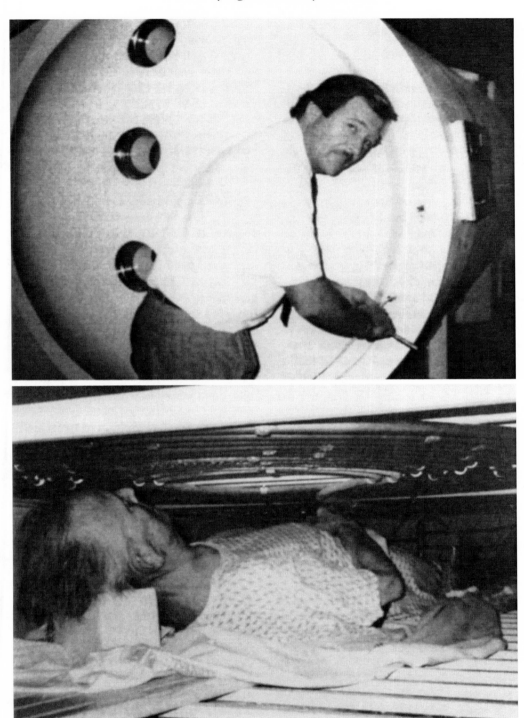

Top: **Harold Pavett sealing shut the master chamber of his Lyo-Tech-Plus freeze-dry preservation system. Photo courtesy of Harold Pavett.** *Bottom:* **the body of Lambert Hultz in the freeze-dry chamber. Photo courtesy of Harold Pavett.**

of human preservation. The editor of the magazine has suggested that the publicity would result in someone willing to ship him a body for preparation.

According to the *Weekly World News*, the preservation of an infant has been successfully accomplished by freeze-drying. In June 1989 the newspaper, known for its sensationalism, reported that parents Karl and Kaitie Hilding of Malmo, Sweden, had the body of their ten-month-old infant son, Christer, freeze-dried. "Some people think we are morbid or sick but I'd rather have my baby at home than six feet under the ground," Kaitie told reporters. She also stated that she picks the body up and hugs it occasionally. The child died hours after drinking household ammonia. The boy's father was quoted as saying, "He was our first child and we just couldn't bring ourselves to give him up.... I was thinking about alternatives to burying him and recalled that a lot of people have dead pets freeze-dried so they can keep them at home. I talked things over with my wife and she agreed that freeze-drying was the way to go." The couple obtained special permission from the Swedish authorities and had the procedure carried out by taxidermist Stig Torekull. The child was freeze-dried in an upright position and now stands in a corner of the Hilding living room near the television where he liked to play. "As far as I know this freeze-dried baby is a first," remarked Torekull. Christer's body is expected to remain lifelike for eighty to 100 years.

More recently, in 1992, taxidermist Harold J. Pavett founded a corporation to preserve the human body using an advanced form of lyophilization that he has trademarked Lyo-Tech-Plus. Preservation Technologists Corporation (PTC) is based in Fountain Hills, Arizona, and has in fact processed its first client. In 1969 Mr. Pavett had learned about the freeze-drying success of researcher Dr. Harold Merrymann and its modification and improvement by Rolland Hower, an exhibit specialist at the Smithsonian Institution. That same year Pavett vis-

ited the Smithsonian and studied their findings in order to design a unit for taxidermists. Pavett redesigned the specimen and condenser chambers in 1970 and was soon called upon by the Chicago Academy of Sciences to assist in building a state of the art freeze-dryer. Within two years Pavett, director of the academy Dr. William Beecher, and curator George Iannarone had completed their task, and other museums nationwide followed suit.

Mortuary Management (April 1997) reports that Pavett's decision to found his own corporation was "inspired by the concerns of people who expressed displeasure in knowing what would happen to their body once they had died. These concerns, coupled with preservation expertise acquired over a lifetime, led to the design of an entirely new system specifically tailored to humans." In little more than a year, Pavett has constructed a chamber measuring 176 cubic feet that is able to accommodate up to eight people. To use the system a body is frozen in position and placed in the refrigerated master chamber. The chamber is sealed, and the atmospheric pressure is removed by means of a vacuum pump. The cold trap is reduced to a temperature significantly less than the master chamber, causing the ice crystals in the body to sublimate. The vapor is drawn to the cold trap and condenses back to ice crystals, a process that does not physically change the appearance of the body.

A man named Lambert Hultz became Pavett's first client. Hultz had learned of PTC's preservation process prior to his death and contracted with Messinger Mortuaries for funeral services and to serve as a medium through which PTC would perform its preservation service. "Being a man of vision," reports *Mortuary Management* (April 1997), "he knew the process would help mankind, as adding an alternative to the present disposition of human remains." On the day of Mr. Hultz's death PTC initiated its process to preserve his body for viewing by his friends and family, as well as by future generations.

The Preservation Technologists Corporation brochure claims that they have broken the barrier in mortuary science, allowing permanent preservation of the body in its entirety. They offer their services to "the person who wants more than what a mortuary offers." To be preserved by Preservation Technologists Corporation, special arrangements must be made. Funeral services may be held at a local mortuary, but if the body is to be embalmed, only Champion H-A-R Cavity Fluid with Entrone should be used, since other embalming fluids will result in oxidation of the preservation equipment (*Mortuary Management*, April 1997). After services, the body is shipped to Messinger Mortuary, in which the paperwork is handled and from which the body is retrieved by PTC. The Lyo-Tech-Plus™ preservation process takes place over the next six to nine months, depending on the weight of the deceased. The length of time required also affects the price of the service, which ranges from $25,000 to $35,000. When all the moisture has been removed from the body, it is shipped back to the original mortuary, which would dress and cosmetize the body and handle its final disposition. A sealed, glass-topped casket may be purchased to allow for practical viewing at that time and easy access once installed in a mausoleum.

Refrigeration and Freezing

Easier than freeze-drying the body is simply freezing it, and not with dry ice and liquid nitrogen but by conventional means. For long-term storage, freezing is desirable. For storage of a few months' duration, refrigeration will, with a few precautions, work just as well. The average funeral home does not have the facilities to refrigerate or freeze the dead. There is, though, an increasing tendency to acquire refrigerators to provide for cases where there is delay in the decision to embalm. Refrigerators with a one-, two-, or three-body capacity are the most common, but walk-in refrigerators are also available.

The Jewett Refrigerator Company of Buffalo, New York, offers a variety of morgue refrigerators to accommodate as many as nine bodies. In addition to the models in stock, they will customize walk-in models to virtually any shape or size. The units have stainless steel exteriors, fiberglass-reinforced polyester resin interiors, and polystyrene insulation. They are furnished with removable stainless-steel trays accessible from the end of most units or from the side of the smaller models. The machines are air-cooled with a self-contained or remote compressor as needed. The refrigerators may be built-in or installed free-standing and may be modified to serve as freezers.

Unlike American morgue refrigerators that store the body out of sight, the refrigeration units in Europe are often equipped with windows through which the deceased remains on view. Unembalmed remains are often maintained in electrically powered refrigerated horizontal containers with clear glass or transparent plastic lids. The container is kept at an angle so that the blood will settle in dependent areas rather than remain visible in the margins of the neck and ears. In Germany, under similar circumstances, remains are displayed in refrigerated rooms and are visible through a viewing window when the lid is removed from the casket. Hygeco, a company in France that specializes in "thanatopraxy," or preservation care, offers cold chambers and in late 1996 was contracted to supply 1,000 to Saudi Arabia, where bodies are sometimes stored for more than a year. The French magazine *L'Express* (October 31, 1996) reported that Hygeco has also designed a large inflatable refrigerated tent that will accommodate forty bodies on stretchers. The tent, which can be erected in an hour, is intended to provide a place for the victims of accidents or disasters to be collected, examined, and identified.

Refrigerated bodies are usually maintained at a temperature of about 38° to 40° F (3° to 4° C). The condition of a body after storage depends on how long it has been refrigerated and how well it has been

Casket with a removable cover in a refrigerated viewing chamber at the municipal mortuary in Frankfurt-am-Main, Germany. Photo courtesy of the Edward C. Johnson Family Collection.

protected. If it is not wrapped or clothed, the body will dehydrate more rapidly than it would at room temperature due to the condensation and circulation of air in the refrigerator. Even if it is wrapped in a cloth sheet, the entire surface of the body will dehydrate. When plastic sheeting or a plastic zippered pouch is used, the body will not dehydrate but instead will be covered with a large amount of moisture condensation (Mayer 1996, 94). In general, bodies kept under refrigeration display marked desicca-

tion of the lips, eyes, nostrils, and fingertips. The lips become thin and dry, the nose becomes pinched, and the eyelids darken and wrinkle (Strub 1989, 388, 408).

After several hours in a cooler the body becomes cold and rigid as tissues constrict and body fats solidify. The cycle of rigor mortis may be slowed. Tissues in deeper areas of the body will become waterlogged with the plasma from the blood. Refrigeration keeps the blood in a fluid state, so it and the tissue fluids slowly gravitate to the dependent tissues while the upper areas of the body lose moisture through gravitation and surface evaporation (Mayer 1996, 371). Within six to twelve hours the dependent tissues may turn a variety of dark hues from red to blue-black. Elevating the head and shoulders of refrigerated bodies will prevent this intense discoloration in the tissues of the neck and face (Mayer 1996, 361). Another form of discoloration, the characteristic green patch of putrefaction often seen in the abdomen, may also be present because decomposition will continue even inside the refrigerator until the body's internal temperature drops enough to inhibit bacterial growth. The plastic that wards off dehydration will also trap heat in the body, allowing autolysis and bacterial activity to continue until the body is thoroughly cooled (Mayer 1996, 338–39).

Refrigerated subjects are often referred to as "frozen bodies," but it is unusual for unintended freezing to occur. Freezing a body deliberately will render it free of decomposition indefinitely (or as long as the power source is uninterrupted) but will test the skills of the embalmer afterward. Bodies that have been frozen present all the problems of refrigerated cases, but to a more extensive degree. Like the refrigerated body, the frozen body is subject to dehydration, especially in thin areas like the fingers and nose. Exposed or dehydrated areas may desiccate and become brown and shriveled. (If allowed to continue, the dehydration would eventually result in mummification.) The body tissues become firm and rigid, a condition that mimics rigor mortis. Joints will crack if bent, due to the fracture of their frozen contents (Strub 1989, 89). The expansion of tissue liquids and the formation of ice crystals will cause damage to the tissues, which will be more pronounced if the body has frozen slowly (Strub 1989, 358, 409).

Freezing is sometimes used by the embalmer as "insurance" in difficult cases. Dry ice may be used by the embalmer to cover a body that has decomposed. It is then wrapped in a heavy blanket or quilt before being placed in the casket. Within an hour or so, the outer shell of the body will be so thoroughly frozen that the odor will be entirely destroyed and all leakage halted. The casket can then be taken into the church or mortuary for the service (Strub 1989, 282). But perhaps the most common reason for cold storage of the corpse is a delay in burial. Across the northern United States (including Michigan, Montana, Maine, New York, North Dakota), the burial of people who have died during the winter or in the early spring is often delayed until the ground has thawed in April or early May. The bodies are stored at the funeral home or the cemetery. Special attention to the eyelids and nostrils and the use of fungicides are necessary, since the bodies are often viewed by the family prior to burial.

Refrigeration and freezing may both pose difficulties for the embalmer: "Refrigeration can never serve as an acceptable substitute for early embalming. Every hour which elapses between death and embalming will result in problems and complications and reduce the possibility of completely successful results. In those cases where a delay cannot be avoided, refrigeration is advantageous. However, even at a low temperature the body will undergo certain objectionable changes which make it desirable to reduce the delay to an absolute minimum" (Strub 1989, 389). When a cold body is exposed to warm air, some airborne moisture will condense on the cold body surface and this will continue until the temperature of the body reaches that of the surrounding air. However, embalming of refrigerated cases should be started before the body warms. Frozen bodies must be thawed to some extent—using cold water and massage—to permit arrangement of the features and distribution of the fluid, but they should be manipulated as little as possible to avoid additional tissue damage.

Bodies that have been frozen or refrigerated require stronger-than-average embalming solution. Arterial injection should be slow and may be prepared with warm or hot fluid. When the body has been frozen, there will be little or no blood drainage. An instant-tissue-fixation method should be used to achieve preservation of the face if there is threat of distension (Mayer 1996, 341). Circulation problems are common with bodies that have been refrigerated: "Delays increase the chances of distension during arterial injection and also increase the preservative demand of the tissues" (Mayer 1996, 189, 305). In addition, bodies can be expected to firm more slowly after refrigeration, and the effects of the cold may mimic the effects of the embalming. The solidification of subcutaneous fatty tissues may cause them to feel firm to the touch and may falsely signal to the embalmer that a reaction has occurred between the preservative solution and the body proteins (Mayer 1996, 362). The postmortem staining caused by the rupture of blood cells as the body cooled cannot be removed by arterial injection or blood drainage. Bleaching may lighten the stain but will not remove it, and it must be covered with opaque cosmetics (Mayer 1996, 339). The benefits of cooling or freezing the body when necessary outweigh the negative effects, which may be successfully overcome.

Storage of the body has been a factor in a few high-profile cases. The body of oilman and philanthropist J. Paul Getty (d. 1976) was refrigerated for nearly three years while his family awaited permission to bury him on the property of the museum he founded. After singer Kate Smith's death in June 1986, her body remained in a cold-storage vault for more than a year. Smith had asked to be buried in the Catholic St. Agnes Cemetery in Lake Placid, New York. She requested in her will that part of the $300,000 she bequeathed to St. Agnes Church be used to construct a pink- or rose-colored granite mausoleum to house her remains. The church, which had a policy against aboveground burial sites, offered to erect a modest sarcophagus-type structure three feet ten inches high. One of the executors of the es-

tate challenged that this would not constitute a mausoleum, and Smith's sister, Helena Steene, insisted that the tomb had to be a walk-in and proposed a height of eleven feet. Smith's body remained in cold storage until the family and the church compromised at a height of six feet eight inches and a cost of $63,400. Smith was entombed in the newly built and blessed mausoleum in November 1987.

When the diminutive Lena de Nobili died in 1975 at age 92, her devoted son Joseph de Nobili, a doctor, spent the next fifteen years developing and improving upon a liquid solution to prevent the bacterial growth that causes bodies to decay. He hoped to preserve his "sweet little mother," as he called her, in a stainless-steel casket with a quartz glass window that he could open to view her. Her refrigerated body was transferred from Holy Cross Cemetery to the Utter McKinley Mortuaries in Los Angeles in July 1976, and Joseph embarked on his quest to preserve the earthly remains of the "Countess Lena de Nobili," as she is known in the mortuary records. Two to four times per month, Joseph used the preparation room and personnel of the mortuary to perform arterial injections, hypodermic treatments, chemical baths, massages with vitamin cream, and gauze wraps. Balance due to the mortuary at the end of this period totaled nearly $7,000. The mortuary kindly did not charge for 300 days of continuous refrigeration of the remains or for the special white dress in which she was reclothed.

In August 1977, probably due to the unpaid balance on Joseph's account, his privileges at the mortuary were temporarily suspended. During the more than two-month hiatus, he found that his mother's left arm had dehydrated, but by injection and the application of preservative cream he was able to restore the limb and reverse the general deterioration and discoloration of the body that had occurred. Plans for the resumption of weekly treatments included the replacement of the brain in Lena's skull and the immersion of her nude body in miraculous waters Joseph claimed to have obtained from "the religious authorities of Lourdes, France." The immersion in the holy waters was to take place in the mortuary chapel or at "a sacred place designated by the ecclesiastical authorities" after the body had been washed and given an alcohol bath.

After additional treatments, the body of Lena de Nobili was immersed in her son's preservative fluid inside a conventional casket that had been re-outfitted to serve as a tank. The casket was then hermetically sealed and locked and re-entombed in a mausoleum in Holy Cross Cemetery, but Lena did not rest in peace. In 1990, while Joseph was having surgery in Italy, workers at the Harbor Lawn-Mount Olive Mortuary in Costa Mesa, California, unplugged the refrigerator in which his mother was then stored and shipped Lena's unrefrigerated body to San Diego for burial, explaining that they had not received the $500 monthly storage fee since 1984. Joseph retrieved the body and found that it was undamaged because it had remained bathed with his solution. Nevertheless, he filed a breach of contract lawsuit against the mortuary for allowing the frozen body to thaw before he could find a way to preserve it (Kohut 1993, 5–6).

The body of Ferdinand Marcos, ex-president of the Philippines, was also placed in cold storage but under very different circumstances. When Marcos died in exile in Hawaii on September 28, 1989, the new president Corazon Aquino would not allow Marcos' widow, Imelda, to bury his body in the Philippines, despite public demonstrations outside the palace. Imelda stubbornly vowed not to bury him until she could bring his body home. She had the body entombed at Valley of the Temple Memorial Park in Kaneohe, Hawaii. The refrigerated mausoleum had a spectacular view, a deck and patio, and a twenty-four-hour guard. Tapes of Marcos's speeches and songs were repeatedly played. Imelda kept the body of her husband in cold storage for four years and reportedly wheeled it out for parties annually on his birthday. Imelda blamed the restlessness of

her husband's spirit for numerous natural disasters, including Hurricane Andrew, and urged that she be allowed to "put the remains of the president to rest so that these negative vibrations will leave us" (Kohut 1993, 49).

In 1993 Marcos' body was finally allowed back into the Philippines. A funeral held in his hometown of Batac was attended by more than 40,000 people. The body of the former president was enshrined in a glass casket inside a marble and granite sarcophagus, illuminated by a spotlight and an eternal flame. *Asiaweek* (vol. 19, no. 38: Sept. 22, 1993) reports, "Thanks to the embalmer's art, the late strongman, who was wasted by disease in later life, looks twenty years younger. Indeed, his features give off such an eerie, life-like sheen that a few visitors thought he had returned to life." After another four years, however, the fate of Marcos' remains was again in question. On March 4, 1997, the *Chicago Sun Times* reported that electricity had been cut off to the tomb, an act that Imelda Marcos called "harassment of the dead." In February the electric co-op in the province of Ilocos Norte had shut off power to the refrigerated crypt. But on March 7, the electricity was restored by order of the mayor upon payment of a portion of the $215,000 owed on the account.

In Ghana, bodies are stored not to await permission for burial but to allow the family time to afford it. The Ashanti people save for as long as three years after the death of a family member to pay for a lavish funeral. Dr. K. A. Boiteng, who has been the chief medical examiner of Kumasi for more than thirteen years, stores the bodies awaiting burial in his mortuary. They were once stored in two large coolers installed by the British in 1958. Now they are stored in a big freezer that has a backup generator in case of a power failure. Greg Palmer writes (1993, 165), "On our tour of his facility, he opened his freezer door, and there must have been fifteen people in there, solid as rocks."

The families call Dr. Boiteng a week or so in advance of when they will be ready to hold the funeral so that the body can be defrosted: "In this climate, it takes about three days," explains Dr. Boiteng (Palmer 1993, 165). The funerals traditionally last three days, so the mortuary is busiest on Friday mornings. Recently thawed bodies are carried by the staff, who wear rubber boots and blue smocks. Other bodies lie on the floor of the hallway in caskets or wrapped in white sheets. The family in its entirety and in full funeral regalia gather outside the back door, at which a police officer is posted, to take possession of the body as soon as the paperwork is completed.

6. Accidents of Nature

Adventurers, Explorers, and a Spelunker

What sets apart the mummies in this section is that their mummification was accidental. Although they risked their fate, they did not plan or pay for it. Freezing was compliments of Mother Nature, not provided by Alcor. But not all of the victims were subject to simple freezing. The exposure to the elements caused some bodies to form adipocere and others to desiccate. The forces that individuals braved during their struggle to the top of the mountain or the center of the continent were the same forces that caused—but did not ensure—their preservation. Cold temperatures don't guarantee survival of a body if it is exposed to sunlight. Being surrounded by ice does not mean the body will emerge intact: a glacier may in fact tear it up. The bodies that have been recovered are therefore doubly remarkable for having been preserved and for having been found.

ADVENTURERS

What goes up doesn't necessarily come down. The bodies of those who die ascending or descending a peak are often unrecoverable. Although the young men who tackled Mt. Cleveland were searched for and discovered months later, the bodies of unfortunate alpinists may not emerge for years or even decades, if at all. Some of these climbers take on a local challenge. Others travel halfway around the world to conquer a famous mountain. Some are amateurs, others have guided climbing tours for years. Neither familiarity nor experience completely protect an adventurer from the possibility of dying in the effort and, once dead, from being subjected to the forces of nature—forces that have the potential to hold them captive for millennia. Although their goals are personal rather than patriotic, the adventurers are to be admired for their daring. When their preserved bodies *are* found, they serve as testaments to the determination of individuals who have literally died in their tracks.

Glacier Bodies

Edda Ambach of the University of Innsbruck calls the discovery of a corpse immersed in glacier ice many years after an accident a "rare event" (Ambach 1991, 1469). But it does occur. In the summer of 1991, six bodies were found on four glaciers in Tyrol, Austria, the large number being ascribed mainly to heavy ice melt (extensive deposition of Sahara sand in the spring of 1991 intensified the absorption of solar radiation and led to increased melting). Dr. Ambach has examined eleven corpses found on Tyrolean glaciers from 1952 to 1991. The bodies had been immersed between eight and fifty years.

Dr. Ambach has described in detail the various paths such bodies take. Corpses are

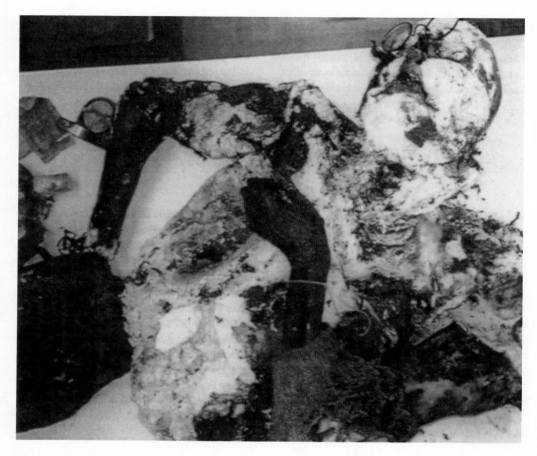

The body of a sixty-two-year-male alpinist recovered from a glacier in the Alps in 1991, fifty-seven years after his accidental death. His preservation resulted from a combination of desiccation and the formation of adipocere. Reprinted by permission of James Bereuter from *Human Mummies*, edited by K. Spindler, et al. (New York: Springer-Verlag, 1996).

transported along a flow line beneath the surface of the glacier and emerge on the surface after reaching the ablation area. If a body is buried in the accumulation area of the glacier where the annual snow accumulation exceeds the annual snow melt, the body will be transported vertically into deeper layers of ice toward the interior of the glacier. The body will pass through the glacier along its flow lines in the deep layers and will surface in the lowest part of the ablation area. If the body is buried in the ablation area where the annual snow and ice melt exceeds accumulation, the body will be directed upwards and will be deposited on the surface. If the body is deposited on the surface of the ablation area, it will remain on the surface and be transported downhill. At the equilibrium line (the intermediate zone where snow melt equals accumulation), flow lines run parallel to the surface, and velocity is highest. Immersion times of up to several hundred years are possible. Immersion times of more than one thousand years are only possible with corpses buried in stagnant or dead ice areas.

Bodies sometimes emerge from the ice partially clothed. Although this may be a result of their movement through the glacier, Dr. Ambach (1993, 1285) points out that paradoxical undressing because of a sudden feeling of warmth is consistent with death by hypothermia. The bodies recovered from glaciers are also often deformed or dismembered by stresses acting in the ice. It is these strong tensile stresses that are responsible for the formation of the crevasses into which hikers sometimes fall. Once it enters the glacial environment, a body may not emerge intact. "As a body can be dismembered by tensile stresses, and because the ice melt varies year by year, parts of the same body may be found at the same site on a glacier but in different years, with several decades passing between the individual discoveries" (Ambach et al. 1992, 376). The stresses are especially high in the accumulation area, where the body may be dismembered by mechanical stress. In the ablation area, the body may be deformed by compressive stresses.

The bodies are subject not only to external processes but internal ones. Inside the glacier soft tissues and organs are generally converted into adipocere, a process that begins when a body is buried in a humid milieu under hermetic seal. Adipocere formation normally takes from three to six months but has been observed in as little as six weeks. If, on the other hand, the body remains on the surface for several weeks and is exposed to dry air and wind, mummification will occur. Low humidity and glacier wind favor mummification, which causes the soft tissues to shrink and the skin to become hard, brown, and leathery. The process takes from a few weeks to several months.

Burial beneath the snow does not preclude mummification. Dehydration may continue when the frozen body is embedded in snow, since snow is porous and permeable to air. When a body is covered with snow after the onset of mummification, further evaporation from the frozen body is still possible. Dr. Ambach estimates that as much as 12 kilograms (26.5 pounds) of the 40 kilograms (88.2 pounds) of water in a frozen body can evaporate beneath snow cover in a winter. If the body is partially snow-covered, the exposed areas will mummify and the buried areas will be converted to adipocere. "Mummification, adipocere and other changes can occur simultaneously in different parts of the body" (Ambach et al. 1992, 376). The processes are not mutually exclusive and often occur in combination.

According to Louis Reynaud of the Laboratoire de glaciologie et géophysique de l'environnement, the majority of alpine glaciers are at the melting point, so there is no deep freezing. Even within these temperate glaciers, however, mummification is rapid. Bodies discovered between three and twenty years after death are similar in appearance. Adipose tissues seem to have been dissolved by the small amount (2 percent by volume) of very pure and acidic water trapped in between the ice crystals. In general only skin, muscles, and bones remain (letter to the author, April 1996). The excellent preservative effect of mummification is illustrated by an interesting anecdote: when the 5,000-year-old "iceman" was discovered in 1992 in the Austrian-Italian Alps, a woman from Zurich tentatively identified the body as that of her father, who went hiking in the area in the 1970s and was never found (Kohut 1993, 200). The bodies that are found answer questions about natural preservation. They also resolve long-standing questions about the fates of the victims, since the site and scene of an accident can be reconstructed by glaciological facts when the time since death is known.

In August 1923 a twenty-eight-year-old woman fell into a crevasse while hiking with two men across the Madatschferner, a glacier 1.1 kilometer (.7 mile) long and as much as .6 km (.4 mile) wide in the Kaunergrat Range of the Oetztal Alps, Tyrol. All three climbers were reported missing. The bodies of the men have never been found, but the woman's body was discovered intact on August 14, 1952. It was found several hundred meters from the site of the accident at the very end of the glacier on the ice-free terrain but not at the terminus of the glacier. She had been immersed in glacier ice for twenty-nine years and had moved with the ice from the ablation area at something less than 25 meters per year. Identification was made by the documents she was carrying and the clothing she was wearing. Her scalp, cheeks, lip area, and chin formed a homogeneous mass of adipocere, with other formations at the neck, breasts, abdominal wall, genitals, and extremities. Her autopsy revealed a shrunken brain, collapsed pulmonary lobes, and a heart and liver that had converted to adipocere. Intestines were partially desiccated and partially saponified. Severe bone fractures of the extremities suggested the woman had fallen into a crevasse. Hypothermia or a pulmonary fat embolism was suggested as the cause of her death.

On August 8, 1934, mountaineers Henna Schlager and Josef Schneider from Vienna were reported missing in the Stubai Alps. Their bodies were found in the middle of the Sulztalferner glacier fifty-seven years later on August 29, 1991, and were identified by personal documents they carried. The site and circumstances of the accident are unknown, but examination of the bodies revealed no bone fractures. The soft portions of the sixty-two-year-old male's head, torso, upper extremities, and internal organs had been transformed into adipocere. The forearms and hands seemed dry-mummified and the skin tight and brown like leather. Samples of the desiccated tissue were taken from the chin and samples of the adipocere were taken from the upper arm for testing. In addition to allowing a profile of the natural lipids, the chin sample indicated that the alpinist had worn sun protection cream (Bereuter et al. 1996, 270).

On September 3, 1953, the body of a thirty-seven-year-old Englishman was found frozen and dismembered by the ice east of the St. Poltener Hutte at the base of Prägrat Kees, a glacier in the Granatspitz Range, Hohe Tauern, in east Tyrol. His identity was assumed by a missing person report dated September 3, 1936—exactly seventeen years earlier—and the accident was reconstructed as a fall into a crevasse. Soft tissue partially mummified and partially transformed into adipocere. The condition of a body found a year earlier on August 8, 1952, is not recorded in the forensic literature. The body of Carlo Capsoni, who died August 25, 1941, was found in the glacier ice on the Hochjoch near the Schone Aussicht refuge. His remains were buried at the cemetery of Unserfrau im Schnalstal.

On May 2, 1953, two alpinists died while participating in a training course for mountain guides. During an exercise that involved crossing an icefall, a hidden snow- or ice-bridge gave way, and a climber from each of two ropes fell down a crevasse at an altitude of 3000 meters and was buried under snow and ice. Due to the danger of more snow and ice breaking off, the victims could not be recovered. The bodies of Odo Strolz, age 28, and Otto Linher, age 31, were found by Horst Frankhauser on August 7, 1991, about 1000 meters from the scene of the accident on the Alpeinerferner glacier in the Stubai Alps. They had been immersed in the ice for thirty-eight years and flowed with it at a rate of 25 meters per year.

In 1965 a mountaineer was seen leaving the common path in an area of crevasses to take some photographs. The climber fell down a crevasse of more than 40 meters in the ablation area of the Gurglerferner, a glacier 6.5 km (4 mi.) long and up to 3 km (nearly 2 mi.) wide in the Oetztal Alps, Tyrol. He could not be rescued because of the structure and exceptional depth of the crevasse. The body was discovered exposed on the glacier surface in the ablation area in 1973 at a distance of 150 meters from the scene of the accident. The corpse had been immersed in glacier ice for eight years, moving with the ice at a rate of approximately 20 meters per year. The man was identified by his clothing and personal objects, including engraved initials. The remains were strongly putrefied and partly mummified. The medical examiner diagnosed severe injuries of the chest and abdomen.

A married couple fell 260 meters down a rock face while climbing on August 25, 1965, when a snow cornice away from the common path collapsed after a fall in temperature. Their bodies came to rest in the accumulation area of the Mitterkarferner, a glacier 2.1 km (1.3 mi.) long and up to 1.2 km (.75 mi.) wide in the Oetztal Alps, Tyrol. On September 21, 1990, their bodies were recovered close to the equilibrium line, one 150 and the other 180 meters from the foot of the rock wall. The uppermost casualty was found immersed in glacier ice, and the lower body was exposed at the surface with the back frozen to a glacier table approximately half a meter high. The immersing component of the glacier's flow lines and a mean flow velocity of less than six meters per year suggested that the bodies should not have been exposed until a much later date. It was due to heavy snow melt between 1984 and 1990 that the casualties were discovered before having passed through the glacier to the ablation area, since the shrinking of the glacier surface had been greater than the immersion rate. The bodies were identified by documents in their knapsacks and found to have been reported missing twenty-five years earlier. The meteorological conditions on the day of the accident and the route taken by the climbers were reconstructed. An examination of one corpse showed severe skull fractures and injuries of the upper cervical spine as the cause of death. The other had died from severe injuries of the chest and multiple bone fractures with pulmonary fat embolism.

On March 5, 1981, mountain guide Dr. Kurt Jeschke fell through a snow bridge into a crevasse 30 meters deep. The accident occurred before he had roped up to lead a guided tour in the Bergglasferner in the Stubai Alps. He was buried under masses of snow between two smooth ice walls 25 centimeters (10 inches) wide. The danger of the crevasse and unfavorable weather prevented recovery of the body. Ten years later, on August 24, 1991, Dr. Jeschke's body was found in the ice, having been carried an average of 35 meters per year down the steep glacier. The corpse had eventually been released by the glacier 350 meters away from the site of the accident.

In Austria responsibility for the recovery of bodies found in glaciers rests with the police and air rescue service. Special helicopter rigs have been used to transport the bodies, which are sometimes freed from the ice with the use of pneumatic hammers. In the absence of suspected crime—and provided the body can be identified—a death certificate indicating the cause of death is made out by the district medical officer. The body is then released to next-of-kin, who must meet costs of recovery. If foul play is suspected or the body cannot be identified, the case is handled by the public prosecutor, and a forensic and criminal examination is ordered (Spindler 1994, 17).

The Mt. Cleveland Tragedy

Like the Austrian authorities, park rangers in mountainous areas of the United States are familiar with tragedies that result in frozen bodies that may or may not be recovered. A number of climbing accidents have occurred in Wrangell-St. Elias National Park in Glennallen, Alaska, over the years, and several of the bodies have never been found. A climber was killed by an icefall in the early 1980s in the Chugash Range, and two climbers were lost on Blackburn later in the same decade. A man was buried by an icefall in the mid–1990s on Mt. Bernard. In 1996 a Mexican man was caught in an avalanche, and his body could not be located during a helicopter search. Park ranger Jay Wells thinks it unlikely that the body will be recovered, since the man was lost in the accumulation zone and is now under approximately twenty to thirty feet of snow (telephone conversation with author, 16 August 1996). In her book *Disappearance: A Map*, Sheila Nickerson poetically documents dozens of disappearances in Alaska.

Chief Park Ranger Stephen J. Frye of Glacier National Park in Montana states that in most cases, the recovery of accident victims is completed within a very short time. There was an incident, however, where the bodies of five climbers were not recovered for six months. He calls the incident "one of the most remarkable and challenging body recovery operations in Glacier National Park's history" (letter to author, 19 July 1996). The story began ominously when five young men notified District Ranger Robert Frauson on December 26, 1969, that they intended to climb the north face of Mt. Cleveland, the highest peak in Glacier National Park, with an elevation of 10,448 feet. Frauson attempted to dissuade them, citing the severe unpredictable winter conditions, avalanche hazards, and the time required to obtain help if needed. The men—James Anderson, age 18, of Big Fork; Jerry Kanzler, age 18, of Bozeman; Mark Levitan, age 20, of Helena; Ray Martin, age 22, of Butte; and Clare Pogreba, age 22, also of Butte—were not discouraged and designated Pogreba as their leader.

Frauson checked the party's climbing gear and found it to be satisfactory, although he felt they lacked the proper type of protective apparel for hands and feet in the event of severe weather. They had enough food for six days with a one- or two-day additional reserve. Frauson suggested that they bring a transistor radio to get weather forecasts. After some consideration, the men decided to ascend and descend the mountain by way of Camp Creek on the west face rather than attempt a climb of the north face. They gave Frauson the names and telephone numbers of a support party located in Bozeman and Butte before they left his house.

The climbers camped overnight at St. Mary and left for Waterton Townsite the following morning, December 27. They did not check in with the Waterton Lakes National Park staff but did clear their climb with the Royal Canadian Mounted Police. They hired a local resident to take them by boat to the south end of Waterton Lake and then went cross-country toward Mt. Cleveland. The temperatures were milder than usual for that time of year, ranging on that day from a low of 21° F (-6° C) to a high of 28° F (-2° C). On December 29 or 30, the climbers began their assent of Mt. Cleveland's west face.

Three of the men shared one rope, and the other two shared another. They reached an elevation above 8,350 feet when disaster struck. They were caught in an avalanche that carried them to the 6,800-foot elevation, where their bodies remained buried.

On December 31, Bud Anderson, the twenty-five-year-old brother of James Anderson, flew over the Waterton and Mt. Cleveland area to check on the progress of the climbers. He observed tracks about halfway up the mountain that led into a fresh avalanche, but he also thought he saw tracks leaving the avalanche. He made a mental calculation that the men would reach the U.S. Waterton Ranger Station on about January 1, 1970. In the early morning of January 2, Anderson and Waterton National Park Warden Jack Christiansen went by boat to the south end of Waterton Lake. They could not see the climbing party or any tracks and contacted the Chief Warden's office at Waterton Lakes National Park.

Bud Anderson also called Ruben Hart, chief ranger of Glacier National Park. Hart brought the matter of the missing climbers to the attention of Superintendent Briggle and his staff. Supervisory Park Ranger William Colony was instructed to contact Anderson for the details necessary to plan a search. Supervisory Park Ranger Joseph Ries was dispatched from St. Mary to the Waterton Townsite to coordinate any potential search and rescue effort and to provide radio communication. In the meantime, Christiansen and Anderson began a hike around the ranger station to look for signs of the climbers.

The emergency situation was brought to the attention of the Midwest Regional Office, and an aerial search was arranged through the Malmstrom Air Force Base at Great Falls. Air Force personnel contacted the Western Air Search Center at Hamilton Air Force Base in California. At the same time, Superintendent Briggle contacted the Montana Aeronautical Commission and arranged for a fixed-wing aircraft out of Cut Bank, Montana, to make a search. The plane flew over the Mt. Cleveland area between 12:15 and 2:15 P.M. but reported no visible signs of the climbers. The pilot did see a fresh avalanche on the west face with tracks leading into and out of it but recommended against additional flights that day due to the extremely turbulent weather.

That afternoon Joseph Ries took up position at the Waterton Ranger Station where he would remain overnight with his radio. William Colony was sent to Waterton townsite to take charge of the search and rescue. A helicopter was requested from the Western Air Center and promised for the following day. Later that afternoon Christiansen and Anderson returned and reported that while tracing the climbers' tracks from the lake towards the north face of Mt. Cleveland, they found skis and snowshoes about a mile and a half from the lake shore. Ground search parties made up of staff from Glacier National Park and Waterton Lakes National Park were planned for the next day. At 6:30 A.M. on January 3, two ground search parties of three men each left by boat from Waterton Townsite to the south end of the lake. One party was led by Park Ranger Jerome DeSanto of Glacier National Park and planned to climb the northwest ridge route of Mt. Cleveland. The other was led by Jack Christiansen and planned to retrace the route on which they had found the skis and snowshoes.

At 9:20 A.M. the promised Air Force helicopter met William Colony at an airstrip a few miles outside Browning, and he accompanied the crew to the Waterton Ranger Station where he took charge of the search and rescue effort. Through the Civil Aeronautics Administration, the air corridor above the Mt. Cleveland area was closed for safety reasons during the helicopter search. After a one-hour delay due to bad weather, the crew flew a search pattern with Colony as observer. They covered both the west side and north face, but visibility was reduced by fog, flat light, and the helicopter's limited observation field of vision. The search revealed what were thought to be human tracks leading down to the northwest from the top of the north col. At 10:30 A.M., the Christiansen search party reported finding two tents, two backpacks, and a cache of food about a quarter mile below the north face of Mt. Cleveland near two snow caves that had apparently not been used. The equipment found at the tent camp included four cargo packs with aluminum frames, a stove, six rock pitons, food for four meals, socks, five sleeping bags, a wool jacket, 200 feet of avalanche cord, and film.

The search operation was joined by alpine specialist Peter Fuhrmann of Banff and wardens from nearby Canadian national parks. Fuhrmann requested that additional technical assistance be sent from Jasper National Park. Superintendent Briggle called on technical climbers from Grand Teton National Park and contacted the support party whose names had been left with Frauson by the missing climbers. Snowmobiles were arranged to transport searchers and supplies, since the lake was expected to freeze during the night and the military aircraft was not allowed to land in Canada. Two inches of snow fell overnight.

On the morning of January 4, volunteer support parties from Bozeman (including Jim Kanzler, the brother of one of the missing climbers) and Butte (including Arthur Martin, the father of one of the young men) arrived at the St. Mary Ranger Station. Jim Kanzler indicated on photographs of Mt. Cleveland's north face the route the climbers had discussed taking. The volunteers, with the exception of Martin, were sent to Waterton townsite. The aircraft was grounded due to the weather, and attempts were being made to bring in a commercial helicopter better suited for search operations. Equipment brought by Peter Fuhrmann was carried by all available personnel to the site of the climbers' tent in preparation for a reconnaissance of the north face by the Canadians from Banff. An alpine specialist and several wardens from Jasper National Park were sent to the Waterton Ranger Station along with the strongest members of the Bozeman-Butte support group.

Assignments were made for the major search operation that was developing. Colony remained in charge in the Mt. Cleveland area, with Frauson assigned to coordinate support from Waterton townsite. Others were assigned to handle press and public relations, timekeeping and records, and cooking. The Weather Bureau forecast warnings for a serious change in weather, but the bad weather did not materialize until January 9. Later in the day the remainder of the support group joined the rest of the men at the Waterton Ranger Station, and some supplies were transported to the station by boat.

The men were reorganized into five search parties and assigned areas of Mt. Cleveland to search. The helicopter from Malmstrom Air Force Base arrived at 11:30 A.M. and returned to the airstrip several times to refuel. The search revealed no human tracks. The military helicopter was released from the search when a helicopter from the Johnson Flying Service arrived. A close search of the upper portions of the north face was made, but no signs of the climbers were found. A party on the ground working the northwest ridge did find tracks and urine marks. "The man tracks discovered seemed to indicate that one or two men climbed at this point on the ridge, making visual study of the possible routes on the north face and returned to the north side of the mountain," reads a report prepared by Glacier National Park in 1970. All but one of the groups, who camped on the west side of the mountain overnight, returned to the base camp at the Waterton Ranger Station.

More supplies, including rations and propane, were carried to Fuhrmann's high camp and transported by boat to the ranger station. Technical climbers from Grand Teton National Park arrived at Great Falls. American park officials met later in the day with the parents and close friends of the missing climbers to apprise them of search efforts and the dim outlook of finding the men alive. The helicopter pilot was grounded for medical reasons, and a relief pilot was dispatched. On January 6, ground search parties continued their work. The relief helicopter pilot shuttled men and equipment to the north face. Sectional probe poles were provided by the Canadian National Park Service. The helicopter searched the proposed climbing routes but found no evidence of the men. Because of the impending weather, plans for an overland retreat of the searchers were discussed.

In the afternoon one of the searchers sighted a pack belonging to the missing climbers. The find was made near the toe of the west side avalanche covered by a light blanket of snow. The helicopter carried most of the other searchers to the site. Probing uncovered a parka containing a camera with film. The pack had also contained a can of black and white film. The films, along with the film found earlier at the tent site, were sent to the townsite to be developed.

At the end of the day most of the searchers were transported back to Waterton Ranger Station by helicopter. The Grand Teton climbers arrived at Waterton townsite, and all but one were flown by helicopter to the ranger station. Plans for the next day's operations were discussed in detail, along with the possibility of having to cancel the search. The men decided against using avalanche dogs. They ordered a magnetometer from Glacier National Park in Canada to detect metal beneath the snow and decided to work the west side avalanche the following day. On January 7, the magnetometer and the last of the Grand Teton climbers arrived at the ranger station. Prints from the black and white film were delivered and showed a strong interest in the north face of the mountain. The helicopter flew an aerial reconnaissance. The ground search parties used probes and the magnetometer to search the west side avalanche, which had deposited snow up to four meters deep in some areas. The searchers were airlifted back to the ranger station at the end of the day. The helicopter was also used to retrieve the register from the summit of Mt. Cleveland, but none of the missing men had signed it.

On January 8, probing continued at the west side avalanche until wind caused more avalanche activity. The magnetometer was used on the north side avalanche. An aerial reconnaissance was flown, but found nothing. The tent camps of both Fuhrmann and the missing climbers were dismantled. All equipment and men were taken off the mountain, and several of the men were released from the search effort. On January 9, the predicted storm struck, grounding the helicopter and halting further search operations. Most of the men involved with the search hiked to Waterton townsite or were transported by snowmobile. A press release announced that the search was being suspended for the winter due to the deteriorating weather conditions and the constant threat of avalanches. The decision had been made after consultation with the parents and relatives of the missing climbers.

On January 10, the men and equipment remaining at the Waterton Ranger Station were flown out or driven out in snowmobiles. During meetings in February and March, plans to resume the Mt. Cleveland search were formulated and approved. On April 20, the entire area for a two-mile radius from the summit of Mt. Cleveland was closed by order of Superintendent Briggle. "The restriction is justified on the basis that we are protecting the integrity of the deceased, their personal property, the safety of recovery teams, and to expedite recovery of bodies," reads his Plan for Resumption of Mt. Cleveland Search.

Briggle's plan created a timetable for sending out fixed-wing flyovers, initiating ground searches, establishing a base camp, and conducting low-level helicopter searches ("If avalanches have carried bodies down into the snow brush, this might be the best method to find them," reads the report). The plan set out the conditions under which outside assistance in the search would be allowed. The plan also covered public information and noted that sightseeing boat operators on Waterton Lake were to be instructed to avoid the subject of the missing

climbers unless asked a direct question by a passenger.

With regard to the recovery of bodies, Briggle's plan stated that no names would be associated with them until identifications were established by the coroner and that a find would be radioed by a preestablished code. The bodies would be removed by helicopter, if possible. If not, they would be carried by a team of twelve men to Waterton Ranger Station, then to the townsite, and then transported to Chief Mountain Customs in a Glacier National Park vehicle. The possibility of a carry-out had been cleared with the Royal Canadian Mounted Police and the coroner agreed to accept photographic and physical evidence collected by park rangers. Families would be notified immediately so that any special handling requests could be made through the coroner. The names of the victims would not be released to the press until the parents had been notified.

Over the next few months several patrols were made into the Mt. Cleveland area by foot and air. Significant finds included a camera containing pictures establishing that the missing climbers were on the west side of the mountain (May 23); an ice ax (May 25); a wool knit cap (June 7); a rucksack frame (June 10); a plastic bag containing flashlight batteries (June 17); another wool cap (June 18); a damaged canteen (June 21); and a shirt and plastic bag (June 25). By June 29, the snow melt had narrowed the possible locations where the bodies would be found. A foot patrol of wardens and rangers followed the climbers' probable route at 5 A.M. Four hours later the party reached the base of the snow in the middle bowl just above the falls at the head of the slide run-out area. The odor of the water from beneath the snow prompted a search upward from the stream bed, and the body of Ray Martin was found about thirty feet from the lowest edge of the snow. The body was under approximately six feet of snow and held in position by a red rope that disappeared into the snow. Assuming the other climbers were attached to the rope, a trench was begun and probes were made. The body of James Anderson was found beneath fourteen feet of snow but was tied to a second rope. The excavation was continued along both ropes in alternating rain and snow flurries.

The searchers ended the day by formulating plans for resuming the recovery. They concluded from the film that had been in Anderson's camera that Mark Levitan would be tied into the middle of the gold line with Clare Pogreba on the other end and that Jerry Kanzler would be found at the other end of the red rope. The searchers knew the ropes to be 150 feet long and decided, despite the difficulty, to continue tunneling along the lines. At the same time, they would trench in the general direction of the lines upslope. Their tools included sharp-pointed fire shovels, square-ended snow shovels, and ice chippers. Preparations were made to use solid-stream, high-pressured, hydraulic mining techniques. Because of bad weather resumption of the recovery effort was delayed until July 1. The plans to tunnel and trench were carried out, but they only advanced about fifteen feet. On July 2, the tunneling continued, and they reentered the creek bed. The searchers discovered Jerry Kanzler's body protruding from the cavern roof about forty feet upstream. After crawling further into the cavern, they found Clare Pogreba's body ten feet beyond Kanzler's. Mark Levitan's arm was spotted protruding from the snow near Kanzler's boot. All of the missing climbers were now accounted for.

The recovery team had two options for removing the three bodies: freeing them from the snow and ice by the use of water or trenching down from above. The second method was decided on as safer and more practical, even though it was more time consuming. "The purpose of the trench technique was to allow several men to work at one time on different levels, to facilitate snow removal, and to provide room for working," explains the report. "The ultimate results were very successful." The men had removed approximately two thirds of the

snow after seven hours of work and returned to Waterton Ranger Station at 7:30 P.M. On July 3, the damaged gravity socks used to create water pressure were replaced by a marine pump. At 11:45 A.M. the end of the trench broke through above Pogreba's body, and it was removed over the next forty-five minutes using shovels and ice chippers. The body of Levitan was freed and removed by 2 P.M. in the same manner. Water was used to remove Kanzler's body at 3 P.M.

The bodies were transported by helicopter to a prearranged site near Chief Mountain to meet with the Glacier County coroner. "This was done in each instance shortly following the removal of the bodies from the ice. The coroner contacted the respective families in each case after identification was made," notes the report. After the recovery of the bodies of the missing climbers, the Mt. Cleveland area was opened to public use. A financial report revealed that the expense of the search and rescue operations in January and the recovery operations in June and July totaled $19,034.57. Although the search and rescue operations did not yield any survivors, the recovery of the bodies was successful.

Carl McCunn

It is not altogether uncommon for the remains of those who have set themselves apart from society to be found weeks or months after their deaths. What is unusual is for those bodies to be perfectly preserved by benefit of having frozen. Such was the fate of thirty-five-year-old Carl McCunn. McCunn had moved from Texas to Fairbanks, Alaska, during the 1970s and found work on the Trans-Alaska Pipeline construction project. In early March 1981 he hired a bush pilot to drop him at a remote lake near the Coleen River, about 75 miles northeast of Fort Yukon on the southern margin of the Brooks Range. He had been planning the trip for the better part of a year and had tried unsuccessfully to convince one of the women who worked at the pipeline camp to accompany him. McCunn had told friends the trip was a photographic expedition and had brought with him 500 rolls of film, two rifles, a shotgun, and 1,400 pounds of provisions. He was to remain in the wilderness through August but neglected to arrange for a pickup at the end of the summer. "I think I should have used more foresight about arranging my departure," he wrote in his diary. "I'll soon find out" (Krakauer 1996a, 81).

McCunn regretted having thrown several boxes of shotgun shells in the river when his provisions began to run short. While using the last of his ammunition to hunt ducks, he was spotted by a plane. The plane circled twice as McCunn waved his fluorescent orange sleeping bag cover. McCunn was sure the pilot would return for him, but Mc-Cunn later realized why he hadn't. The back of his hunting license contained drawings of emergency hand signals for communicating with aircraft from the ground. The motions he had used to signal the pilot indicated that everything was okay and that no assistance was necessary. Two upraised arms would have indicated distress. "They probably blew me off as a weirdo," lamented McCunn in his diary (Krakauer 1996a, 82).

By the end of September McCunn was eating rose hips, attempting to snare rabbits, and scavenging meat from a dead caribou. He was surprised that no one from town had come looking for him. While he waited he metabolized most of his body fat. He had difficulty keeping warm, and his fingers and toes became frostbitten. With few provisions left and temperatures dipping to -5° F (-20° C), McCunn began to get scared, but by then he didn't have the strength to walk out. He finished the last of his rations in November. He was weak and dizzy. He had chills, and the frostbite on his hands and feet—and now his nose—worsened. "This is sure a slow and agonizing way to die," he wrote (Krakauer 1996a, 83–84).

In late November McCunn wrote, "I can't go on like this, I'm afraid. Dear God in Heaven, please forgive me my weakness and my sins. Please look over my family"

(Krakauer 1996a, 84). Inside his tent he placed the muzzle of his .30-.30 against his head and pulled the trigger with his thumb. Two months later, on February 2, 1982, Alaska State Troopers discovered his camp, looked inside the tent, and found McCunn's emaciated corpse frozen hard as stone (Krakauer 1996a, 84).

Mt. Everest Tragedy

Despite the lengths taken to recover the bodies in cases like the Mt. Cleveland tragedy, it is a tradition—and often a necessity—to leave the dead on the mountains they were unable to conquer. Mt. Everest claimed eleven of the eighty-seven climbers who reached (or attempted to reach) its 29,028-foot summit during the 1996 season. Sir Edmund Hillary, who in 1953 became the first Westerner to reach Everest's peak, blames the tragedy on commercialization and overcrowding. Although 1996 was the deadliest season yet, its victims were far from the first. Andrew Irvine and George Leigh Mallory died on the mountain in 1924 and remain in its glaciers. In all, 142 of the approximately 4,000 who have tried to climb Mt. Everest (3.5 percent) have died (Dowling 1996). Dozens of cenotaphs have been erected near base camp, and those the tombstones and boulders memorialize remain at higher altitudes.

In mid–May 1996 there were several teams of climbers ready to challenge the five and a half vertical miles of Everest. Scott Fischer of the United States, his assistants Neal Beidleman and Anatoli Boukreev, and five Sherpas (including Lobsang Jangbu, who died accidentally later that fall) were ready to lead clients Martin Adams, Charlotte Fox, Lene Gammelgaard, Tim Madsen, Sandy Pittman, and Klev Schoening to the summit. Rob Hall of New Zealand, his guides Mike Groom and Andy Harris, and four Sherpas (Ang Dorje, Lhakpa Chhiri, Nawang Norbu, and Kami) were prepared to lead eight team members to the top: Frank Fischbeck, Doug Hansen, Stuart Hutchison,

Lou Kasischke, Jon Krakauer, Yasuko Namba, John Taske, and Beck Weathers. Also ready to ascend were a Taiwanese team led by Ming Ho Gao, who had a bad reputation after an earlier disaster on Mt. McKinley in Alaska, and a South African team known to have very limited experience. "With so many incompetent people on the mountain," said Hall in late April, "I think it's pretty unlikely that we'll get through this without something bad happening" (Krakauer 1996b).

The clients of Fischer and Hall, who had paid as much as $65,000 each for the opportunity, were acclimatized on several daily ascents from the 17,500-foot base camp, but neither the money nor the practice was a guarantee of success or even survival. The members of the two teams set out for the summit on May 5. After a four-day trek to an altitude of 26,000 feet, they reached Camp IV on the South Col, a barren plateau of ice and boulders, by 5 P.M. Hall's team left camp at 11:30 P.M. for the final push and Fischer's team at midnight. At 5:30 in the morning Krakauer reached the 27,500-foot crest of the Southeast Ridge and waited for the whole group to assemble on a level area known as the Balcony. He was surprised to see that Fischer's head Sherpa Lobsang was hauling Pittman up the mountain with a short rope, a task that kept him from installing ropes with Ang Dorje ahead of the climbers.

Beidleman ran out the rope while the climbers waited at the 28,000-foot base of a series of giant rock steps for nearly an hour. Hall's clients began to doubt that they would reach the summit by the 1 P.M. turn-around time their guide had mandated. Fischbeck had already turned around, and soon Hutchison, Taske, and Kasischke followed. The Sherpas fixed ropes along the corniced summit ridge. After taking turns on the safety ropes up the difficult Hillary Step, those still ascending began to reach the summit in the early afternoon of May 10, 1996. Krakauer, Harris, and Boukreev reached the peak shortly after 1 P.M. and headed back down. Beidleman waited for Fischer's clients to

summit but called for them to descend shortly after 3 P.M. Twenty minutes later they passed Fischer, who was still on his way up.

At a little after 2 P.M. Hall reached the summit and waited for more than an hour for his client Hansen to join him. It began to snow as Harris and Krakauer reached the South Summit and fresh oxygen bottles. The sky darkened, the wind blew at 70 miles per hour, and the temperature measured -40° F (-40° C). When Beidleman's group reached the South Summit, Pittman collapsed and was revived with an injection of steroids. Krakauer reached the Balcony at about 4 P.M. and found a shivering Beck Weathers, whom Hall had prevented from further climbing due to vision problems made worse by the altitude. Weathers and Namba were led down by Groom. By the time Fischer had summited with Lobsang at about 3:30 and descended to the South Summit, he had trouble standing and was kept upright and moving by the Sherpa. Fischer asked Lobsang to continue without him, but the Sherpa refused.

By 4:30 P.M. Hall and Hansen had only descended to the top of the Hillary Step. At that point Hansen ran out of oxygen and collapsed. Hall struggled over the next twelve hours to get Hansen down the fixed rope, a stretch that usually only takes half an hour. A friend urged him by radio to abandon his client, but Hall refused. Beneath the Step, Hansen accidentally made the decision for him: he slipped and fell 7,000 feet down the Southwest Face to his death. But by the time Hall reached the South Summit alone at 4:43 A.M. on May 11, he was too weak to move in the hurricane-strength wind, so he hunkered down and waited for help. He was patched through by radio to his wife in New Zealand. Before his trip the couple had talked about the impossibility of being rescued from the summit ridge, and Hall had explained, "You might as well be on the moon" (Krakauer 1996b). Hall found two full oxygen bottles that he was able to put into use at about 8:30 A.M. Despite regular urgings by radio, he was unable to descend and became increasingly frostbitten. At 6:20 P.M. he was again patched through to his wife and had a final conversation with her.

At about 5 P.M. the day before, Groom, Namba, Beidleman, and five of Fischer's clients had reached the Balcony. An hour later Krakauer had reached his tent in Camp Four: "It would be many hours before I learned that everyone had in fact not made it back to camp—that one teammate was already dead and that 23 other men and women were caught in a desperate struggle for their lives," he writes (1996b). Krakauer had seen Harris stumbling toward camp, but footprints seen the following day suggested that Harris had accidentally walked off the Lhotse Face, a 4,000-foot drop. At 8 P.M. on the night of May 10, Beidleman, Groom, two Sherpas, and seven clients became disoriented by the hurricane and wandered the South Col for the next two hours in search of their tents. Hutchison attempted to look for the missing climbers six times but was unable to venture more than a few yards from the tents. They huddled, ironically, only 350 yards from the camp, until Beidleman and three others went for help at midnight. Forty-five minutes later most of the party reached Camp IV and sent Boukreev to retrieve Fox, Namba, Pittman, and Weathers, who were all semiconscious and unable to walk. Madsen, unwilling to abandon his girlfriend Fox, stayed with the group to await rescue. When Boukreev found them, Namba and Weathers appeared to be dead. He gave Hill and Madsen a bottle of oxygen to share and carried Fox to camp on his back, a task that took an hour. He carried Hill and led Madsen down the mountain, then collapsed from exhaustion. Altogether, he had made five trips up and down. Thanks to Boukreev all of Fischer's team had been rescued by 5 A.M.

In the early morning of May 11, Hutchison organized a team of four Sherpas to locate the bodies of Weathers and Namba. Following Boukreev's directions, they found the bodies at the edge of the Kangshung Face. Hutchison chipped a three-inch-thick cara-

pace of ice from the face of the first body. It was Namba, and she was still breathing. Weathers lay twenty feet away, and his face was also caked with frost and ice. He too was alive, but barely. Lhakpa Chhiri, an Everest veteran, urged Hutchison to leave the two where they lay, since they would certainly die before they could be carried down to camp, and a rescue attempt would needlessly jeopardize the other climbers. Hutchison returned to camp at 8:30 A.M. and told the others his decision.

At 9:30 A.M. on May 11, Ang Dorje and Lhakpa Chhiri made an attempt to bring Hall down, but the wind forced them to turn back 700 feet below his position. Four other Sherpas left at the same time to rescue Fischer and Gau. At 9 P.M. the night before, Fischer had collapsed 300 vertical feet below the Balcony. Lobsang had anchored him to a snow-covered ledge when he was no longer able to drag him any further. The Sherpa was joined by two other Sherpas who were struggling to bring down Gau. They tied the two semiconscious men together and went for help. When the Sherpas returned for them twelve hours later, they found Fischer barely breathing and unresponsive, so they descended with Gau. That afternoon, against all odds, a nearly blind Weathers staggered back to camp.

At 7 P.M. Boukreev climbed back up the mountain in search of Fischer. He found the lifeless guide without gloves and with his jacket unzipped. Boukreev dragged Fischer's body off the path, used climbing rope to lash him to the mountain, and covered his face. It would have been impossible to carry the body at that altitude. Boukreev believes bodies should remain on the mountain as a warning but should be decently covered. He intends to cover Fischer's body with stones on a future ascent. Fischer's wife Jeannie said in an interview after his death (Dowling 1996) that they had made wills before his first trip to Mt. Everest in 1987 and that in the event of his death Fischer wanted to be left in a crevasse on the mountain. "I would feel cheated if Scott had been killed in a car crash," she said. "He deserved to die on Mount Everest."

The frozen bodies of Scott Fischer and Rob Hall were seen twelve days later by David Breshears and his climbing partner Ed Viesturs, who had postponed their ascent to the summit to avoid the crowds. "I never thought they'd die on Everest," Viesturs said later (Dowling 1996). When they climbed over the South Summit on their way to the top, they discovered Hall lying on his right side in a shallow ice-hollow with his upper body buried beneath a drift of snow (Krakauer 1996b). Sir Edmund Hillary, who believes the Nepalese government should limit the number of Everest expeditions to two or three per year rather than the dozens it now allows, is sympathetic despite his criticisms: "While I expected it, I was obviously shaken. We actually heard a man die on the mountain, talking to his wife as he was dying. This was very dramatic, very sad stuff. My own personal feeling—I would have preferred to die peacefully alone, and let the world find out about it later" (Dowling 1996). Although the story has been told, the bodies remain to tell the tragic tale to future climbers.

EXPLORERS

Another group of men challenged themselves physically, mentally, and emotionally to reach new terrain—to go where no one had gone before. A subset of these men reached the ends of the earth but lived to tell about it only in their posthumous memoirs. Bodies were, of necessity, left by the wayside as the expeditions continued. It was impossible for explorers to expend their valuable resources to bring the dead to their destination and home to loved ones. In some cases it was impossible even to recover the victims' bodies from the deep chasms and crevasses that claimed their lives. In the most famous ill-fated trek, Robert Falcon Scott and the members of his expedition to the South Pole knew at the end that their tent

was their tomb. The search party learned their fate and recovered their diaries and scientific samples, but Antarctica claimed—and still claims—their bodies.

Antarctica is "the highest, windiest, coldest, driest, most inhospitable and desolate continent on earth" (Gordon 1981). Ice averaging more than a mile thick covers over 5.5 million square miles (98 percent) of Antarctica. Less than a foot of snow a year falls (an average of two inches in the interior), but winds of up to 200 miles per hour cause drifting. The temperature is rarely above freezing and has reached -117° F (-83° C). And yet it is still a sought-after destination for some. Explored earlier in the century, it is now studied. Today there are sixty research stations on the continent, which is shared by the forty-one countries that have signed the Antarctic Treaty. Although less than 25,000 living Americans have been to Antarctica, any one of them could have been accidentally killed. To prevent such a tragedy new visitors to Antarctica are required to attend a two-day field safety school. To prepare for the possibility they must provide a full set of dental x-rays and wear a set of dog tags to assist in the identification of their remains. The South Pole is a more elusive goal than it would seem from looking at a globe. Today, the geographic South Pole is marked each year, since the polar ice cap moves over it at a rate of thirty-three feet per year.

At the turn of the century, reaching it was still an unrealized dream. In 1898 Norwegian explorer Carstens Borchgrevink headed a scientific expedition to Antarctica. The ship left ten men at Cape Adare for the winter of 1899 and as the winter ended, Nicolai Hanson, a zoologist from the British National History Museum, fell ill from an apparent intestinal disease. He died in October: "It made a strange scene, that first burial in Antarctica. The grave was blasted open with explosive to receive the rigid corpse. A forlorn group of men stood around in the pale light, the ice crunching under their feet. One hand moved automatically towards a hat and was quickly withdrawn as the icy air breathed a warning. In the distance the penguins squeaked and chattered to each other, flapping their rudimentary wings as if shrugging their shoulders, while the black cliffs loomed above the glacier and the two Lapps, tears frozen on their leathery cheeks, sang a strange northern dirge on the Southern Continent" (Mountfield 1974, 138). The ship returned for the remaining men and brought them to the Ross Ice Shelf where, with British naval officer William Colbeck, they made a sledging journey that established a "farthest south" record and opened the way for Scott. The continent had been breached, but it had also claimed its first victim.

Australian scientist and explorer Sir Douglas Mawson made an expedition to explore the area around the Magnetic South Pole in 1912. In December, not long after he set out with his two companions Ninnis and Mertz, Ninnis disappeared—along with his team of dogs and a heavily loaded sledge—into a deep crevasse. An injured dog could be seen on a shelf 150 feet down, but there was no trace of Ninnis or anything else. Without the food and tent the sledge had contained, Mawson and Mertz made a dash for their base camp, now more than 300 miles away. They used the remaining dogs as food and when Mertz weakened he was added to the load on the remaining sledge. Mertz died of food poisoning when they were still 100 miles from camp. Mawson cut the sledge in half, piled his few supplies on it and continued on. He found cairns containing food left by search parties, but when he reached the base camp in February 1913 (two weeks late), the ship that had arrived to pick them up was disappearing into the distance. He spent another winter in the Antarctic with five men who had volunteered to stay at the hut and await his return (Mountfield 1974, 180, 185).

After Robert Falcon Scott and Roald Amundsen had reached the South Pole—only the latter living to tell about it—Ernest Shackleton led an expedition hoping to cross Antarctica in 1914. He sailed aboard the

Endurance, which got iced in off the Weddell coast, and Captain A. Mackintosh sailed the *Aurora*, which headed for McMurdo Sound to establish a base camp. After the *Endurance* cracked under the pressure of the ice, Shackleton led a party of five men to a whaling station in May 1915. After four attempts to reach the rest of the stranded men by boat, they were all rescued in August 1916. Captain Mackintosh and two other men of the second party, whose ship had drifted away before all the supplies had been unloaded, perished.

The research of Antarctica and of previous expeditions continues to claim victims just as its exploration did. In 1993 Jostein Helgestad was part of an expedition to recover the tent and sledge that Roald Amundsen left at the South Pole in 1911. He plunged down a hidden crevasse 130 feet deep. The rescue team based at McMurdo station flew 1,200 miles to the location in which Helgestad had disappeared. The team worked its way to the crevasse and team member Steve Dunbar was lowered to within three feet of Helgestad's body. But because the walls of the crevasse narrowed at that point to ten inches, the body could not be recovered. Like the bodies of mountaineers, Antarctic adventurers are often left in what may be bluntly called natural cold storage with little hope of recovery.

Robert F. Scott's Antarctic Expedition

The British Antarctic Expedition (also called the Terra Nova Expedition) to the South Pole from 1910 to 1913 was organized and led by Captain Robert Falcon Scott of the Royal Navy, who had commanded his first Antarctic expedition in 1899. Scott knew the potential danger of the expedition. He told the press, "None can foretell our luck. We may get through, we may not. We may have accidents to some of the transports, to the sledges, or to the animals. We may lose our lives. We may be wiped out. It is all a question that lies with providence and luck"

The camp in which Robert Falcon Scott and his men were found after the snow had been cleared away. The tent was collapsed and the men remained entombed inside it. Photo courtesy of UPI/Corbis-Bettmann.

(Huxley 1977, 203). During his earlier Discovery expedition to Antarctica from 1901 to 1904, Scott lost one of his men. George Vince slipped down an abyss as the men headed back to the ship after a blizzard stranded them about four miles from shore. Before the ship left the Antarctic, the company carried out a memorial service and erected a wooden cross in his honor (Huxley 1977, 71, 130).

Scott was a strong man, five feet nine inches tall and weighing 160 pounds, but he was not invincible. He was subject not only to the ironies of fate but to the ultimate fate of us all. He is described by expedition member Apsley Cherry-Garrard: "He will go down to history as the Englishman who conquered the South Pole and who died as fine a death as any man has had the honour to die. His triumphs are many—but the Pole was not by any means the greatest of them. Surely the greatest was that by which he conquered his weaker self, and became the strong leader whom we went to follow and came to love" (Cherry-Garrard 1989, 248).

The Terra Nova sailed from Cardiff,

Wales, on June 15, 1910. When the ship reached Lyttelton, New Zealand, Scott received a telegram from Norwegian explorer Roald Amundsen notifying him of Amundsen's plans to go south. The Terra Nova—loaded with men, dogs, ponies, sledges, equipment, and supplies—entered pack ice on December 9. On December 31, they set up winter quarters in a hut that still stands at Cape Evans on McMurdo Sound. In April and May Scott and a team of eleven men spent several weeks laying a depot along their intended route to the Pole. On June 22, 1911, an expedition of three men, one of them Cherry-Garrard, set out for an unexpectedly difficult trek to Cape Crozier to collect Emperor penguin eggs. During the journey Cherry-Garrard wrote, "I for one had come to that point of suffering at which I did not really care if only I could die without much pain. They talk of the heroism of the dying—they little know—it would be so easy to die, a dose of morphia, a friendly crevasse, and blissful sleep. The trouble is to go on..." (Cherry-Garrard 1989, 284). Their mission was almost fatal, but they returned five weeks later.

Two parties of men (twelve in all) started on the 800-mile polar journey, one on October 24, 1911, and the other eight days later. They mounted the Beardmore Glacier and erected the Upper Glacier Depot. Four of the men, including Cherry-Garrard, returned to the base camp. By December 31, Scott and his men established Three-degrees Depot at a latitude of 87 degrees, 150 miles from the South Pole. Scott sent back all but four of the men on January 3, 1912. For the last stretch of the expedition, he retained Dr. Edward Adrian Wilson (a.k.a. "Uncle Bill"), chief of the scientific staff and zoologist; Lieutenant Henry R. Bowers (a.k.a. "Birdie"), Royal Indian Marine who organized the stores; Captain Lawrence E. G. Oates (a.k.a. "Titus" or "The Soldier") of the Inniskilling Dragoons, who had taken care of the ponies; and Edgar Evans (a.k.a. "Taff "), petty officer in the Royal Navy who had served in Scott's Discovery expedition and was known as the "strong man" of the Terra Nova Expedition. Of Wilson and Bowers, Cherry-Garrard (1989, 294–295) writes, "These two men went through the Winter Journey and lived: later they went through the Polar Journey and died. They were gold, pure, shining, unalloyed. Words cannot express how good their companionship was…. It is hard that often such men must go first when others far less worthy remain."

For thirteen days the five men made steady progress. But on January 16, 1912, they came upon evidence that Roald Amundsen's party had preceded them. Amundsen had reached the South Pole on December 17, 1911. Scott reached the Pole exactly one month later, writing, "Great God! … this is an awful place and terrible enough for us to have laboured to it without the reward of priority" (Savours 1975, 152). During Amundsen's four-day stay at the Pole, his party had raised the Norse flag and named the continental plateau after their king, Haakon VII. Their return journey took thirty-eight days (Henry 1950, 101). Cherry-Garrard (1989, 606) writes, "On the one hand, Amundsen going straight there, getting there first, and returning without the loss of a single man, and without having put any greater strain on himself and his men than was all in the day's work of polar exploration. Nothing more business-like could be imagined. On the other hand, our expedition, running appalling risks, performing prodigies of superhuman endurance, achieving immortal renown, commemorated in august cathedral sermons and by public statues, yet reaching the Pole only to find our terrible journey superfluous, and leaving our best men dead on the ice." Scott's party fixed the precise location of the Pole less than a half-mile from that established by Amundsen.

A deflated Scott and his men began their return on January 18, 1912. They reached Three-degrees Depot on January 30 and Upper Glacier Depot on February 7. Descending Beardmore glacier took them ten days. On February 17, Evans fell ill, having previously received a concussion and an injury to his hand during a fall into a crevasse. Also weakened by the meager rations, Evans was found kneeling in the snow, with disheveled clothing, slurred speech, and a "wild look in his eyes" (Huxley 1977, 252). He became unconscious and died shortly after midnight. Scott ordered Wilson to distribute opium tablets to be taken if they could no longer endure (Henry 1950, 93). Wilson kept a tube of morphine for himself and gave the others thirty tablets each, but they were never used.

The men reached Shambles Camp on February 18 and were met by several unfortunate circumstances: they did not have enough oil to carry them to the next depot seventy-one miles away, Oates's feet were badly frostbitten, and the temperature had dropped. They managed to reach Mount Hooper Depot on March 10, but much of the fuel there had evaporated. On March 15, Oates asked the others to continue without him, but they struggled on a few more miles. The following morning, Oates told his companions, "Well, I am just going outside, and I may be some time" (Cherry-Garrard 1989, 544). He never returned and Cherry-Garrard

(1989, 581) explains, "Practically any man who undertakes big polar journeys must face the possibility of having to commit suicide to save his companions, and the difficulty of this must not be over-rated, for it is in some ways more desirable to die than to live, if things are bad enough...."

On March 16 or 17, Scott wrote the following passage in his diary: "I take this opportunity of saying that we have stuck to our sick companions to the last. In case of Edgar Evans, when absolutely out of food and he lay insensible, the safety of the remainder seemed to demand his abandonment, but Providence mercifully removed him at this critical moment. He died a natural death, and we did not leave him till two hours after his death. We knew that poor Oates was walking to his death, but though we tried to dissuade him, we knew it was the act of a brave man and an English gentleman. We all hope to meet the end with a similar spirit, and assuredly the end is not far" (Cherry-Garrard 1989, 598).

By the 18th of March, the men were within twenty-one nautical miles of One Ton Camp. On March 19, they pitched their tent for the sixtieth and last time. On March 22 and 23, Scott wrote: "Blizzard bad as ever—Wilson and Bowers unable to start—tomorrow last chance—no fuel and only one or two of food left—must be near the end. Have decided it shall be natural—we shall march for the depot with or without our effects and die in our tracks" (Cherry-Garrard 1989, 599). A week later, Scott was still writing:

> Every day we have been ready to start for our depot 11 miles away, but outside the door of the tent it remains a scene of whirling drift. I do not think we can hope for any better things now. We shall stick it out to the end, but we are getting weaker, of course, and the end cannot be far.
> It seems a pity, but I do not think I can write more.
>
> R. SCOTT
>
> For God's sake, look after our people.
> [Cherry-Garrard 1989, 599]

In preparation for certain death Scott put his affairs in order. He requested on a page in his diary that it be sent to his widow (Huxley 1977, 255). In addition to writing in his diary, Scott penned twelve letters, including notes to Wilson's wife: "I can do no more to comfort you than to tell you that he died as he lived, a brave, true man—the best of comrades and staunchest of friends" (Cherry-Garrard 1989, 600); Bowers' mother: "I write when we are very near the end of our journey, and I am finishing it in company with two gallant, noble gentlemen. One of these is your son..." (Cherry-Garrard 1989, 600); and his friend Sir J. M. Barrie: "We are pegging out in a very comfortless spot.... I am not at all afraid of the end.... I may not have proved a great explorer, but we have done the greatest march ever made and come very near to great success" and later added, "We did intend to finish ourselves when things proved like this, but we have decided to die naturally in the tracks" (Cherry-Garrard 1989, 600–601).

Scott also wrote a message to the public, listing the specific causes of the disaster, including the weather and Edgar Evans' death from a concussion of the brain. The message concluded: "We arrived within 11 miles of our old One Ton Camp with fuel for one last meal and food for two days. For four days we have been unable to leave the tent—the gale howling about us. We are weak, writing is difficult, but for my own sake I do not regret this journey, which has shown that Englishmen can endure hardships, help one another, and meet death with as great a fortitude as ever in the past.... These rough notes and our dead bodies must tell the tale, but surely, surely a great rich country like ours will see that those who are dependent on us are properly provided for" (Cherry-Garrard 1989, 602-3).

On November 12, 1912, at nearly midday, a search party led by Lieutenant E. L. Atkinson found Scott's tent eleven to twelve nautical miles south of One Ton Camp (longitude 169.15 east, latitude 79.38 south). The top of the tent was spotted by Charles "Silas"

Wright and the flap was pulled aside by Atkinson. "That scene can never leave my memory," writes Cherry-Garrard (1989, 541). At the side of the tent, the top half of two pairs of ski sticks and the bamboo mast of the sledge stuck up out of the snow. The tent was covered with two to three feet of drifted snow and had been pitched close to a snow-covered cairn from the year before. An extra gathering of snow showed where the ventilator was and enabled them to find the door. Two of the men entered through the funnel of the outer tent and through the bamboos on which the lining of the inner tent was stretched. They could see nothing until they dug the tent out.

The final tableau was revealed. Scott lay in the center and had thrown back the flaps of his sleeping bag and opened his coat. His left hand was stretched toward Wilson, his lifelong friend, and his skin was yellow and frostbitten. There was tobacco and tea by his head. Under his shoulder was the green wallet in which he carried his diaries, with the brown books inside. On the floor were the letters he had written. Everything was tidy and the tent was taut. Near Scott was a lamp formed from a tin and some lamp wick used to burn the little methylated spirit which remained. "I think that Scott had used it to help him to write up to the end," speculated Cherry-Garrard (1989, 542). "I feel sure that he had died last—and once I had thought that he would not go so far as some of the others. We never realized how strong that man was, mentally and physically, until now." Wilson was on his left with his head towards the door and his hands folded over his chest. Bowers was on his right, lying with his feet towards the door. Both were in an attitude of sleep, with their sleeping bags closed over their heads. The early stages of scurvy had weakened the men, but they had died of exposure, fatigue, and starvation.

Cherry-Garrard (1989, 540) marveled that the doomed men had continued keeping records, making photographs, and collecting the scientific specimens that were later found on their sledges: "It is magnificent that men in such case should go on pulling everything that they have died to gain. I think they realized their coming end a long time before." Atkinson's men sorted out Scott's gear, records, papers, diaries, spare clothing, letters, chronometers, finnesko, socks, a flag, a book Cherry-Garrard had lent Bill for the journey, and the notes they had left for them on the Beardmore glacier. They uncovered the sledge and found more odds and ends, Bowers's meteorological log, thirty-five pounds of geological specimens, the harnesses, ski and ski-sticks.

The instructions in Scott's diary said that the finder was to read it and bring it home. Atkinson sat in the search party's tent and read, but only enough to know what had happened. When he had the outline of the story, he gathered his men and read the "Message to the Public" and the account of Oates' death, as Scott wished. He then read the Burial Service and a chapter from Corinthians. The men sang Scott's favorite hymn, "Onward Christian Soldiers." They left the bodies of Scott and his men in their sleeping bags, kept the floor-cloth under the bodies, and collapsed the tent above them by removing the bamboo poles. They built a cairn over them and fixed a cross from two skis above it. On either side the two sledges were fixed upright and dug in. A note signed by all members of the search party was left at the cairn on a bamboo standing by itself.

Cherry-Garrard wrote about the burial later that night: "I cannot think that anything which could be done to give these three great men—for great they were—a fitting grave has been left undone. A great cairn has been built over them, a mark which must last for many years. That we can make anything that will be permanent on this Barrier is impossible, but as far as a lasting mark can be made it has been done.... The whole is very simple and most impressive" (Cherry-Garrard 1989, 543–44). The cairn could be seen from more than eight miles away.

Atkinson's party retraced Scott's route in an attempt to recover Oates's body, but it remained buried in the snow. They found only his sleeping bag and built another cairn to mark the spot near which Oates had walked out to his death. They erected a cross and lashed a record of his death to it: "Hereabouts died a very gallant gentleman, Captain L. E. G. Oates of the Inniskilling Dragoons. In March 1912, returning from the Pole, he walked willingly to his death in a blizzard to try to save his comrades, beset by hardship" (Huxley 1977, 258).

Upon the return of the search party, Atkinson presented Scott's diary and last letter to his widow Kathleen. The establishment of the Scott Memorial Fund raised more than enough money to repay the debts of the expedition. The additional funds were used to found the Scott Polar Research Institute at Cambridge. Statues of Scott were raised in Waterloo Place, London, and Christchurch, New Zealand. On January 22, 1913, a wooden cross was erected on Observation Hill at McMurdo Station in memory of the Polar Party. It bears their names and an inscription from the last line of Tennyson's "Ulysses": "To strive, to seek, to find, and not to yield." The monument is nine feet high and can be seen nine miles away.

When the Terra Nova reached New Zealand, the men remained at sea for twenty-four hours while a cable was sent to England to inform relatives before news of the tragedy was published in the newspapers. Cherry-Garrard writes, "To a sensitive pre-war world the knowledge of these men's deaths came as a great shock: and now, although the world has almost lost the sense of tragedy, it appeals to their pity and their pride. The disaster may well be the first thing which Scott's name recalls to your mind ... but Scott's reputation is not founded upon the conquest of the South Pole. He came to a new continent, found out how to travel there, and gave knowledge of it to the world" (Cherry-Garrard 1989, 638–39).

Not a trace of Scott's funeral cairn was found by Ernest Shackleton's men in 1916 (Cherry-Garrard 1989, 613). Lecturing sixty years after Scott's death, Charles "Silas" Wright, a member of both the Terra Nova

Expedition and the search party, was asked why the bodies had not been taken back to England to be buried with full honors in a British national mausoleum. "He could only reply that it had never occurred to any of the search party to do so. The bodies belonged to the Barrier—or to the Ross Ice Shelf, as it has now become—and there they should remain" (Huxley 1977, 271). The bodies do remain, but not in place. American scientists have calculated that the grave is now more than fifty feet under the surface of the snow and fifteen miles nearer to the edge of the ice shelf. In the distant future, the bodies will be carried by an iceberg out into the antarctic seas (Mountfield 1974, 178). The "ice-embalmed" bodies of Scott and his men will be preserved indefinitely in the natural refrigeration and insect-free environment of Antarctica (Henry 1950, 42–43).

Because Robert F. Scott and his party died, Roald Amundsen's victory was overshadowed. The British showed disdain for Amundsen as if he had somehow been responsible for Scott's death. Amundsen was not given his due. Scott's journey was described in heroic terms, whereas Amundsen, who had reached the Pole and returned safely, was considered by some to have been "lucky" (Gordon 1981, 40). In fact, Amundsen lost his life near the North Pole in 1928. His body was never recovered from the arctic sea after his plane went down. "Amundsen and Scott, who had dramatically raced each other for glory and achievement at the South Pole, ended up sixteen years apart, entombed at the opposite ends of the earth, each in eternal snow and ice" (Gordon 1981, 43).

The Exploration of Greenland

Like the antarctic explorers, the men who explored Greenland sometimes had to pay the ultimate price. Like Antarctica, Greenland is inhospitable. An ice cap covers 665,000 of its 845,500 square miles and local glaciers cover another 29,500 miles. In all, 82 percent of Greenland is covered with ice (Banks 1975, 22–23). And the ice has claimed many lives.

In June 1906 a twenty-seven-man expedition led by thirty-four-year-old Ludwig Mylius-Erichsen left Copenhagen in a ship called the *Danmark*. They intended to survey the last unmapped section of Greenland's east coast. The men wintered near Cape Bismarck and laid depots for their journey. In the spring of 1907 the men headed north by dog-sledge. On May 1, they split into two parties. Lieutenant J. P. Koch, artist Aage Bertelson, and hunter Tobias went north to Cape Bridgman. Their task complete, they turned back and met Captain Mylius-Erichsen on May 27 at Danmark Fjord. Koch headed south and reached the ship at Danmarkshavn on June 23, having sledged 1,200 miles in 88 days.

Captain Mylius-Erichsen became overdue, so relief parties went north in search of him. With the onset of winter, it became clear that the men had perished (Banks 1975, 171). In the spring Koch and Tobias sledged north and found the body of Greenlander Brønlund near the depot in Lambert Land. Brønlund's diary indicated that his two companions had died earlier in an attempt to go south by way of the ice cap. Open water stopped the return journey, hunting was disappointing, and the men starved to death.

When the Danmark Expedition returned, there was a feeling that a search should be made to find the bodies of the missing men and retrieve their diaries. In 1909 a five-man Danish expedition led by Ejnar Mikkelsen set out to do just that in a small vessel called the *Alabama*. They wintered on Shannon Island and Mikkelson and Iver Iversen, a relief stoker, made a journey to Lambert Land the following fall. They found Brønlund's grave but were unable to locate the bodies of the other two men. After journeying north and finding records Erichsen had left, the men nearly died returning to the *Alabama*, and when they reached it, they found that the ship had been crushed by the ice. A relief ship was not able to pick them up until 1913.

In 1930 Alfred Wegener headed a German project to establish three stations, one on each coast and one in the center of the ice cap. A small east-coast party based themselves on Scoresby Sound. A larger expedition of seventeen men camped on the west coast north of Disko Bay and attempted to transport cargo to the central Eismitte Station. When Sorge and Georgi, the two scientists living in snow caves at the station, began to run short of supplies, Wegener recruited a large convoy of sledges to carry the essentials to them. Hard conditions deterred the native Greenlanders until only one, Rasmus Villumsen, remained with Wegener and his companion Loewe. Loewe's feet became frostbitten, and when they arrived on October 30, the cold had set in, and the food they had brought was insufficient for five men. Wegener and Villumsen took some provisions and sledged for the coast but died during a snowstorm. A search was made in the spring and Wegener's body was found. It had been sewn into his sleeping bag and marked by a ski. He had died of exhaustion or a heart attack and Rasmus had buried him, taken his diary, and set off for the coast. Rasmus's trail petered out, and it is probable that he fell into a crevasse (Banks 1975, 189).

The Last Voyage of the Karluk

The *Karluk* was a brigantine with an auxiliary steam engine built in 1880. It saw many uses before being reoutfitted for arctic waters. By the time it became the main ship for the Canadian Arctic Expedition in 1913–1914, it had seen better days and soon reached the end of its career. The ship was owned by Vilhajalmur Stefansson, who planned the expedition—funded in part by the Canadian government—to survey the western arctic and to search for new polar lands. The ship was captained by Robert Bartlett of Newfoundland, who had captained many of Robert Peary's ships.

The *Karluk* left Esquimalt, British Columbia, on June 17, 1913, with 24 white men, including Stefansson, and 7 Eskimos aboard. The expedition headed through the Beaufort Sea on the way to Herschel Island but made poor time. The ship got iced in and began to drift. On September 20, Stefansson went ashore to hunt caribou but was unable to return to the ship. The ice had broken up, a gale raged, and the amount of daylight had diminished. The ship, which was now near Point Barrow, could not reach open water and suffered more storms in October. It continued to drift northwest toward Wrangell Island off Siberia. Knowing they would probably have to abandon the ship, Captain Bartlett put the Eskimo crew members to work making fur clothing for the expedition members. By November 11, they were without sun 24 hours a day.

Christmas and New Year's Day were spent locked in the ice. On January 10, 1914, the ice split away from the starboard side of the ship, but it was still frozen to the port side. This left the ship prone to being crushed by the moving ice sheet and prompted Captain Bartlett to prepare to abandon the ship. That very evening a point of ice pierced the ship's planking and the timbers of the engine room, ripping off the pump fixtures and causing irreparable damage. Bartlett ordered the men to leave the ship, but he remained on board until 4 P.M. the following day, when it began to sink. The men camped in igloos and houses made of boxes and crates for more than a week, since it was too dark for ice travel and land was some 70 miles away.

On January 21, two parties—one led by the Eskimo Mamen and the other by the ship's mate—were sent to make a trail to shore, relay supplies, and establish a camp. Four days later the sun returned. In late January Dr. Mackay and three of the men requested permission to set out on their own. After signing a waiver releasing the captain from responsibility, they were outfitted with supplies and left Shipwreck Camp on February 5. Mamen and his party had returned two days earlier, stopped by open water three miles from land. The land they had nearly

reached was not Wrangell Island, as had been supposed, but Herald Island.

With all but eight of the men (the mate's party and the doctor's party) reassembled, eight men were chosen as an advance team and set out over the ice on February 19. The others waited for the weather to clear. After leaving a record of the shipwreck, along with the names of expedition members and their actions, in a copper tank on the ice, the balance of the men left Shipwreck Camp on February 24 in two groups eight hours apart. Covering 30 miles in two days, they caught up with the advance party on the 28th and helped them carve a path through three miles of raftered ice. They made it through the rafters, some of which were 100 feet high, on March 4. The men relayed supplies, including rations that would last them 80 days, and reached a spit on Wrangell Island on March 12. Captain Bartlett later wrote, "We were on land but were a long way from civilization; we need not drown but we might starve or freeze to death if we could not get help within a reasonable time" (Mowat 1976, 265–66).

Once established on shore, three men returned to Shipwreck Camp for more food. Captain Bartlett and Kataktovick headed for Siberia. They crossed many lanes of open water, repaired their sledge numerous times, nearly lost their dogs, and killed a polar bear, but reached the Siberian coast on April 4. They had traveled more than 200 miles in 17 days but were warmly received by the native Chukchee. With their assistance the two men reached Emma Harbour and were taken across the Bering Sea to St. Michael, Alaska, by the skipper of an American whaler. Captain Bartlett had an S.O.S. message transmitted at the U.S. Army telegraph station and the U.S. Coast Guard cutter *Bear* agreed to proceed to Wrangell to rescue the balance of the party. Captain Bartlett became impatient aboard the *Bear*: "Until someone came to rescue them they would not know whether I had ever succeeded in reaching the Siberian coast or not.

Every day of this suspense must be telling on them and bringing them face to face with the thought that they might have to spend another winter on the island, an experience which would be likely to kill them all" (Mowat 1976, 274). The ship left on July 13, but returned to Nome for coal on August 27. In Nome, Captain Bartlett convinced the U.S. Coast Guard vessel *Corwin* to try to reach the men on Wrangell Island and learned that the schooner *King and Winge* would also be in the vicinity.

The *Bear* left Nome on September 4. Four days later it met up with the *King and Winge* that had picked up the *Karluk* party. Captain Bartlett was relieved to be reunited with most of his men as they joined him on the *Bear*. The mate's party and that of Dr. Mackay had not been heard from. In addition, three other men had been lost. On the spit the men had divided into smaller parties for general harmony and larger hunting areas. Two of a party of three, Mamen and Malloch, became ill with nephritis and died within days of each other toward the end of May. Another man, Breddy, who had remained with a group that moved down the coast to Waring Point, fatally shot himself in what was attributed to an accident but speculated to be suicide. Although the fate of the mate's party is not known, the skeletonized remains of Dr. Mackay's party were discovered on the shore of Herald Island in 1929. The corpses of Malloch, Mamen, and Breddy may still remain entombed intact in the ice.

SPELUNKER

Floyd Collins was not exploring the ends of the earth but its bowels. He was driven by an urge to investigate his natural surroundings, despite the risks. Like the arctic and Antarctic explorers in this way, he differed from them in many respects. He was not subject to temperature extremes, he was not part of a team, and he was not making his attempt on behalf of his country. In ad-

dition, the cave that killed Collins was not the entity that preserved him. In fact, Floyd's preservation was only partly natural. The restoration of his intact exhumed body was deliberate. But perhaps what most sets Collins apart from the other adventurers and explorers—and what allies him with carnival mummies—is that his body was displayed to the public. The cave that claimed Floyd Collins was allowed to reclaim him.

Floyd Collins

The life of cave explorer Floyd Collins ended nightmarishly, and he did not rest in peace. Collins became trapped 60 feet underground in Sand Cave on January 30, 1925, when his ankle was pinned by a boulder. The accident occurred at the beginning of his third week of work at Sand Cave, after he had penetrated 150 feet through a narrow passageway. He was trying to find a connection between Kentucky's Crystal Cave and Mammoth Cave, which became a national park several years later in 1941. Collins was missed and found, but could not be pulled free. On the fourth day trapped in the cave, Collins told a friend who had reached him, "I've faced death afore … it don't frighten me none. But it's so long—so long" (Murray and Brucker 1979, 102).

The boulder at Collins' feet could not be budged and the narrow space of the tunnel did not allow room for mechanical means of reducing the boulder or even the surgical removal of Collins' lower leg. All his would-be rescuers could do was to keep him as comfortable as possible under the circumstances until the authorities could find a way to help. A military court of inquiry convened in Cave City on February 10 to determine what action to take. Unfortunately, they did not move quickly enough. By February 12, Collins had been trapped 13 days, his voice had not been heard in more than five, and he had not eaten in over a week. The court moved to Sand Cave on February 13 to take testimony from some of the miners working there. Final hearings were held on February 14.

The rescue attempt, when it finally got underway, was a massive effort to tunnel through the solid rock next to the tunnel where Collins was pinned. The activity drew an estimated 10,000 to 50,000 spectators (Murray and Brucker 1979, 170) from 20 states. The National Guard was called in to maintain order. Several planes, including one piloted by Charles Lindbergh, stood by in a field outside Cave City to fly photographs of the rescue attempt to the big-city papers. The total cost of the rescue operation was estimated at $200,000. But by the time the rescuers reached him, the 37-year-old Collins had died of exhaustion and exposure anywhere from a few hours to a few days before.

Edward Brenner, a professional miner from Cincinnati, was the first to see Collins after the rescue tunnel reached the passageway. The light bulb they had put on his chest to warm him and give light had gone out. Only his head and part of his left arm were free. A steady stream of water ran onto his cheek, leaving a red mark. His left eye was closed, his right slightly open. His mouth gaped at least an inch, revealing his gold tooth, and his face was bearded and dirty (Murray and Brucker 1979, 209). Brenner examined Collins under the instructions of Capt. J. F. Francis of the medical detachment of the 149th Infantry. He reported that Collins was cold, that he couldn't feel a pulse in front of his ear or in his wrist. He could not get at the lids of Collins' eyes to shine a light in them because they were too sunken. Dr. Francis and Dr. William H. Hazlitt of Chicago stated to the media that Collins' death had been due to a combination of exposure, exhaustion, and starvation. From the condition of the body as described by Brenner, they estimated that he had been dead at least 24 hours.

Collins became a Kentucky folk hero. His fate had been predicted by his brother

Floyd Collins in his thirties. Photo courtesy of Ken Sherman.

Homer (who told him he would get caught in Sand Cave) and his stepmother Jane (who was convinced that Collins' own dream of being trapped by a rockfall and rescued by angels was a warning from God). His story is told in books, movies, poems, novels, articles, television specials, and songs, including "The Ballad of Floyd Collins." One of his chroniclers, a small Louisville newspaperman named William B. "Skeets" Miller, who had squeezed into the tunnel to interview Collins, won a Pulitzer Prize on May 4, 1926. The theme of most of the newspaper articles was how impotent and vulnerable people are individually and how much they need one another in the face of whatever destiny has assigned to them. Collins' resignation to divine will was held up as an example of how to live and die. But the region's experienced cavers pointed out that Collins was partly responsible for his own fate by going where it was not within the power of anyone to rescue him.

Several rumors attached themselves to the Collins tragedy. Some observers believed that the accident was a stunt to advertise Crystal Cave, that Collins really was only pretending to be trapped. Others believed it was intended to stimulate sales of the *Louisville Courier-Journal* newspaper. Still others thought the L&N Railroad had concocted the scheme to increase its passenger traffic. And a few thought Collins and friends simply intended to bilk money out of a gullible public or that Collins' two business associates did not want him rescued and had left him in the cave to die (Murray and Brucker 1979, 177). The theories coalesced into four varieties: Collins was part of a hoax to lure tourists to the Kentucky cave country; he was murdered after he entered the cave; food and water had been purposely withheld so he would die; or he was still alive and went out and back in every night (Murray and Brucker 1979, 181). Several people purporting to be the escaped Floyd Collins were exposed as frauds. In Washington, D.C., false reports circulated that Collins was found weighing only 80 pounds after his release had been effected by the State Department.

To counter rumors of a hoax, the Collins family decided to recover the body for burial rather than leaving him entombed in the cave. Henry St. George Tucker Carmichael, general superintendent of the Kentucky Rock Asphalt Company (Kyroc) that had sunk the shaft, asked Collins' father Lee Collins for permission to amputate Collins' leg to more easily remove the body, but his request was denied. He therefore announced that the body would remain where it was and that a coroner's jury would handle final legal details. A chairman and six others who knew Collins descended into the shaft one by one to view the body after Everett Maddox had washed Collins' face, brushed back his hair, propped up his head on several small stones, and turned his face so it could be seen

clearly. The coroner's jury completed its formal inquest in Cave City on February 17, with Carmichael testifying that Collins' removal would probably result in the death of one or more of the rescue party. The jury's verdict was unanimous: "...that Floyd Collins is now dead and that he came to his death from exposure caused by being accidentally trapped in what is commonly called Sand Cave" (Murray and Brucker 1979, 215). Later that day the military court of inquiry was reconvened for a final session. Carmichael offered to bring one of Collins' fingers, hands, or even his head to the surface as tangible proof that he had been trapped below but was convinced to allow a photograph to be taken instead. John W. Steger of the *Chicago Tribune* was chosen to take the photo for national distribution, but only the *Tribune* received an exposed negative and published a photo showing a bald head, out-of-focus patches of dark and light, and a round shape supposed to be the light bulb on Collins' chest.

A 55 minute funeral service was held at the cave on February 17 by the Reverend Roy H. Biser, minister of the First Christian Church of Glasgow, Kentucky. Biblical texts were read, hymns sung, and prayers offered. The Reverend C. K. Dickey, pastor of the Horse Cave Methodist Church, offered a prayer and said, "Floyd Collins' body lies in yonder cave ... but his soul is with God, and he is happy" (Murray and Brucker 1979, 217). A. F. Pearson, a Glasgow funeral director, dropped a piece of ash, a tiny fern, and a bit of earth into the mouth of the shaft and the Reverend Mr. Dickey committed Collins' unseen remains to his Maker. Plans for Collins' body to lie in state for two days in the Cave City High School gymnasium and to be buried at the entrance to Crystal Cave could not be carried out.

On February 18, Carmichael rounded up about 75 people to move rocks, dirt, and trees into the shaft and had announced that concrete would be used to seal in the body and permanently block the entrance to Sand Cave. Bee Doyle, who owned

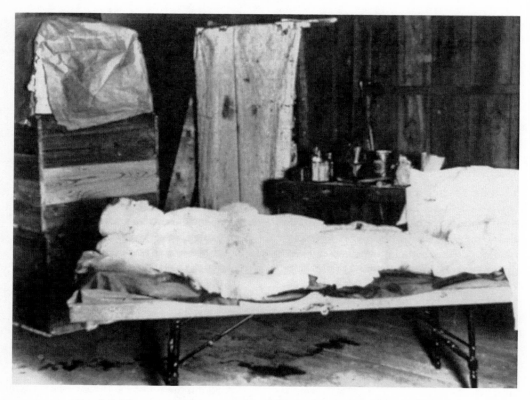

Floyd Collins on the embalming table. Photo courtesy of Roger Brucker.

the land above Sand Cave, collected 50 cents each from tourists who wished to see where Collins had died and remained entombed. Homer Collins declared his intention to raise enough money to bring his brother's body to the surface and took matters in hand. Homer and his other brothers, Marshall and Andy Lee, filed petitions in the Hart County court to have their father, Lee Collins, disqualified as administrator of Floyd's estate as *non compos mentis*. Lee was removed temporarily and the Union Trust Company of Glasgow substituted. Homer then contracted with W. H. Hunt, a miner from Central City, to recover Collins' body. Hunt and six other men began digging on April 4 and reached the body on April 17. The rock pinning Collins' left ankle was shaped like a leg of lamb and was estimated to weigh 50 to 75 pounds but weighed in at only 27. (The rock was claimed as property by Bee Doyle, who put it on display.)

Collins' body was brought to the surface on April 23, 1925, with about 100 people present. It was wrapped in a cloth, hoisted to the surface by a hook, and lowered onto a handmade stretcher. Hunt and his workmen gathered around the body to have their pictures taken. The cloth was slit to reveal Collins' face and those present were requested to file past to view the body. The corpse was then placed in a wicker basket and taken to Cave City, where it was embalmed by J. T. Geralds. Collins' body had begun to decompose, and cave crickets had eaten off his ears and part of his face. Restoration took three days and included the replacement of the destroyed facial features: eyes, nose, and mouth (Johnson, Johnson, and Williams 1996, 469). The body is said to have been substantially reduced in weight. While on the embalmer's table, Collins was photographed by Wade Highbaugh, who claimed that the body displayed bruises on the left leg and a dislocated right shoulder, but the negatives were later lost in a fire.

Floyd Collins' mother reportedly expressed satisfaction with his appearance after restoration (Johnson, Johnson, and Williams 1996, 469). On April 26, the body was buried in a casket borne by six pallbearers with sashes on their arms that read "Sand Cave." An estimated 400 people heard the brief funeral service in the rain, and the casket was placed in a grave beside the Flint Ridge family homestead and near the path to Crystal Cave. The spot was marked by a huge stalagmite.

In 1927 Lee Collins sold Crystal Cave for $10,000 to Dr. Harry B. Thomas, a Horse Cave dentist, along with the right to move his son's body into Crystal Cave if he wished. Collins was disinterred and placed in a glass-covered bronze metal casket after considerable remedial embalming work to make his corpse presentable. On June 13, 1927, with suitable publicity, Collins' new casket was placed in the middle of the tourist trail in Crystal Cave's main concourse (the "Grand Canyon"), where visitors could pass by and look in at him. A large red granite tombstone was placed at his head, calling him the "Greatest Cave Explorer Ever Known." The casket was included on tours of the cave and visitors were allowed to view the body until about 1948. Collins had a waxy white face, wore a black suit, and had gloved hands.

Floyd Collins' brothers were outraged and sued Dr. Thomas in late June 1927, but in 1929 a judge ruled that the cave and body had been legally obtained by Dr. Thomas. On the morning of March 19, 1929, Dr. Thomas discovered that Collins' body had been stolen the night before. He alerted authorities, who dusted the casket for fingerprints and used bloodhounds to track the corpse. Eight hundred yards from the cave, wrapped in a gunny sack and half-hidden in the brush on the edge of the Green River, the body was found minus its left leg. Collins was back in his casket on March 20. The thief was never apprehended, and the leg was never found. Some attribute the theft to a rival cave owner. Some believe it was staged by Dr. Thomas to stimulate his cave's tourist trade. Others believe Homer Collins hired some men to snatch the body, but they had dropped it.

The remains of Floyd Collins were returned to Crystal Cave in a 1,200-pound coffin with a glass cover under a metal lid that could be lifted for viewing. The body was no longer continuously displayed, but tours paused at the casket and interested visitors were still permitted a peek under the lid for the proper tip as late as 1952. The body had been frequently restored to keep it presentable, and the casket had been replaced several times. Meanwhile, the affronts to Collins' dignity continued. In 1939 Dr. Thomas erected a monument to Collins in the center of the town of Horse Cave, Kentucky, but the memorial was knocked down by a truck in 1965.

Mammoth Cave was dedicated as the nation's twenty-sixth national park in 1946. In 1961 the National Park Service bought Crystal Cave from Dr. Thomas' widow, Mrs. Carrie B. Thomas, and her two daughters for $285,000 and closed it to tourists. Eleven years later the connection Collins had sought was finally made between Crystal Cave and Mammoth Cave (which eventually totaled 144.4 miles of passages). Collins remained inside the cave but off limits to tourists. Local cave explorer Dane Raque, who mapped the underground tunnels for the Park Service, said, "You always paid your respects to Floyd when you did work down there, and invited him to go along. He was a kindred spirit."

Collins' family sued the federal government to release Floyd's body, and officials agreed to do so, eventually but local opposition slowed their efforts down. Carol Collins, wife of brother Marshall's grandson Donnie Collins of Horse Cave, repeatedly wrote to the Park Service requesting reburial of Collins' body, but nothing ever came of it until late 1988, when park ranger Phil Veluzat informed them that the Park Service was looking into the matter. Veluzat's investigations had revealed that a federal ruling issued back in 1961 stated that the Interior Department had no obligation to perpetuate anything so "totally repugnant" as making Collins' body another roadside attraction. A prompt reburial in a local cemetery at government expense was recommended, and the details were worked out by Mammoth Cave Park historian Bob Ward and Park superintendent David Mihalic.

Leona Ashe, Collins' half-sister who had been born five years after the accident, was contacted as next-of-kin for permission to bury Collins near his mother and believed it was the right thing to do. The plan was objected to by a member of the Cave Research Foundation, who wrote that the removal of Collins' body "appears to be callous, disrespectful" and that the plan also threatened to diminish Collins' place in history. A former director of the foundation charged that the action "flies in the face of Collins' wishes, as expressed to his father when he first found Crystal Cave. It's a slap in the face to every caver in the country" (Fincher 1990, 150). Foundation members pointed out that in Europe, the bodies of cavers who die during exploration efforts are often left in the caverns where the accidents occurred.

Nevertheless, a block and tackle was rigged outside the entrance to Crystal Cave. A steel sled was welded together and thick plywood siding laid down in the first large gallery below the entrance. A 15-man crew pushed, pulled, and lifted the coffin, the massive tombstone, and its base (weighing around 1,000 pounds each) up a narrow path and out of the stone grotto. The move took three days. Collins' casketed body was taken by hearse to the Hatcher & Saddler Funeral Home in Glasgow, where it was housed while services were arranged at the cemetery in Mammoth Cave National Park. Some restorative work was done on the exterior of the glass-sealed casket, but it remained unopened and the body was not viewed by any member of the family or staff. Leona Ashe states that she had "no desire to see the body" and had been told "there were bones coming through" (telephone conversation with author, 12 June 1996).

Tommy G. High, vice president of Hatcher & Saddler, writes, "In regard to my personal feeling concerning the display of Mr. Collins' remains and family efforts to reclaim it, I feel it was a disgrace for anyone to exploit a family tragedy for personal gain.... I applaud the family efforts to reclaim the remains of Mr. Collins in order to give him a 'final' resting place with dignity. I also feel that the request to remove him from the cave was too long in receiving approval" (letter to author, 23 January 1995).

Collins was finally buried in the family plot on Flint Ridge beside the Mammoth Cave Baptist Church on Good Friday morning, March 24, 1989, with 40 family members present. He was interred in the bronze-hued metal coffin with its inner top of transparent glass sealed from view. The service was read by the Reverend Gary Talley, including Psalm 40: "I waited patiently for the Lord; and he inclined unto me, and heard my cry. He brought me up also out of a horrible pit, out of the miry clay, and set my feet upon a rock..." (Fincher 1990, 137). At the conclusion of the service, the Reverend Mr. Talley did not sprinkle the customary clods of earth on the lowered casket, saying later, "Somehow ... it wouldn't have seemed appropriate in Floyd's case" (Fincher 1990, 150). Reporters, including a representative of the *Chicago Tribune*, gathered some distance away from the grave site. Only family members, including Leona Ashe, attended the burial. Another family member, Mary Lou Carney, of Chesterton, Indiana, said, "There is a real sense of relief now. It's been a nightmare for three generations the way he has been treated."

7. Acts of Faith

Servants, Patriarchs, and Believers

Some bodies are said to be too pure to decay, but always after the fact. The grave of a monk or nun is opened years after death to reveal a body that is whole and incorrupt. The find is marveled over and used as evidence in the individual's progression to sainthood. But not all saints are incorruptibles, and incorruption does not guarantee sainthood: "It is not only the multitude of examples of bodies naturally preserved from decay which creates a difficulty against any premature appeal to the interference of supernatural agencies. There is also the fact that the occurrence of the phenomenon is extremely arbitrary, and, to judge by human standards, inconsistent" (Thurston 1952, 240). Enshrining those whose bodies do remain incorrupt is a time-honored religious tradition. Conversely, in many religions it is customary to enshrine patriarchs whose bodies have been prepared for what is hoped will be perpetual preservation. Whether planned for or serendipitous, preservation is associated with those who have dedicated their lives to their God. There have been a handful of secular incorruptibles, but their preservation is also attributed to their faith or that of their families. Whether incorruptibility is a measure of holiness may be debated, but one thing is clear: preservation cannot be predicted.

SERVANTS

Holy incorruptibles are set apart from other mummies because they are not pre-served by the hands of humans or the forces of nature but supposedly by divine intervention: "Of course it must be recognized throughout in dealing with this subject that cases of a remarkable and seemingly unaccountable preservation of human remains are sufficiently common to make it rather difficult to decide in any individual instance that the absence of corruption is due to anything more than mere coincidence" (Thurston 1952, 238).

The incorruptibles are not desiccated like many mummies, but usually remain supple and therefore in a category of their own: "The incorruptibles have been incorrectly classified as natural mummies, but…the products of the deliberate and accidental preservations, without exception, have been not more than shriveled specimens, always rigid and extremely dry. Most of the incorruptibles, however, are neither dry nor rigid but quite moist and flexible, even after the passage of centuries" (Cruz 1977, 33). The bodies of the holy have been found incorrupt despite the adverse circumstances of their burial (delayed interment, frequent transfer, rough handling) and the unfavorable conditions in the tomb (temperature, moisture, proximity to decaying bodies). Their resistance to the decay that would normally take place is not attributed to ascetical diets during life or to embalming after death. It is claimed that the majority of incorruptibles were not embalmed or treated in any way yet were found not only lifelike but "sweetly scented" many years after burial (Cruz 1977, 27).

This special distinction is occasionally bestowed upon those who lived lives of virtue. Although the pope is reluctant to accept the incorruption of the body as a miracle supporting proof of a person's sanctity, exceptions have been made (Cruz 1977, 40).

The facts that many incorruptibles are on public display, that they periodically undergo scientific and medical testing, and that their fellow religious are unlikely to have participated in deception are given to counter claims that the incorruptibles are hoaxed (Cruz 1977, 42). Although the Catholic Church may not consider them miraculous, the possibility that they may have been deliberately rather than divinely preserved cannot be ruled out. Embalming historian Edward C. Johnson points out that embalming can be concealed in a number of ways: cavity fluid may be introduced through the navel which is then closed with a circular stitch, arterial fluid may be injected in the popliteal artery behind the kneecap so that the incision wouldn't show from the front, or the body may simply be covered with a preservative-saturated cloth (telephone conversation with the author, 29 July 1996).

In the case of Sister Maria della Passione, decomposition did not ensue upon her death on July 27, 1912. Although embalming isn't mentioned, much was made of the fact that rigor mortis did not occur. The body of the forty-six-year-old nun was conveyed in a shallow, open casket to the chapel of her convent in southern Italy some eight or nine hours after her death. Crowds of visitors came to pay their respects and were able to move her hands to kiss them and place them on the afflicted parts of their bodies. The body of Sister Maria remained perfectly flexible, as though it were that of a living person. In a biography of the nun, L. Fontana notes that it was the hottest season of the year and states, "Although it [the body] was pulled about by the constant handling of

those who stood close to it, to the astonishment of all, it remained without a trace of corruption and without giving off the least unpleasant odour; on the contrary it was remarked that the face became more and more beautiful and the features more clear-cut" (Thurston 1952, 273). A doctor objected to the body being held above ground for three days but withdrew his protest when he saw the condition of the remains.

Whether divine, deliberate, or merely accidental, the bodies of twentieth-century servants of God continue to join their brothers and sisters in this highly variable state of preservation. Santa Savina Petrilli da Siena's body, which had not been embalmed after her death in 1923, exhibited a very poor natural mummification when examined by anthropologists in this decade (Fulcheri 1996, 220). The body of Blessed Maria Assunta Pallotta was presumably better preserved but poorly documented. Maria was sent to the Chinese mission of Tong-Eul-Kiou by the Franciscan Missionaries of Mary in 1904, only to die of typhus within a year of her arrival. In April 1913, eight years after her death at age twenty-seven, Maria's remains were found perfectly preserved during their transfer to Tai-Yuan-Fou. The Communists took over the mission in 1949, and according to author Joan Carroll Cruz (1977, 300), "It is impossible to obtain any information concerning the present condition of the relic. It is also not known if the grave of the Beata has been respected." Her memory, however, has been. Maria was beatified by Pope Pius XII on November 7, 1954, and her feast day is celebrated annually on April 7. More spectacular and better-documented examples include the incorruptible bodies of Jacinta of Fátima and Father Solanus.

Venerable Jacinta Marto

Jacinta was the ninth child of Manuel Pedro Marto and Olimpia de Jesus dos Santos (who had two children from a previous marriage). She was born in 1910 in the village of Aljustrel in the Portuguese parish of

Top: Jacinta of Fatima (d. 1920) upon her exhumation in 1935. Photo by Baptisat R. 28 Maio, E. Venda Nova-Amadora. Photo courtesy of Fatima Archives. *Bottom:* Jacinta of Fatima upon exhumation. Photo courtesy of Fatima Archives.

Fátima, which lies about one hundred miles north of Lisbon. Jacinta was an ordinary child, though said to be of a very sensitive temperament. In 1916 Jacinta, her brother Francisco, and their cousin Lucia de Jesus dos Santos saw an Angel of Peace three times—twice on a rocky hillside overlooking the village of Aljustrel and once at the well in Lucia's backyard. The angel urged them to pray, do penance for the remission of sins, make sacrifices, and obtain the conversion of sinners.

On May 13, 1917, the three children saw the Virgin Mary in Cova da Iria, near Fátima, where they had been grazing sheep. At the time, Lucia (who saw, heard, and spoke to the Lady) was age 10, Francisco (who saw the Lady) was age 9, and Jacinta (who saw and heard the Lady, but did not speak to her) was age 7. During the first apparition of the brilliant Lady in white, she asked the children to return to the same spot at the same time on the 13th of each of the following six months. On June 13, the Lady requested that the children establish a devotion to the Immaculate Heart of Mary. On July 13 the children were given a vision of hell. She asked the children to keep the contents of both visions secret, but they were finally revealed by Lucia twenty-five years later. After Lucia's revelation, Pope Pius XII consecrated the whole church to the Immaculate Heart of Mary and assigned a Feast Day of August 22. A third secret revealed to the children has never been disclosed.

On October 13, 1917, the Lady appeared and asked the children to have a chapel built on the location in her honor as the Lady of the Rosary. She also performed a miracle as she had promised by causing the sun to become especially brilliant and to dance in the sky, an event witnessed by the large crowd that had gathered (not all of whom were convinced that it was not a natural phenomenon) and others who saw it from a distance. After this vision the children were revered by many and ridiculed by others. They were even arrested and detained for several days by authorities who threatened to boil them in oil unless they revealed the Lady's secrets.

In October 1918 Jacinta and Francisco were afflicted by the Spanish influenza that was epidemic at the time. Both of them insisted that prayers and doctors would not cure them and Jacinta predicted that she would die alone in a hospital, far from her family. Francisco's health deteriorated rapidly. He died on April 4, 1919, and was buried in the family tomb of the Barons of Alvaiázere in the cemetery of Vila Nova de Ourém. Jacinta's health continued to deteriorate, and she was moved in July 1919 to the Hospital of St. Augustine in Vila Nova de Ourém, where she remained for two months and then returned home with a large open sore on her side. Father Formigao wrote, "Jacinta is like a skeleton and her arms are shockingly thin. Since she left the local hospital where she underwent two months of useless treatment, the fever has never left her. She looks pathetic. Tuberculosis, after an attack of bronchial pneumonia and purulent pleurisy is undermining her enfeebled constitution" (Rengers 1986, 70).

Jacinta's body continued to waste away. She was taken to a hospital in Lisbon, where she was visited by the Lady and told the day and hour of her death. She was diagnosed with purulent pleurisy of the large left cavity (an inflamed chest membrane) and fistulous osteitis (inflammation and abscess) of the seventh and eighth ribs on the left side. Jacinta was operated on by chief surgeon Dr. Leonardo de Castro Freire but grew worse. On February 20, 1920, Jacinta—knowing she was dying—requested the sacrament of Holy Viaticum but instead received the Sacrament of Penance. She died at 10:30 that night without receiving Holy Communion. At the time of her death a beautiful fragrance was said to have been exuded from her wasted body.

Jacinta's body was dressed in a white First Communion dress with a blue sash, in accordance with her wishes to be buried in the garb of the Lady. She was laid in a coffin that was placed on two stools in the sacristy of the parish Church of the Holy Angels by the arrangement of Dr. Lisboa. A steady stream of pilgrims arrived to pray and touch rosaries, statues, and religious medals to Jacinta's dress. The pastor, Father Reis, was worried about premature veneration and possible health risks, so he moved the coffin to a locked office upstairs that was used by the Confraternity of the Blessed Sacrament. He deposited the key with the undertakers, Antonio Almeida & Company. Almeida took responsibility for leading small groups of the faithful upstairs to see the body. Dr. Lisboa wrote, "He was deeply impressed by the respect and devotion with which the people approached and kissed the little corpse on the face and on the hands, and he remembers very clearly the live pinkness of the cheeks and the beautiful aroma which the body exhaled" (Rengers 1986, 78).

On the morning of February 24, Jacinta's body was sealed in a lead casket in the presence of Antonio Almeida, the authorities, and a number of women who remarked on the beautiful floral aroma that the diseased body emitted when the coffin was closed. The casket was carried to the train station in the company of a large crowd and transported by rail to the cemetery of Vila Nova de Ourém to be entombed in the family sepulcher with that of her brother. Lucia said later, "My aunt took me to see the mortal remains of her little daughter, in the hope of distracting me in that manner, but for a long time my sadness seemed to increase more and more" (Galamba de Oliveira 1982, 186).

On September 12, 1935, Jacinta's casket was opened in preparation for its removal to Fátima. "...all the spectators were struck with amazement as they beheld the face of Jacinta perfectly preserved. Miracle? Natural phenomenon?....Was the rest of it in the same condition? The haste with which everything was done precluded further investigation" (Galamba de Oliveira 1982, 45–46). Several people touched handkerchiefs and religious articles to the body, after which the casket was closed and the small four-car procession that included the children's parents made its way to Fátima. The "urn" containing the remains of Jacinta was

carried by the Baron of Alvaiázere and his son. The cortege entered the place where the apparitions had taken place, and mass was said by the Archbishop of Evora. Pilgrims came to touch religious articles to Jacinta's urn. After the service the remains of Jacinta and Francisco were transferred to a simple white tomb in the parish cemetery of Fátima that had been erected by Dr. José Alves Correia da Silva, bishop of the diocese of Leiria.

The tomb was visited by the Cardinal Patriarch of Lisbon and several bishops during a spiritual retreat on May 13, 1938. On May 1, 1951, the remains of Jacinta (still intact) and Francisco were finally translated to the sanctuary built on the spot where the Virgin Mary had appeared. Pope John Paul II made a pilgrimage to Fátima on May 13, 1982. He prayed in the chapel at the site of the visions, met with Lucia, and prayed at the tombs of Francisco and Jacinta in the basilica.

The cause for the canonization of Jacinta and Francisco had been initiated in 1946. An informative process was introduced for each child in 1952 and concluded in 1979, when they became approved candidates for beatification. Testimony was taken from Jacinta's cousin Lucia, who had become a Carmelite nun in Coimbra and was still living in 1986. On May 13, 1989, Pope John Paul II granted the title of Venerable Servants of God to Jacinta and Francisco Marto by decree. If canonized, Jacinta and Francisco will be the youngest nonmartyrs ever to become saints.

Father Solanus Casey, O.F.M. Cap.

Bernard Francis "Barney" Casey was born in Prescott, Wisconsin, in 1870. He entered the diocesan seminary of St. Francis de Sales in Milwaukee at age 22 and arrived in Detroit at age 26 to begin his novitiate. He made his religious profession at age 28, adopted the brown Franciscan habit, and was given the name Frater Francis Solanus. Father Solanus resumed his study of theology

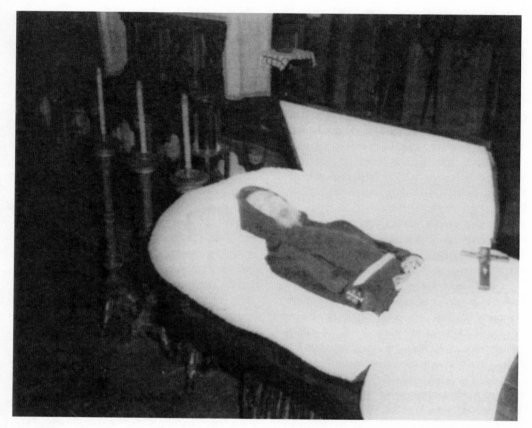

Father Solanus Casey, O.F.M. Cap., in an open casket prior to his burial in 1957. Photo courtesy of the Father Solanus Guild.

for the priesthood at St. Francis Capuchin Seminary in Milwaukee. He was ordained *sacerdotas simplex* (simplex priest) at age 34, with the condition that he would not preach publicly or hear confessions. Father Solanus began a long career as a sacristan and doorkeeper dedicated to the poor and needy. He was assigned to friaries in Yonkers; Harlem; Detroit; Brooklyn; Huntington, Indiana; and again in Detroit.

Father Solanus displayed the virtues of faith, piety, goodness, charity, humility, and simplicity. He was generous and tolerant and had unshaken faith in God, reciting the rosary daily and sometimes spending entire nights in prayer. He also had gifts of prophecy and healing. He referred to his miracles as favors from God and remained humble about his own part in them. On No-

vember 8, 1923, Father Solanus was asked to keep a log of prayer requests and to note when the prayers had been answered. The answered prayers included the recovery of a dying woman from pneumonia, the disappearance of a woman's life-threatening heart condition, and the restoration of a woman's memory. By July 28, 1924, Father Solanus had made 96 entries in his journal and 41 of these indicated that prayers had been answered (Odell 1995, 89).

From 1935 to 1945, Father Solanus saw some 150 to 200 people per day at St. Bonaventure's Monastery in Detroit. Despite the number of his intercessions, he did not practice his healing on his fellow monks because he believed that they were not to seek healings but as religious men were instead to follow Christ and to see sufferings as blessings. Father Solanus himself was hospitalized in Detroit in September 1942 for eczema and fever and used the time for penance and prayer. In May 1949 he was hospitalized in Fort Wayne, Indiana, for "weeping eczema" and his legs were covered with painful open sores. Solanus also suffered from erysipelas, or St. Anthony's fire, an acute infectious disease of the skin.

Father Solanus celebrated the 50th anniversary of his priestly ordination on July 28, 1954. His health had weakened, and he was thereafter hospitalized several times. In 1956 some skin cancers on his legs were diagnosed and removed. In 1957 he was again admitted to the hospital, where he intervened on behalf of a woman who had miscarried three times and afterward successfully delivered a twin son and daughter. On July 31, 1957, after receiving the sacraments and pronouncing, "I give my soul to Jesus Christ," Father Solanus died in the hospital at age 86. "The eyes closed and he fell backward a bit, exhaling his last breath. It was just 11:00 A.M." (Odell 1995, 201).

The body of Father Solanus was transported to Van Lerberghe Funeral Home, chosen for the large numbers of mourners it could accommodate. He was dressed in his Capuchin habit with the hood pulled up over his head. A rosary and copies of the Rule and Constitution of the Order were placed inside the casket. Visiting hours began on the morning of August 1. Capuchins stood near the casket to receive expressions of sympathy and to prevent any attempt to acquire relics. Two columns of approximately 5,000 people filed by the body until the doors were closed late that night. The next morning the body was scheduled to be taken to St. Bonaventure's Monastery Chapel, but hundreds more mourners had gathered at the funeral home and were allowed to pay their respects.

The body of Father Solanus was taken to St. Bonaventure's later in the day and was viewed by another 6,000 followers. By the morning of August 3, 20,000 people of every order and religious persuasion had paid their respects. The funeral mass that day was celebrated by Father Solanus' brother, Monsignor Edward Casey. In Father Solanus' words, "Death is the climax of all humility, when we must finally give up all and turn all over to God. Death can be very beautiful—like a wedding—if we make it so" (Odell 1995, 222). Father Solanus was buried in the cemetery of the Detroit Capuchins near the monastery. The small graveyard, which already held the bodies of seventeen other friars, was frequently visited by the faithful.

In 1960 the Father Solanus Guild was formed to spread word about the life and work of Father Solanus. Five years after Father Solanus' death, seven notebooks documenting some 6,000 prayer requests, 700 of which had been answered, were discovered among his things. His miracles included medical cures, averted bankruptcies and divorces, and the prevention of mental breakdown. In 1966 Father Gerard Hesse, O.F.M. Cap., the Capuchin provincial, gathered reports of Solanus' favors and cures and sent them to Rome. In the same year, Father Paschal Siler was appointed vice-postulator to gather information about Solanus. In 1972 the first official step was taken toward further study of his holiness: the National Council of Catholic Bishops gave a *nihil obstat*, a statement that nothing hinders further investigation.

In 1974 Brother Leo Wollenweber succeeded Father Siler as vice-postulator and two years later petitioned Cardinal John F. Dearden to initiate the Cause of Beatification and Canonization within the archdiocese. The Cause was initiated by the Archbishop Edmund C. Szoka, who had succeeded Cardinal Dearden. Szoka conducted the *Processus Cognitionalis*, or informative process, and in 1984 the official testimony of fifty-three witnesses was taken from Detroit to Rome and given, along with other records totaling 3,600 pages, to the Sacred Congregation for the Causes of Saints. The decree was promulgated on November 7, 1986.

Part of the diocesan investigation in the Cause for Canonization included the exhumation of Father Solanus' body. Shortly before sunrise on July 8, 1987, the grave in St. Bonaventure Cemetery was opened. The casket was carried into a room adjoining the chapel. The body was viewed by Archbishop Szoka, other Church officials, Capuchin witnesses, two Casey family members, and mortuary authorities (Odell 1995, 207). The examination was conducted by Dr. Gordon Rose, head of the Department of Mortuary Science at Wayne State University. When the casket was opened, the body was readily recognizable as that of Father Solanus. According to the report that was to be sent to Rome, the structural and tissue integrity of the body was extensive, but some decomposition in both arms had occurred. The body was found to be about 95 percent intact. Although this was not deemed miraculous, the doctor who conducted the examination declared the preservation to be "remarkable" in his official report. The body of Father Solanus was washed, dressed in a fresh habit, and placed in a new bronze-colored steel casket. The casket was sealed and entombed in the chapel.

In the fall of 1994 and again near Christmas, the story of Father Solanus Casey was aired on NBC's *Unsolved Mysteries*. After the television exposure, Father Solanus received an increased number of visitors. In the first half of 1995 some 15,000 people arrived to pay their respects at the tomb of Solanus inside the chapel.

The published *Positione super virtutibus* was approved on April 7, 1995, by the Designated Committee of Theological Consultants. On June 20, 1995, the Cardinals, Bishops in Ordinary Session, and William Wakefield Baum, the Cardinal Ponens of the Cause, acknowledged that Father Solanus had cultivated the theological and other virtues to a heroic degree. The facts concerning these findings were brought to the attention of Pope John Paul II, who ordered that a decree be written. The decree, given at Rome on July 11, 1995, reads as follows: "There is proven evidence that the theological virtues, Faith, Hope and Charity to-

wards God and neighbor and also the cardinal virtues, Prudence, Justice, Temperance and Fortitude and other virtues, have been exercised to a heroic degree by the Servant of God, Francis Solanus Casey, professed priest of the Order of Friars Minor Capuchin, concerning whom, this decree is promulgated." The decree was made public and entered into the Acts of the Congregation for the Causes of Saints. Father Solanus Casey had been declared "venerable."

The Decree of Heroic Virtue is the most important step in the Process for Canonization. As Vice Postulator Brother Leo Wollenweber, O.F.M. Cap., explains, "The way is now opened to Beatification which could follow upon acceptable proof of at least one miraculous cure attributed to Fr. Solanus' intercession. We are presently working to document a few of the hundreds of cures that have been reported over the past years. When we have sufficient documents, including hospital records and doctors' statements, these will be submitted to the Congregation for Causes of Saints in the hope that one may be accepted" (letter to the author, 25 July 1996). If Father Solanus is beatified, he will be given the title "blessed." If a miracle is proven to be attributed to him after beatification, he may be canonized and would thus become the first American-born male saint.

Brother Stephen Nehme

A case more difficult to confirm is that of Brother Stephen Nehme, a monk in the Kfeifan Monastery in Lebanon. According to a newspaper clipping from 1966, Brother Stephen died on August 28, 1938, while he was praying after dinner. He was buried directly in the ground in the monks' cemetery under the monastery. When his grave was breached ten years later during the burial of another monk, his body was found to be intact. After immediate prayers at the grave site, the monks removed Brother Stephen's body to a special tomb and placed it in a glass-covered casket. The darkening of the skin was supposedly the result of one of the monks, who was dismissed after it was learned that he had several times undressed the body, washed it with oil and gasoline, exposed it to the sun, and then washed it with hot water before returning it to the casket.

Bukkai Shōnin

Not all incorruptibles are Roman Catholics. Some are not even Christians. Bukkai Shōnin was a Japanese priest who practiced asceticism at Mount Yudono and died in 1903 at age 76. Immediately after his death, he was put in a wooden coffin that was placed in an underground stone chamber prepared in accordance with his will. The chamber of hewn stone was one meter beneath the stone slab covering the grave. It was two meters deep and one and a quarter meters wide. Near the floor was a shelf of iron bars upon which the strong wooden coffin had been placed. After three years, the priests were supposed to exhume and mummify the body, but by that time, exhumation became forbidden by law, so Bukkai remained buried at the Kanzeonji Temple, Murakami City, Niigata prefecture.

Bukkai's tomb was excavated in 1961. Parts of the body had skeletonized and other parts had mummified. The scientists described what they found: "Many bones were separated at the joints. The soft parts had decomposed and were attached to the bones like dirt, but some skin of his back was mummified. There is no evidence that the brain and viscera were extracted. The body was probably in a sitting position when it was placed in the coffin, but it was not so at the time of our excavation" (Sakurai and Ogata 1980). Upon exhumation, the body was 158.2 centimeters in height and weighed 7.2 kilograms. Unlike similar mummies, Bukkai had not been damaged by rats, but the scientists were not able to determine blood groups because of corrosion of almost all of the soft parts.

Preservation of soft tissue is rare in Japan. But by gradually reducing the intake of nutrition over a long period during life, the body's constitution is altered to one that is strongly resistant to decomposition after death. Some of the ascetics abstain from the five cereals (rice, barley, corn, millet, and beans) for this purpose. After interment for three years in an underground stone chamber, their bodies are exhumed and dried.

PATRIARCHS

Like many other centuries, the twentieth century is bracketed by the deaths of religious leaders whose power and popularity are so great that they are embalmed with special care. This careful embalming, intended to allow prolonged enshrinement and funeralization, has a long tradition in many religious cultures. When Joakim, patriarch of Constantinople, died in 1912 his body was enthroned for homage, as documented in a contemporary photograph. When Archbishop Sergei Ochotenko, head of the Byelo Russian Autocephalic Church of Australia and Abroad, died in 1971 he too was enthroned. Although enthronement is the equivalent of lying in state, it has the benefit of allowing the hand to be posed in benediction. Many religious figureheads, however, are enshrined in less unusual positions. The Catholic popes recline; the Dalai Lamas sit.

Some religious leaders have little name recognition but had large followings. To allow the faithful to pay their respects, Bishop McCullough of the House of Prayer was embalmed in the District of Columbia in the early 1990s, placed in a glass casket, and transported to several locations across the United States so that funerals could be conducted by his followers. Some find it important to preserve the body of a religious figure, not only to pray for his soul, but to wait for him to reinhabit his body. The followers of Indian guru Thakur Balak Brahmachari believed he would be resurrected within a couple of weeks of his death, so they put his body on ice. They washed him and changed his robes daily for weeks. Thousands of pilgrims, who had come to see him come back to life, were given holy water from the melted ice to drink. Two months later 1,200 Calcutta policemen stormed the Ashram, captured the body, and took it to a crematorium (Carlton 1995, 164).

Embalming with preservative fluids rather than preventing the onset of decomposition with ice offers—but does not ensure—a better chance at preservation for saints-to-be: "Some mummies of saints are natural mummies, due to the particular conditions of the tomb, of the micro-climate, and of the local climate....Other mummies derive from partial artificial mummification processes. The body was anointed with unguents, perfumes and spices before burial out of devotion, but also to allow for a long public exposure before being buried. Still other mummies have been properly artificially preserved and in some cases dissected and eviscerated (Fulcheri 1996, 221). But even in cases where preservation is a deliberate objective, it does not always succeed. Whether they loom above their followers or lie in their midst, the bodies of religious leaders are at the mercy of their embalmers, experienced or not, and subject to the whimsy of their craft. All the same, Archbishop Ochotenko most likely remains upright on his throne in the darkness of his tomb, his hand still raised in blessing....

Pope Pius X (Giuseppe Melchiorre Sarto)

The future St. Pius X was born in Italy in 1835 and ordained in 1858. He was named archpriest of Salzano in 1867 and was made chancellor of the Treviso Diocese in 1875. He served as bishop of the Diocese of Mantua from 1884 to 1893. Pope Leo XIII appointed him cardinal and patriarch of Venice. When the pope died, Pius X was elected to take his place. Pius X died August 20, 1914, was beatified in 1951, and was canonized in 1954. "Before the pope's beatification his

body was exhumed and was found in an incorrupt state, authentic in all respects, with the skin a delicate white. The physician of Pope Pius XII, in order to maintain the condition of the corpse, injected a special preserving chemical that unfortunately turned the body a medium brown. The incorruption, however, has been maintained" (Cruz 1984, 282). The body of Pope Pius X is enshrined in a side altar of St. Peter's Basilica but is not wholly visible. His face is covered with a bronze mask and the body covered with fine vestments.

Pope Pius XII (Eugenio Pacelli)

Pope Pius XII died October 9, 1958, of strokes in the papal summer palace at Castel Gandolfo. His death was witnessed by his personal physician Dr. Riccardo Galeazzi-Lisi. Afterward, the physician stated that the body was embalmed in the room in which he died and that an entirely new process invented by Professor Oreste Nuzzi of Naples would preserve the body indefinitely in a "natural state." The embalming method, which the physician helped to develop, requires no incisions or injections. It is based on the principle of osmosis, the tendency of fluid to flow from a low to high concentration of salt. During the treatment, which took three and a half hours, pungent fluids were sprinkled on the Pope's clothing and volatile resins were absorbed through the skin. No further treatment was required, according to contemporary dispatches from Rome.

Although newspapers have claimed that the body should remain preserved for one hundred years, this was not the case. The body decomposed rapidly, and exposure of the remains to the view of the faithful was terminated. Swiss honor guards stationed at each corner of the open casket were reported ill during their vigil, another indication that the embalming was a complete failure. Embalming historian Edward C. Johnson points out that medical men do not embalm often enough and with only limited experience are unlikely to do so successfully.

Pope John Paul I
(Albino Luciani)

Pope John Paul I died on September 28, 1978, at age 65 after a reign of only thirty-three days. It has been speculated that he was poisoned, and the time of death is in dispute among researchers, but the stated cause of death was a heart attack occurring at 11 P.M. Sister Vincenza found him sitting up in bed in his pajama bottoms and day shirt. His back and feet were warm to the touch. The body was laid out by his doctor Renato Buzzonetti, Bishop John Magee, and John Paul's secretary Don Diego Lorenzi. His body was not incontinent and did not need to be washed. He was dressed in his white cassock, and a piece of silk was tied around his head to keep his jaw in place.

According to one account, the Signoracci brothers embalmed the pope on the night of his death to avoid the swelling and smell that had occurred with the body of Pope Paul VI and to ensure that the body could be exposed to the faithful for several days. Ernesto and Arnaldo Signoracci prepared the fluid, checked the nose and mouth for seepage, and injected the fluid into the femoral arteries. They are uncertain of the time, but it is assumed it was about 7 o'clock that evening. They insist that they did not remove any organs or blood (Cornwell 1989, 277), despite testimony by those on the scene: "Every day during the lying in state they came with other specialists and put up screens and locked the doors. On the first day they took away parts of the body, possibly bowels and so on. But after two or three days he was unrecognizable," remembers Don Diego Lorenzi (Cornwell 1989, 111).

According to Dr. Buzzonetti, the body of the Pope was moved to the Sala Clementina, where it was exposed from noon until about seven o'clock in the evening on September 29 and where the president of Italy, Sandro Pertini, paid his respects. The body was then moved to the Sala dei Forconi, the "Hall of the Preachers," where it was undressed and treated for hygienic preservation without the removal of organs, intestines, or blood. Dr. Buzzonetti claims that the embalming was not carried out until at least nineteen or twenty hours had passed, in accordance with Italian law that insists that a body be observed for fifteen hours before being touched (Cornwell 1989, 222).

Dr. Buzzonetti states that the preservation process was done by a team directed by Professor Cesare Gerin, director of the Istituto di Medicina Legale at the State University of Rome. He was assisted by Professors Fucci, Mariggi, and Maragin. One of the Signoracci brothers was present as a technical assistant. The treatment began at about 7 P.M. on September 29 and was completed at about 3:30 the following morning. The body was clothed with vestments again and exposed (Cornwell 1989, 220–21).

The body of Pope John Paul I lay in state in St. Peter's Cathedral for four days as people filed past at the rate of 12,000 per hour. The body was guarded around the clock by Swiss guards. On October 3, the gates were closed and screens erected around the body. An examination, that some speculate was an autopsy, was conducted by doctors (Yallop 1984, 238–39). The pope's remains were hermetically sealed in three coffins of cypress, lead, and ebony and placed inside a marble sarcophagus in the crypt of St. Peter's Basilica.

Thirteenth Dalai Lama
(Thupten Gyatso)

Thupten Gyatso, the Thirteenth Dalai Lama, died in 1933 at age 58. In November of that year he had summoned a photographer to take his picture, an act the people of Lhasa took to signify his imminent death. The Dalai Lama went to the "Honorable Field" (died) in mid–December. His only symptom had been a cough, so his death is attributed to everything from a weak heart to uremia, pneumonia, or overwork (Bell 1987, 441). That he died on a Sunday was considered a bad omen for his family and for the country of Tibet. Public mourning began a few days after the Dalai Lama's death and was reduced from the usual seven weeks to three weeks in the hope that the new Incarnation would come quickly. No one wore new clothes, ornamented themselves, danced, or sang. Lamps were lighted on the rooftops. A biography by the Tibetan government states that the chief lamas "performed sacrificial ceremony before his precious body continually" and "composed a poem asking him to reincarnate soon" (Bell 1987, 446).

The body of the Thirteenth Dalai Lama was "embalmed and treated at intervals with salt" (Bell 1987, 446). Lamas, government officials, and members of the public came before the ornate throne and offered sacrifices in honor of the holy man, who was seated in a lotus position.

The Tibetan biography recounts that during the Dalai Lama's period of sitting in state, his head was discovered to have turned: "The face was turned towards the south. The people kept coming to pay their homage. One day when we opened the box to put in fresh salt, we found the precious body with the face turned towards the northeast. We were astonished, and we and all the attendants who were there are eye-witnesses of this. And we saw many rainbows and clouds going towards the north-east. This must be a sign that the coming Incarnation will be born in the same direction" (Bell 1987, 451). This sign, along with a vision experienced by the Regent who had been appointed, led a government search party to Kumbum monastery and from there to the house in which they found a child not yet three years old whom they determined to be the true incarnation of the Thirteenth Dalai Lama (as well as the previous twelve Dalai Lamas). This boy became the Fourteenth Dalai Lama.

Unlike the bodies of most Tibetans that are exposed to scavengers, or the bodies of great teachers that are sometimes cremated, the holy incarnations of the Dalai Lamas are embalmed by members of the monastic community (Goodman 1986, 29). Today the Thirteenth Dalai Lama remains preserved in salt like his predecessors and entombed on the fourth floor of the Potrang Marpo (the red palace) in the Potala in Llasa, Tibet, but he had to wait patiently for his tomb to be built: "All the while his hastily embalmed body, swathed in cotton, the face covered by a life-like effigy, kept mute watch over the palace in which he had spent most of his earthly life (Goodman 1986, 8). The Potala was the residence of the Dalai Lama and his entourage, site of all ceremonies of state, and destination for pilgrims. The palace contains the golden tombs of eight Dalai Lamas. The structures rise from the lower floor and shoot up through the upper stories to the roof, where their domes become golden canopies that can be seen for miles (Goodman 1986, 90). The tomb of the Thirteenth Dalai Lama is an ornate structure built between 1934 and 1936 with gold, silver, and precious gems, and other wealth acquired during his lifetime and donated after his death. A silver statue of its occupant stands in front of the tomb, which stands over sixty feet high and is said to incorporate more than a ton of gold. The room also contains paintings of the Dalai Lama with his contemporaries and wall murals tracing the principal events in the Dalai Lama's life, as well as other works of art.

According to the Fourteenth Dalai Lama, Tenzin Gyatso, "...many of the great spiritual masters take release from earthly existence—that is, they die—whilst meditating. When this happens, it is often the case that their bodies do not begin to decay until long after they are clinically dead" (Dalai 1990, 208). The Fourteenth Dalai Lama speaks from experience. Ling Rinpoché, his senior tutor, died on December 25, 1983. The Dalai Lama writes, "...as if any further evidence of his being a remarkable person were needed, his body did not begin to decay until thirteen days after he was pronounced dead, despite the hot climate. It was as if he still inhabited his body, even though clinically it was without life" (Dalai 1990, 217). When

Joakim III, Patriarch of Constantinople, enthroned for homage after his death in 1912. Photo courtesy of the Carpenter Center for the Visual Arts, Harvard University.

the exiled Fourteenth Dalai Lama is released from his body, it too will surely be preserved like the bodies of his predecessors in the Potala.

Patriarch Joakim III

Joakim III was intelligent and eloquent and destined for an ecclesiastical career from an early age. He was ordained a deacon in Rumania at age 18, afterward serving at Orthodox churches and continuing his studies in Vienna. In 1860 he joined his spiritual guide Joakim of Kyzikos, whom he would later succeed, when he became Patriarch Joakim II of Constantinople. Three years later the future Joakim III was or-

dained a priest, becoming the Metropolitan Bishop of Borne the following year and Metropolitan Bishop of Thessalonike ten years later. In October 1878, after the death of his mentor, Joakim was elected as Patriarch of Constantinople at the young age of 44. Although he resigned in March 1884 because of restrictions on the Orthodox Church by the Turkish government, he returned to his patriarchal office in May 1901 after governmental relations with the church were relaxed. He served for more than a decade, keeping abreast of the changes occurring in Turkey in the Balkans and witnessing the outbreak of the first Balkan War before falling gravely ill. After his death on November 13, 1912, at the age of 78, he was

Archbishop Sergei Ochotenko enthroned for homage after his death in 1971. Photo courtesy of Blackwell Funerals.

seated in the official patriarchal cathedra in the Phanar at Constantinople. The photograph taken at that time depicts his enthroned body surrounded by ecclesiastical and civil dignitaries. Joakim's funeral was carried out with unprecedented honors from the Orthodox Church and the Osmanli government. He was buried in the patriarchal cemetery near the Monastery of Our Lady of the Spring at Balukli, a short distance outside the eastern wall of Constantinople.

Archbishop Sergei Ochotenko

Archbishop Sergei Ochotenko died on October 2, 1971 at age 92. After fleeing Russia in 1917 Archbishop Ochotenko had settled in Adelaide, Australia. He became the head of the Byelo Russian Autocephalic Church of Australia and Abroad and was considered the spiritual father of the several thousand Greeks in Australia. His body was discovered approximately twelve hours after his sudden death in his residence to the rear of the Greek Orthodox Church of the Archangels Michael and Gabriel. He was lying on the floor on his right side with cyanosed fingertips. Large bruises on the right thigh and forehead indicated that he had struck an object and the floor in his fall. The cause of his death was progressive cardiac insufficiency. The archbishop had also suffered from hypertension and diabetes. The death was certified by a doctor.

The remains were removed from the residence by Blackwell Funerals of Torrensville, South Australia. The body was stored in a refrigerated chamber until the decision to bury the archbishop in a seated or horizontal position could be made. Because it would cause the body to become firm, embalming could not proceed until the decision had been reached.

Four days after the archbishop's death, the Very Reverend Archbishop Spyridon and the Greek Orthodox Church Committee agreed that Ochotenko should be buried in the ancient tradition of kings, patriarchs, and clergy. He was to be entombed seated on a throne and robed in full vestments. His right hand was to be raised in benediction to symbolize that he would never be dethroned, even in death. The fingers of the raised right hand were to be formed to depict the letters "V" and "X," which in the Orthodox Church means "Christ Always Wins." The enthroned body was to be placed on view in the church from the evening of October 12 through the services that would be conducted all night and until the funeral service that would take place from 12:30 until 3 P.M. At that time the throne would be conveyed to the West Terrace Cemetery and lowered into a tomb for final interment. The clergy believed that the Archbishop would be the first in Australia to be buried in this traditional manner. The Reverend Father A. Marinakis, vicar of the Church of the Archangels, told reporters that a seated burial had been Ochotenko's wish.

The plans posed several problems to the funeral directors: how to preserve and present a body in a sitting position to the public for nearly twenty-four hours eleven days after sudden death, how to manufacture a throne of suitable strength and ornamentation that had a top cover to enclose the remains for burial, how to convey such a large structure to the cemetery, and how to lower it into the tomb. Peter Elberg and others at Blackwell Funerals began their task by placing the body in a seated position. They took measurements from the top of the head (including the crown) to the buttocks, from the buttocks to the rear of the knees, and from the knees to the bottom of the shoes. They also measured the width of the body with the right hand raised and the left arm clutching a Bible. From the measurements, they designed and built a throne with the correct seat height and depth and properly positioned armrests. The archbishop was six feet three inches tall and weighed 210 pounds.

The gross measurements of the throne were 36 inches square and 68 inches high without the detachable carrying arms.

The throne was made from polished timber, upholstered with gold, padded material, and adorned with silver-plated crosses, purple and black ribbons, and carpet underfoot. Long arms would be attached to the sides of the throne so that it could be carried as a sedan chair by rotations of fourteen men. The throne would be enclosed for burial by securing a board across the front and attaching a canopy that would be screwed to the back of the throne.

During the four days that had elapsed before embalming could begin, the remains had deteriorated. There was little purging, but the skin had begun to slip in the bruised areas of the body. Edema was present in the arms and legs. However, the arteries showed no signs of arteriosclerosis and the funeral home reported that the physical condition of the body was that of a man of sixty years of age.

The embalmers at Blackwell raised five points for the injection of Demosol embalming fluid: the left brachial artery, the right and left carotid arteries, and the right and left femoral arteries. The blood was drained from the right jugular vein. First, approximately two pints of a mild solution (three ounces to the half gallon) were injected into the brachial artery. Immediately afterward, twelve pints of a stronger solution (eight or nine ounces to the gallon) were injected. The drainage was good, the discoloration disappeared, and little purging was evident. "At this stage the body looked quite presentable," reads the funeral director's report.

The following afternoon, another four pints of strong embalming fluid were injected. When clear embalming fluid oozed from the jugular vein, injection was discontinued. A trocar was used to search and drain the viscera, including the heart and lungs. Cavity fluid was injected into the hollow organs. The skin was rubbed with petroleum jelly and all orifices were plugged. The body was then placed on a chair to establish the necessary sitting posture. The fingers were fixed to the desired form with splints and adhesive tape. The archbishop's head was slanted slightly to the right to give him a more natural appearance.

On October 11, the day before Archbishop Ochotenko was to be placed in the church, the clergy visited the funeral home. They anointed Ochotenko's body with holy oils and advised the embalmers in correctly dressing the body, which was arrayed in gold vestments and a jeweled crown. The deceased was then placed on the finished throne. The raised right arm was supported in position by strapping a strong metal band around it, passing the band through the sleeve, and screwing the band to the armrest. The body was maintained in position by leather straps that were screwed to the throne. The straps were passed through holes made in the vestments and buckled around the shins, stomach, chest, and neck. The shoes were secured through their soles to the floorpiece. Cosmetics were applied to the face, and the hair and beard were combed.

The next day the throne was transported from the funeral home to the Greek Orthodox Church of the Archangels Michael and Gabriel. It was placed near the sanctuary steps a few feet from the front pews. At 6 P.M. on October 12, 1971, the religious service commenced. The service was conducted by Archbishop Spyridon and clergy from the Byelo Russian Church, the Ukranian Orthodox Church, and the Serbian Orthodox Church. The eighty-minute service was attended by about 500 mourners, including clergy of many denominations.

The church remained open to visitors all night. During the evening and the following day, people of all nationalities and ages arrived to pay their respects or satisfy their curiosity. Some ascended the steps to the throne and kissed Archbishop Ochotenko's garment, bowed and made the sign of the cross, and laid flowers at his feet. The services were also attended by the media. A local television station conducted interviews

with clergy and bystanders and aired them throughout Australia. All local newspapers and the *Adelaide Advertiser* published articles about the funeral, most accompanied by photographs of the archbishop on the throne.

Ten minutes before the procession was to leave for the cemetery, the carrying arms and the front piece were attached to the archbishop's throne. The clergy carried it through the front door, around the church grounds, and to the front gate. The crown was replaced with an ornamental headpiece and the gold Bible was exchanged for a less ornate edition. Afterward, the canopy was affixed. The funeral procession resumed and with the aid of the police and the city council progressed through the streets to the cemetery.

Two heavy wooden bearers were laid across the tomb and two lowering straps were laid both across and along the grave. Two men steadied and kept the throne upright during its slow descent eight feet down into the concrete brick-lined vault. The tomb was then sealed with a concrete slab and would later be marked with a specially constructed monument. Of the monument, the funeral home writes, "This memorial will remind all of a tribute paid in a very special way and we, the funeral directors, will be reminded of a challenge upon which, in retrospect, we can look back and say was met with great success. We believe that occasions such as these can do much for the regard and respect with which the public may hold the funeral profession." The funeral directors, the mourners, and the memory of Archbishop Ochotenko all benefited from this painstaking—and more importantly, successful—preparation of the body.

BELIEVERS

Distinct from cases where deaths have gone unreported for practical reasons despite objectionable odors, as discussed in the next section, are cases in which bodies are retained because they have not become repugnant. These bodies of ordinary laypersons have been absolved of the requirement to decay. Their bodies have remained fresh for months or years after death or are found intact upon an often divinely inspired exhumation. As secular incorruptibles they are objects of as much devotion as their saintly counterparts. When the body is kept secretly in the home, this devotion is shown by the immediate family members. When the secret becomes known, the public either denounces it or joins in the worship of a body believed to be miraculously preserved by an act of God.

Secular incorruptibles may be found worldwide. *Fortean Times* (no. 91, October 1996) reported that a woman from Hubei province in China who had died of heart failure in November 1992 was still perfectly preserved. According to the woman's grandson, her temperature was normal and her muscles were flexible ten hours after her death. Two days later rigor mortis had still not set in, so the family decided to keep the body. Three years later, despite fluctuations in temperature ranging from 32° to 93° F (0° to 34° C), the face of the corpse is described as radiant, the head still turns on the shoulders, the body has not decomposed, and many of the joints are still supple. Chinese scientists are said to be baffled.

Here in the United States the preservation of such bodies—which is not always perfect—is almost always attributed to the religious beliefs of the deceased or those who attend to their posthumous needs. An old woman who lived in Brooklyn with her five grown children discovered that she had a brain tumor. Being religious, she stopped taking her medicine and told her children that God would heal her. After she died they waited patiently for the promised cure, taking care of their mother's body and washing and changing her clothes for more than a year (Carlton 1995, 163–64). Police in Lubbock, Texas, responded to a man's complaint that his niece Marsha was preventing him from seeing his sixty-four-year-old sister, Wynona Fuller. They went to the women's apartment and found Wynona's decomposing body in bed, covered by a white blanket. They determined that she had died of natural causes five months earlier. Marsha Fuller explained to Sergeant Randy McGuire that she had stayed with her mother's body in hope of her resurrection. "[God] had taken her mother's soul out of her body so he could repair it cell by cell," after which he would revive her (Kohut 1993, 6).

Miguel Ángel Gaitán ("The Miracle Child")

Just before his first birthday in 1966, Miguel Ángel Gaitán succumbed to meningitis. He was buried in Villa Unión, the town of 600 people in northwest Argentina where he lived briefly and died. In 1973 Miguel Ángel's coffin was unearthed during a violent rainstorm. A cemetery worker opened the coffin and was surprised to find the remains of the child inside virtually intact. The worker built a makeshift tomb of stones to shelter the coffin, but when he returned the next day the tomb had collapsed. It was rebuilt, but when it tumbled down again the coffin was left out in the open. Subsequently, the lid of the coffin would not remain in place despite being weighed down with rocks and heavy objects. Miguel Ángel's mother, Argentina Gaitán, explained to the *New York Times* (August 10, 1996), "...every morning we found the lid removed. Finally we realized that Miguel did not want to be covered. He wanted to be seen, so we placed him in this coffin with a glass lid."

More than twenty years later, Miguel Ángel's small, wrinkled body is still preserved in a two-story concrete tomb in Villa Unión. The corpse is attended daily by his sixty-four-year-old mother. Mrs. Gaitán sometimes allows visitors to touch the baby's head. "Normally they don't get to touch him, but if they ask, I unlock the case and let them," Mrs. Gaitán told the *New York Times*. "But you'll get a miracle whether you touch him or not," she adds. She will occasionally dress the body in the clothes brought as gifts, for instance the small

Top left: **The gravestone of Julia Buccola Petta (d. 1921) in Mount Carmel Cemetery in Hillside, Illinois. Photo courtesy of Barbara Rotundo, The Association for Gravestone Studies.** *Top right:* **The photo on Julia Buccola Petta's gravestone said to show her when she was exhumed six years after her death. Photo courtesy of Barbara Rotundo, The Association for Gravestone Studies.**

soccer uniform given by a fan of Argentina's championship team Boca Juniors. She also sells cards and trinkets with her son's picture on them for $2 and pamphlets that chronicle his life and death for $15.

Miguel receives offerings of flowers, toys, clothing, and money from people who attribute miracles to his intervention, though he is not a saint. He also receives cards and letters of thanks for recoveries from disease, survival of hardships, proposals of marriage, passing grades on exams, and lesser accomplishments. Miguel's body is believed to be preserved so that it can be visited by those asking for blessing. The priest of Villa Unión, the Reverend Ricky Alberto Martínez, points out that the Roman Catholic Church officially recognizes as saints only those who have been canonized by the Vatican but that the church cannot ignore "unofficial saints" like Miguel Ángel: "We can't negate the feelings that people have for

this child and the faith that he has inspired in them" (the *New York Times*).

Father Martínez intends to conduct a scientific investigation to determine why Miguel Ángel's corpse has not decomposed. He also plans to document the miracles that have been attributed to the baby. With this evidence he will apply to have the child beatified. Meanwhile, Miguel's fame continues to spread, and people arrive in cars and tour buses from all over Argentina. Ramón Ricardo Poblete, a municipal official, says, "Miguel Ángel has been good for the town and for the people. We all have to believe in something" (the *New York Times*).

Julia Buccola Petta ("The Italian Bride")

A story surfaces occasionally about a family member hearing a voice urging disinterment of a dead relative. The deceased, when brought to the surface, looks very much like he or she did when buried. One such story comes from Rome: Maria Mattei dreamed for twelve years that she could hear her dead daughter pleading to be fetched from the coffin. The child had been buried at the age of two. In May 1977 she could bear the dreams no longer and, with the help of her parish priest, obtained permission to open the coffin. "But on opening the grave, the mystery only deepened. For though the child had obviously been dead all those years, the body looked as if it had only been buried the day before" (De'ath 1993, 375).

Another of these stories, which admittedly read like urban legends and are in fact difficult to substantiate, comes from the American Midwest: Julia Buccola Petta died during childbirth in 1921 at age 39. After her death her mother (or by another account, her daughter) heard Julia's voice telling her to open the grave. Finally, after six years, the body was exhumed. It was found completely intact, and a photograph was taken. The photo appears on her tombstone in Mount Carmel Cemetery in Hillside, Illinois, but whether it was taken during her life or after death is an unresolved question. Helen Sclair of the Association for Gravestone Studies is of the opinion that the photo was taken at the time of the funeral rather than at the reinterment, although she notes that photos of brides in the casket are rare on tombstones (letter to author, 16 February 1997). The cemetery in which Julia is interred is owned by the Catholic Archdiocese who is very reticent to give out information about the case. However, some say that Julia, known locally as "The Mother" or "The Italian Bride," haunts the cemetery and that her wedding bouquet of roses can sometimes be smelled.

Medgar Evers

The remarkable preservation of the buried body of Medgar Evers has been substantiated in federal court during the third trial of his assassin Byron De La Beckwith.

Evers, Mississippi field secretary of the NAACP, was ambushed by Beckwith shortly after he arrived home at 12:30 A.M. on June 12, 1963. Beckwith shot the thirty-eight-year-old civil rights leader in the back with a rifle and left him bleeding in his driveway in front of his wife Myrlie and their children. Evers was rushed to University Hospital but died less than an hour later.

Evers's body was cared for at the Collins Funeral Home on North Farish Street in Jackson, Mississippi. His brother Charles, who assumed Medgar's role at the NAACP, made sure he was dressed and his hair was styled properly. A viewing was held at the funeral home. Although Evers had told his wife he wanted a brief funeral, without expense or long-winded eulogies, the funeral arrangements were handled by the NAACP. The funeral was held at the Masonic Temple and was well attended by those who had known and worked with Evers—including Martin Luther King, Jr.—but was also crowded with reporters and photographers. Evers was dressed in a suit Myrlie had chosen, with a blue NAACP tie imprinted with the scales of justice, a white Masonic apron trimmed in blue, and an Elks emblem around his neck (Vollers 1995, 140). His casket was draped with the American flag. The funeral lasted an hour and a half, after which the casket was lifted into a white hearse that led a procession back to the Collins Funeral Home. Outside the funeral home, the growing crowd began to get violent in their demand for the killer until they were convinced to disperse.

The body of Medgar Evers was prepared by Clarie Collins Harvey for its journey by train to Washington, D.C. The casket was driven to the station in Meridian and accompanied on the unembellished train by Harvey and Mary Cox, who were surprised at the numbers of mourners who turned out at the stations along the way. Myrlie, Medgar's brother Charles, and the Evers' two older children, Reena and Darrell, flew to Washington for the burial. Medgar, a World War II veteran, had wanted to be buried in Jackson, Mississippi, but the NAACP had made arrangements for his burial at Arlington National Cemetery. He was given a full military burial with a six-man honor guard and a three-gun salute. Taps were sounded, and the flag that had covered the casket was folded and handed to his widow.

During Byron De La Beckwith's first trial, which began on January 27, 1964, Dr. Forrest Bratley testified to having performed the autopsy on Medgar Evers's body while it was still warm. The cause of death had been hemorrhage. The entrance wound was about ten inches below the right shoulder blade and was a little smaller than a dime. The path of the bullet was tracked through the body and exited in a jagged gash roughly the size of a half-dollar (Vollers 1995, 168). Despite the prosecution's evidence and witnesses, both the first and second of Beckwith's trials ended in the all-white juries being unable to reach a verdict.

On December 17, 1990, Beckwith was rearrested to be tried again for the murder of Medgar Evers. Because the original autopsy report was missing from the first trial, prosecutors Bobby DeLaughter and Charlie Crisco obtained Myrlie's permission to have Evers's body exhumed. In June 1991, Myrlie's younger son, James Van Dyke ("Van") Evers, flew to Washington to meet DeLaughter and Crisco and oversee the disinterment. The grave was opened with a backhoe: it was dry and the casket was well sealed. The casket was placed in a hearse and driven to Albany, New York. Van accompanied the remains of his father and DeLaughter and Crisco followed in a separate car. They arrived at the Albany Medical Center before dark.

The second autopsy was performed by New York State's chief pathologist, Dr. Michael Baden, who had volunteered to conduct the post mortem examination and to testify at the trial at no charge. The casket was opened the morning after it had arrived, with Van staying outside the room until the condition of the remains was known. Dr. Baden pried open the casket and Crisco

recorded the event with a camcorder. The moment the casket was opened was later described as "emotional" and "spiritual": "Everyone in the room gasped. Evers' body was perfectly preserved. His burial suit was still neat and dry; his face was only slightly altered from dehydration, as if he had been dusted with a thin coat of ashes. Medgar Evers looked as if he were sleeping, certainly not like someone who had been dead for almost thirty years" (Vollers 1995, 288). Van was brought in and left alone for a time with his father's body. Evers' body was undressed and opened by Dr. Baden, while Crisco photographed the autopsy. Dr. Baden took x-rays that revealed bullet fragments still in the chest.

During the third trial of Byron De La Beckwith, which began on January 18, 1994, and ended in a sentence of life imprisonment, Myrlie Evers was asked to identify a small color photograph. She was surprised to realize that the photo of her husband had not been taken at the time of his funeral, but at the time of the recent exhumation. Despite the objections of Beckwith's defense team, the photo of the well-preserved body of Medgar Evers was circulated among the jury. Dr. Michael Baden was later called to testify about his autopsy of Evers' body. He explained that he had identified the body by noting an old football injury in his left ankle and by the bullet wound that had fractured two ribs. He said that the slug had left a starburst pattern consistent with a high-powered rifle and that he had removed lead fragments that had splintered off the bullet. Three of the less gory photographs of the autopsy were allowed to be shown to the jury. Baden testified that Evers' corpse was the "most pristine" body he had ever seen in his many years of experience. "The body was as if it had been embalmed the day before," he said with some awe (Vollers 1995, 342).

Carl Stevens

Carl Stevens' decision during life led to his death. His prolonged posthumous history is now a matter of public record. Stevens lived in Knoxville, Illinois, with his wife, Carole, her two children, Cindy (age 8 at the time of his death) and Craig (age 5 at his death), and family friend Richard Kunce. Stevens and family were part of what the media referred to as a "health cult." Carole practiced holistic health care, including the use of healing crystals, exorcism, channeling, and the administration of health supplements. Carl Stevens was convinced to stop taking insulin for his severe diabetes. Predictably, he went into a diabetic coma and died in May 1979.

Coincidentally, the Stevens family became reclusive in May, shortly before Carl's "disappearance." His brother Roger helped to keep Carl's death a secret by threatening legal action against the police, family, and friends who attempted to contact Carl. These included the children's godparents, Pat and Frank Walker of Knoxville, who were worried about their well-being, and Carole's nephew Curt Poutch of Cudahy, Wisconsin, who informed the authorities. Poutch, who had been in the house, reported that Carl appeared to be dead and was dried out. The corpse was lying in bed, brown and shriveled, having been preserved by natural dehydration.

Despite evidence to the contrary, the Stevens family believed that Carl was literally, figuratively, or religiously alive and that they could speak to him through prayer. The children made statements that they had seen dead people and that their father didn't look that way. They mentioned a cat that had died and decomposed in their front yard with the ribs showing, whereas their father was still in a solid state. During Carl's posthumous tenure at the residence, the family moved his corpse around the house to different rooms and chairs. Police later surmised that the body may have dried in the basement, where it had been seated in a lounge chair. The family also took Carl for occasional walks around the house and changed his clothes and bed linens daily.

Police finally entered the home on January 29, 1988. Official photographs show the corpse lying on the bed with white diaper-like underwear, pajama pants, and white socks. The skin was dried like shoe leather. The body was emaciated, with orange-brown skin, and weighed fifty pounds. Stevens, age forty-eight at the time of his death nine years earlier, was pronounced dead at 3:15 that afternoon. The cause of death was stated to be complications of diabetes due to lack of insulin. Mrs. Stevens later told authorities that her husband had died in her arms on May 12, 1979. The case became known in the media as the "Knoxville Mummy" and was discussed on a 1988 television episode of *Oprah*. The case was investigated by Knox County sheriff Mark Shearer, who worried that without a prosecution the body might be returned to the family, and by Dick Flanagan of the Illinois State Police Division of Criminal Investigation.

Knox County coroner Roger Hannam performed an autopsy shortly after the body was recovered. The exact cause of death was listed as "metabolic and electrolyte imbalance due to diabetes mellitus." Lawrence Blum testified about the white sheets, pajama bottoms, and socks. He stated that the outer tissue was drying and the shrinkage was consistent with mummification. "Chewing marks" on the left thumb had occurred after death. The internal examination showed fibrous tissue in the lung area which could have been the result of pleurisy or pneumonia, marked atrophy of the pancreas, other organs dry and shriveled, spinal cord absent due to deterioration, and insect pupa casings in the cranial cavity. Carl's hair tested negative for drugs and poisons. The mummification, depending on temperature and humidity, would have taken weeks to months. There was some lividity in the back and legs. Color varied from brown to golden brown to mahogany in areas of lividity. There was no evidence of embalming, and the brain was decomposed and absent. The body had a sheen, possibly from the application of cream.

State's Attorney Raymond Kimbell

expected Carl Stevens' burial to be a condition of sentencing. This was no longer a point of contention after his funeral was arranged through the Hurd-Hendricks Funeral Home in Knoxville, Illinois. The funeral, conducted by the Reverend Milton Marquith, was attended by Stevens' wife, children, and mother. But only his mother was present at his burial in Wataga Cemetery in Knoxville on February 7, 1988. The children were temporarily placed in foster homes. Jennifer McPhail of the Illinois Department of Child and Family Services evaluated the children and testified in court that they had been living in a closed delusional system and suffered from an induced psychotic disorder.

Richard Kunce was charged with failing to report a death, but the charge was dropped at his 1989 trial on the grounds that the statute of limitations (eighteen months) had expired. According to Kunce's testimony, Carl had instructed his wife that there should be no funeral. Kunce said he had had many conversations with Carl and that he was happy and content. Kunce had seen Carl take an occasional breath and felt an occasional pulse and did not believe the pathologist's report. Kunce moved on to Corpus Christi, Texas, after his trial and taught public school in the Flour Bluff School District.

Carole Stevens testified that she was solely responsible for Carl's body, that she had found Carl with no respiration or heartbeat on the floor of their bedroom in mid–May 1979. She claimed Carl had sporadic respirations and heartbeats in September 1986. She claimed he looked like he was in a coma for the first six to eight weeks, then swelled up. Fluid came from his nose and mouth. He later shrank to skin and bones, the brownish-black color turning over the years to brown, orange-brown, and beige. According to her testimony, the signs of death she had been taught to look for as a nurse were not present. She allowed the body to remain on the floor for some months, later put it on the bed, and at some point moved it to the basement. Carole had previously been ordered to undergo psychiatric evaluation, but a judge ruled in July 1988 that she could resume custody of the children under the guardianship of the Department of Child and Family Services.

8. Mummy Miscellany

Eviction, Collection, and Neglect

Like many of the other mummies discussed in this book, these individuals did not choose their fate. In some instances, the bodies were decently interred and their mummification only revealed when the money for their perpetual care ran out or when the cemetery flooded. Others were prevented from resting in peace from the moment of death—death caused by killers collecting bodies or death unreported by family members benefiting from the continued presence of the corpse. With the help of natural mummification, the bodies kept the secret of their presence under floorboards, in closets, in attics, and in basements. Bodies have also accumulated legally when the coolers in county and city morgues have filled with those awaiting autopsy. And in one curious and infamous instance, bodies that accumulated accidentally underwent natural refrigeration and dissection of another sort.

EVICTION

According to some sources, disinterment of the dead does not often reveal intact remains: One sexton of a large cemetery who had supervised the opening of vaults both above and below the ground for over twenty-eight years, related that only one such preservation was found during that time and that it was as dry and hard as stone. Other sextons, with as many as fifteen years experience each,

had never seen such a preservation but had heard that at least one of these rigid conservations had been found previously in their cemeteries. The mummified condition of these remains is believed by them to have been effected by strong embalming fluids, which halted dissolution until the desiccation of the tissues was completed under prolonged drying conditions (Cruz 1977, 30).

Although the preservation of buried bodies may not be common, it is not that unusual. Mike Dodge of the Dodge Company, which manufactures embalming chemicals and products, reports that many exhumed bodies have been found intact. He writes, "Over the years, I've heard of a great many instances of bodies being disinterred in excellent condition. We have made no effort to keep a record of such reports and I don't happen to know of anyone who has" (letter to author, 13 August 1996).

As discussed in the introduction, modern embalming chemicals that preserve the body above ground also alter the odds in favor of its preservation underground. Retired British embalmer Desmond Henley, O.B.E., has been entrusted with the care of various cases in which bodies have been exhumed after being buried in waterlogged graves for periods exceeding one year. "I can vouch that all of these cases were completely viewable (following a small amount of cleaning) and were viewed by relatives," he says ("Lenin's Embalming" 1994, 24). He also notes in the same interview that sixteen months after his treatment of the body of King Freddie of Uganda, the remains were repatriated from London to Kampala, Uganda, and were viewed by the populace in Namirembe Cathedral day and night for one week. Although the preservation and condition of the body of Liberia's former president Samuel Doe (d. 1990) is not noted, it too was put on display. Rebel leader Prince Johnson, Doe's torturer and assassin, had the body exhumed and publicly shown on a slab of zinc when Doe's father visited town and asked to see it (Kohut 1993, 96).

Perhaps more remarkable are cases in which bodies are "embalmed" by the soil or the underground conditions rather than by the embalmer. In Greenland, the mummification of inhumed bodies does not happen deliberately but as a "lucky" result of dry air, drainage, and frost. In Naples, Italy, the volcanic properties of the soil have led the people of the region to retain a custom that was established by Roman times and was never forbidden by Roman Catholicism. The deceased is buried directly in the ground. The soil, rich in minerals, causes dehydration and mummification. The corpse is exhumed eighteen to twenty-four months later. By then the body is desiccated, stiff, brown, and light in weight. It is wrapped in a shroud and placed in the family vault.

Museo De Las Momias

The most famous naturally occurring mummies are probably those of Guanajuato, Mexico. Guanajuato, one of the country's wealthier cities, has become a popular vacation spot among natives. It has also become a destination for international tourists interested in its macabre offerings.

In 1896 the deceased relatives of families who couldn't pay burial-plot fees for their perpetual care underground were disinterred by city officials. "To the horror of the authorities and the relatives of the dead, what they unearthed were not skeletons but flesh mummified in grotesque forms and fa-

cial expressions. The soil's chemical content combined with the region's atmospheric conditions to preserve the flesh in this unique way" (Noble 1989, 745). Most were in excellent condition with remnants of hair and skin. The cadavers were judged fit for display in a local museum and continued to be exhumed until the law changed in 1958 (Meacham 1992, 153). Cemetery buff Tom Weil writes (1992, 264), "On the face of a body labelled Gabino Castro (d. 1904) remain well formed and fluffy looking hairs, never again to be shaved, while a woman wears a long braid of hair across her left breast in a permanent coquettish pose.... In the figures one sees both the living and the departed, death with a human face and humanity with the skull beneath the skin."

The most expressive of the mummies, which embalming historian Edward C. Johnson calls "nightmares," were displayed behind glass in a museum, and the others were cremated. "The mummy museum is Guanajuato's very own Little Shop of Horrors, proudly displaying 119 mummified bodies, one dignified as the 'smallest mummy in the world'" (Meacham 1992, 153). Some of the mummies are clothed and others are not. Shiny teeth, intact genitals, fingernails, eyebrows, heads of hair, and folds of skin are among the sights seen in the museum. Weil writes (1992), "Down in the darker precincts of the Pantheon thirteen glass cases line one wall of a long narrow hallway, each case holding about eight bodies, their skin yellowish and leather-like." A number of infant corpses rest on an upper shelf.

The museum's occupants were photographed by Archie Lieberman in 1978 using available light. The photographs appear in *The Mummies of Guanajuato* (1978), accompanied by a story about the mummies that Ray Bradbury had written thirty years earlier. "I began making pictures hoping that there was no curse on what I was doing and that I was not disturbing the spirits of the dead," writes Lieberman in the book's preface. "I rationalized that since there was a charge of a few pesos to see the mummies,

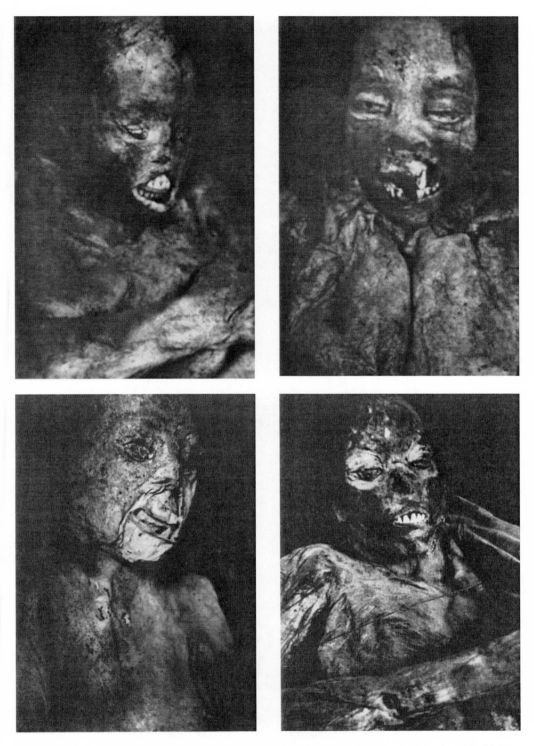

Four of the mummies preserved in Guanajuato, Mexico. Reprinted by permission of Archie Lieberman from *The Mummies of Guanajuato* by Ray Bradbury (New York: Harry Abrams, 1978).

this was their job. It was like paying to see a freak show at a carnival." The mummies reminded Lieberman of sculptures, although he never lost sight of the fact that his subjects had once lived. Weil (1992) compares them to Edvard Munch's painting *The Scream*. Bradbury (1978) writes, "They resembled nothing more than those preliminary erections of a sculptor, the wire frame, the first tendons of clay, the muscles, and a thin lacquer of skin. They were unfinished, all one hundred and fifteen of them. They were parchment-colored and the skin was stretched as if to dry, from bone to bone. The bodies were intact, only the watery humors had evaporated from them."

Bradbury wrote that the burial fees were twenty pesos a year or 170 pesos for permanent interment. The depth at which the bodies were buried was inversely proportional to the likelihood of their being disinterred. An exhumed body for which a fee was subsequently paid would be reburied; otherwise it would remain standing in the museum. "They looked as if they had leaped, snapped upright in their graves, clutched hands over their shriveled bosoms and screamed, jaws wide, tongues out, nostrils flared. And been frozen that way. All of them had open mouths. Theirs was a perpetual screaming.... Long ago the clothes had whispered away. The fat women's breasts were lumps of yeasty dough left in the dust. The men's loins were indrawn, withered orchids." However similar their desiccation, each of the mummies retains an individual identity: "How talented was death. How many expressions and manipulations of hand, face, body, no two alike" (Bradbury 1978).

Locals attribute the preservation of the Guanajuato mummies to underground gas and soil conditions. The museum is located at the Esplanada del Pantéon and may be toured between the hours of 9 A.M. and 6 P.M. for a small fee (and a tip for the tour guide). There is an additional charge for cameras, but flashes are allowed. Although the crowd may be surprisingly large and the sale of commemorative items outside quite brisk, the atmosphere is said to be respectful and almost religious.

Mummies of San Bernardo

In San Bernardo, Colombia, a town of 12,000 people forty miles southwest of Bogotá, the local custom was to transfer human remains from the ground to urns five years after burial. When gravedigger Eduardo Cifuentes began working at the cemetery seventeen years ago, he found the burial pit to be full of bodies. The town's dead had not decomposed and he told reporters, "I didn't like stepping on them because they were humans like us, so I started organizing them" (*Fortean Times*, no. 91, Oct. 1996). A dozen of the mummies are displayed in a small, dank underground crypt nearby.

Another dozen of the better-preserved mummies were moved in late 1994 to a pantheon behind the cemetery. For a fee of about 500 pesos, one can view the remains displayed on concrete slabs under glass. They include three small children huddled together, one still wearing clothes and white shoes, but with a large hole in the top of her head. A woman identified as Prudencia Acosta is dressed in a dark brown shawl and cape and clutches a red carnation. The well-preserved body of a man stands neatly attired in a jacket, tie, and trousers. Some of the bodies appear peaceful, while others are contorted. Some are clothed and others are naked. Both clothes and skin have become earth-brown.

Scientists have examined the mummies, but have not been able to explain the lack of decomposition. Locals compare the mummies to those of Guanajuato, Mexico, but point out that the San Bernardo dead were entombed above ground and didn't come into contact with the ground like those in Mexico. They suggest the mummification is a result of the purity of the water, the lack of chemical additives in the food, the fact that the cemetery attracts solar radiation, or the ingestion of large amounts of guatila and balu (native produce). One elderly resident confesses that he never eats vegetables so that he can decompose properly after death and won't become a mummy. Others have asked that the remains of their relatives be chopped up and burnt if they are found mummified upon disinterment. Still others watch to be sure this is done.

Hardin Cemetery Flooding

Occasionally, natural disaster does to the dead what has been done deliberately in some cultures. They are unearthed and the sometimes surprising status of their preservation is revealed. During the flooding in the midwestern United States in 1993, the town cemetery at Hardin, Missouri, was nearly obliterated. Of the 1,576 graves, 769 burials were eroded from the cemetery and washed toward the Missouri River. The seven-acre cemetery, containing burials from 1810 to the present, was bordered on the south side by a levee. Flood waters crested the levee on July 10, 1993, and began to flow down the roads within the cemetery. As the force of the water increased, the graves were eroded away and their contents washed eastward into the adjoining cornfields. The waters receded two weeks later.

Caskets, vaults, markers, and human remains had been scattered over twenty-six square miles of farmland. A local volunteer force of medical personnel, funeral directors, and other authorities recovered what they could and placed the remains in refrigerator trucks or in barns on the county fairgrounds. Assistance in the recovery, identification, and reburial was provided by a disaster mortuary team sponsored by the Office of Emergency Preparedness. The team consisted of three funeral directors, a forensic anthropologist, a fingerprint expert, and a mortuary search/recovery expert from the U.S. Army Quartermaster Corps. Their arrival was followed by the arrival of an identification team of forensic anthropologists, dentists, pathologists, FBI fingerprint experts, and support personnel.

A large pole barn on the county fairgrounds was converted to a morgue. Bodies floating in stagnant waters, hanging in trees, caught in fencerows, and spread out over the fields were brought to the morgue for identification. The remains of 66 complete or partial bodies were recovered, along with hundreds of crania and bones. Ten of the bodies were completely mummified, including one interred in 1937 and another in 1950. The criteria for positive identification were flexible because of the lack of antemortem records, which consisted of biomedical data and personal information supplied by surviving family members. In addition, the cemetery association had incomplete records about the placement of graves and the number of graves per plot and the local funeral homes had failed to complete personal information cards that are placed in containers within the caskets. To help in crossmatching against existing antemortem data, representatives from casket manufacturers were on site to provide estimated dates of manufacture of the various casket styles.

Complete and partial remains had a greater chance of being identified because of the amount of anthropological information that could be obtained and because they had generally been interred more recently and therefore had a better availability of antemortem records. The remains were examined and photographed. Personal effects and clothing were documented. Dental examinations were conducted on all remains and an anthropological or pathological examination was made, depending on the condition. Fingerprints were taken when possible and x-rays made in some cases. Documentation and identification took two weeks and yielded 119 positively identified remains. Most of the remains were decomposed, mummified, incomplete, or skeletal. When bodies were mummified, specific areas of the skeleton (pubic symphysis, sternal end of the right or left fourth rib, dentition, and the left or right femur) were exposed for a more accurate determination of sex, age at death, and stature.

The results of the identification project revealed that preservation of the remains was remarkably variable. There appeared to be no relationship between the condition of the remains (whether mummified or skele-tonized) and length of interment. However, exposure of the remains to the flood water and to air once recovered contributed to the differential preservation (Sledzik and Hunt, 1977). Most of the complete bodies, includ-ing those that had mummified, had been buried between the 1920s and the 1960s. Some of the remains revealed cause of death, and a majority showed evidence of embalm-ing. Evidence of autopsy was observed in both soft tissues (ventral incisions and su-tures) and skeletal remains (cut ribs and sterna).

Each individual consisting of at least an essentially intact cranium was reburied in a separate casket and vault. All remaining skeletal material was reburied according to sex (female and male material in separate caskets). "Because of the Hardin disaster, efforts are being made by the funeral indus-try to permanently mark remains before in-terment in areas where cemeteries may be impacted upon by natural forces. This strat-egy would also be advantageous for burials which may become at risk in the future from cultural actions such as road construction and other types of development" (Sledzik and Hunt, 1977).

COLLECTION

According to a September 1996 story in the *Washington Post*, the District of Co-lumbia Morgue is more than 50 percent above capacity. Of the sixty or so bodies stored at the facility at the time of the report, forty were unclaimed, and some had been there since 1994. But what is more disturb-ing than this legal backlog is the accumula-tion of bodies by those who have robbed them of life. Several infamous murderers of the twentieth century have made collections of their kills, sometimes for company, some-

times for lack of an easy way to dispose of them, and sometimes for reasons still un-known to us. Mummification or partial mummification made the presence of the bodies inconspicuous enough to avoid de-tection by the authorities for months or even years.

One way murderers prevent the bodies of their victims from deteriorating is to freeze them. This allows them to dispose of the bodies at their leisure or at a more op-portune time. Freezing may also confuse the authorities with regard to the time of the vic-tim's death. When a skull and other remains were found in November 1987 at a Boy Scout camp near Farmington, Missouri, they were identified by facial reconstruction and sub-sequent photo superimposition as Bun Chee Nyhuis, a thirty-three-year-old native of Thailand last seen by her friends in Decem-ber 1983. Her husband, Richard Nyhuis, con-fessed to accidentally killing her during an argument when he pushed her and caused her to hit her head on a steel post. After she died, he hid her body in a freezer in the base-ment of his St. Charles home for three months until the spring of 1984 and then buried her at the camp, where he was a scoutmaster. Nyhuis was brought to trial, convicted of first-degree murder, and is serv-ing a life sentence without parole in a Mis-souri state prison. Occasionally, frozen bod-ies are found before they can be disposed of. California health inspectors carrying out a routine check on a fast-food diner in Los An-geles in October 1992 discovered two human corpses in the deep freeze. They were identified as the owner, Lydia Katash, and her lover who had been strangled at least eight months previously. Police arrested Katash's ex-husband and partner in the busi-ness, but the restaurant remained open, since no California law prevents human bodies from being stored next to food (Moore 1994, 102).

In some cases, the bodies *are* the food. They are preserved out of dread desire or dire necessity. After the well-known aircraft accident in the Andes in the early 1970s, the snow provided natural refrigeration of the dead, whose flesh was resorted to when all other means of sustenance were exhausted. For Karl Denke, human meat was not a last resort but a first choice. As the operator of a rooming house in Munsterberg, Silesia (now Ziebice, Poland), from 1918 to 1924, Denke had an unlimited supply of potential meals until one of his victims survived long enough after being axed to name his attacker. Police arrested Denke and found the papers and belongings of twelve men in his possession. The most compelling evidence against him consisted of two large tubs of brine in the kitchen that held human meat. The authorities estimated that he had killed at least thirty of his boarders, pickling some for future use and eating the choice portions of others. In a ledger, he had listed names and dates with the respective weights of the bodies he had pickled dating back to 1921. After his arrest Denke confessed to having eaten nothing but human flesh for the past three years. He hanged himself with his suspenders in his cell before his trial.

As industrious as Denke, but perhaps not as utilitarian, other killers have amassed bodies out of what would seem mere laziness. Harrison Graham kept the corpses of women he had killed stacked up on the floor of his squalid Philadelphia apartment. John Christie was surrounded by the corpses of his victims—under the floorboards, in the cupboard, in the washhouse—until he moved out. Walter Knocke of Erfurt, Germany, began killing and collecting women in 1982. When police caught up with him in 1986, they found the bodies—some mummified and others decayed—of seventeen of his victims, dressed in wedding gowns and propped up around his apartment. Fritz Honka killed at least four prostitutes from Hamburg's red light district in his small attic room between 1971 and 1974. Instead of disposing of the bodies, he kept them in his flat, fortifying himself with alcohol against the stench and frequently dousing the room with quarts of deodorant. He torched the apartment in January 1975, but firemen found the mummified

leg of a woman wearing a gold sandal among the ashes. Honka confessed and was arrested, convicted, and sentenced to the maximum punishment of life imprisonment.

Like Honka, Dennis Nilsen resorted to deodorizing his apartment, lined as it was with the victims he manipulated like dolls. He, too, is serving a prison term. Of those that collect the dead, the majority conceal them rather than cavort with them. But despite the captive state of the victims, not all of their killers are captured. Cecil Maltby, a London tailor, shot and killed his mistress Alice Hilda Middleton on August 24, 1922, and lived with her decomposing body in the flat above his shop for several months. Police kept a watch over Maltby, who refused to let them enter his shop after Middleton's husband reported her missing in December. On January 10, 1923, a health order was issued enabling the authorities to break in. Maltby shot himself through the mouth in the bedroom as they entered to find the decomposing remains of Mrs. Middleton wrapped in a sheet in the bathtub in the kitchen (Gaute and Odell 1989, 206). In the case that follows, the concealer died more than a decade before her deed was discovered.

Trunk Babies

On September 20, 1967, John Hartnett was cleaning out the cluttered basement room of a six-story apartment house. Hartnett was the superintendent of the sixty-five-year-old building at 812 West 181st Street in the Washington Heights neighborhood of New York. He came upon an old-fashioned steamer trunk that had belonged to the deceased wife of Jacob Solomon, a sixty-seven-year-old man living on the third floor. The Solomons had moved into the building in the mid–1930s, about two years after they married. Anne Solomon had died in 1954.

Hartnett brought the find to the attention of Mr. Solomon, who said he had no knowledge of the trunk. Solomon came down to the basement and instructed Hartnett to

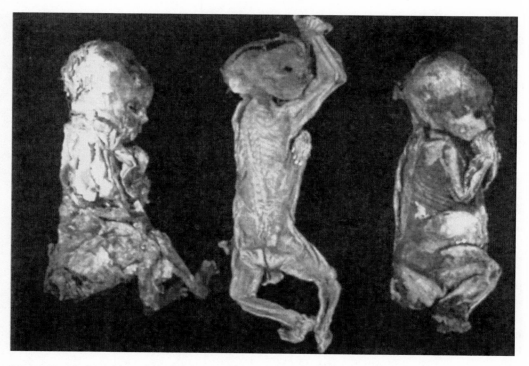

Mummified babies found in a trunk in the basement of a New York City apartment building in 1967. These specimens are in the collection of the National Museum of Health and Medicine, Armed Forces Institute of Pathology. Photo by Robin-anna Ferris, M.F.S., courtesy of the National Museum of Health and Medicine, Armed Forces Institute of Pathology. (Accession number 1990.0003.1660.)

break open the lock to determine if the trunk contained any valuables. Inside they found a large package wrapped in brown paper and newspapers and tied with cord. The large package contained three smaller packages wrapped in newspapers. The men unwrapped the smaller packages and were surprised to find three mummified babies. The babies were wrapped in New York newspapers: the *Evening Sun* of January 20, 1920, the *Evening World* of March 4, 1922, and the *Evening Journal* of October 17, 1923. The dates of the papers indicated that the babies had been dead for more than forty years. Mr. Solomon related that his wife had been married previously at about the time of World War I when she was sixteen. Her first husband had died within two or three years and Solomon had no knowledge of any births.

The infants were examined by Chief Medical Examiner Dr. Milton Helpern. X-

rays were taken and showed well-preserved skeletons. Helpern told the *New York Times* (September 22, 1967), "Because of advanced mummification, we'll never know if they were born dead or alive, or if alive, what caused their deaths. There are no obvious signs of traumatic injuries." He determined that the infants were newly born and full-term when wrapped in the newspapers. One baby was identified as male and another still had the umbilical cord attached. Helpern concluded that three medically unattended births had been concealed and explained that the natural mummification could have taken place within less than a year's time.

The mummified infants became part of the Milton Helpern collection of the New York City Medical Examiner's Office (the so-called "Black Museum"). In 1990 or 1991 the entire collection of 1700 gross pathological specimens and 300 skeletal specimens

A body lying in the snow outside the wreckage of the chartered Uruguayan airplane that crashed in the Andes Mountains in 1972. Photo courtesy of UPI/Corbis-Bettmann.

was acquired by the National Museum of Health and Medicine in Washington, D.C. The infants are not on exhibit.

Accident in the Andes

Daniel Juan, president of the "Old Christians" rugby team, chartered a Uruguayan Military Air Transport (TAMU) airplane for the team from Montevideo, Uruguay, to Santiago, Chile, on October 12, 1971, for $38 a seat. He recruited 40 people—19 team members, the team physician and his wife, and 20 supporters—for the trip, which was at the invitation of the "Old Boys," an English rugby team. After a cancellation the extra seat was sold to Graziela Mariana, who wished to attend the wedding of her oldest daughter.

The plane took off as scheduled but due to bad weather the captain made a one-night stopover in Mendoza, Argentina, where the passengers stocked up on items hard to find in Chile, including chocolate and whiskey. The plane left Mendoza on the afternoon of Friday, October 13. The 370-mile trip south to Malargue, west through the Planchon Pass to Curico, and north to Santiago should have taken an hour and a half. The pilot turned north, believing they had reached Curico, but they were in fact still in the heart of the Andes Mountains among peaks that reached 17,000 feet. At an altitude of 14,100 feet, the right wing of the plane struck a rocky peak, folded back, and cut the fuselage in half. The left wing and engine broke away.

Five people fell out of the plane at the point of impact and died quickly: Lieutenant Ramon Martinez, the plane's 30-year-old navigator; Ovidio Ramirez, the 26-year-old steward; Gaston Costemalle, a 23-year-old law student; Guido Magri, a 23-year-old agronomy student; and Alejo Hounié, a 20-year-old veterinary student. Of the two people sucked out of the plane during the crash, one (24-year-old cattle rancher Daniel Shaw) died instantly; the other (18-year-old prep school student Carlos Valeta) survived the impact, but fell to his death in a soft spot in the snow trying to reach the others. The passengers still inside the plane were thrown forward as the fuselage plowed downhill some 6,500 feet. As the nose of the plane collapsed, the pilot and copilot were crushed: Colonel Julio Cesar Ferradas, age 39, was killed instantly, but Lieutenant Colonel Dante Hector Lagurara, age 41, survived for several hours before he died.

As the bodies in the fuselage were untangled, at least three were dead or died within minutes: Fernando Vazquez, a 20-year-old medical student; Dr. Nicola, the team physician; and Dr. Nicola's wife, Esther. The dead and those expected to die were dragged outside the fuselage into the snow so that the seats could be cleared from the plane. An hour later it began to get dark, snow fell, and the temperature dropped to well below zero. The wounded were carried back inside the fuselage for the night.

The Air Search and Rescue Service (SAR) in Santiago was notified of the missing plane an hour after its last transmission. Four search planes flew that afternoon, the first within two hours of the crash, until it was too dark to see. The news reached the Uruguayan media sometime after six o'clock that evening. The families of the passengers began to gather, some believing the boys would be found, some believing they had been killed in the crash. Majors Juan Ivanovic, Carlos Garcia, and Jorge Massa of the SAR listened to the tapes from the control towers in Mendoza and Santiago to calculate the likely track of the airplane and deduced that it must have crashed within a 400-square-mile area that happened to be one of the most inaccessible in the Andes. They alerted the Andes Rescue Group of Chile (CSA). In fact, the plane had crashed in Argentina, less than five miles from Hotel Termas, a summer resort that was closed but held firewood, canned food, and maps.

On October 14, searches were conducted by five Chilean planes, three Argentine jets, a police aircraft, and two other planes. The Air Search and Rescue Service

alone had mounted 15 missions that flew for 36 hours. None of the searchers found a trace of the plane.

At the wreckage that same morning, Francisco Abal, a 21-year-old cigarette factory worker, was found to be dead. The survivors—many of whom had never seen a dead body before—dragged the dead to a level place near the fuselage, removed their clothing for the use of the survivors, and buried them in the snow, scooping out shallow indentations with luggage and scraps of metal. They included, in addition to the pilot and copilot, Dr. and Mrs. Nicola, Fernando Vazquez, 50-year-old Eugenia Parrado (mother of survivor Fernando Parrado), Graziela Mariani, 22-year-old economics student Felipe Maquirriain, and twenty-four-year-old bank clerk Julio Martínez-Lamas. The men removed the body of Lagurara from the cockpit and buried him but were forced to leave the jammed body of Ferradas where it was. Fernando Parrado, a 22-year-old mechanical engineering student, had been believed dead and spent the night in the snow but was found during the makeshift burial to have a pulse.

There were eight people unaccounted for: the five who had fallen out of the plane (including the navigator and the steward), the two who had been sucked out (including Valeta, who had disappeared in the snow), and Juan Carlos Menéndez, a 22-year-old law student. The total of 17 people who died in the crash or shortly thereafter left 28 survivors. They believed they would be rescued in a matter of days and had even seen a private search plane overhead, but the pilot had not spotted them.

Nine more search missions, totaling more than 29 hours, were mounted by the SAR on October 15 and 23 missions, totaling 55 hours, the following day. On October 17, the Uruguayan Air Force assembled a plane and crew to duplicate the flight path of the lost plane, but weather prevented them from taking off. The SAR mounted only two missions that day, totaling 2 hours and 45 minutes, due to the weather conditions and 8 missions, totaling 14 hours, over the next three days. The visual searches and examinations of aerial photographs had revealed nothing. On October 21, after a total of 142 hours and 30 minutes in the air, the SAR terminated the search. The survivors heard the announcement on a transistor radio one of them had found in the wreckage. They were believed dead, and a search for their bodies would be resumed after the spring thaw. The search was carried on privately by Carlos Páez Vilaró, the father of survivor Carlos Páez, an 18-year-old agriculture student.

After strenuous efforts by Fernando Parrado to revive her, Parrado's 20-year-old sister, Susana, died on October 21 and was buried the next day in the snow beside their mother. On the same day, their rations of food—including eight chocolate bars, two tins of mussels, three small jars of jam, some scattered dates and dried plums, some nougat bars and caramels, a packet of crackers, a small tin of almonds, and several quarts of wine—gave out, and all the toothpaste they had with them was also soon gone. Because of the altitude the mountain had no vegetation of any kind. They continued to drink snow melted on aluminum seat backings and drained into empty bottles. The survivors' gear included a heavy stainless-steel ax found in the cockpit, ponchos they crafted by wiring seat covers together, and sunglasses made from pieces of tinted plastic found in the plane.

"For some days several of the boys had realized that if they were to survive they would have to eat the bodies of those who had died in the crash. It was a ghastly prospect. The corpses lay around the plane in the snow, preserved by the intense cold in the state in which they had died. While the thought of cutting flesh from those who had been their friends was deeply repugnant to them all, a lucid appreciation of their predicament led them to consider it" (Read 1975, 63). Roberto Canessa, a 19-year-old medical student, was the first to openly broach the subject of eating the dead by explaining that they were all dying slowly of malnutrition, that there was little hope of finding the plane's tail section, and that even if they did, that food too would run out. "Soon we shall be so weak that we won't have the strength even to cut the meat that is lying there before our eyes," he reasoned (Read 1975, 63). If they excluded the three family members, there were seven bodies in the "cemetery" that would sustain them for at least a month. Other survivors agreed that it would not be immoral, since their spirits had already departed, and that in this way their deceased friends would help them go on living. They made a pact among themselves that if any more of them were to die, their bodies were to be used as food.

Canessa, Daniel Maspons (20-year-old student), Gustavo Zerbino (19-year-old medical student), and Adolfo Strauch (24-year-old agronomy student) found a body whose buttocks protruded from the snow a few yards from the plane. Canessa used a piece of broken glass to slice 20 match-stick-sized slivers from the frozen body. He laid the meat on the roof of the plane and offered it to the others. Canessa then set the example by swallowing the first piece. Several of the others did the same later that evening. Canessa cut more meat from the same corpse the following day, and it was eaten by even more of the survivors. Thereafter, the meat from their *compañeros* (comrades), as they called them, was served at midday after it had dried in the sun. Most of the men ate without hesitation, but a few refused the food or could not keep it down. They found it more palatable when cooked, but there was only a small amount of wood on the plane so this was only allowed once or twice a week. Canessa insisted that the proteins died off when heated, and Daniel Fernandez (26-year-old agronomy student) pointed out that cooking the meat caused it to shrink so that there was less of it.

On the night of October 29 an avalanche covered the survivors sleeping in the wreckage of the plane with five feet of snow. Eight people were killed: Diego Storm, a 20-

year-old medical student; Gustavo Nicolich, a 20-year-old veterinary student; Juan Carlos Menéndez; Marcelo Perez, the team captain; Carlos Roque, the plane's 30-year-old mechanic; Daniel Maspons; Enrique Platero, a 22-year-old dairy farming student; and Liliana Methol, 34-year-old wife of Javier Methol. The 19 remaining survivors huddled together with the dead bodies for the rest of that night and the next to keep warm until they had the strength to dig themselves out. After his wife's death, Methol (36-year-old cigarette factory executive and uncle of Francisco Abal, who had already died) huddled with her body, withdrew from the group, and later demanded that her body be excluded from use as food.

On the morning of October 31, the hungry men tunneled out of the fuselage. The Strauch cousins Adolfo and Eduardo (a 25-year-old architecture student) uncovered a victim of the avalanche and cut meat off the body in full view of the others. "The meat before had either been cooked or at least dried in the sun; now there was no alternative but to eat it wet and raw as it came off the bone, and since they were so hungry, many ate larger pieces, which they had to chew and taste. It was dreadful for all of them; indeed, for some it was impossible to eat gobbets of flesh cut from the body of a friend who two days before had been living beside them" (Read 1975, 104). Over the next eight days, the survivors were able to remove the rocklike snow and the bodies from the cabin. "The corpses, frozen into the last gestures of self-defense, some with their arms raised to protect their faces like the victims of Vesuvius at Pompeii, were difficult to move" (Read 1975, 105).

The survivors' fear of dying was heightened by their constant contact with the dead bodies and the knowledge that they could easily join them. Rather than touch the dead, some of the men would tie a nylon luggage strap around the shoulders and drag the corpse out. Others removed clothing from the bodies to supplement their own. Some of the corpses inside the entrance were left encased in a wall of ice as a reserve in case the survivors were unable to get to or to find those outside. "There was one important offshoot of the avalanche: a dramatic change in the food arithmetic. It cut by seven the number to be fed and raised by six the number of bodies in the cemetery that could be eaten" (Blair 1973, 161).

The butchering of the bodies was done by the Strauches and Daniel Fernandez, with the frequent help of Gustavo Zerbino. The corpses were dug out of the snow and thawed in the sun. "The cold preserved them just as they had been at the moment of death. If the eyes remained open, they would close them, for it was hard to cut into a friend under his glassy gaze, however sure they were that the soul had long since departed" (Read 1975, 112). The large pieces of meat were passed to another team of men who would slice them into smaller pieces with razor blades, often sneaking a piece into their mouths. The heart (and the blood around it), liver, kidneys, intestines, and bone marrow of the dead were eaten and only the head, skin, lungs, and genitals were discarded. Soon they were consuming one body every three days, faster than anticipated in spite of their rationing. Fat, taken off the bodies in sheets and dried in the sun, was not rationed, nor were the hands, feet, and other bits left over from earlier carcasses.

To keep the fuselage more tidy, they made a rule that no bones were to be brought inside and that any fat brought in had to be removed from the plane the same day. To prevent ulcers they believed would be caused by stirring up their digestive juices with fantasies they conjured up and shared, they tacitly agreed to refrain from talking about food. They occasionally joked about eating human flesh, which had first caused constipation and later diarrhea, and about dying, asking, "How would I look in a piece of ice?" (Read 1975, 139).

By mid–November the snow that remained compressed itself into a relatively firm mass that was soft during the day and solid ice at night. To preserve their food supply, the men had to cover the shallowly buried dead every few days and used cardboard or plastic to shield the graves from the sun. At first they continually reburied the remains but gave this up as a waste of energy. At the same time, they had to hunt for the bodies buried earlier and now covered with a thick layer of snow from the avalanche. Digging by José Algorta (a 21-year-old economics student) revealed red-painted toenails, indicating the restricted body of Liliana Methol. The men began to sink exploratory holes by urinating on a single spot, but only found bodies they had agreed not to eat. Because of their increasing hunger and their cravings for salt, they began eating flesh that had partially rotted. They also ate the brains, frozen or mixed with other organ meats.

To insulate the feet of expeditionaries, the men devised a means of making rudimentary socks, using the flesh and subcutaneous fat of the forearm pulled off and sewn up at one end. On the 15th Parrado and 19-year-old law student Antonio Vizintín located the tail section of the plane, which included the galley and the luggage compartment. They found a box of chocolates, a packet of sugar, three meat patties, some moldy sandwiches (parts of which were salvageable), and plenty of warm clothing (including woolen socks). They created a cross in the snow with the suitcases, left a note on the tail section, and returned to the plane hauling a makeshift sled laden with their finds. They made more expeditions to the tail, filling rugby socks with human meat to sustain them.

On November 23, 21-year-old economics student Arturo Nogueira died in his sleep and was buried the next day. Rafael Echavarren, a 22-year-old dairy farming student, died after three days of delirium, before which he told the men, "Please tell my father not to abandon my body in the Andes" (Blair 1973, 164). Numa Turcatti, a 24-year-old law student who had refused to eat from the bodies, was the last of the survivors to die. Six-

teen men remained alive. When two condors appeared in the sky, the men were afraid the birds would carry off the carrion. Parrado told the Strauch cousins in confidence that they should use the bodies of his mother and sister if absolutely necessary.

On December 12 Fernando Parrado, Roberto Canessa, and Antonio Vizintín packed food, water, and whiskey, made safety lines from seatbelts, and set out to the west. Three days into the trek, they sent Vizintín back to make their food supply last longer. Those left in the fuselage realized they would have another shortage of food if they continued to exclude the bodies of survivors' family members. They began a hunt for the missing bodies, which having died sooner would be fatter and contain more vitamins. Gustavo Zerbino, Adolfo Strauch, and Eduardo Strauch found the body of Carlos Valeta uphill and brought it to the cemetery. Farther uphill they found the body of Daniel Shaw, which they strapped to a sled and brought down over a period of two days. Because Shaw was a cousin of the Strauches, his body was placed in reserve with the other family members. "The boys assumed correctly that the last five of the missing bodies were uphill from the place they found Shaw. They left them there for the time being. It was too difficult a climb to retrieve them: there was the ever-present danger of starting an avalanche. It was colder up there and the snow was deeper. The bodies would be well preserved until they were needed" (Blair 1973, 177).

When Páez and Algorta climbed up the mountain later, they found another body. The skin that had been exposed to the sun had turned black and the eyes were missing, either burned out or eaten by condors. They covered the body with snow and a second party returned over the next two days to butcher it where it lay. Meanwhile, melting snow revealed the bodies buried more deeply near the fuselage. The Strauches supervised the digging of two pits, one for the bodies of family members that were still kept in reserve and the other for bodies they could eat. Though they now no longer needed to eat putrid meat, many of the men continued to do so for the stronger taste. "It was still more difficult … to eat what was recognizably human—a hand, say, or a foot—but they did so all the same" (Read 1975, 209).

The men learned on their radio that Páez's father was organizing another search for the missing plane. On December 17 an SAR plane on the last day of the new search initiated by Carlos Páez Vilaró and other family members flew overhead but did not notice the snow-covered wreckage, the waving men, or the cross they had fashioned from the plane's seats. Having heard nothing from Parrado or Canessa after ten days, the men made plans to walk out on their own on January 8, estimating that their food supply would last until the 15th.

On December 20 Parrado and Canessa found help in the form of Sergio Catalan, who was on horseback on the other side of a river. Catalan came back the following morning with food that he threw across to them. He learned who they were through notes thrown back and forth around a rock. Catalan informed the police and a rescue party on horseback reached the two men. They had buried what was left of their store of human meat. The news of their survival leaked out, and the survivors on the mountain heard it on the radio on December 22, debating afterward whether they should cover up the evidence of their cannibalism before their impending rescue. The two men who had reached civilization after 70 days in the Andes were examined by doctors and found to be fit except for cracked lips, conjunctivitis, and weight loss. They explained what they had eaten and were told not to mention it to the press.

Parrado rode in one of the two SAR rescue helicopters to help locate the plane. The survivors were to be brought out four at a time. Carlos Páez, Eduardo Strauch, Antonio Vizintín, and Daniel Fernandez jumped into one helicopter and José Luis Inciarte, a 24-year-old agronomy student, and Alvaro Mangino, a 19-year-old prep school student, jumped into the other containing Parrado. After reaching Los Maitenes the men were physically examined and found to be suffering from undernourishment and vitamin deficiency. At a press conference later in the day, they said they had survived on the food they had brought with them, followed by lichens, roots, and herbs. The eight survivors were transported to the hospital of St. John of God in San Fernando and all but Inciarte were found to be in good health. Their confessions were heard individually by Father Andres Rojas, who explained to each of them that their survival cannibalism had not been a sin. The men were reunited with their families—and with teammate Gilberto Regules, who had flown to Chile on a commercial airplane instead of the charter—and later released from the hospital. Inciarte and Mangino left in ambulances and the other six in private cars.

The remaining survivors—Javier Methol; Gustavo Zerbino; José Algorta; Alfredo Delgado, a 24-year-old law student; Roy Harley, a 20-year-old mechanical engineering student; Roberto Francois, a 20-year-old agriculture student; and Ramon Sabella, a 21-year-old agronomy student—spent another night on the mountain with four men that had arrived on the helicopters: nurse José Bravo and climbers Sergio Diaz, Claudio Lucero, and Osvaldo Villegas. The survivors objected to the men taking photographs but were told it was a necessary record for the Chilean Army and that the photos would not be published. Diaz later said, "The boys had a lot of things they wanted to get off their minds…. Principally, they were concerned about how the fathers of the boys they had eaten would react, and how society would react…. I told them, candidly, that it was going to be very difficult for them. Because of the terrible circumstances fate had placed them in, all their lives would change significantly, perhaps drastically. I told them they could best compensate the families of the eaten by being humble. That is, adopting a lifestyle of humility" (Blair 1973, 241).

Diaz located the intact bodies of Eugenia and Susana Parrado, Liliana Methol, and four men. He had been told the headless body of Ferradas was still in the cockpit. Diaz consulted with Zerbino and made a drawing showing the location and names of all the bodies. Excluding Ferradas, 13 of the bodies had been untouched and the other 15 were mostly bones. One of the survivors told the rescue team, "God helped us.... When the avalanche hit us on the sixteenth day, killing seven or eight people, we buried five of the bodies in the frozen snow; so it was like having a refrigerator to keep them from spoiling and getting putrid" (Lopez 1973, 117).

On December 23 two of the three arriving helicopters landed on the mountain. Captain Eduardo Sanchez got out and surveyed the site. Under ordinary circumstances SAR personnel would have retrieved the bodies and they would have been inspected by a judge who would issue burial permits to the relatives. But because cannibalism was involved, and because they had died in Argentina and not Chile, the bodies were left at the site until decisions could be made by higher authorities. Captain Jorge Massa conducted an aerial inspection and located, mapped, and photographed the area, including the five bodies remaining uphill: "They seemed to be sitting in a circle, heads bowed ... as though participating in some strange rite," he described (Blair 1973, 245). The last of the survivors were taken to Public Assistance Hospital in Santiago and treated. Harley was sent to intensive care. That afternoon the other eight survivors were driven to Santiago for a reunion with their fellows, and later they all flew nervously to Uruguay in a jet.

News reports of cannibalism began to surface on December 23 and were published worldwide, with the exception of Uruguay. On December 26 two papers printed photographs of a half-eaten human leg in the snow. Back in their hometown, members of the rugby team elected Alfredo Delgado to

speak for them at a press conference. He compared their actions with Christ dividing his body and blood among the apostles at the Last Supper. The crowd applauded and cheered. Afterward, Dr. Helios Valeta, whose son had been eaten, said, "Thank God there were forty-five so that sixteen could live." Later he elaborated, "I wondered if my son had helped them survive. Now I know they did eat him. I accept this, as a father and as a doctor. In spite of my grief I believe my son's body had a more beautiful destiny than just decaying in the earth..." (Blair 1973, 266–67). Not all the families were so forgiving.

The Chilean authorities and the fathers of the victims decided to bury the bodies on the mountain in a common grave. Ricardo Echavarren, whose son's last wish had been conveyed to him, was opposed. He requested official help in Chile to bring down the body but was refused. After several days, officials agreed that the death certificates would be issued in San Fernando and signed by Dr. Eduardo Arriagada, who had flown on the first rescue mission. The date of the crash was used as the date of death for all 29 victims.

The mass burial was to be conducted by the Chileans, and no relatives would be permitted to attend. Echavarren met privately with Sergio Diaz, who reluctantly agreed to attach a tube containing his First Communion Certificate to Rafael's body and to see that the body was buried last, on top of the others. On January 18, 1973, 12 men were transported to the site by helicopter. They divided into teams. Some bagged the remains of bodies that had been eaten. Others placed the intact bodies in bags. Diaz bagged Rafael Echavarren's body and attached the tube. It took all 12 men to pry the instrument panel back so that the decomposing body of Ferradas could be freed. Four men used pickaxes to dig a grave between a quarter and a half mile east of the fuselage. Their efforts caused two avalanches, the second of which carried down two of the five bodies that had remained uphill. The contents of the wreckage were doused with gasoline and burned, but afterward the charred fuselage remained. After spending the night in tents, the men completed the square 20-foot grave and brought to it the remains from near the fuselage, the body near the tail of the plane, and the three bodies remaining on top of the mountain. The following morning, Father Ivan Canviedes held the burial service, scattered a handful of Uruguayan dirt over the rocks, and planted a small iron cross over the grave. A few hours later the helicopters arrived to bring them off the mountain.

After several weeks Ricardo Echavarren had still not received permission to retrieve his son Rafael's body. Echavarren therefore mounted his own expedition with experienced friend Gustavo Nicolich and two newspaper reporters, Francisco Fernandez Quintana and Juan Antonio Dominguez. They met in Mendoza and drove into the Andes to meet up with mountain men Rene Lima and Antonio Ayala, who had agreed to serve as guides. They left on horseback on March 20 with three mules (two to carry supplies and one to carry the body). They picked flowers along the way to place on the grave.

The expedition reached the site the following day, visiting the fuselage and then the grave. After lifting off the rocks, they found the bag marked by the tube that contained Rafael's body. To be certain, Echavarren opened the bag and identified the body. They placed it on a sled they made out of an aircraft seat, lowered it down the slope, and tied it on the mule. They reached the Hotel Termas late that night, and there Echavarren and Nocolich were arrested by police for grave robbing. The police took them to San Rafael and refused to release them until a federal judge intervened. The judge released the men on the condition that Echavarren report to officials in Malargue the following morning. The police kept the body, which was stored in a niche in the San Rafael Cemetery. In Malargue, Echavarren was released through the intervention of the mayor

of San Rafael. He later began legal proceedings in Buenos Aires to allow his son to be returned to Uruguay.

As an offshoot of the movie *Alive*, which was released by Touchstone/Paramount in 1992, a video, *Alive Twenty Years Later*, was filmed. Several of the 16 survivors, who still live in the Montevideo suburb of Carasco and have remained close friends, were interviewed. Fernando Parrado, now a businessman and television personality, served as technical advisor on the *Alive* film and spent three months on location in the Canadian Rockies. The set was also visited by Ramon Sabella and Carlitos Páez, who at the time had announced he would be running for president of Uruguay. The men found the recreation—complete with buried bodies—disturbing. Gustavo Zerbino recounted the near-death experience he had after the avalanche. Looking back on their act of cannibalism, Daniel Fernandez admitted it was disturbing, saying that they didn't know who they were eating, but they knew it was a friend. José Incarte explained that they felt *not* eating the bodies would be turning their backs on the miracle of having survived the crash itself. Because they had only a limited supply of bodies, even the human meat had to be rationed, so the task of cutting it up was carried out exclusively by the Strauch cousins. Most of the men have come to terms with their past and say they would do it again if they had to.

The Victims of Richard Kuklinski

Richard Kuklinski dispatched his victims, whom he said numbered more than 100, by numerous methods. One of those victims, Louis Masgay, Sr., of Forty Fort, Pennsylvania, was killed with a gunshot to the occipital-parietal region of the head. Masgay had been lured into buying some videotapes from Kuklinski. Instead, he was killed and robbed of the $90,000 he had brought with him. Kuklinski then hung Masgay's body in a walk-in freezer compartment in his warehouse in North Bergen, New Jersey. There the body remained for more than two years.

Masgay's body, wrapped in about 20 consecutive layers of garbage bags and rope, was discovered in a wooded area of Rockland County, New York, in September 1983. Examination of the body revealed the peculiar decomposition pattern in which there was more external than internal decomposition and no distension of the tissues or intestines. In addition, "The body emitted a peculiar, foul odor not representative of the usual odors associated with decomposition" (Zugibe and Costello 1993, 1405). The surface of the body appeared greasy. The head was less well-preserved than the rest of the body, the brain had liquefied, and a bullet and two fragments were found inside the cranial cavity.

The peculiar pattern of decomposition suggested that the victim had been frozen for some period of time. Freezing would kill or alter the growth pattern of enteric flora. The external aspects of the body would be the first to thaw and therefore the first to be exposed to micro-organisms from outside the body (Zugibe and Costello 1993, 1406). The head may have decomposed more rapidly because of the bullet hole, which allowed entrance to micro-organisms, and because it may have thawed rapidly due to its small size. Examination of tissue sections of the heart muscle indicated damage by ice crystals, also suggesting that the body had been frozen prior to being discarded. The Rockland County Medical Examiner writes: "This case is a good example of the cautions that must be exercised in interpreting the time of death.... We propose that in any case involving a decomposing body that had been dumped during the months of the year when the climate is cool or warm, (not freezing), it behooves the medical examiner to consider the possibility of the body having been frozen prior to dumping" (Zugibe and Costello 1993, 1407). Clues include greater external than internal decomposition, a pastiness to the skin, and ice crystal artifacts in the tissue sections.

The Rockland County Medical Exam-

iner's Office cataloged the anthropomorphic findings, dental charts, physical characteristics, clothing, shoe size, jewelry, glasses, and—using a special technique for mummified bodies—fingerprints. The body was subsequently identified as Masgay, who had last been seen about two and a quarter years earlier. Masgay had left home on July 1, 1981, to buy videotapes from a Mr. Richard Kuklinski and was never seen again. The M. E.'s office was later contacted by authorities in New Jersey, where Kuklinski was being held as a suspect in a series of homicides. An informant had provided the New Jersey attorney general's office with a sworn statement that he had observed a body hanging in a freezer compartment within Kuklinski's warehouse.

Kuklinski was unsuccessful in his attempt to confuse the authorities about the victim's time of death. He was arrested on December 17, 1986, for the murder of five people over a two-year period. On March 16, 1988, he was found guilty of two counts of homicide and several other felonies. On May 25, 1988, he pleaded guilty to the murder of Louis Masgay and another man in return for dropped weapons charges against his wife and drug and weapons charges against his son. He also confessed to another murder. In a prison interview, he was later quoted as saying, "In a freezer nothing changes, my friend.... It's like pulling a steak out of the fridge" (Zugibe and Costello 1993). Kuklinski was dubbed "The Iceman," although Masgay was purportedly the only victim he froze.

Elena Hoyos

After an unsuccessful marriage that was later annulled, Elena Hoyos was courted by Karl Tanzler Von Cosel. Elena refused the eccentric Von Cosel's offer of marriage and shortly thereafter, in 1931, died of tuberculosis at the age of 22. Von Cosel received permission from Elena's sister Maria Medina to build a tomb for his beloved in City Cemetery in Key West, Florida. The tomb, which he built himself, was described in the *American Funeral Director* (January 1984) as "a baroque sanctuary suitable for the resting place of a saint." Von Cosel visited the tomb often and would remove the lid of the casket to stare at the face and hands of the deceased. When the body began to deteriorate, Von Cosel decided to use an experimental fluid he had developed. Von Cosel, a hospital technician, believed that the fluid would not only keep Elena's body intact but restore her to life.

Late one night Von Cosel transferred the body from its casket to his laboratory in Key West City Hospital. He spent the night filling the body with tissue preservatives and before dawn carried it to the fuselage of an airplane he hoped to rebuild to fly them both to his German homeland. He hired a taxi driver to tow the fuselage to his shack on the town's outskirts. He then dressed Elena like a bride, complete with a veil and a gold wedding band, and allowed her to lie in state for the next seven years. He used wax when necessary to build up sunken tissue, held parting joints together with piano wire, and used cosmetics to give the skin a lifelike color (the *American Funeral Director*, January 1984). Mrs. Medina was unaware that her sister's body was missing from her tomb until October 6, 1940, but she knew where to find it. When she peeked into Von Cosel's shack, she saw the body of her sister—lifeless but with open eyes—reclining on the bed.

After obtaining a search warrant, sheriff's deputies arrested Von Cosel for grave robbery. Elena's body was removed to the Benjamin Lopez Funeral Home, where it was viewed by more than 2,000 people who waited in line for as long as two hours to see the remarkably lifelike remains. Later, the remains were casketed and returned to the tomb that Von Cosel had built for her. Von Cosel was freed on bond posted by his sister. Charges were dropped at the trial when the judge ruled that the statute of limitations had expired. Von Cosel then filed suit for possession of the body, stating that he had

greater claim to it than the dead woman's sister, but his request was denied.

To prevent history from repeating itself, Mrs. Medina and her husband Mario made arrangements with the W. Warren Sawyer Funeral Home and Otto Bethel, the sexton of the City Cemetery, to have Elena's remains interred. Mr. and Mrs. Medina were present when the casket was removed from the tomb, wheeled to a newly opened grave, and quietly buried. Von Cosel, no longer employed by the hospital, was soon evicted from his home and sought refuge with his sister in Zephyrhills, Florida, until his death in 1952 at the age of 83. Elena's unusual (and empty) tomb was destroyed, and the secret location of her grave presumably died with her sister and brother-in-law (the *American Funeral Director*, January 1984).

The Victims of John Reginald Halliday Christie

Englishman John Reginald Halliday Christie had a criminal record for minor offenses. He married Ethel Waddington in 1920, but the marriage broke up after three years. He lived alone at No. 10 Rillington Place until his second marriage. The victim of his first murder was Ruth Margarete Christine Fuerst, with whom he had been having an affair. He hid her body under the floor boards in the front room before his wife returned from a trip and moved the body to the washhouse while she was shopping. He later carried it to the front garden and buried it. He killed another victim by compelling her to inhale gas, the odor of which he disguised with Friar's Balsam. The body of Muriel Amelia Eady, one of his coworkers, was placed in the washhouse until she too could be buried in the garden.

On November 8, 1949, Christie gassed and strangled Beryl Evans, the wife of his upstairs neighbor Timothy, and convinced her husband that she had died during an abortion attempt. Police found the bodies of Mrs. Evans and her 14-month-old infant in the washhouse, and Timothy Evans was hanged in 1950 for the death of the child.

Christie strangled his wife of 25 years on December 14, 1952, and explained away her absence to family and friends when necessary. He left her body on the bed for two days before depositing it beneath the floorboards in the front room covered with dirt brought in from the garden. The murder of his wife was followed by the gassing and strangling of three more women. Prostitute Rita Nelson, age 25, was killed before or after sexual intercourse on January 2, 1953, and placed in a cupboard in the kitchen the following morning. On January 12, Kathleen Maloney, a 26-year-old prostitute, was also strangled and stashed in the cupboard before or after intercourse. Both women had been left partially clothed and wrapped in a blanket. Twenty-six-year-old Hectorina McLennan, a recent acquaintance of Christie's, met the same fate on March 3, 1953. Her body was nude except for a brassiere.

Christie left his flat on March 20 and sublet it to a Jamaican man named Beresford Brown four days later. While planning to redecorate the kitchen, Brown discovered one of its walls to be hollow. He peeled off the wallpaper and discovered behind the broken cupboard door "a naked corpse bent forward to show a large expanse of her posterior" (Jackson 1975, 79). Authorities were summoned and the remains photographed. When the corpse was pulled out, the bodies of the two other women were discovered, photographed, and removed. All three were taken to the Kensington mortuary. The front room of the house was searched, and the fourth body, discovered under the floorboards, was guarded until morning when it was also conveyed to the mortuary. Christie was arrested on March 31, 1953. He confessed to all the murders but claimed that of his wife was a mercy-killing, two others were in self-defense, and the murder of Mrs. Evans was an assisted suicide.

The body of 54-year-old Mrs. Christie had been wrapped in a blanket that was fastened with a safety pin at the top. The body was unclothed except for stockings on both legs. The head was wrapped in a pillowcase and a vest had been used as a "diaper." Her death from asphyxia was estimated by pathologist Francis Camps to have taken place 12 to 15 weeks earlier. During their search of the house and grounds, police discovered bones in the garden, some of which were later identified as human and coming from two women of different heights and ages. They were identified as belonging to Fuerst and Eady.

The three semiclothed bodies found in the cupboard were in a good state of preservation. The kitchen alcove had provided cool, dry surroundings with some air movement. Two of the bodies exhibited a cherry-pink color, indicating poisoning by carbon monoxide, and all three tested positive for being exposed to the gas. "I think he got some feeling of satisfaction in continuing to live in Rillington Place with the dead bodies nearby," said Dr. J. A. Hobson, psychologist and defense consultant (Jackson 1975, 83).

In May 1953 police exhumed the bodies of Beryl Evans and her daughter Geraldine from a cemetery in Kensington. The slightly warped lid of the casket was raised to allow the escape of gases before it was transported to Kensington mortuary. The bodies were examined by pathologists Francis Camps, Keith Simpson, and Donald Teare, psychiatrist Jack Abbott Hobson, several officers from the Metropolitan Police and Scotland Yard, and Chief Inspector George Jennings, who had identified the bodies at the original autopsies. The bodies were covered with a shroud that was overgrown with white mold. The child lay on top of the mother on a bed of damp brown sawdust.

Jennings easily recognized the bodies a second time because both had been remarkably preserved by the formation of adipocere. "Adipocere is seldom well developed in bodies buried in coffins, which seem to decompose more rapidly than those with-

out, but it had been favoured by some unusual conditions: the cold weather at the
time of death, the position of the bodies in
the outside wash house, and the effect of the
rather wet common grave and the well-
drained sandy soil" (Simpson 1978, 197).
Both bodies were whitish-yellow, but the
thighs of the mother were pink until shortly
after being exposed to the air. Mrs. Evans'
body was reopened along the original autopsy incisions. The organs were remarkably
preserved, with the lungs pink until shortly
after exposure to the air. The bodies were
reinterred the same day. Specimens tested
negative for carbon monoxide.

Christie was tried and found guilty for
the murder of his wife in June 1953 and was
hanged at Pentonville prison on July 15.
Camps conducted his autopsy. Fifteen years
later the Evans case was reopened, and it was
found probable that Evans had killed his
wife Beryl and that Christie had killed their
daughter Geraldine. If so, Evans had been
hanged for the wrong murder. He was given
a posthumous pardon, exhumed, and reburied outside the prison.

The Victims of Dennis Nilsen

Dennis "Des" Nilsen of 195 Melrose
Avenue in London was fascinated by the
image of a lifeless body. He would arouse
himself by lying very still in front of a mirror with his head beyond the reflection so
that he could imagine his body was someone
else's corpse. Toward the end of 1978 he pow-
dered his body and used makeup to apply
gunshot wounds before engaging in his au-
toerotic fantasies. After he had murdered, he
explained, "It was as if the spirit of the man
still dwelt within and the decay of death was
a consummation of life itself. I compared my
own 'living' body with the dead body and
thought how strange it was that they were
now beyond pain, problems and sorrow and
I was not" (Masters 1984, 271).

Nilsen killed his first victim, an Irish
eighteen-year-old he brought home from a
pub, on December 30, 1978. He strangled the

young man to unconsciousness with a nearby
necktie, then drowned him in a bucket of
water. He placed the body upright in an armchair and stared at it for some time until carrying it into the bathroom. He washed the
body and shampooed the hair, seated it with
some difficulty on the toilet, patted it dry, and
carried it to his bed. "His face was slightly
discoloured (pinkish) and his eyes were half
open. His face seemed to be slightly puffed
up and his lips (bluish) slightly parted.... I
turned him over on the bed and ran my
fingers down the length of him ... he was still
warm to the touch. His wet hair left a mark
on the pillow. I straightened him up (on his
back) on the bed and pulled the bedclothes up
to his chin," Nilsen writes in his prison journal (Masters 1984, 111).

Nilsen clothed and fondled the body,
but decided against having sex with it because it had grown cold and moved it to the
floor. "The coldness of a corpse has nothing
endearing in it," Nilsen wrote later (Masters
1984, 302). He decided to store the body beneath the floorboards, but it had stiffened up
with rigor mortis. He leaned the corpse
against the wall until morning, when the
joints had loosened enough to fit him under
the floor. A week later Nilsen became curious, took the body out of its hiding place, removed the clothes, bathed it, and examined
it closely. The body was pale but not discolored, and the limbs were relaxed. After
twenty-four hours, part of which time the
corpse had been suspended by the ankles
from the bed, Nilsen replaced it under the
floorboards. "I laid him on the kitchen floor
and decided to cut him up, but I just couldn't
do anything to spoil that marvellous body,"
writes Nilsen (Masters 1984, 113). The body
remained in the apartment until August 11,
1979, when he took it outside in a bag and
cremated it in a bonfire.

Nilsen's next killing was that of Canadian tourist Kenneth Ockendon on December 3, 1979, again by strangling after luring
the man home from a pub. Nilsen stripped
the body, bathed it, and kept it in bed with
him for the rest of the night. He put the body

in the cupboard before he went to work and removed it, wiping away a brown liquid that had dripped from his nose, upon his return. He dressed the corpse in clean socks and underwear and arranged the body in poses for photographs (which he later burned), covering up any puffiness or discoloration of the skin with makeup. Nilsen arranged the body on top of him as he watched television. He interred the body beneath the floor but resurrected it on four separate occasions over the next two weeks. In Nilsen's words, "It was cold down there and he was still very fresh.... I thought that his body and skin were very beautiful, a sight that almost brought me to tears after a couple of drinks. He had not a mark on him save for red lines on his neck. Before he returned to his 'bed' I would sit him on my knee and strip off the underwear and socks, wrap him in curtain material and put him down (actually saying, 'Good night, Ken')" (Masters 1984, 119).

Nilsen killed Martyn Duffey in May 1980 by strangling and submerging his head in the kitchen sink. He undressed the body, washed it as it lay on top of him in the bathtub, and dried it after propping it up in a kitchen chair. After some fondling, he stored the body in a cupboard for two days, during which time it became bloated, so it was relegated to the floor. Later, he brought up the bodies of Ockendon and Duffey, dismembered them, put the remains in two suitcases, and stored the luggage—which he occasionally doused with disinfectant—in the garden shed.

Billy Sutherland was strangled that summer, used as a companion for two days, and interred beneath the floorboards. Sutherland was followed by a Mexican or Filipino boy whose body was placed under the floor and later dismembered. Of one of his unidentified victims, Nilsen wrote, "His naked body fascinated me. I remember being thrilled that I had full control and ownership of this beautiful body.... I was fascinated by the mystery of death. I whispered to him because I believed he was still really in there.... I would hold him towards me standing up and view in the full length mirror (my arms around him). I would hold him close often, and think that he had never been so appreciated in his life before" (Masters 1984, 125).

Three more murders followed in quick succession as maggots fed ravenously under the floorboards. Nilsen decided it was time for another bonfire but decided it was necessary to cut the bodies up first. He fortified himself with rum, undressed to avoid soiling his clothes, took up the floorboards once again, and dragged the bodies one by one by the ankles onto plastic sheets he had spread on the kitchen floor. Using a sharp kitchen knife, he cut off the head, hands, and feet and washed, dried, and bagged each piece after it was severed. He made an incision from the navel to the breastbone and took the internal organs out as a unit. The rest of the body he cut into large chunks, brushing the maggots off with salt. The remains of four bodies and the suitcases in the shed were burned in a huge bonfire in early December 1980, with an old tire to disguise the smell. Nilsen saw the fire through to completion, raking the ashes afterwards and breaking up a skull that had survived intact.

After three more victims met their fate and were sealed beneath the floorboards, Nilsen killed his twelfth victim, a skinhead with a tattoo around his neck reading "cut here." Having learned his lesson about the causes of the odor in his apartment, Nilsen routinely relieved his victims of their internal organs, which he deposited over the fence in the garden. In addition, he dismembered and parceled the pieces for easier removal before placing them under the floor with earth and deodorant tablets. Epileptic Malcolm Barlow was killed in September, and his small body was stashed in a kitchen cabinet, there being no more room under the floor. Then Nilsen accepted an offer from his landlords to move to 23 Cranley Gardens. The day before his move on October 5, 1981, he kindled a final bonfire to destroy the remaining evidence.

Within six months of living in his new

apartment, Nilsen had killed another man. In March 1982 he drowned John Howlett in the bathtub when strangling proved ineffective. He stored the body for several days in the wardrobe, then cut it up into small chunks, boiling certain parts to reduce them and flushing them down the toilet. The pieces he was unable to cut up were thrown out with the trash or bagged and stored in a wooden tea chest. Nilsen kept down the smell with air fresheners and deodorant sprays. In September he killed alcoholic Graham Allen. Nilsen left Allen's body in the bathtub for three days, periodically changing the cold water in which he lay. He then dissected, boiled, flushed, and stored parts of the corpse like that of his previous victim.

Stephen Sinclair, a drug addict, became Nilsen's sixteenth and last victim in January 1983. The body was bathed and enjoyed, then placed in the wardrobe. Portions of his body were flushed down the toilet a week later. Plumbing problems in the apartment building brought the police, who arrested Nilsen for suspicion of murder on February 9, 1983. Nilsen was relieved to finally confess to the murder of 16 people. On May 26 he was committed for trial at the Central Criminal Court on six charges of murder (Ockendon, Barlow, Duffey, Howlett, Sutherland, and Sinclair) and two of attempted murder. The jury trial began on October 24, 1983, with Nilsen pleading not guilty. On November 4, by a majority verdict, Nilsen was found guilty of the six murders and the two attempted murders. The judge sentenced him to life imprisonment with a recommendation that he serve a minimum of 25 years.

NEGLECT

Last but not least are bodies that are left where they fall, whether the fall is due to natural causes, accidental death, suicide, homicide, or "undetermined." Murder victims have been dispatched but not disposed of. People who live alone die and are occasionally not missed until their bodies have mummified. Sometimes the cause of death is not known, but the consequences are feared, so a body is tucked away and forgotten—only to be discovered years or even a generation later. In the most curious of cases, the body of a dead household member is literally ignored: stepped over and worked around until authorities intervene.

When police discover that a death has taken place, those confronted with failing to report it almost always have a ready excuse. When 42-year-old Deborah Josh was charged in Kissimmee, Florida, with failing to report the death of her 82-year-old employer, she explained to Osceola County Sheriff's Captain Gary Pearce that she wanted to continue receiving his monthly pension checks. After the man's apparently natural death, Josh, his live-in caretaker, had stored the man's body in a small freezer for two years (Kohut 1993, 7). When the body of three-year-old Muriel Makinson, first believed to be a large yellow doll, was found on top of a cupboard in a house in Highbury Hill, North London, in August 1951, her parents at first claimed they had never seen it before. Pathologist Francis Camps noted that the skull had been fractured in two places and estimated that the death may have occurred ten years before. Mrs. Ernest Makinson finally told police that she had slapped her disobedient daughter, who struck her head on a gas stove and died the following morning after some sort of seizure: "I just panicked. I thought I would keep the body. I didn't put it in the sack for several weeks. I put it in a chest of drawers with a nightdress on" (Jackson 1975, 167). The corpse was left behind when the family temporarily evacuated the house during the Blitz. After Camps found burns on the body, Mrs. Makinson also admitted to trying to destroy it, but since the cause of death could not be ascertained, the authorities let the matter drop.

When the body of retired mechanical engineer Long Lu Lee was discovered in the home he shared with his wife, 62-year-old

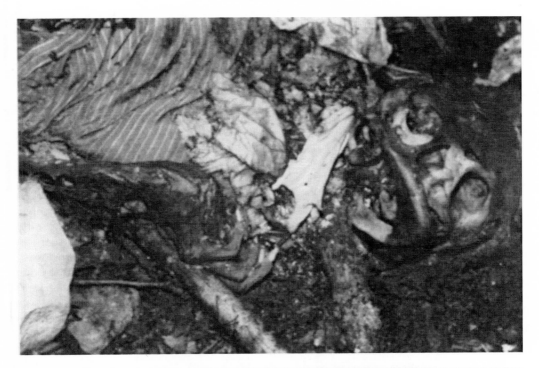

The upper body and the leg of a 75-year-old white female missing for three months, from June 20 to September 16. Photos courtesy of William Bass, University of Tennessee.

Thuc Khoanh Lu seemed genuinely surprised to learn that he had been dead in her basement all year. Although she was not considered a suspect in his death, she had neglected to file a missing person report when her husband disappeared the previous winter. On December 1, 1994, Long Lu Lee was discovered in the Queens, New York, house by the Brooklyn Union Gas Company. The corpse was dressed in a blue bathrobe, white sweater, jogging pants, white socks, and sandals. It was seated on a patio chair near the boiler and behind a huge cobweb. The head had fallen off and was found beneath the chair.

The excuse of a man in Florida was not that he didn't know his roommate was missing, but that he didn't know he was dead! Forty-three-year-old William Delaney fell in the house he shared in Key West with his 78-year-old roommate. The body lay facedown in the doorway between the kitchen and the bathroom. The roommate often asked Delaney if he wanted something to eat or drink or would like to be taken to the hospital, but he didn't receive a response. He therefore continued to step over the body for two months until police officers entered the residence. The roommate told the police that he thought Delaney was alive because he seemed to change positions and stretch his legs. According to police, however, the body had decomposed to the point that it "seemed to be melting into the floor" (Kohut 1993, 9).

Like failure to report a death, failure to bury a body is often justified in the eyes of those at fault. In 1988, 44 decomposing bodies were found stacked like cordwood in a closet at the Lewis J. Howell Mortuary in Jacksonville, Florida. Mr. Howell blamed the delay on paperwork, despite the fact that one of the bodies had been there for ten years. In *Death to Dust* (1994), Kenneth V. Iserson reports that as of 1992, Flint, Michigan, funeral director J. Merrill Spencer was still holding the body of James McDill—who had died on February 26, 1989—pending payment of the family's past due account of

$3,605.29. "The body is still in the basement of my parlor, and will stay there until they pay me," Spencer is quoted as saying. Although U.S. common law prohibits retaining a corpse as security for the payment of funeral costs, there are no Michigan state laws requiring burial if no payment is made (Iserson 1994, 559).

Sometimes deaths are undiscovered and bodies unburied because neighbors are not missed. The body of reclusive Adele A. Gaboury was discovered four years after her death in her Worcester, Massachusetts, home. In April 1996 the body of 47-year-old Gabriella Villa was discovered in Monza, Italy. She had died of natural causes approximately seven years earlier in her home. Neighbors and her estranged husband had assumed that she had moved to another town. During the severe winter of 1981, police entered the Bronx apartment of 47-year-old Jessie Smalls and found her encased in a block of ice. A water pipe had burst and flooded the place, forcing the police to chop the ice away before they could recover the body (Moore 1994, 35). A 77-year-old woman in the Sydney suburb of Punchbowl was also found frozen to death in her home. She had apparently leaned over her top-opening freezer, overbalanced, and hit her head. She was found inside it. A woman in Stockholm sat on her balcony for two and a half months during the winter before neighbors realized she was dead. Police theorized that the woman, who was discovered in March, had died while watching New Year's Eve fireworks. She was seated in a chair on the balcony and wore a hat and coat. Her head was leaning against the railing. Neighbor Margaretha Marsellas eventually became suspicious after seeing the woman there at all hours in frigid temperatures (Kohut 1993, 9–11).

Complaints rather than concern often lead authorities to the not-so-recently deceased. In the late 1980s, police entered an apartment in an abandoned building in the slum section of an eastern city to investigate the report of an overpowering odor. In the doorway to one of the bedrooms they found a body. The police report read, "The body is fully extended face down with the face tilted left. The right cheek and entire body is stuck to the floor. There are no body fluids visible and the body is dried out. It appears to have been chewed and the bones are exposed. The fire department responded and assisted with shovels in prying the body from the floor" (Ubelaker 1992, 160). Much of the body was desiccated, but some of the soft tissue was still moist and contained maggots: "It is not unusual for active arthropod feeding to continue in the moist tissues of bodies that are otherwise dried up, even in cases where the body appears to have become mummified" (Ubelaker 1992, 161). Forensic anthropologist Douglas Ubelaker verified that the body was that of a black male and estimated his age to be between 26 and 36 years. He estimated time since death to be about three months. When the remaining soft tissue was removed, fractures in the skull indicated homicide.

In certain rare instances recovery of bodies from the location of their deaths is ruled out for practical reasons and they are left in place. In the case of the Swedish ferry boat *Estonia*, which sank in 1994 with 852 people on board, the bodies remain with the wreck in the freezing Baltic Sea. Approximately 80 percent of the relatives of the victims want the bodies recovered, but the government plans to entomb the wreck in concrete. The soft sea bed in the area is being strengthened. Concrete brackets will be used to strap the vessel to the sea floor and it will be sealed forever. The low temperatures of the water ensure that the bodies will decompose very slowly, but to bring them up and identify them would be an enormous task. Unfortunately, as reported in the *Funeral Monitor* (June 24, 1996), one body has washed up on a beach, and more are expected to come ashore in ones or twos unless something is done quickly.

Sometimes bodies simply turn up, separated from their families, their histories, and often their own identities. An Associ-ated Press story (February 28, 1996) reported that a block of ice containing the body of a man age 20 to 25 with Asian features was found on a beach at Roedvig in southeastern Denmark. Because the body was unclothed, police considered suicide unlikely; because there were no wounds on the body, the man had probably not been murdered. Suicide was the cause of death of a body found in London's Chinatown. In her 1955 memoir *Evidence for the Crown*, Molly Lefebure recounts pathologist Keith Simpson's investigation of an unidentified Chinese man whose body had mummified after hanging in a bombed-out house for several months.

Occasionally, great pains are taken to identify recovered bodies. The methods may involve continued preservation of the body to keep the features recognizable. On September 1, 1934, the partly burned body of a young woman dressed in embroidered pajamas was found in a culvert near Albury, New South Wales. She had a gunshot wound in the head but had been killed by blows to the skull. The woman appeared to be English but could not be identified. Her only distinctive feature was her lack of ear lobes. Photographs, fingerprints, and a full description of the body were widely circulated, and the body itself was placed in a tank of formalin at Sydney University. A number of people viewed the body and tentatively identified it as Linda Agostini, wife of an Italian restaurant worker. Police interviewed Antonio Agostini in July 1935 and showed him pictures of the dead woman but declared the case unsolved when he denied that it was his wife. In 1944 the newly appointed Commissioner of Police for New South Wales, W. J. Mackay, reopened the case, had the body taken out of the formalin bath, and had her face made up and her hair dressed. Seven people identified her from photographs as Linda Agostini. Antonio Agostini confessed, stating that Linda had begun to drink heavily and had threatened him in bed with a revolver. In the struggle the gun had gone off and killed her, so he drove her body to the culvert, poured gasoline over it, and set it on fire. Agostini was tried, convicted by a jury of manslaughter, sentenced to six years of hard labor, and then deported to Italy (Gaute and Odell 1989, 244).

Katherine Howard

In August 1975 Wilbur Howard reported his wife missing. He flunked a polygraph test, but no body had been found. In April 1976 the headless, handless body of a woman was discovered floating in Greenwood Lake, which borders the Appalachian Trail between New York and New Jersey. She had a gash under her left breast, and her slim, athletic body was covered with green algae. An autopsy was performed by a hospital pathologist, who estimated her age to be in the twenties and time since death to be about three weeks. Police posters and broadcasts for missing persons of that age brought no leads.

Six days after her discovery troopers Dan Reidy and Jimmy Curtis brought the body to New York's chief medical examiner Michael Baden in a coffin. Dr. Baden determined that the woman was about 55 years old and that the gash under her breast had been made to remove a scar distinctive enough to identify her. Her stomach contained the remains of a fruit and vegetable meal. A sample of the algae was scraped off the torso and sent to a biologist who identified two generations: fresh green algae from that year and dead algae from the year before. The woman had therefore been dead for at least a year and a half.

The new description reported in the newspapers and on the radio brought a call from a woman claiming the body was probably that of her sister Katherine Howard of Elmont, New York, and that she had most likely been killed by her husband Wilbur Howard. When asked if her sister had any distinguishing characteristics, the woman described a scar under her left breast. The last time the two had been together—two years before— they had eaten a meal of fruit and vegetables.

After being questioned again Wilbur Howard said he thought his wife had run away. Police could find no x-rays to prove the body was Katherine's, even though a podiatrist in Elmont recognized the toes of one of the feet the authorities had disarticulated. The police appealed to Wilbur Howard to allow them to eventually close the case by making a confession in his will. Howard died two years later but left no confession. The body is still officially unidentified (Baden 1989, 86–88).

Joan Pearl Wolfe

On October 7, 1942, one of a party of Marines exercising in the sand dunes high up on Hankley Common, near Godalming, England, spotted a dried brown hand sticking out from a mound of earth. When he took a closer look, he saw part of a shriveled and discolored leg. The Surrey Police were summoned by field telephone and Superintendent Richard Webb posted a guard, covered the mound with a mackintosh sheet, and sought out experts. The group he summoned included Major Nicholson (chief constable), Detective Superintendent Roberts (head of the Surrey criminal investigation department), several police officers, a photographer, Dr. Eric Gardner (instructed by the coroner), and Keith Simpson (medicolegal advisor to the Surrey police), with Detective Inspector Ted Greeno (Scotland Yard) arriving later.

The area was cordoned off and photographed. Simpson collected soil samples and examined the hand: "The thumb and first two fingers had been bitten away close to their roots, as by rats. Both the hand and the leg were becoming mummified, so death had occurred at least a few weeks before" (Simpson 1978, 60). Simpson and Gardner excavated the shallowly buried body with gloved hands, and Gardner determined, based on the growth of heather on an overturned clod of earth, that the body had been buried five or six weeks. The body was female and lay face downward with the right arm outstretched. The back of her skull had been shattered by a heavy implement (later determined to be a wooden branch found at the scene) and her head was disintegrating as a result of vermin action.

The mummy was wearing a worn green and white summer frock with a lace collar, belted at the waist by a string. Her underclothes consisted of a slip, a vest, a brassiere, and panties, none of which were disarranged. She wore socks; her shoes were found several hundred yards away. A scarf was tied loosely around her neck and knotted in front. Lacerations and scrapes on her ankles and feet indicated that she had been dragged to the site, probably by her right arm. The body smelled strongly of putrefaction and was filled with maggots, indicating it must have been exposed to the air for as long as a day or two before burial or that it was incompletely covered by loose leaves or a cloth.

Simpson secured permission from the coroner, Dr. Wills Taylor, to remove the body to his laboratory at Guy's Hospital in London. It was rolled into a waterproof sheet and placed in a carbolic bath in the mortuary upon arrival. After the bath had killed the maggots, Simpson removed the clothes. The age was estimated at 19 or 20 and the woman's height was determined to be five feet four inches. Her bobbed hair was fine and sandy brown and had been bleached some weeks before death. She had buck teeth, which had been knocked out by a fall or a blow.

Parts of the woman's breasts and thighs had been converted to "the white substance, foul-smelling and unctuous to the touch, called adipocere" (Simpson 1978, 62). Adipocere formation usually takes five or six weeks in a temperate climate, but the heat generated by the maggots may have accelerated the formation to within a month. The woman had been stabbed in the face and had defensive wounds on her right hand and arm. A crush fracture of the right cheekbone showed that she had been bludgeoned while lying on her face. The skull, which Simpson and Gardner pieced together with wire and

rivets, had been shattered into 38 pieces by a single blow that would have caused immediate unconsciousness and death a few minutes later. Superintendent Webb remembered a woman of the appropriate description named Joan Pearl Wolfe, who had come to his office, told him she was pregnant, and been referred to a hospital. She had been living in the woods in an improvised wigwam made out of branches, twigs, and leaves by her lover August Sangret, a soldier stationed at the nearby army camp. Sangret had visited Webb the following day looking for Joan so that he could ask for her hand in marriage. Sangret was picked up but was not told of the discovery of the body. He answered questions impassively, made a 17,000-word statement to police about himself and Joan, and said, "I guess you found her. I guess I shall get the blame," followed by "She might have killed herself" (Simpson 1978, 65). Because he had not incriminated himself, Sangret was released. The case became known as the "wigwam murder."

Sangret was picked up by police a second time after a knife that matched the wounds was found in Witley Camp. He identified it as belonging to Joan and was arrested and charged with the murder. Sangret was tried five months later. Simpson exhibited the knife and the skull in court, and the jury found Sangret guilty but recommended mercy. He was hanged at Wandsworth Jail, and Simpson performed the autopsy. A tattoo on his arm read "Pearl" (Simpson 1978, 69).

William and John Higgins

In June 1913 two men found the bodies of two children floating in water-filled Hopetown Quarry near Winchburgh, England. The bodies had been tied together with window-cord, which broke when the men tried to lift them out of the water. The children were fully and identically clothed, but the inexpensive garments had almost completely rotted from immersion. They wore stockings with garters under the knees and boots. Their shirts were imprinted with the stamp of a poorhouse at Dysart in Fife.

The bodies had been almost wholly transformed into adipocere, a slow but permanent process. Sir Sydney Smith writes, "We were interested from a purely medical point of view, because extensive transformations are rarely come across, and these specimens were quite exceptional. In each body the formation was complete apart from the feet, which had been covered by the boots, and in which the adipocerous condition was therefore not so far advanced" (Smith 1959, 41). He performed an autopsy on each body in the mortuary at Linlithgow and took the opportunity, while Professor Harvey Littlejohn distracted the two police officers who were present, to remove some samples of adipocere for teaching purposes.

Smith guessed the bodies had been in the water from 18 months to 2 years. Though the external appearance gave little indication of gender, the internal examination revealed them to be males. Their heights were three feet seven and a half inches and three feet two inches. Based on an examination of the teeth and bones, Smith estimated the taller boy to be six or seven years of age at death and the smaller boy to be between three and four. Both scalps were nearly bare, but they each had tufts of brown hair on the back that had been cut shortly before death. The internal organs were remarkably well preserved, as were the stomach contents: "The extensive adipocere formation was responsible for preserving this valuable evidence over such a phenomenally long period" (Smith 1959, 42).

The meal had been eaten about an hour before death, suggesting that they lived locally, but because the area was remote it was theorized that they had instead walked to the quarry with their killer. Based on all the evidence, police found that two boys matching the descriptions had disappeared in November 1911. Their mother had died, and the boys were cared for in a poorhouse. Their father, Patrick Higgins, had been imprisoned for

two months in 1911 for failing to maintain them. On his release he collected the boys and boarded them with a widow but refused to pay her. Threatened with imprisonment again, he tried to get the boys into a home but wouldn't pay for their board. They then disappeared.

Witnesses saw Higgins walk towards Winchburgh with the boys and saw him later without them. Higgins offered several excuses for their absence, including adoption by a woman he met on the train. Police collected evidence and arrested Higgins a few days after the bodies were found. The trial was held three months later, and the jury returned a unanimous guilty vertict, with a recommendation of mercy due to the length of time that had elapsed between the murder and the trial. After the judge pronounced sentence of death and Higgins was led out of the courtroom, he looked back at his relatives and friends in court and gave them a smile and a wink. He was hanged on October 1, 1913. Smith examined the body, which was afterward cut down and buried on prison grounds.

In a contemporary university magazine, someone wrote:

Two bodies found in a lonely mere,
Converted into adipocere.
Harvey, when called in to see 'em,
Said, "Just what I need for my museum"
    [Smith 1959, 50]

In fact, the samples removed from the bodies by Smith and Littlejohn included the boys' heads, stomachs, internal organs, and an arm and a leg from each. The parcels rode back to Edinburgh with them on a crowded train, causing much puzzlement about the resulting odor, but arrived safely and without question: "We put the purloined specimens in the Forensic Medicine Museum at the University, and you can see them there to this day. They are still used to illustrate adipocere formation to students. So complete is their state of preservation that most of the details—including the small injury to William Higgins' scalp—can still clearly be discerned" (Smith 1959, 51).

Mrs. Knight

Sarah Jane Harvey, whose husband had left her in 1936, took in lodgers at her home at 35 West Kinmell Street in Rhyl, North Wales. Mrs. Knight, lame and good-natured, took a room for which she paid 30 shillings a week.

In April 1960 Mrs. Harvey's son Leslie, who had lived with her until his marriage two years earlier, decided to clean and paint her house while she was in the hospital for some tests. He forced open the doors of a floor-to-ceiling pinewood cupboard on the stair landing that had often aroused his curiosity when he was growing up. A wave of dank air hit him as he pulled the door open, and his flashlight revealed a brown human foot protruding from a blanket-covered mound. After Leslie Harvey summoned his father-in-law, the police were called in.

The body was as hard as a statue and later described as a shell of skin and bones. A garden spade was required to pry it loose from the floor, a task made more difficult by generating clouds of choking dust. The dust, dead flies, spiders, and rotting clothes were brushed off the body. It was determined to be female. Signs of maggots were present on the skin, and they had eaten the internal organs. The body had no hair on the scalp, no teeth, no tongue, no eyelashes, and no blood vessels. Pathologists discerned that the woman had been about five feet four inches tall, was aged 50 to 65, had been right-handed, and had walked with a limp. Her condition of disseminated sclerosis was deduced and would probably have caused her death soon if she had not been killed. Bits of a ligature around her neck may have been used to strangle her or may instead have been a superstitious remedy worn to cure a cold.

The body was identified as that of the lodger Mrs. Knight, whose alimony of two pounds a week was collected by Mrs. Harvey as she mummified in the cupboard. Mrs. Harvey, upon being questioned, explained that a few weeks after Mrs. Knight began to board with her, she collapsed on the floor. Mrs. Harvey could not lift her onto the bed and left her to dress and make tea. When she returned, Mrs. Knight had died. Being alone and scared, Mrs. Harvey pulled her along the landing and put her in the empty cupboard. She hung up flypapers, wedged an eiderdown between Mrs. Knight's thighs and legs, and locked the doors. Mrs. Harvey continued to take in lodgers, one of whom attempted unsuccessfully to force the lock.

In the Assize Court at Ruthin, Denbighshire, in October 1960, Mrs. Harvey pleaded not guilty to the murder of Mrs. Francis Alice Knight. Pathologist Francis Camps, brought into the case by the defense, commended the work of pathologist Dr. Edward Gerald Evans in examining the body, "which resulted in much fresh scientific knowledge coming to light about mummies" (Jackson 1975, 88). Nevertheless, the cause of Mrs. Knight's death, whether natural or unnatural, could not be ascertained. Mrs. Harvey, who had received more than £2,000 of Mrs. Knight's alimony, was sentenced to 15 months' imprisonment for fraud.

Mr. Ellis

An 80-year-old man fell asleep one afternoon in the bar that he frequented at the Equestrian Public House on Blackfriars Road in Southwark, England. After closing time the barman roused him, and the half-awake Ellis opened the door leading to the cellar instead of the street and fell down the steps to the floor nine and a half feet below. The man broke his neck in the fall and the barman later found the body when he went down for coal. He had once been in trouble with the police and panicked. He wrapped the body in a cocoon of curtains and propped it in the corner, after which he gave his notice and disappeared.

The old man had been missing for nearly a year when his body was found in June 1935 by a man tidying up the cellar, which was used to store coal, pieces of furniture, and other odds and ends. He moved a large bundle of old carpets tied with electric flex, which stood upright in the recess at one end of the large triangular-shaped cellar. He cut the flex, found more wrappings of curtains and oil-cloth, and discovered the dehydrated corpse inside. The brown skin was like parchment, the flesh had withered, and the bones were standing out. The head had come apart from the neck. The body was light and stiff and could easily be held erect with one hand. The face was unrecognizable, and there was no clue to his identity. Superintendent Robert Fabian was summoned to the scene by the manager of the Equestrian, and he called in specialists from Scotland Yard, who were accompanied by Sir Bernard

Spilsbury. Routine police work discovered the identity of the victim "and how he came to be wrapped up like a package for the post" (Browne and Tullett 1988, 370).

Though Ellis had been healthy for his age, the shock of the fall, a fractured skull, and other injuries caused his death, which may have been instantaneous. Mummification was brought about by the combination of sudden death, a fairly rapid cooling of the body in the cellar, and its being rolled up in an air-tight bundle. The barman pleaded guilty to concealment of the body, was sentenced to three days' imprisonment, and was immediately released (Browne and Tullett 1952, 434–36).

9. Conclusion

The display of human remains is for some a very sensitive issue. Even scientists have been known to issue blanket condemnation of the practice in one of its most legitimate contexts, the museum: "In my opinion the public display of mummies or parts of mummies or of human preparations is intrinsically inhuman and quite inappropriate to our cultural consciousness—regardless of their historical and scientific importance, their state of conservation or public interest … these bodies deserve some remnant of human dignity which we must try to retain for them, irrespective of their academic and historic testimonies. After all, the humane treatment and respect for the human remains of our past also honours the sciences concerned" (Seipel 1996, 6).

The most important consideration seems to be dignity, but this means different things to different people. In the midst of dissection a cadaver is decidedly undignified in its presentation, but most people would not deny the value of its preservation. The enshrinement of Vladimir Lenin is done with some decorum but is considered by many to be a vulgar display. Perhaps more important than the dignity with which mummified remains are handled is whether or not they are displayed to the public. When the public voices its collective objection to an exhibit, even in a medical or natural history museum, the exhibit may be shelved but may or may not be deaccessioned. When mummies are privately owned, the owners necessarily become secretive about their holdings to avoid having to defend their collections against those who would lobby for burial. The result of the actions of those individuals whom embalming historian Edward C. Johnson refers to as "the well-intentioned" is that most modern mummies extant today are kept behind closed (and locked) doors.

And yet mummies are kept—and bodies continue to be preserved—for a number of reasons. The field of medicine requires cadavers. The field of science, including forensic anthropology, benefits from examples of natural desiccation and the formation of adipocere. Archaeologists have learned from the experiment to replicate ancient Egyptian embalming techniques. Other reasons are harder to justify objectively. Believers in miracles seek out the miniature mummy of Miguel Ángel Gaitán in the hope that he will cure their woes or ills. Family members tend to the bodies of the dead in their homes believing that they will regain consciousness. The bodies of political leaders are preserved and enshrined as symbols of their ideals. And mummified bodies have, of course, been used merely to educate and entertain. The examples that fly in the face of all objections are those individuals, eccentricity aside, who have provided for their own mummification and sometimes their own posthumous display. Clients of Summum and Alcor pay tens of thousands of dollars to ensure that their bodies will be preserved after death. Samuel Dinsmoor's instructions for the placement of his body within the tomb he built for himself were unequivocal, if egotistical.

ETHICS

The formal display of the bodies of political leaders after death is a practice often condemned as archaic. Although it is a fact that without senses the deceased cannot be "hurt," his or her memory may be. Powerful symbols to the government and to the many that visit their mausoleums, the embalmed bodies of Vladimir Lenin and Chairman Mao were preserved against their wishes and over the objections of their closest relatives. Even when consent has been given, preservation carries with it a duty that the physical remains be kept from harm—a duty that was reportedly shirked by many of the custodians of the body of Eva Perón.

Bodies that are formally enshrined in a religious atmosphere or displayed in a museum context are less controversial than bodies exhibited by the state. The beautifully preserved corpse of little Rosalia Lombardo rests in a children's chapel in the Capuchin Monastery. The bodies of other babies—less than perfect in form, but well preserved—may still be seen in the teratology collections of medical museums. In fact, museums are looked to by those who are ready to relinquish the mummies in their private collections but are less willing to consign them to the ground. "Deaf Bill" was only buried after offers to donate him to the Alton Museum of History and Art were declined. Offers to house Hazel Farris permanently at the Bessemer Hall of History Museum are still on the table.

Whether the *informal* display of a body after death constitutes exploitation is open to debate. A blanket condemnation of the exhibition of mummies in carnivals and the occasional funeral home does not consider the circumstances of each case. The embalmer should not be faulted for preparing for delayed claim of the body and could not have been expected to pay for the burial out of his own pocket when the family never surfaced. The embalmer may be criticized for retaining the body and letting visitors view it or for actively or passively allowing the mummy to pass into the hands of showmen, but this is to judge by today's standards. And although the methods that showmen used to obtain the mummies may have been unethical, the attempt to improve their sideshows and increase their profits was a valid and ongoing objective.

Proprietary interest in mummification and mummified bodies causes concern to some. That the only bodies on display in Guanajuato, Mexico, are those whose families could not afford perpetual care for their graves may raise eyebrows in this country, but those same bodies provide a source of revenue—however small it may be—for the living locals. Summum in Salt Lake City and the Scientific Research Institute in Moscow charge exorbitant sums for their services, but their clients are well informed of the procedures and quite willing to pay the necessary fee. In some cases the financial burden is taken up by survivors, including those willing to pay for the privilege of having their loved ones freeze-dried. In other cases, the financial and physical burdens are insurmountable, so the bodies of those who have died ascending or descending Mt. Everest are left on the mountain and occasionally exposed by the wind to their wary successors. Buried as best they can be under the circumstances, the unrecovered bodies are considered to have been laid to rest in a way that is both fitting and traditional, regardless of the fact that the bodies will remain undecayed indefinitely.

Rather than allowing them to decay, embalmers and scientists put unclaimed and donated bodies to good use. Purposes such as the testing of experimental embalming chemicals are allowed by state law or mitigated by the prior voiced or implied consent of the deceased. Dr. Katsusaburo Miyamoto preserved the body of his wife with the understanding that it had been her wish that he use her body to perfect his technique. A. Z. Hammock sought the permission of the local coroner to permanently preserve the body of his friend "Speedy" Atkins. Dr. Masaichi Fukushi preserved the skins of tattooed

Japanese men and women with their full cooperation so that the otherwise transitory artwork would not be destroyed. And more commonly, body donors sign a document bequeathing their anatomical gift—a document that may be revoked by next-of-kin and that details any limitations restricting the use and disposition of the remains.

In addition to being subject to the expressed wishes of the deceased and the decisions of the next-of-kin, dead bodies are subject to the needs of local and other law enforcement agencies. In cases where victims have been hidden by serial killers, bodies have been illicitly stockpiled, and deaths have gone unreported, preservation of the remains may be maintained in a morgue cooler until the deaths can be investigated and autopsies performed. Similarly, bodies that have been buried in the traditional manner may be legally exhumed and may in fact reveal well-preserved remains. Historians have also waged a legal and social battle for the right to examine mummified remains. Scientists interested in determining whether John Wilkes Booth survived being shot after Lincoln's assassination have attempted through the courts to have Booth's grave opened to compare the remains with any (as yet unfound) "Booth mummies." Beyond the questions of legality and identity are the simple facts that keeping mummies in hiding or limiting their audience prevents against the chance that someone with an opposing viewpoint will call for their immediate burial and that the burial of all modern mummies, without regard to the individual circumstances of their preservation and conservation, will irreversibly lay to rest the work of some excellent amateur and professional embalmers.

"A curator's task is never easy: he must come to terms with prohibitions of religious dogmas, prejudices, his own inner fears, and the ceaseless inroads of organic decomposition. Nevertheless, and in spite of secular difficulties, anatomical dissection and preservation … have been assiduously performed," writes F. Gonzalez-Crussi (1993, 84–86). Cadavers continue to be prepared

for each new semester of medical students, test subjects continue to demonstrate benefits and shortcomings of new embalming chemicals, the bodies of those who put their faith in cryonics continue to be immersed in liquid nitrogen, the corpses of political leaders and religious figures continue to be enshrined, the frozen bodies of amateur adventurers continue to surface at or near the sites of their accidents, and—although they may only rarely be seen at the carnival today—more modern mummies continue to come to light in both funeral homes and private homes.

CONSERVATION

The owners of mummies, whether they are individual or institutional, have—in addition to ethical considerations—a very practical obligation toward them: to ensure their continued preservation. Museum curators, mortuary owners, and private individuals do their best to maintain the bodies in their care. Companies that offer long-term preservation may or may not offer perpetual care. The purveyors of some methods conceal the end result, freeing themselves of accusations of "malpractice" by opaquely wrapping and permanently sealing the body. Others, including the Russian Scientific Research Institute, offer periodic maintenance of the embalmed remains. Modern science and the continued improvement of preservation techniques offer the best opportunity for carefree conservation. Freeze-drying requires only protection against insect damage. Plastinated remains are virtually indestructible. And the bodies of the Visible Man and the Visible Woman require only electronic maintenance.

In many cases conservation of a body is a duty carried out with the future in mind. Those convinced of a mummy's value and interest seek to preserve it for future generations. Subjects used by developers of mortuary chemicals will affect the quality of embalming fluids used henceforth. The body donor preserved by the means of the ancient Egyptians remains bandaged in a glass-topped box for periodic testing and continued assessment of his preservation. In other cases examination of mummified remains is brief, and conservation is not a concern. The incorruptible bodies of those with the potential for sainthood are briefly exhumed, documented, and reburied. The bodies disinterred from the Missouri cemetery by floods were collected, studied, identified when possible, and reinterred. In still other cases where preservation was accidental and bodies have not been recovered, conservation continues at the whim of nature. Whereas bodies that have saponified are stable, bodies that have frozen in glaciers will remain so only until exposed.

On the other hand, careful maintenance of the frozen bodies of cryonics clients is necessary for two reasons. First, the preservation method requires a substantial outlay of money by the deceased, with whom the cryonics organization has signed a legally binding contract. Second, and more important, is the fact that this method was chosen because cryonicists both living and dead believe that it offers the potential for revival. Whereas mummies in the more traditional sense may suffer some minor damage and still be presentable, the cryonically preserved must remain wholly intact to minimize any repairs necessary upon future resuscitation. The promise to cryonics clients is therefore both legal and ideological—and their situation is necessarily very different from that of the conservators of other embalmed, mummified, and even frozen bodies.

Removing bodies from the situation in which they mummified poses several potential problems and may require a secondary means of preservation. Dry human remains are susceptible to damage from many environmental factors once removed from the conditions that resulted in their preservation. They may be contaminated by handling them without gloves. Changes in relative humidity and temperature can cause the skin layers to split and separate. High visible and ultraviolet light levels can cause collagenous materials to become faded and brittle. High humidity may lead to mold growth and may initiate renewed putrefaction. The remaining proteins in the mummy are a rich food source for rodents and for insects such as the clothes moth, carpet beetle, and biscuit beetle. Mummies are also delicate: "Whilst bodies may appear robust, the desiccation which had led to their preservation inevitably results in a loss of the natural flexibility of the epidermis and subcutaneous tissues which may become friable and detached. Bones also become increasingly brittle so that rough or careless handling can easily lead to fractures" (Rae 1996, 33). Dust is a three-fold problem: the dust or the handling required to remove it may be disfiguring, the dust layer holds moisture in close proximity to the skin leading to mold growth, and the dust also provides an additional food source for insects. The British Museum recommends a relative humidity of 50 percent, a temperature of 64° to 77° F (18° to 25° C), and light levels of below 200 lux (Rae 1996, 33). The Getty Conservation Institute has devised a hermetically sealed display and storage case for mummified remains and other artifacts prone to biodeterioration. The nitrogen-filled case guards against air pollutants and changes in humidity and oxygen levels (Maekawa and Lambert 1993).

In addition to careful upkeep, the conservators of modern mummies have other obligations to the deceased and to his or her family members. Medical schools have a duty to respectfully dispose of the remains or, upon request, to return them (often after cremation) to the family for burial. Museums, mausoleums, and other institutions are charged with keeping the remains safe from vandalism and other threats. When obligations cannot be met or mummies become too cumbersome to care for physically or because of public pressure, they are usually buried rather than cremated. Traditional disposition of the remains absolves the owners of criticism and unwanted publicity. The National Museum of the American Indian is keeping the bodies of the "little men" out of sight until their burial in a Native American cemetery can be arranged. Bodies that have outlived their usefulness are also entombed or interred. Joseph Stalin was installed in the Kremlin wall; Eva Perón was placed in an Argentine tomb. When the decision is finally made to bury a body that has remained above ground for generations, the casket is often covered with several feet of cement to avoid the possibility that the grave may be tampered with.

Although they are not high-maintenance and are rarely high-profile, many of the bodies that have been in circulation as carnival mummies or local curiosities have undergone well-publicized funerals and burials. Those that have not been interred, however, do not suffer from lack of attention. The bodies of Marie O'Day and Hazel Farris are occasionally cleansed of mildew. "Speedy" Atkins was regularly washed and redressed in his tuxedo. Whether the caretaker is a carny or a funeral director, most mummies are well cared for. They are given a periodic change of clothes, a casket in which to repose, and repairs to the body when necessary. They are thought of with affection and spoken of with nicknames but retain their living identity. Occasionally the butt of jokes or pranks, they are also the object of flattery about their remarkable state of preservation. These mummies are, however, subject to a unique occupational hazard. Because they have been exposed to close and somewhat casual public scrutiny, they often show the scars caused by skeptics. Elmer McCurdy is missing some digits, George Stein has a large nick on the bridge of his nose, and "Deaf Bill" is missing part of his ear.

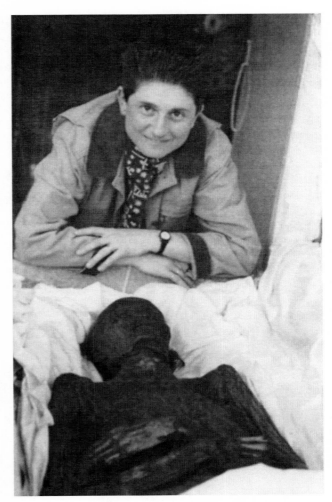

The author with the mummified remains of Hazel Farris.

The ethnic heritage of these mummies differs: African American, Italian, German, Russian, Mexican, Portuguese, and Argentine. The causes of their deaths vary: suicide, homicide, accident, natural. For some, family members are their most outspoken advocates. The family of cave explorer Floyd Collins had to bring suit against the federal government to recover his body for burial. The father of Rafael Echavarren, one of the rugby players killed in the 1971 aircraft accident in the Andes, defied the law to recover his son's frozen body. Among those who are not claimed by next-of-kin, the common bond is the very lack of a familial bond. With no relatives to look after them after death, the mummies become like old friends to their custodians. In many cases these custodians are the sons and daughters, grandsons and granddaughters of the men who so suc-cessfully embalmed them. It is the prerogative of these custodians to determine the best interest of these men and women who did not ask to be mummified but are unable to voice their objection.

Bibliography

Albert, J. S. No date. "The Enigma of People Who Petrify Human Bodies." *Vision*.

Alexander, Caroline. 1994. "Little Men: A Mystery of No Small Significance." *Outside* (April): 98–101, 174–79.

Ambach, E. 1991. "Fatal Accidents on Glaciers: Forensic, Criminological, and Glaciological Conclusions." *Journal of Forensic Sciences*, September: 1469–73.

____. 1993. "Paradoxical Undressing in Fatal Hypothermia (Homo tirolensis). *The Lancet* 341 (May 15): 1285.

Ambach, W., E. Ambach, and W. Tributsch. 1997. "Unusual Discoveries of Corpses Immersed in Glacier Ice After Fatal Accidents: Glaciological Aspects." *Journal of Glaciology* 37, no. 125: 185–86.

Ambach, W., E. Ambach, W. Tributsch, R. Henn, and H. Unterdorfer. 1992. "Corpses Released from Glacier Ice: Glaciological and Forensic Aspects." *Journal of Wilderness Medicine* 3: 372–76.

Ariès, Philippe. 1981. *The Hour of Our Death*. Translated by Helen Weaver. New York: Vintage.

Baden, Michael M., with Judith Adler Hennessee. 1989. *Unnatural Death: Confessions of a Medical Examiner*. New York: Ivy Books.

Banks, Michael. 1975. *Greenland*. Totowa, N.J.: Rowman and Littlefield.

Barnes, John. 1978. *Evita, First Lady: A Biography of Eva Perón*. New York: Grove Press.

Barry, Dave. 1988. "I Remember Mummy." *Miami Herald/Tropic Magazine*, June 26.

Barth, Jack, Doug Kirby, Ken Smith, and Mike Wilkins. 1986. *Roadside America*. New York: Simon & Schuster.

Basgall, Richard J. 1989. *The Career of Elmer J. McCurdy, Deceased: An Historical Mystery*. Dodge City, Kans.: Trail's End.

Bates, Finis L. 1907. *The Escape and Suicide of John Wilkes Booth*. Memphis, Tenn.: Finis L. Bates.

Bell, Sir Charles. 1987. *Portrait of a Dalai Lama: The Life and Times of the Great Thirteenth*. London: Wisdom Publications.

Ben-Abraham, Avi. 1989. "Putting Death on Ice." *Saturday Evening Post* (March): 60–62.

Bereuter, T. L., et al. 1996. "Postmortem Alterations of Human Lipids, Part I. In Spindler et al., eds. *Human Mummies*. New York: Springer-Verlag/Wien.

Bergheim, Laura A. 1988. *Weird Wonderful America: The Nation's Most Offbeat and Off-the-Beaten-Path Tourist Attractions*. New York: Collier Books.

Berryman, Hugh E., et al. 1997. "Recognition of Cemetery Remains in the Forensic Setting." In Haglund and Sorg. *Forensic Taphonomy*. Boca Raton, Fla.: CRC Press.

Bianchi, James L. 1986. *Cryonic Suspension Legal Forms Manual*. Oakland, Calif.: Trans Time.

Blair, Clay, Jr. 1973. *Survive!* New York: Berkley Medallion Books.

Blair, I. W. 1994. "Embalming of Chairman Mao." *The Embalmer* 37, no. 4 (autumn): 16.

The Body in the Barn: The Controversy Over the Death of John Wilkes Booth. 1993. Clinton, Md.: Surratt Society.

Boffey, Melissa Johnson. 1978. "Is This the Man Who Killed Lincoln?" *American Cemetery* (July): 24–26.

Bortoli, Georges. 1975. *The Death of Stalin*. New York: Praeger.

Bowen-Jones, Carys. 1993. "How to Become a Mummy." *Marie Claire*, U.K. Edition (June): 18–19, 50.

Bradbury, Ray. 1978. *The Mummies of Guanajuato*. Photographs by Archie Lieberman. New York: Harry N. Abrams.

Brier, Bob. 1994. *Egyptian Mummies: Unraveling the Secrets of an Ancient Art*. New York: William Morrow & Co.

Brier, Bob, and Ronald S. Wade. 1995. *The Use of Natron in Human Mummification: A Modern Experiment*. Paper presented at the

Second International Conference on Mummies in Cartagena, Colombia.

Browne, Douglas G., and E. V. Tullett. 1952. *The Scalpel of Scotland Yard: The Life of Sir Bernard Spilsbury*. New York: E. P. Dutton.

Browne, Douglas G., and Tom Tullett. 1988. *Bernard Spilsbury: His Life and Cases*. New York: Dorset Press.

Bryan, George S. 1940. *The Great American Myth*. New York: Carrick & Evans.

Bylinsky, Gene. 1993. "A Digital Adam." *Fortune*. vol. 128, no. 11 (Nov. 1): 123.

Calloway, Earl. 1974. "Black Hobo Immortalized in Don McLean's Song." *Chicago Defender*, December 3: 18.

Carlson, Lisa. 1987. *Caring for Your Own Dead*. Hinesburg, Vt.: Upper Access Publishers.

Carlton, Bronwyn. 1995. *The Big Book of Death*. New York: Paradox Press.

Caruso, Dorothy Park Benjamin. 1945. *Enrico Caruso: His Life and Death*. New York: Simon & Schuster.

Cherry-Garrard, Apsley. 1989. *The Worst Journey in the World*. New York: Carroll & Graf.

Clark, Michael A. et al. 1997. "Postmortem Changes in Soft Tissues." In Haglund and Sorg. *Forensic Taphonomy*. Boca Raton, Fla.: CRC Press.

Cockburn, Aidan, and Eve Cockburn, editors. 1980. *Mummies, Disease, and Ancient Culture*. Cambridge, England: Cambridge University Press.

Cornwell, John. 1989. *A Thief in the Night: The Mysterious Death of Pope John Paul I*. New York: Simon & Schuster.

Cronin, Xavier A. 1994. "Waxing Lenin." *The Embalmer* 37, no. 4 (autumn): 20.

Cruz, Joan Carroll. 1977. *The Incorruptibles: A Study of the Incorruption of the Bodies of Various Catholic Saints and Beati*. Rockford, Ill.: Tan Books and Publishers.

_____. 1984. *Relics*. Huntington, Ind.: Our Sunday Visitor.

Dalai Lama. 1990. *Freedom in Exile: The Autobiography of the Dalai Lama*. New York: HarperCollins.

Daniels, V. 1996. "Selection of a Conservation Process for Lindow Man." In Spindler et al., eds. *Human Mummies*. New York: Springer-Verlag/Wien.

De'ath, Richard. 1993. *Tombstone Humour*. London: Chancellor Press.

de Jonge, Alex. 1986. *Stalin and the Shaping of the Soviet Union*. New York: William Morrow.

DeSpelder, Lynne Ann, and Albert Lee Strickland. 1983. *The Last Dance: Encountering Death and Dying*. Palo Alto, Calif.: Mayfield Publishing Co.

Dowling, Claudia Glenn. 1996. "Death on the Mountain." *Life*. August: 32–46.

Drimmer, Frederick. 1981. *Body Snatchers, Stiffs and Other Ghoulish Delights*. New York: Citadel Press.

Fierro, Marcella Farinelli. 1993. "Identification of Human Remains." In Spitz, ed. *Spitz and Fisher's Medicolegal Investigation of Death*. Springfield, Ill.: Charles C. Thomas.

Fincher, Jack. 1990. "Dreams of Riches Led Floyd Collins to a Nightmarish End." *Smithsonian* 21, no. 2 (May 1): 137–50.

Fischer, Christian. 1980. "Bog Bodies of Denmark." In Cockburn and Cockburn, eds. *Mummies, Disease, and Ancient Culture*. Cambridge: Cambridge University Press.

Fischer, Louis. 1964. *The Life of Lenin*. New York: Harper & Row.

Fraser, Nicholas and Marysa Navarro. 1980. *Eva Perón*. New York: W. W. Norton.

Fulcheri, E. 1996. "Mummies of Saints." In Spindler et al., eds. *Human Mummies*. New York: Springer-Verlag/Wien.

Galamba de Oliveira, Joseph. 1982. *Jacinta: The Flower of Fatima*. Trans. Humberto S. Medeiros and William F. Hill. Washington, N.J.: AMI Press.

Galloway, Alison. 1997. "The Process of Decomposition." In Haglund and Sorg. *Forensic Taphonomy*. Boca Raton, Fla.: CRC Press.

Galloway, Alison, et al. 1989. "Decay Rates of Human Remains in an Arid Environment." *Journal of Forensic Sciences* 34, no. 3 (May): 607–16.

Garland, A. Neil, and Robert C. Janaway. 1989. "The Taphonomy of Inhumation Burials." In Roberts, Lee, and Bintliff, eds. *Burial Archaeology*. Oxford: B.A.R.

Gaute, J. H. H., and Robin Odell. 1989. *The New Murderers' Who's Who*. New York: Dorset Press.

Gilligan, T. Scott, and Thomas F. H. Stueve. 1995. *Mortuary Law (Ninth Revised Edition)*. Cincinnati: The Cincinnati Foundation for Mortuary Education.

Gonzalez-Crussi, F. 1993. *The Day of the Dead and Other Mortal Reflections*. New York: Harcourt Brace.

_____. 1995. *Suspended Animation: Six Essays on the Preservation of Bodily Parts*. San Diego: Harcourt Brace.

Goodman, Michael Harris. 1986. *The Last Dalai Lama: A Biography*. Boston: Shambhala.

Gordon, Paul C. 1981. *The Exploration of Antarctica*. Paramus, N.J.: ITT Antarctic Services.

Haglund, William D., and Marcella H. Sorg. 1997. *Forensic Taphonomy: The Postmortem Fate of Human Remains*. Boca Raton, Fla.: CRC Press.

Hardy, D. E. 1988. "Remains to Be Seen." *Tattoo Time,* no. 4. Honolulu: Hardy Marks Publications, 74–78.

Harner, Michael J. 1984. *The Jívaro: People of the Sacred Waterfalls*, Berkeley: University of California Press.

Harrington, Alan. 1969. *The Immortalist*. New York: Discus Books.

Hawley, Dean A. et al. 1991. Specimens for Teaching Forensic Pathology, Odontology, and Anthropology. *The American Journal of Forensic Medicine and Pathology*. vol. 12, no. 2: 164–69.

Henry, Thomas R. 1950. *The White Continent: The Story of Antarctica*. New York: William Sloane Associates.

Hunter, Jack. 1995. *Inside Teradome: An Illustrated History of the Freak Film*. London: Creation Books.

Huxley, Elspeth. 1977. *Scott of the Antarctic*. Lincoln, Neb.: University of Nebraska Press.

Huyen, N. Khac. 1971. *Vision Accomplished? The Enigma of Ho Chi Minh*. New York: Collier.

Iserson, Kenneth V. 1994. *Death to Dust: What Happens to Dead Bodies?* Tucson, Ariz.: Galen Press.

Jackson, Robert. 1975. *Francis Camps: Famous Case Histories of the Most Celebrated Pathologist of Our Time*. London: Granada Publishing Ltd.

Jackson, Stanley. 1972. *Caruso*. New York: Stein & Day.

Johnson, Edward C., and Melissa Johnson. 1986. "Dr. Pedro Ara." Parts 1 and 2. *American Funeral Director* (April): 23–24, 60–61; (May): 22–24, 66–67.

Johnson, Edward C., and Melissa Johnson. 1987. "The Man Who Embalmed Evita." *The Embalmer* 30, no. 1 (Jan./Feb.): 14–26.

Johnson, Edward C., Gail R. Johnson, and Melissa Johnson Williams. 1993. "The Salafia Method: Alfredo Salafia's Embalming Produced Long-Term Success, But How Did He Do It?" *The American Funeral Director* (May): 24–25, 64–68.

_____. 1996. "The History of Modern Restorative Art." In Mayer. *Embalming*. Stamford, Conn.: Appleton & Lange.

Johnson, Robert. 1988. "After the Good Life, What Better Death Than as a Mummy?" *Wall Street Journal*, October 28: 1+.

Journal of the International Society for Plastination. 1995. Vol. 9, No. 1.

Joyce, Christopher and Eric Stover. 1991. *Witnesses from the Grave: The Stories Bones Tell*. Boston: Little Brown.

Kimbrell, Andrew. 1993. *The Human Body Shop: The Engineering and Marketing of Life*. New York: HarperCollins.

Klinger, Rafael. 1991. "Going in Style: Yuppiedom Moves to the Hereafter with New Mummy Process." *XS* (August 7–13): 12–14.

Kohut, John J., and Roland Sweet. 1993. *News from the Fringe: True Stories of Weird People and Weirder Times*. New York: Plume.

Krakauer, Jon. 1996a. *Into the Wild*. New York: Villard.

_____. 1996b. Into Thin Air. *Outside* (Sept.): 48–66+.

Kurtzman, Joel, and Phillip Gordon. 1976. *No More Dying: The Conquest of Aging and the Extension of Human Life*. Los Angeles: J. P. Tarcher.

"Lenin's Embalming Comes Under the Media Spotlight." 1994. *The Embalmer* 37, no. 1 (winter): 24.

"Lenin's Face-Saver." 1994. *The Embalmer* 37, no. 2 (spring): 31–32.

Lewis, Arthur H. 1970. *Carnival*. New York: Trident Press.

Li Zhisui. 1994. *The Private Life of Chairman Mao*. Trans. Tai Hung-Chao, with editorial assistance of Anne F. Thurston. New York: Random House.

London, Marilyn R. et al. 1997. "Burials at Sea." In Haglund and Sorg. *Forensic Taphonomy*. Boca Raton, Fla.: CRC Press.

Lopez, Enrique Hank. 1973. *They Lived on Human Flesh*. New York: Pocket Books.

MacDougall, Curtis D. [1940] 1958. (reprint) *Hoaxes*. New York: Dover Publications.

Maekawa, Shin, and Frank Lambert. 1993. *The Getty Conservation Institute's Inert Atmosphere Display and Storage Case for the Pharaonic Mummies of the Egyptian Museum, Cairo: Final Report*. Malibu, Calif.: The Getty Conservation Institute.

Main, Mary. 1980. *Evita: The Woman with the Whip*. New York: Dodd, Mead & Co.

Maples, William R., and Michael Browning. 1994. *Dead Men Do Tell Tales: The Strange and Fascinating Cases of a Forensic Anthropologist*. New York: Doubleday.

Martínez, Tomás Eloy. 1996. *Santa Evita*. New York: Alfred A. Knopf.

Masters, Brian. 1984. *Killing for Company: The Case of Dennis Nilsen*. New York: Stein & Day.

Mayer, Robert G. 1996. *Embalming: History, Theory, and Practice* (2d edition). Stamford, Conn.: Appleton & Lange.

McHargue, Georgess. 1972. *Mummies*. Philadelphia: J. B. Lippincott.

Meacham, Deborah, editor. 1992. *On the Loose in Mexico 1993*. New York: Fodor's Travel Publications.

Mellen, Paul F. M., Mark A. Lowry, and Marc S. Micozzi. 1993. "Experimental Observations on Adipocere Formation." *Journal of Forensic Sciences* 38, no. 1 (January): 91–93.

Micozzi, Marc S. "Frozen Environments and Soft Tissue Preservation." In Haglund and Sorg. *Forensic Taphonomy*. Boca Raton, Fla.: CRC Press.

Micozzi, Marc S., and Paul S. Sledzik. 1992. "Postmortem Preservation of Human Remains: Natural and Technical Processes." *Proceedings of the First World Congress on the Mummy Study*, vol. 2. Tenerife, Canary Islands: Museo Archeologicao y Etnografico de Tenerife, 759–64.

Miller, Elaine Hobson. 1995. *Myths, Mysteries and Legends of Alabama*. Birmingham: Seacoast Publishing.

Moore, Steve. 1994. *The* Fortean Times *Book of Strange Deaths*. London: John Brown Publishing.

Morgan, Ernest. 1984. *Dealing Creatively with Death: A Manual of Death Education and Simple Burial*. Burnsville, N.C.: Celo Press.

Mountfield, David. 1974. *A History of Polar Exploration*. New York: Dial Press.

Mowat, Farley. 1976. *The Polar Passion: The Quest for the North Pole*. Toronto: McClelland and Stewart.

Murray, Robert K., and Roger W. Brucker. 1979. *Trapped!* New York: G. P. Putnam's Sons.

Newton, Michael. 1990. *Hunting Humans: An Encyclopedia of Modern Serial Killers*. Port Townsend, Wash.: Loompanics Unlimited.

Newton, Michael. 1992. *Serial Slaughter: What's Behind America's Murder Epidemic?* Port Townsend, Wash.: Loompanics Unlimited.

Noble, John, Dan Spitzer, and Scott Wayne. 1989. *Mexico: A Travel Survival Kit*. Victoria, Australia: Lonely Planet Publications.

Noguchi, Thomas T. with Joseph de Mona. 1985. *Coroner at Large*. New York: Pocket Books.

O'Brien, Tyler G. 1994. *Human Soft-Tissue Decomposition in an Aquatic Environment and Its Transformation into Adipocere*. Masters' Thesis, University of Tennessee, Knoxville.

Odell, Catherine M. 1995. *Father Solanus: The Story of Solanus Casey, O.F.M. Cap., Updated*. Huntington, Ind.: Our Sunday Visitor.

Ollove, Michael. 1994a. "Maryland Man Being Mummified." *Baltimore Sun*, June 17.

_____. 1994b. "UM Scientists Wind Up a Job: Our Mummy Is a Mummy." *Baltimore Sun*, June 26.

Ortiz, Alicia Dujovne. 1996. *Eva Perón*. Trans. Shawn Fields. New York: St. Martin's.

Palmer, Greg. 1993. *Death: The Trip of a Lifetime*. New York: HarperCollins.

Payne, Robert. 1964. *The Life and Death of Lenin*. New York: Simon & Schuster.

Perper, Joshua A. 1993. "Time of Death and Changes After Death." In Spitz, ed. *Spitz and Fisher's Medicolegal Investigation of Death*. Springfield, Ill.: Charles C. Thomas.

Phillips, Archie, and Bubba Phillips. 1981. *Freeze Dry Taxidermy*. Fairfield, Ala.: Archie Phillips.

Rae, A. 1996. "Dry Human and Animal Remains." In Spindler et al., eds. *Human Mummies*. New York: Springer-Verlag/Wien.

Read, Piers Paul. 1975. *Alive: The Story of the Andes Survivors*. London: Pan Books.

Rengers, Christopher. 1986. *The Youngest Prophet: The Life of Jacinta Marto, Fatima Visionary*. New York: Alba House.

Richardson, Rosamond. 1994. *Stalin's Shadow: Inside the Family of One of the World's Greatest Tyrants*. New York: St. Martin's Press.

Rivenburg, Roy. 1993. "The Ancient Art of Mummification is Alive in Utah." *Gannett Suburban Newspapers*, January 31.

Roberts, Charlotte A., Frances Lee, and John Bintliff, editors. 1989. *Burial Archaeology: Current Research, Methods, and Developments*. Oxford, England: B.A.R.

Rodriguez, III, William C. 1997. "Decomposition of Buried and Submerged Bodies." In Haglund and Sorg. *Forensic Taphonomy*. Boca Raton, Fla.: CRC Press.

Sakurai, Kiyohiko, and Tamotsu Ogaga. 1980. "Japanese Mummies." In Cockburn and Cockburn, eds. *Mummies, Disease, and Ancient Culture*. Cambridge: Cambridge University Press.

Sava, George. 1976. *Mourning Becomes Argentina*. Bognor Regis: New Horizon.

Savours, Ann, editor. 1975. *Scott's Last Voyage Through the Antarctic Camera of Herbert Ponting*. New York: Praeger Publishers.

Schechter, Harold. 1989. *Deviant: The Shocking True Story of the Original "Psycho"*. New York: Pocket Books.

Schell, Orville. 1992. "Once Again, Long Live Chairman Mao." *Atlantic* 270 (Dec.): 32–36.

Schemann, Serge. 1992. "Preserving Lenin, the High-Tech Icon." *New York Times*, December 16.

Shearer, Lloyd. 1976. "Traveling in China with James Schlesinger." *Parade: The Sunday Newspaper Magazine*, 24 October.

Simpson, Keith. 1978. *Forty Years of Murder: An Autobiography*. New York: Charles Scribner's Sons.

Sledzik, Paul S. In press. "Forensic Taphonomy: Postmortem Decomposition and Decay." *Forensic Osteology II*. Ed. by Kathy Rechs. Springfield, Ill.: Charles C. Thomas.

Sledzik, Paul S., and D. H. Hunt. 1977. Disaster and Relief Efforts at the Hardin Cemetery. *In Remembrance: Archaeology and Death*. Ed. D. Poirier and N. Bellantoni. Westport, Conn.: Greenwood Press.

Sledzik, Paul S., and Marc S. Micozzi. 1997. Autopsied, Embalmed, and Preserved Human Remains." In Haglund and Sorg. *Forensic Taphonomy*. Boca Raton, Fla.: CRC Press.

Smith, Sir Sydney. 1959. *Mostly Murder*. New York: David McKay.

Snow, Clyde. 1977. The Life and Afterlife of Elmer J. McCurdy: A Melodrama in Two Acts. Special Supplement (September). Detroit: Paleopathology Association.

Soloviov, Michael. 1996. "Embalming in Russia." *The Embalmer* (winter): 15.

Sorg, Marcella H. 1997. "Forensic Taphonomy in Marine Contexts." In Haglund and Sorg. *Forensic Taphonomy*. Boca Raton, Fla.: CRC Press.

Spindler, Konrad, Harald Wilfing, Elisabeth Rastbichler-Zissernig, Dieter zur Nedden, Hans Nothdurfter, editors. 1996. *Human Mummies: A Global Survey of Their Status and the Techniques of Conservation*. New York: Springer-Verlag/Wien.

Spindler, Konrad. 1994. *The Man in the Ice*. New York: Random House.

Spitz, Werner U. 1993. "Drowning." In Spitz, ed. *Spitz and Fisher's Medicolegal Investigation of Death*. Springfield, Ill.: Charles C. Thomas.

Spitz, Werner U., editor. 1993. *Spitz & Fisher's Medicolegal Investigation of Death: Guidelines for the Application of Pathology to Crime Investigation* (3d edition). Springfield, Ill.: Charles C. Thomas.

Sternthal, Susan. 1989. "Will Soviets Finally Bury What Is Left of V.I. Lenin?" *Washington Times*, 28 November.

Stewart, T. D. 1979. *Essentials of Forensic Anthropology*. Springfield, Ill.: C. C. Thomas.

Stone, Judith. 1990. "Of Human Bandage." *Discover* 11 (January): 8–10.

Strub, Clarence G., and L. G. Frederick. 1989. *The Principles and Practice of Embalming* (5th edition). Dallas: Professional Training Schools and Robertine Frederick.

Summum Web site: http://www.summum.org/mummification

Tanner, Adam. 1994. "Lucky Stiff." *National Review* 46 (Nov. 7): 32–34.

Taylor, James. *Shocked and Amazed! On and Off the Midway*.Baltimore, Md.: Dolphin-Moon Press and Atomic Books.

Terrill, Ross. 1980. *Mao: A Biography*. New York: Harper & Row.

Thurston, S. J., Herbert. 1952. *The Physical Phenomena of Mysticism*. Chicago: Henry Regnery.

Tinsley, Russell. 1990. *Taxidermy Guide: The Complete Illustrated Guide to Home Taxidermy* (3rd edition). Hackensack, N.J.: Stoeger Publishing Co.

Tumarkin, Nina. 1983. *Lenin Lives! The Lenin Cult in Soviet Russia*. Cambridge, Mass.: Harvard University Press.

Ubelaker, Douglas, and Henry Scammell. 1992. *Bones: A Forensic Detective's Casebook*. New York: Edward Burlingame Books.

University of Carlifornia, Irvine, College of Medicine Web site: http://www. com.uci.edu/~anatomy/willed_body/wbpe1.htm

Volkogonov, Dmitri. 1994. *Lenin: Life and Legacy*. Translated and edited by Harold Shukman. New York: HarperCollins.

Vollers, Maryanne. 1995. *Ghosts of Mississippi: The Murder of Medgar Evers, The Trials of Byron De La Beckwith, and the Haunting of the New South*. Boston: Little, Brown.

von Hagens, Gunther, Klaus Tiedemann, and Wilhelm Kriz. 1987. *Anatomy and Embryology*. vol. 175: 411–21.

Vraney, Mike. 1994. "Dan Sonney: Last of the 40 Thieves." Ed. Lisa Petrucci. *Cult Movies*, no. 12: 24–27+.

Vreeland, James M., Jr., and Aidan Cockburn. 1980. "Mummies of Peru." In Cockburn and Cockburn, eds. *Mummies, Disease, and Ancient Culture*." Cambridge: Cambridge University Press.

Waldrop, M. Mitchel. 1995. "The Visible Man Steps Out." *Science* 269 (September 8): 1358.

Wallechinsky, David, Irving Wallace, and Amy Wallace. 1977. *The People's Almanack Presents The Book of Lists*. New York: William Morrow.

Wang, B. H. 1996. "Excavation and Preliminary Studies of the Ancient Mummies of Xinjiang in China." In Spindler et al., eds. *Human Mummies*. New York: Springer-Verlag/Wien.

Weil, Tom. 1992. *The Cemetery Book: Graveyards, Catacombs and Other Travel Haunts Around the World*. New York: Hippocrene Books.

Weiss, Rick. 1992. "Looking Good—Forever." *Health* 6 (Nov./Dec.): 30+.

Wheeler, David L. 1996. "Creating a Body of Knowledge: From the Cadaver of an Executed Murderer, Scientists Produce Digital Anatomical Images." *Chronicle of Higher Education* 42, no. 21 (February 2): A6–A7+.

Wilkins, Robert. 1990. *The Bedside Book of Death: Macabre Tales of Our Final Passage.* New York: Citadel Press.

Wilson, Francis. 1929. *John Wilkes Booth: Fact and Fiction of Lincoln's Assassination.* Boston: Houghton Mifflin.

Yallop, David A. 1984. *In God's Name: An Investigation into the Murder of Pope John Paul I.* New York: Bantam.

Zimmerman, M. R. 1996. "Mummies of the Arctic Regions." In Spindler et al., eds. *Human Mummies.* New York: Springer-Verlag/Wien.

Zugibe, Frederick T., and James T. Costello. 1993. The Iceman Murder: One of a Series of Contract Murders. *Journal of Forensic Sciences* 38, no. 6 (November): 1404–8.

Index

Abrikosov, A. I. 28
Ackerman, Michael 110
Adams, Eleanor 152
Adams, Martin 177
Adipocere formation 21–26, 168–70, 235–36, 243, 244; rate of 23–24
Agostini, Linda 241–42
Alcor Life Extension Foundation 142–46
Alexander, Caroline 119, 122
Allegranza, Antonio 122–24
Almeida, Antonio 199
Ambach, Edda 167–69
American Cryonics Society 143
Amundsen, Roald 181–83
Anderson, Bud 172
Anderson, James 172, 176
Ara, Pedro 33, 44, 45–47, 48, 49
Arambúru, Pedro Eugenio 47, 48–49
Ashe, Leona 194
Atkins, Charles Henry 94–96
Atkinson, E. L. 184–85
"Aunt Mary" 106–7
Autopsy 9, 11, 21, 36, 37, 61, 65–67, 78, 82, 85, 126, 170, 205, 214, 215, 222, 236, 242, 244, 249; tissue testing 19, 36, 52, 55, 68–69, 75, 85–87, 118–19, 139, 146, 170, 196, 235

Babcox, Robert 129
Baden, Michael 214, 242
Baglivo, James 145
Bailey, George "Bill" 102
Barbour County Historical Museum 124
Barnes, Joseph K. 78, 82
Barnum, P. T. 124
Bartlett, Robert 187–88
Bates, Finis L. 78–82
Bedford, James H. 142, 143
Beichert, Bernie 138, 139
Beidleman, Neal 177–79
Benjamin, Dorothy Park 50
Benjamin Lopez Funeral Home 234
Bessemer Hall of History 72, 75
Biaggi, Mario 91
Black, L. O. "Hoot" 92–93

"Black Museum" 224–25
Blackwell Funerals 208–10
Boiteng, K. A. 165
Bonch-Bruevich, V. D. 28
Bonnette, Angela 122–24
Booth, John Wilkes 60, 77–87, 92, 249; autopsy of 78; death of 77; family of 78, 80
Borchgrevink, Carstens 180
Boswell, Capt. Harvey Lee 59, 77, 89, 93–94
Boukreev, Anatoli 177–79
Bowers, Henry R. 183–84
Bradbury, Ray 218–20
Brahmachari, Thakur Balak 203–4
Brenner, Edward 190
Brier, Bob 7, 115–19
Brooks, Luther 72–75
Brooks, O. C. 72–74
Byrer, Frank 124
Bukkai Shonin 203
Buzzonetti, Renato 205

Cadavers 4, 103–7, 109, 112, 116; storage of 105–6; use of 24–26, 32, 104, 112–14, 135, 140, 248
Campbell, Charlie 92
Camps, Francis 235–36, 238, 245
Campuzano, Lydia 137
Canessa, Roberto 227, 229–30
Capsoni, Carlo 170
Carmichael, Henry St. George Tucker 191
Carney, Mary Lou 194
Caruso, Enrico 43, 49–50
Casey, O.F.M. Cap., Father Solanus 199–202
Casper's Law 16
Celesia, Michaelangelo 50–51
Chamberlain, Arlene 143
Chamberlain, Fred R., III 145
Chamberlain, Linda 145
Champion Company 6
Cherry-Garrard, Apsley 182, 185
Chew, John A. 36, 134–35
Chicago Press Club 82
Choi, Joseph 65–67
Christ, Chris 128–30
Christiansen, Jack 172–73

Christie, John Reginald Halliday 223, 234–36
Clair, Richard 143
Collins, Floyd 189–94; family of 1, 190, 192–94, 251
Collins Funeral Home 213
Colony, William 172–73
Crispi, Francesco 50
Cryonic preservation 8–9, 138, 140–46, 250; neuropreservation 8, 9, 143, 145
Cryonics Institute 141, 143, 144, 145
Cryonics Society of California 142–43, 144
Cryonics Society of New York 143
Cryopreservation 146–47

Dalai Lama, Thirteenth 205–7
Davis, Jimmy 75–77, 84
"Deaf Bill" see Lee, William
DeBlasio, Ann 143
Debov, Sergei S. 35
Dehydration 3, 13–14, 20, 72, 92, 107, 115–18, 162–63, 169, 195, 218, 241
Denke, Karl 223
de Nobili, Lena 164–65
DeSanto, Jerome 173
Desiccation 3, 6, 13, 15, 17–20, 89, 118, 250; rates of 19
Dewhurst, Neil 153–54
Dickey, The Rev. C. K. 191
Dimitrov, Georgi 139
Dinsmoor, Samuel 27, 54, 55–58, 247
Disinterment see Exhumation
Dissection 52, 103–6, 247
Dodge Company 13, 113–14, 217
Dodge Correctional Institute 151
Doe, Samuel 218
dos Santos, Lucia de Jesus 198–99
Doyle, Bee 191, 192
Dufour, Lou 128
Dunphy, John J. 99–102
d'Urre of Aubais, Maurice 58
Duryea, Maynard 114

East Coast College 107, 109
Echavarren, Rafael 229, 231–32
Echavarren, Ricardo 231–32, 251
Ellis, Mr. 245–46
Embalming: anatomical 6, 44, 50, 104–6, 109; ancient Egyptian 1, 3, 4, 94, 115; by immersion 6, 35, 45, 105, 118, 135, 158, 165, 241; by injection 5, 6, 14, 39, 44–45, 51–52, 72, 89, 102, 122, 163–64, 205, 209; by osmosis 116, 204; by salting 57, 116–17, 206; cavity treatment 5, 14, 57, 117, 204, 209; concealment of 196; "eonosmia" 54; evisceration 5; experimental 113–19, 122–24, 234; legal requirement of 10; licensing of 10–11; machines 6; powder 15, 44; Russian-style 139–40; Salafia Permanent Method 51–52; traditional 5, 109–10, 135, 158

Embalming fluid: Argon 80; arsenic-based 6, 61, 72, 98; Bisga 12; Champion H-A-R Cavity Fluid 161; Demosol 209; formaldehyde 6, 10, 40, 72, 89, 129, 151; formalin 6, 80, 105, 108, 126, 241; Hydrolan 12–13; Hydrolite 13; ingredients of 13, 35, 94, 96, 105, 124, 135–36; Nasco Fluid Medium 114; research and development of 12, 113–15; Ruffer's Solution 19, 126; Sandow Cavity Fluid 114; Tufts Human Anatomical Solution 105
Epstein, Anatol 143
Esper, Dwain 63
Ettinger, Robert 140–42
Evans, Beryl 234–35
Evans, Edgar 183–84
Evers, Medgar 213–14
"Evita" see Perón, Eva
Exhumation 7, 11, 15–16, 48, 50, 78, 82, 84–86, 151–52, 199, 201–2, 203, 211, 213, 214, 217–21, 232, 235, 249; in Guanajuato, Mexico 218–20; in Naples, Italy 218; in San Bernardo, Colombia 220–21

Farmica, Cancetto 87, 88–92
Farris, Hazel 70–75
Federal Trade Commission 12
Fernandez, Daniel 227–28, 232
Fischbeck, Frank 177–78
Fischer, Scott 177, 180
Flinch, John 51
Flynt, Althea 145
Fox, Charlotte 177, 179
Frauson, Robert 172–73
"Freak babies" see Teratology specimens
Freddie of Uganda, King 218
Freeze-drying 7, 20, 157–61
Freezing 163–66, 203–4, 222, 232–33, 238, 241; accidental 7, 167–89, 240; in Ghana 165–66; and time of death 222, 233; see also Cryonic preservation
Friedman, Dave 59, 64, 65, 67
Frye, Stephen J. 171–72
Fuerst, Ruth Margarete Christine 234
Fuhrmann, Peter 173, 175
Fukushi, Katsunari 152–53
Fukushi, Masaichi 152–53
"Funeral Rule" 12

Gaboury, Adele A. 240
Gaitán, Miguel Angel 211–12
Gammelgaard, Lene 177
Garden of Eden 55–56, 58
Garvin, Julie 137
Gein, Edward 7, 150–52
Genteman, Paul 143
George, David E. see Booth, John Wilkes
Georgetown University 105
Georgia Marble Company 136

Geralds, J. T. 192
Getty, J. Paul 164
Getty Conservation Institute 250
Glacier bodies *see* Freezing, accidental
Glennie, Jim 143
Gobbo, Evelina 122–24
"Gold Tooth Jimmy" *see* Davis, Jimmy
Gooding's Million Dollar Midway 128
Gottwald, Clement 139
Graham, Harrison 223
"Graham, Sylvia" 144
"Grave wax" *see* Adipocere
Great Patterson Carnival Shows 63
Greco, Janet 137–38
Griffith, John T., Jr. 154
Groom, Mike 177–79
Guanajuato mummies 7
Gyatso, Thupten *see* Dalai Lama, Thirteenth

Hall, Rob 177–80
Hall, Ward 128–30
Hammock, A. Z. 94–96
Hamrick, Graham 124
Hansell, Leslie 27, 58
Hansen, Doug 177–78
Hardin Cemetery 221–22
Harmur Sideshows 130
Harris, Andy 177–78
Hart, Ruben 172
Hatcher & Saddler Funeral Home 194
Hawkes, Ken 79, 80, 85–87
Hazard, Tom 145
Hazlitt, William H. 190
Helpern, Milton 224–25
Henley, O.B.E, Desmond 36, 44, 217
Henry, Kay 137
Hesse, O.F.M. Cap., Father Gerard 201
Heye Foundation 120, 122
Higgins, John and William 243–45
High, Tommy G. 194
Highbaugh, Wade 192
Hilding, Christer 160
Hillary, Sir Edmund 177, 180
Hizone Company 6, 114
Ho Chi Minh 27, 41, 42
Hogan, Mary 151
Honka, Fritz 223
Howard, Katherine 242
Howell, Lewis J. 240
Hower, Rolland 160
Hoyos, Elena 233–34
Hudson, Walt 130
Huffman, Bill 157–60
Hultz, Lambert 159–60
Hurd-Hendricks Funeral Home 216
Hutchison, Stuart 177–79
Hydrol Chemical Company 12
Hygeco 161

"Iceman" 169
Incorruptibles 7–8, 250; religious 195–203; secular 210–16
Indiana University 107
"Italian Bride" *see* Petta, Julia Buccola

Jacinta of Fátima 196–99
James, Jesse 60
Jangbu, Lobsang 177–78
Jay Gould's Million Dollar Spectacle 82, 84
Jenkins, David 52
Jernigan, Joseph Paul 110
Jeschke, Kurt 171
Jewett Refrigerator Company 161
Jívaro mummies 7, 119–22; preparation of 121
Joakim III 203, 207–8
John Paul I, Pope 205
John Paul II, Pope 199, 202
Johnson, Joseph L. 61–63
Johnson, Walter E. 154

Kanzler, Jerry 172, 176
Kanzler, Jim 173
Karwowski, Joseph 147–49
Kasischke, Lou 178
Katash, Lydia 222
Kazir, Andan 150
Kent, Dora 145
Khomatov, Boris 36
Kim Il Sung 42–43, 139
Knight, Mrs. 245
Knocke, Walter 223
"Knoxville Mummy" *see* Stevens, Carl
Koch, Ilse 150
Koch, J. P. 187
Krakauer, Jon 178
Krasin, Leonid 31, 32
Krateil, Juan 120
Kuklinski, Richard 232–33
Kunce, Richard 215–16

Lee, William 99–102
Lenin, Vladimir 1, 5, 27, 28–37, 39, 44, 133, 139–40, 247–48; autopsy of 28, 30; family of 29, 33, 37; mausoleum 28, 30, 31, 32–33, 36, 38
Levitan, Mark 172, 176
Li Zhusui 39–41
Lieberman, Archie 218
Liersch, E. D. 64, 67
"Little men" *see* Jívaro mummies
Lombardo, Rosalia 43, 50, 52–54
Los Angeles Cryonics Society 142
Lovejoy, Alan 145
Luciani, Albino *see* John Paul I, Pope
Lying in state 4, 27–58, 59–60, 201, 204–5, 234, 248
Lynn University 135
Lyon, Mrs. Oscar D. 125
Lyophilization *see* Freeze-drying

Maddox, Everett 191
Madsen, Tim 177, 179
Makinson, Muriel 238
Maltby, Cecil 223
Mammoth Cave National Park 189, 194
Marcos, Ferdinand 165
Maria Assunta Pallotta, Sister 196
Maria della Passione, Sister 196
Martin, Arthur 173
Martin, Ray 172, 175–76
Marto, Francisco 198–199
Marto, Jacinta see Jacinta of Fátima
Masgay, Louis, Sr. 232–33
Mattei, Maria 213
Mawson, Sir Douglas 181
May, John Frederick 78
McCrew, Anderson 96–98
McCrew, Andrew see McCrew, Anderson
McCunn, Carl 176
McCurdy, Elmer 1, 6, 60–70; autopsy of 65–67
McDougald, Beacham 89, 90
McDougald, Hewitt 88, 90–91
McDougald, John 89
McLean, Don 97–98
Merryman, Harold 160
Michaels, Paul 145
Michigan Cryonics Society 141
Mikkelson, Ejnar 187
Miller, William B. 190
Miyamoto, Katsusaburo 54–55
"Mother" see Petta, Julia Buccola
Mulestein, Blaine 145
Mummies: burial of, 12, 37, 38, 46, 47–48, 49, 69–70, 79, 89–91, 96–97, 99, 101–2, 122, 170, 194, 216, 222, 231–32, 248–50; claiming of 63, 67–68, 80, 98, 100; computerized tomography (CT-scan) of 110, 111, 119; conservation of 9, 35–36, 57, 62, 75, 203, 249–52; discovery of 169–71, 175–76, 224, 233, 235, 238–40, 242, 245–46; display of 4, 12, 59, 64, 72–74, 76–77, 80–84, 87, 90, 92–98, 100–1, 125–31, 161, 193–94, 211–12, 218–20, 247–48; identification of 18, 19, 21, 46, 61, 67–69, 78, 82, 90, 170, 221–22, 241, 242, 245, 246; magnetic resonance imaging (MRI) of 110, 111; purchase of 60, 62–63, 80–84, 87, 92, 121, 125; x-rays of 46, 116–17, 129
Mummification: artificial 5; cost of 136, 139–40, 143, 154, 158, 161; definition of 3–4; natural 5, 16–26, 196, 215, 224, 235, 238, 245–46; partial 3, 17, 19, 20, 169–70, 203, 222
Museum Vrolik 126
Mütter Museum 124–25, 126
Mylius-Erichsen, Ludwig 187

Namba, Yasuko 178–79
National Funeral Directors Association 138
National Geographic Explorer 115, 118

National Library of Medicine 111, 112
National Museum of Health and Medicine 107–8, 122, 124–27, 153, 224
National Museum of the American Indian 119–22, 250–51
Nehme, Bro. Stephen 202–3
Neto, Augustinho 139
Nilsen, Dennis 223, 236–38
Noguchi, Thomas 68–69
Nuzzi, Oreste 204
Nyhuis, Bun Chee 222

Oates, Lawrence E. G. 183–84, 186
O'Brien, Tyler G. 24–26
Ochotenko, Archbishop Sergei 203, 208–10
O'Day, Marie 87, 92–94
Olds, Fred 68–69
Olizable, The Rev. Francisco 115
Orlowek, Nathaniel 84, 85

Pace, Elgie 96–97, 98
Pacelli, Eugenio see Pius XII, Pope
Paravicini, Giuseppe 122–24
Parrado, Fernando 226–27, 229–30, 232
Parsons, Sue 138
Pavett, Harold J. 159–61
Pearson, A. F. 191
Penniman, W. B. 79–80
Penska, Stanislas 143–44
Perón, Eva 1, 27, 43–49; family of 48, 49
Perón, Isabelita 48–49
Perón, Juan 27, 43, 46, 47, 48
Petrification 80, 92, 122–24
Petta, Julia Buccola 212–13
Phillips, Archie 157
"Pickled punks" see Teratology Specimens
Pittman, Sandy 177–79
Pius X, Pope 204
Pius XII, Pope 45, 47, 198, 204–5
Plainfield Cemetery 152
Plastination 107–10; polymerizing emulsion technique 109; sheet plastination technique 109–10
Pogreba, Clare 172, 176
Preservation 29, 54; and temperature 19–20, 250; in dry ice 163; in glass 147–49; in water 20, 241
Preservation Technologists Corporation 159–61
Price, Brian 154, 157
Prosection see Dissection
Purvis, John 65

Ra, "Corky" 134–39
Ra, Gracey 135, 139
Refrigeration 7, 19, 42, 161–66, 208; in morgue 222, 249
Research Center of Biostructures see Scientific Research Institute for Biological Structures
Restoration 3, 28, 32, 34, 101, 105, 124; after exhumation 16, 192–93, 202, 217, 234

Reynaud, Louis 169
Reynolds, Bobby 130
Ries, Joseph 172–73
Rinpoché, Ling 206
Romakov, Yuri 139–40

St. Helen, John *see* Booth, John Wilkes
Salafia, Alfredo 5, 50–54
Saponification *see* Adipocere
Sarto, Guiseppe Melchiorre *see* Pius X, Pope
Savina Petrilli da Siena, Sister 196
Schieding, Brent 145
Schoening, Klev 177
Scientific Research Institute for Biological Structures 36, 42–43, 133, 139–40
Scott, Robert Falcon 181–86
Shackleton, Ernest 181, 186
Sibly, Walter K. 128
Signoracci, Arnaldo 205
Signoracci, Ernesto 205
Simpson, Keith 242–43
Singh, Spoony 64
Sledzik, Paul 85, 126, 127
Smalls, Jessie 240
Smith, Kate 164
Smith, Pervis 152
Smith, Sidney 244
Smithsonian Institution 119–20, 124, 160
Smoke curing 7, 147–50
Solomon, Jacob 223
Sonney, Dan 64, 67
Sonney, Louis 63–64, 67
"Spaghetti" *see* Farmica, Cancetto
"Speedy" *see* Atkins, Charles Henry
Spencer, J. Merrill 240
Spilsbury, Sir Bernard 246
Spitzer, Victor 112
Stalin, Joseph 29, 30, 35, 37–39
Stefansson, Vilhajalmur 187
Stein, George 98–99
Stevens, Carl 6, 214–16; family of 215–16
Stevens Brothers Circus 129
"Stone Man" *see* Stein, George
Strauch, Adolfo 227–30
Strauch, Eduardo 228–30
Struve, Gustave 120–22
Sublimation *see* Freeze-drying
Summum organization 6, 8, 133–39
Sweet, Marie Phelps 144
"Sylvester" 92
Szoka, Archbishop Edmund C. 202

Talley, The Rev. Gary 194
Tanning 21, 150–53, 155

Taske, John 178
Tattooing 152–53, 248–49
Taxidermy 1, 151, 153–61
Temu, Ron 134, 137
Teratology specimens 6, 125–31; confiscation of 127, 128–29
Thanos, John 116
Thomas, Harry B. 193
Trans Time 145
Tse-tung, Mao 5, 27, 39–42, 248; mausoleum of 41–42
Tulane Medical School 126

Ubelaker, Douglas 85, 241
Uniform Anatomical Gift Act 8, 104, 145; whole-body donation 9, 104–5, 110, 116, 126, 153, 158
United States Patent Office 147
University of California 105
University of Colorado 112
University of Maryland 116, 119
University of Wisconsin 151
Utter McKinley Mortuaries 164–65

Van Lerberghe Funeral Home 201
Villa, Gabriella 240
Vince, George 182
Visible Man 110–13
Visible Woman 113
Von Cosel, Karl Tanzler 233–34
von Hagens, Gunther 107, 110
Vonner, Erhard 153
Vorobyov, Vladimir 31, 32, 34

Wade, Ronald 7, 113, 115–19
Weathers, Beck 178–79
Wegener, Alfred 187
Weird Museum 127
Werner, Karl 141
White, Jerome B. 143
Wilson, Donald E. 116
Wilson, Edward 183–85
Wolfe, Joan Pearl 242–43
Wollenweber, O.F.M. Cap., Bro. Leo 201–2
Worden, Bernice 150
Wright, Charles 184–86

Xu Jing 39, 40

Zbarsky, Boris Ilich 31, 32, 33, 34, 37
Zbarsky, Ilya 34, 35, 38
Zedong, Mao *see* Tse-tung, Mao
Zerbino, Gustavo 227–31
Zhang Bingchang 39, 40